THE CORPSE AS TEXT

THE CORPSE AS TEXT

DISINTERMENT AND ANTIQUARIAN ENQUIRY,
1700–1900

Thea Tomaini

THE BOYDELL PRESS

First published 2017
The Boydell Press, Woodbridge

ISBN 978 1 78327 194 8

The Boydell Press is an imprint of Boydell & Brewer Ltd
PO Box 9, Woodbridge, Suffolk IP12 3DF, UK
and of Boydell & Brewer Inc.
668 Mt Hope Avenue, Rochester, NY 14620–2731, USA
website: www.boydellandbrewer.com

A catalogue record for this book is available
from the British Library

The publisher has no responsibility for the continued existence or accuracy of URLs for external
or third-party internet websites referred to in this book, and does not guarantee that any content
on such websites is, or will remain, accurate or appropriate

This publication is printed on acid-free paper

Printed and bound by TJ International Ltd, Cornwall

For Zsa Zsa Eleni

CONTENTS

ILLUSTRATIONS

ACKNOWLEDGMENTS

This book would not have been possible without the assistance and cooperation of the Reader Services staff of the Huntington Library, San Marino, CA. Special thanks to the Munger Reading Room staff for managing my numerous and sometimes odd requests. Many thanks to the Reader Services staff at the British Library and to the Library staff at the University of Southern California.

Many thanks to the archivists and librarians who assisted me in my research for this project, especially: David Morrison of the Worcester Cathedral Library and Archive, Derek Maddock of Sudeley Castle and Gardens Archives, Enid Davies of St George's Chapel Archives and Library, and Christina Tse-Fong Tai of the National Portrait Gallery Archives.

Special thanks to my colleagues who read chapters, gave feedback and advice, and engaged in discussions with me about this project, especially: Tina Boyer, Chris Freeman, Jay Paul Gates, Bruce Gilchrist, Stefanie Goyette, Lawrence D. Green, Ana Grinberg, Heather James, Mary Leech, Nicole Marafioti, Asa Simon Mittman, Melissa Ridley-Elmes, Martina Saltimacchia, Robert Savage, Larry Swain, Larissa Tracy, Wendy Turner, Kelly De Vries, and Renée Ward. The members of MEARCSTAPA have been particularly helpful, and I thank them wholeheartedly.

Very special thanks to my family and friends, who listened politely and smiled somewhat uncomfortably while I talked excitedly about disinterments in restaurants, in pubs, on holidays, at the beach, at parties, at concerts, during sporting events, during fireworks displays, and at the theatre. And thank you to my dear friend Jill Ragaway for describing me on Facebook as 'erudite and slightly demented'. I am genuinely, unironically flattered. Hugs.

1

INTRODUCTION

The Corpse as Text

Of all the manners in which a culture attempts to relate to the dead, disinterment is the most radical. Its very directness is shocking, as it is characterised by the ultimate taboo of death: immediate contact with the corpse. But rather than producing disgust and horror exclusively, ritual disinterment also produces fascination and even emotional gratification. This is true when disinterment is performed ritually, as a religious practice, but it is also true when it is performed as an academic or scientific exercise. During the eighteenth, and also through the nineteenth century, antiquaries and 'proto' archaeologists[1] in Britain engaged in the disinterment of figures from English history and literature. Their mission was to validate their own cultural and political values by looking, literally, into the faces of the dead.

During the period 1700–1900, the subject of remembrance and its connection to the historical, literary, or noble body in death attracted the attention of antiquaries who viewed disinterment for academic purposes as an essential element of study.[2] A corpse

---

[1] I use this term to make a distinction between the twenty-first-century science of archaeology and eighteenth- and nineteenth-century antiquarianism. Antiquaries did excavate meticulously, and they contributed largely to the development of the discipline of archaeology; but some of them also engaged in the unfortunate practices of tomb robbing, souvenir trafficking, and exotic collecting for private markets. As Jason Kelly states in his book *The Society of Dilettanti*, 'A modern understanding of professionalisation has shaped contemporary discussions of eighteenth-century *dilettanti* and *virtuosi*. Generally, nineteenth- and twentieth-century histories of the disciplines define a profession by such common traits as a self-regulating institutional structure, full-time occupation, and authority in the professional–client relationship because of professional expertise.' In today's terminology, most antiquaries are considered amateurs. Jason M. Kelly, *The Society of Dilettanti: Archaeology and Identity in the British Enlightenment* (New Haven, CT, 2009), p. 9.

[2] The chapters of this book describe disinterments that span this time frame but the chapters do not trace a development of the practice over time. This is because, where disinterment is concerned, there is a great variety of methods, expertise, and opinions concerning the men who performed the disinterments. Some are historians, some are physicians, some are clergy, and some have architectural interests. Some of them knew the others personally or by reputation, while others were unknown to the rest entirely. The relevance of each disinterment to its specific period (such as Georgian, Regency, or Victorian) are discussed in the respective chapters. The use of the phrase 'eighteenth-and-nineteenth century' in this Introduction is for general purposes, to frame the overall theory of the book and prepare the reader for the

could be seen as a document in and of itself, in which truths could not only be perceived, but *read*; for twenty-first-century scholars this idea is rooted essentially in the Derridean idea that memory can be inscribed upon an object, a person, or, in this case, a corpse.[3] This concept is reflected in contemporary studies that use interdisciplinary methods to engage with objects and read them as texts. These studies include *Untimely Matter in the Time of Shakespeare* by Jonathan Gil Harris (in which the objects in Shakespeare's plays are connected to the fabric of the dramatic narrative)[4] and *The Key of Green*, by Bruce R. Smith, in which the colour green is connected to the construction of a comprehensive cultural narrative in the late sixteenth and early seventeenth centuries.[5] Susan Zimmerman discusses the particular subject of the human corpse as a facet of 'thing studies' in *The Early Modern Corpse and Shakespeare's Theatre*.[6] In cooperation with these studies, this book will present an interdisciplinary analysis of the culture of disinterment, by which a corpse is the 'thing' around which a theory of reading becomes possible. The corpse itself is a text that becomes part of a comprehensive tradition of intertextual analysis that involves a myriad of literary, ecclesiastical, academic, and artistic sources. The corpse as text is, in some ways, an extension of the idea that a grave is a text. As Howard Williams states, a furnished grave is a 'tableau' that creates a display of the identity of the deceased that is perceived by the mourners not literally, but imaginatively and even dramatically.[7] This tableau is textual – Guy Halsall calls it 'the grammar of display'.[8] Martin Carver, in his discussion of graves as texts, states that a grave is a poem in and of itself: 'a palimpsest of illusions'.[9] Burials, therefore, do not merely contain language; they *are* language.[10] As this book shows, the corpse is one aspect of that language. What Williams calls the 'mnemonic performance' of the grave (and per this study, the corpse) accomplishes the same thing that other texts, and particularly poetic texts do: it renders temporal distinctions ambiguous, allowing past, present, and future to be conflated.[11] Burials are in a sense 'multimedia performances'.[12] This study demonstrates that a disinterment is

forthcoming specifics of each chapter. The actual period covered by the individual chapters ranges from the late seventeenth century to the end of the Victorian period in 1901.

[3]   This idea is also rooted in important studies of memory by Mary Carruthers and Frances Yates. See Mary Carruthers, *The Book of Memory* (Cambridge, 1990); and Frances Yates, *The Art of Memory* (Chicago, 1966).

[4]   Jonathan Gil Harris, *Untimely Matter in the Time of Shakespeare* (Philadelphia, 2009).

[5]   Bruce R. Smith, *The Key of Green* (Chicago, 2008).

[6]   Susan Zimmerman, *The Early Modern Corpse and Shakespeare's Theatre* (Edinburgh, 2005); see also M. De Grazia, M. Quilligan, and P. Stallybrass, eds., *Subject and Object in Renaissance Culture* (Cambridge, 1996).

[7]   Howard Williams, *Death and Memory in Early Medieval Britain* (Cambridge, 2006), p. 118.

[8]   Guy Halsall, 'Burial Writes: Graves, 'Texts', and Time in Early Merovingian Northern Gaul', in *Erinnerungskultur im Bestauttungsritual*, ed. J. Jarnut and M. Wemhoff (Munich, 2003), p. 67.

[9]   Martin Carver, 'Burial as Poetry: The Context of Treasure in Anglo-Saxon Graves', in *Treasure in the Medieval West*, ed. Elizabeth M. Tyler (York, 2000), p. 37.

[10] Carver, p. 37.

[11] Williams, p. 119.

[12] Williams, p. 118, and Halsall, pp. 66–7.

essentially this type of text read backwards; meaning is complementary to that of burial, but innovated and envisioned in an inverse way. Although they did not use twenty-first-century terminology, scholars of the eighteenth and also those of the nineteenth century were aware of the concept and employed it in antiquarian investigation and academic enquiry into the graves of the historical dead. In the case of antiquarian scholarship between 1700 and 1900, the idea of 'reading' the dead can be traced to two sources: the ancient tradition of hagiographic inspection of corpses, and the interpretive habits of those engaging in academic or ecclesiastical studies.

By the eighteenth century, disinterment had been a common practice in England for over a thousand years. Noblemen and kings were often buried in temporary tombs while more lavish and costly monuments were built. When translation of the remains was called for, it was common for the coffin (or lead envelope) to be opened, the corpse inspected, and remarks recorded as to its condition. Family and loyal admirers could find great comfort in knowing that the deceased looked well upon inspection, and that his or her identity was verified. A candidate for sainthood could be checked for incorruptibility, and relics could be collected.[13] Sometimes the disinterment and translation of noble or royal remains exonerated parties suspected of foul play: Henry V famously staged a public disinterment of Richard II before the erstwhile king's reburial at Westminster Abbey.[14] The display of Richard's corpse was meant to show that there were no marks on the body indicating murder.[15]

Commoners also experienced disinterment and the translation of remains, although for them the process was far more practical. Medieval burials of commoners were not generally marked with headstones, and such graves were not considered permanent in any case.[16] After the corpse was devoid of its flesh, the bones were disinterred by the sexton and carried to the local charnel house for storage. When the charnel house was full the bones were carted away for any number of purposes, which were decided upon

---

[13] The issue of fetish and the body where translations are concerned is related to discrete issues of sacredness that I will not be dealing with here. The hagiographic inspection and translation of corpses within sacred spaces is a subject that has been exhaustively researched, especially concerning the period 800–1500 CE. Similarly, the destruction of shrines and disinterment of corpses during the Reformation is also a subject about which much has been published. Some recent and helpful sources are John Crook, *English Medieval Shrines* (Woodbridge, 2001); Patrick J. Geary, *Living with the Dead in the Middle Ages* (Cornell, 1994); Eamon Duffy, *The Stripping of the Altars* (New Haven, CT, 1992); Peter Marshall, *Beliefs and the Dead in Reformation England* (Oxford, 2002); and Nancy Mandeville Caciola, *Afterlives: The Return of the Dead in the Middle Ages* (Ithaca, NY, 2016).

[14] Raphael Holinshed, *Chronicles of England, Scotland, and Ireland*, 6 vols. (London, 1807–8), vol. III, cap. 13, pp. 14–15; and Paul Strohm, 'The Trouble with Richard: The Reburial of Richard II and Lancastrian Symbolic Strategy', *Speculum* 71, no. 1 (January 1996): 92.

[15] At least there were no outward signs of murder; had Richard II starved to death or died of dysentery (either of which is likely), there would be no visible evidence of violence on his corpse.

[16] Philip Schwyzer, *Archaeologies of English Renaissance Literature* (Oxford, 2007), pp. 108–9.

by local government.[17] In 1549, for example, the charnel house of St Paul's Cathedral was emptied and the bones of the dead were used as landfill for three windmills outside the city.[18] Most people understood that graves were impermanent; as Philip Schwyzer states in *Archaeologies of English Renaissance Literature*, '…there seems to have been little sense (aristocratic tombs aside) that the resting place of one's body could or should constitute a kind of inalienable private property'.[19] Although there were stories of saints who spent their lives as members of the Commons, such persons were rare; for the most part, saints adopted the ecclesiastical life and were buried in church or abbey grounds. After inspection for the signs of sainthood, their remains were translated to better tombs in finer churches.

Death rituals in Early Modern England were based largely on the idea that the relationship between life and death was largely the relationship between a present and a future state. This is true both before and after the Reformation, as Sarah Tarlow points out in her study of English death rituals.[20] But during the eighteenth century attitudes began to change. Tarlow says:

> The living maintained highly individualised relationships with individual dead kin and friends, and the relationship after death corresponded to the kind of relationship in life. These were relationships characterised by the same emotions which increasingly articulated relationships between the living; that is to say, love, pity and sensibility. In contrast to the attitudes of the seventeenth century, the relationship was not between past and future states, but a synchronic relationship between a living and a dead person.[21]

These attitudes became even more pronounced as the eighteenth century passed and the nineteenth century began. As Tarlow explains, the growth of sentimentalism where mortality was concerned caused people to view the dead as unique persons just as they had been in life. Moreover, the celebrated dead (such as royalty or other important people) could be mourned with the same depth of grief as one's own kin or friends.[22] Relationships between the living and the dead therefore achieved a wider context, one that was more sentimental and open to interpretation than it had been before.

Developments in English attitudes toward the dead over the course of the period 1700–1900, therefore, call for the corpse to be understood in diverse ways. As Nigel Llewellyn states, the body's biological matter is only one of its aspects; the social body

---

[17] For a full discussion of burial customs and the management of Medieval and Early Modern churchyards, cemeteries, and charnel houses, see Peter C. Jupp and Clare Gittings, eds., *Death in England: An Illustrated History* (New Brusnwick, NJ, 1999).

[18] Schwyzer, *Archaeologies*, p. 108.

[19] Schwyzer, *Archaeologies*, p. 108.

[20] Sarah Tarlow, 'Wormie Clay and Blessed Sleep: Death and Disgust in Later Historic Britain', in *The Familiar Past?* ed. Sarah Tarlow and Susie West (London, 2002), pp. 192–3.

[21] Tarlow, pp. 192–3.

[22] Tarlow, p. 193.

is another. He says that the Early Modern English funeral '...is a liminal, transitory moment set between the polarities of life and death'.[23] This is true, and in this sense the funeral is not the ultimate act of the Early Modern English death ritual, nor is the act of commemoration, whether it is textual (epitaph or elegy) or material (monuments). The ultimate act of the English death ritual between 1700 and 1900 is disinterment: it is an ironic reversal of burial and an extension of the liminal state between life and death. It argues against polarity and finality, creating a transitory moment that is relevant to the lives of both rich and poor, clergy and laity. This is true precisely because the corpse is comprised of two elements: the physical body and the social body.[24] As Nigel Llewellyn explains, narratives of death set in the past retained their didactic potency because these two elements could be observed individually. Doing so allowed antiquaries to imagine the bodies of the commemorated dead in diverse ways.[25] The natural body in death, the bearer of meaning, acts as the signifier. The social body, the body imagined in a social context, acts as the signified.[26] This is also true concerning the body imagined in a narrative context, whether that narrative is literary, folkloric, or historical. As Stephen Bann states in his discussion of the subject, during the eighteenth century it became common to use the terms of rhetoric and literary criticism to refer to historical events and personages; by the nineteenth century those terms were used in historiographical discussions.[27] As this book shows, the reading of a corpse as a text allows for rhetorical and literary terms to be used in a similar way.

Although disinterment for the purposes of canonisation or hagiography had a solid precedent, antiquaries of the eighteenth and also the nineteenth century made important distinctions between their work and that of the Medieval Church when viewing the long-dead figures of the past. For a hagiographic inspection of a corpse, a doctrinal standard based on textual precedents determines whether the present will be validated by the past. Those standards are inscribed upon the corpse by its 'incorruptible' condition; the viewer literally 'reads' the corpse for signs of sainthood that are measured against the Church's institutional and textual standard. The present is thereby made to serve the past. The antiquaries discussed in this book produce the opposite effect by their research: they inspect corpses in order to validate suppositions about the past that are generated from their own contemporary experiences rather than from an established standard of the past. Interestingly, this is true of scholars of both Catholic and Protestant faiths–it is a cultural, rather than religious, distinction. In looking at a corpse they expected to 'read' truths about their own present time. The past is thereby made to serve the present. A corpse disinterred in this manner is different from an exhumed saint in that an individual (or small group), rather than an institutional body,

---

[23] Nigel Llewellyn, *The Art of Death: Visual Culture in the English Death Ritual* (London, 1991), pp. 13 and 48–9.
[24] Llewellyn, p. 31.
[25] Llewellyn, pp. 47–9.
[26] Llewellyn, p. 51.
[27] Stephen Bann, *The Clothing of Clio* (Cambridge, 1984), p. 3.

determines the truths that proceed from the corpse. The antiquary communicates those truths to the public based on his or her own ideas of nobility, patriotism, faith, or artistic appreciation. The scholar then awaits confirmation of these truths by others who share the same sentiments. Those sentiments are expressed via texts: in academic journals and books, in newspapers, in letters, and in works of literature. This method is, however, quite problematic: people see what they want to see. The excavator, no matter how well-meaning he or she is, brings suppositions of his or her own to the site of disinterment, inscribes his or her experiences in the present onto the corpse, reads them, and then congratulates him or herself on perceiving the truth of the past. Interest in the corpse and its past amounts to a fascination with the Self and one's present. It is an absurd and narcissistic practice, and it occurs in every case presented in this study.[28]

As Clare Simmons states, the absurdity of such a practice is connected to a sense of national identity and public duty, and particularly the rights claimed as part of that identity.[29] Especially during the period 1800–1900, scholars, clergymen, and politicians who were engaged in this type of anachronism employed a view of 'Medieval England' (a term that includes the sixteenth and early seventeenth centuries) in order to impose a definition of 'authenticity' that served their purposes. A nostalgic image is therefore generated – one that can be recognised, admired, and pronounced 'authentic' when it reflects upon its maker. In this sense disinterment presents an interesting paradox: the corpse must reflect (or be made to reflect) the subjective conclusions already determined by the investigative parties engaged in the study. When this happens, the corpse is given 'authentic' status – not because the corpse is more real than others, but because it is materially and conceptually 'genuine' in that it reflects national character and national identity in a satisfactory way.[30] Such disinterments catered to a longing for the past that drew heavily upon this idea, and such methods were appreciated by politicians, clergy, novelists, and playwrights, who found this idea useful and practical. Such historical anachronism, although it causes temporal displacement, also encourages an understanding of past realities that enhances an awareness of one's place in the present. D.R. Woolf comments on this irony, saying that antiquarianism extracted (literal) pieces of the past that might be considered banal and gave them a new sense of exotic usefulness and relevance. The effect was similar on the collector, who developed a new sense of his past and himself.[31] Philippa Levine calls these

[28] This is not to say that the system of exhuming corpses for hagiographic inspection was not narcissistic. It certainly was, but the organised institutional narcissism of the Medieval Church is the subject of another (and much larger) study. See the aforementioned works by Patrick Geary and Eamon Duffy, and see also Robert Bartlett, *Why Can the Dead Do Such Great Things?* (Princeton, NJ, 2015).

[29] Clare Simmons, *Popular Medievalism in Romantic-Era Britain* (New York, 2011), p. 7.

[30] See Anthony Smith, *National Identity* (London, 1991), pp. 80–100 for a discussion of 'national character' in the seventeenth, eighteenth, and nineteenth centuries.

[31] D.R. Woolf, *The Social Circulation of the Past: English Historical Culture 1500–1730* (Oxford, 2003), p. 20 and pp. 44–9.

methods of academic enquiry and their political and ecclesiastical applications part of a 'gospel of heritage' that developed over the course of two centuries and culminated in the Victorian period.[32] The devotees of this 'gospel' were committed to authenticating and legitimising their heritage rather than simply preserving it in an effort to prevent its stagnation for the sake of posterity.

Calling these efforts a 'gospel of heritage' is not mere hyperbole. The interpretive habits of members of educated groups were heavily influenced by the manner in which they were trained to read their Bibles.[33] For centuries religious tracts, sermons, lectures, and commentaries had anticipated Christ in the books of the Old Testament and encouraged a comprehensive technique by which texts were interpreted retrospectively.[34] This technique influenced secular thought throughout the eighteenth century and also through the nineteenth; and eventually became what Peter Sinnema calls 'an appropriate interpretive paradigm for secular texts'.[35] As Joseph Levine points out in his study of historical method, chroniclers of the Middle Ages (namely Geoffrey of Monmouth but also Matthew Paris, William of Newburgh, Ralph of Coggeshall, and Roger of Wendover, among others), '...invented fictions and passed them off as histories, or [wrote] histories into which they intruded fictions, almost without criticism'.[36] Their focus was on the didactic point of the story, which had a value all its own. Early Modern historians like Raphael Holinshed and Edward Hall followed their example in the sixteenth century. Erasmus wrote in *De Copia*, that if a fictional narrative were used to make an applicable point, it could be accepted as true; and in More's *History of Richard III* the distinction between history and poetry is blurred – as Levine says, 'without embarrassment'.[37] Antiquaries who became interested in disinterment in later years were quite used to the idea that history and legend – even fable, as Levine suggests – could coexist as foundations for study.[38] They knew that an understanding of one's subject relied upon what Levine calls a 'fruitful cooperation' between disciplines, by which a comprehensive understanding

---

[32] Philippa Levine, *The Amateur and the Professional: Antiquaries, Historians, and Archaeologists in Victorian England 1838–1886* (Cambridge, 1986), p. 4.

[33] Peter Sinnema, *The Wake of Wellington: Englishness in 1852*. (Athens, OH, 2006), p. 5. See also R.J. Smith, *The Gothic Bequest: Medieval Institutions in British Thought, 1688–1863* (Cambridge, 2002).

[34] Sinnema's discussion of this particular type of typological interpretation is traced to the evangelical movements of the late seventeenth and early eighteenth centuries. His analysis of this particular tradition of reading focuses on the public reaction to Wellington's death in 1852 and extends to the early twentieth century. He acknowledges that it continues to this day in various forms.

[35] Sinnema, p. 5.

[36] Joseph M. Levine, *The Autonomy of History: Truth and Method from Erasmus to Gibbon* (Chicago, 1999), p. 17.

[37] Erasmus, 'De Copia', ed. Craig R. Thompson, trans. Betty Knott and Brian McGregor. *Collected Works*, vol. XXIV (Toronto, 1978), p. 634.

[38] Joseph M. Levine, *Humanism and History: Origins of Modern English Historiography* (Ithaca, NY, 1987), p. 37.

of the subject might be formed.[39] This was an important understanding: as Levine states, between 1700 and 1900 antiquarian interest was often ancillary to a profession, such as medicine, the law, or the church, although many undertook antiquarian study for its own sake.[40] Levine also notes a significant concern among antiquaries about fraudulence: although historical re-creation could be imaginative, deceptive interpretation was discouraged.[41] The antiquary was expected to be imaginative and interpretive but not overuse his imagination. As Stephen Bann notes, the production of forgeries, especially between 1750 and 1850, threatened antiquarian study.[42] The creation of 'historical poetics' was meant to have an integrative effect, creating a form of communication between the antiquary, his subject (here, the corpse), and the audience of his published study or book. A comprehensive epistemology is the goal. Frauds and hoaxes, whether of texts or material items (such as false bones, hair, or teeth) interrupt that communication, causing a linguistic gap in the integrative poetics of disinterment.[43] Still, an antiquary with an active sense of fantasy might turn his talents toward historical novels. As Bann states, the literary efforts of Sir Walter Scott and others could be constructive: 'And who can doubt that the Waverley Novels, though in the strictest sense a deception, gave their readers a new capacity for fine discrimination between what was authentic and what was false in a historically concrete milieu?'[44]

This mode of reading also contributed to the development of the narrative of hero worship. The generation of heroic narratives is a distinctive and dramatic aspect of political, historical, and literary texts of the eighteenth and also of the nineteenth century. Writing heroes was a complex process, and although much can be attributed to Thomas Carlyle's *On Heroes and the Heroic in History* (as it certainly should),[45] the process by which heroic narratives connected figures of history and literature to contemporary patriotic and religious values was multifaceted. One of the most interesting facets of this subject is the retrospective 'reading' of the life and character of a celebrated person (who might be seen as either a hero or a legendary villain). According to Peter Sinnema, the construction of a heroic narrative involves deep communication with its audience via 'a recognisable, culturally acceptable structure

---

[39] Levine, *Autonomy of History*, pp. 123–4.

[40] Levine, *Autonomy of History*, p. 99.

[41] Levine, *Autonomy of History*, p. 99.

[42] Especially Charles Bertram's forgery *The Description of Britain*, purportedly by Richard of Westminster/Cirencester (1757). This document (published under the auspices of the antiquary William Stukeley) managed to retain a measure of academic currency well into the nineteenth century. It was even republished in 1878, a decade after it was exposed as a hoax. See Stephen Bann, *The Clothing of Clio*, pp. 2 and 6.

[43] Bann, pp. 4–6, and 77.

[44] Bann, p. 3.

[45] Thomas Carlyle, *On Heroes, Hero-Worship, and the Heroic in History*, ed. Michael K. Goldberg, Joel J. Brattin, and Mark Engel (Berkeley, 1993).

which has many powerful associations attached to it'.[46] The practice of disinterment was one type of 'structure' that cooperated with retrospective life-reading. Disinterment had a recognisable and culturally acceptable set of descriptive terms attached to it, and it was the source of many powerful associations between the present and the past. These associations established the dead as continually relevant members of society. As Elizabeth Fay discusses in her study of the relationships between historical and literary ideals in the Romantic period, figures of centuries past are allowed to come close enough to late eighteenth- and early nineteenth-century culture to reflect its values comfortably, while at the same time retaining enough historicity to remain emblematic of an exotic Other. As Fay shows, this Otherness becomes an important trope for the anachronism that developed during the Romantic period and eventually stands in as a metaphor for the 'Medieval past', even if the definition of that term is extremely loose.[47] There was little effort to establish anything resembling what scholars now term 'historical accuracy' or 'authenticity' where such ideals were concerned. The term 'Medieval knight' might describe an Anglo-Saxon hero, a character from the Arthurian romances or from one of Shakespeare's plays, or an allegorical figure from Spenser's *Faerie Queene*. Where the term 'Medieval' is concerned, the most influential literary example – the dedication of Tennyson's *Idylls of the King* to the late Prince Albert – the most influential artistic examples – those of the pre-Raphaelites (namely Millais and Rossetti) – and the most influential historico-political example – Carlyle's praise of Shakespeare – demonstrate that there was an extraordinary sense of elasticity with which the term 'Medieval' was used.

'Reading' objects (and bodies) changes how people look at connections between history, literature, and material culture. It becomes possible to examine an historical period or literary genre with a material object at the centre, from which literary and historiographic discussion proceeds. Such a discussion treats the object itself as text, rather than something that is described by text. Disinterment represents a form of historical materialism in which the corpse is the 'thing' that generates intellectual energy. This is different from the type of 'thing studies' that revolves around a shard of pottery, a shoe, or a piece of jewellery (although Joseph Addison, in his *Dialogue upon the Usefulness of Ancient Medals* (1726), does call his collection 'a body of history').[48] Quite simply, the corpse is too big to fit into the antiquary's Wonder Cabinet.[49] The wholeness of the body is an issue, and it bears directly upon the fact that the corpse is

---

[46] Sinnema, p. 5.

[47] Elizabeth Fay, *Romantic Medievalism: History and the Romantic Literary Ideal* (New York, 2002).

[48] Joseph Addison, *Dialogue upon the Usefulness of Ancient Medals* (London, 1726), p. 20. For a discussion of the Victorian fascination with gems, see Stephanie Markovitz, 'Form Things: Looking at Genre Through Victorian Diamonds', *Victorian Studies* 52, no. 4 (Summer 2010): 591–619.

[49] The exception to this statement is the example of the Egyptian mummy, which, although it is a fascinating aspect of corpse studies for the period 1800–1930, is not a part of this study.

seldom translated where antiquarian excavations are concerned. The examples of this study are those in which an academic inspection is for the most part conducted in the context of the corpse's current resting place.[50] Although this study does not discuss tomb-robbing or souvenir culture as a primary subject, it will describe the occasional theft of items from graves opened for academic inspection. Bones, teeth, and locks of hair do find their way into the Wonder Cabinets of antiquaries and collectors, and they do become objects of fetish, but they nevertheless represent the objectification of fragmentary remains. They do not represent wholeness. Bones, teeth, and locks of hair are objects; the whole human body in death is both object and subject. The souvenir object is allowed to retain its temporal moment as an artefact of an earlier time, whereas the disinterred corpse is appropriated and reimagined so that its relationship to the current time is relevant. Moreover, objects in the Wonder Cabinet are on continuous display, usually in a private home; but the disinterred corpse is examined and then reburied, most often in or very near its current burial space.[51]

A human corpse does not go from being a subject to an object when a person dies. As one important study of materiality in Early Modern culture points out, anyone who has ever been to a funeral knows that in death human beings continue to be subjects.[52] The human corpse retains such a strong power of attachment that it has a sovereignty of its own. Where the noble body or the royal body is concerned this sovereignty acquires an important double meaning. As De Grazia, Quilligan, and Stallybrass discuss in *Subject and Object in Renaissance Culture*, present-day archaeologists make a series of distinctions between subject and object when excavating, classifying, and exhibiting human remains; but antiquaries between the Georgian and Victorian periods did not make the same distinctions. Although sepulchral monuments and epitaphs described the finality and permanence of death, the remains of noble, historical, or literary persons were seen more as subjects than objects,[53] and antiquaries were very sensitive to the latent humanity of the celebrated dead.[54] Antiquaries sought to perceive the past not only via the body of work – the *corpus* – of a celebrated deceased person, but also via

---

50 The exception is my chapter on Katherine de Valois, who was examined forensically nearly three hundred years after her disinterment and then reburied in another location within the same building.

51 Again, the exception is Katherine de Valois, whose corpse was in continuous view from 1503 to 1778.

52 The interrelation between subject and object is essentially Hegelian, but a discussion of the issue as it pertains to the Tudor and Stuart eras is found in De Grazia, Quilligan, and Stallybrass, eds., *Subject and Object in Renaissance Culture*.

53 One exception to this rule is Egyptian mummies that were displayed in private homes as *objets d'art*, but that is the subject of another study.

54 Zimmerman correctly points out that much of the fascination for the *persona* of the dead stems from Christian theology concerning resurrection. The resurrection of the body is the union of sign and signified, and the body of Christ as an incarnation of God in man represents a similar union. The Eucharistic sacrament recreates this incarnation mystically and was part of the discourse of daily life in Medieval Europe. Zimmerman, pp. 5–7.

the corpse itself. Theirs was a consideration of the body memorialised, commemorated, and – most importantly – fantasised about. In this sense the corpse of a celebrated figure becomes fetishised and acquires a phantasmic quality that drives the power of the subconscious and ultimately the imagination. This is less common with parts of corpses (like teeth or locks of hair) than with entire bodies.

The period between 1700 and 1900 produced and cultivated a popular mythology of the dead that was different from that of centuries before. This mythology concerned presumptions about the public and private relationships between the celebrated dead and the nation. Such connections were subtler in earlier centuries (with the exception of saint veneration). The rise of antiquarianism is a major factor in the development of these issues. Often defined mistakenly by his (or in some cases, her) proclivity for collecting, the antiquary was a key figure in the study, appreciation, and preservation of monuments and tombs, and the churches, castles, and chapels that housed them. This book does not contain a history of antiquarianism, but it does recognise the important contributions made by antiquaries to dialogues about national character and memory. Antiquarian interest in disinterment accompanied and encouraged the growth of the disciplines of archaeology (including the budding discipline of Egyptology), anatomy, and social history, a facet of history that was often dismissed by 'serious' academics. The fascination of antiquaries with excavation of the dead was part of a discourse of acquisition and investigation that aided in the establishment of the great museum collections in Britain and the Continent (and eventually the United States). It was also part of an ongoing discourse about the continuing relationship between the living and the dead concerning public space and private life.

Almost exclusively male (with some exceptions), antiquaries sought organisation into clubs, groups, and factions, and from the late eighteenth to the mid-nineteenth century membership grew exponentially. By 1886 there were fifty-six county and local antiquarian societies in addition to the Society of Antiquaries in London.[55] Antiquaries disliked epithets like 'self-taught', that held them apart from scholars at the universities, and they resisted the stereotype that they were hobbyists, souvenir hunters, or worse – grave robbers.[56] They drew much of their inspiration from predecessors who had sought to modernise the work of chronicling and collecting during the sixteenth and seventeenth centuries. John Bale (who, before his conversion, wrote a history of the Carmelite order to which he belonged) wrote an alternative history of the Roman Church that was meant to expose the deep corruption of its clergy and thereby promote Henrician ecclesiastical policies.[57] Richard Mulcaster and his cohorts in the Society of Archers lent imaginative energy to their acquisitions of chivalry-themed books and objects.[58] Robert Cotton's library was widely varied, and he had a strong interest in the

[55] Philippa Levine, *The Amateur and the Professional*, pp. 182–3.
[56] Levine, *The Amateur and the Professional*, pp. 2–3.
[57] Bale, John, *Acts of the English Votaries* (London, 1546).
[58] See Charles B. Millican, 'Spenser and the Arthurian Tradition', *The Review of English Studies* 6, no. 22 (1930): 167; and *Spenser and the Table Round: A Study in the Contemporaneous*

context that resulted from the juxtaposition of different manuscript sources in the same library or even in the same volume. This is definitely true of sources describing rituals like coronations and funerals.[59] The Norfolk antiquary Thomas Browne was among the first to excavate and describe Anglo-Saxon and Romano-British graves, cataloguing and illustrating their contents in the mid-seventeenth century.[60] Over the course of the period 1700–1900, antiquaries viewed their efforts (at various moments and in various ways) as contributions to the development of a nation that valued its past but was unconstrained by it; thus they also viewed their work as distinct from the hagiographic agenda of monastic chroniclers or relic peddlers. Objects belonging to a political or literary figure were historical artefacts, not relics.

Because the sixteenth and early seventeenth centuries were often accepted as part of the 'Medieval' period in the popular imagination,[61] the Reformation was an important aspect in academic discussions of national character. Peter Marshall makes a very interesting point when he states that people of the sixteenth and seventeenth centuries were not quite sure how they wished to be remembered; they only knew that they did not want to be forgotten.[62] This is true. The sixteenth and seventeenth centuries produced what Marshall calls a 'schizophrenic attitude' toward remembrance of the dead.[63] Ornate Italianate tombs shared sacred space with the 'decent' gravesites of the Protestant dead, which, although they could be lavish, employed neo-Platonic allegorical figures rather than religious symbolism.[64] Both types of tombs shared sacred space with the shrines of saints of earlier centuries, some of which were literally torn out of the walls during the Dissolution of the Monasteries in 1538–9, the bones of their occupants scattered or burnt or thrown into nearby rivers. Similar events between 1649 and 1660 created more confusion as to how the dead were to be remembered. Scholars of the two centuries following compensated for such confusion by making determinations about the past that were generated by their own reading habits. Myth, stereotyping, and what Peter Mandler calls 'a surge in popular historical consciousness',[65] caused these scholars

    Background for Spenser's Use of the Arthurian Legend (Cambridge, 1932), p. 94.

[59] See Kevin Sharpe, *Sir Robert Cotton, 1586–1631: History and Politics in Early Modern England* (Oxford, 1979). Cotton's collection was strong in other subjects attractive to antiquaries of the eighteenth century, such as state offices and Medieval history.

[60] Unfortunately, Browne mistakenly identified the graves as Roman; but his recognition of the need to associate memory with material culture is an important one. See Williams, *Death and Memory*, p. 2.

[61] References of this type most often appear in novels, plays, poems, and paintings, as the subsequent chapters of this book will demonstrate. The tendency to include the Elizabethan and Jacobean eras in the umbrella term 'Medieval', has much to do with popular attitudes about Shakespeare's life and work.

[62] Marshall, *Beliefs*, p. 265.

[63] Marshall, *Beliefs*, p. 265.

[64] Marshall, *Beliefs*, p. 265.

[65] Peter Mandler, 'Revisiting the Olden Time: Popular Tudorism in the Time of Victoria', in *Tudorism: Historical Imagination and the Appropriation of the Sixteenth Century*, ed. Tatiana String and Marcus Bull (Oxford, 2011), p. 13.

to define the past according to their understandings of the present. As Mandler states, whatever once constituted remembrance of the dead between the Reformation and the Restoration now took second place to what constituted remembrance of the dead between the lives of Queen Anne and Queen Victoria.[66] 'Heritage' was not a word that described the past – it was one that described contemporary national pride. This view of the past was practical and material; it was informed by a broad national consciousness and it included the dead and their burial places, as parts of a wide-ranging, and compellingly inclusive, modern body of knowledge.[67]

Antiquaries fought vigorously against the stereotype that they were merely tomb-robbers or relic hunters. The Society of Antiquaries disavowed the very idea of tomb-robbing and disdained the practice of relic hunting as an unpleasant remnant of Catholicism as early as 1600.[68] John Weever, a seventeenth-century forerunner of eighteenth-century antiquarianism, regretted the vandalism of the Dissolution during the reign of Henry VIII. He condemned sixteenth-century iconoclasts in his book *Ancient Funeral Monuments*,[69] which became a standard for antiquaries of later years. In Weever's view, these broken tombs, emptied of their abbots, bishops, and saints, should provoke sympathy and repentance on the part of the reverent and investigative viewer:

> Marbles which covered the dead were digged up, and put to other uses … Tombs hackt and hewn apieces; Images or representations of the defunct broken, erased, cut or dismembered. Inscriptions or Epitaphs, especially if they began with an *orate pro anima*, or concluded with *cuius anime propitietur Deus*. For greedinesse of the brasse, or for that they were thought to be Antichristian, pulled out from the sepulchres, and purloined; dead carcases, for gaine of their stone or leaden coffins, cast out of their graves…not so much for taking out the money…but for the drawing out and dispersing abroad the bones, ashes, and other sacred remains of the dead.[70]

In his lengthy rumination on monuments, Weever ultimately concludes that there is a connection between monument, text, and memory, and that this relationship is enhanced by the concept of disinterment when the practice is conducted with respect. He recounts his own experiences with scholarly detachment:

> In the North Isle [sic] of the Parish church of Newport-Paintell in Buckinghamshire, in the yeare 1619, was found the body of a man whole and perfect; laid downe, or rather leaning downe, North and South; all the concavous parts of his body, and the

---

[66] Marshall, *Beliefs*, p. 265; and Mandler, p. 13.

[67] Levine, *The Amateur and the Professional*, pp. 2–4.

[68] Thomas Hearne, *A Collection of Curious Discourses*, 2 vols. (London, 1773), vol. I, p. 228.

[69] John Weever, *Ancient Funerall Monuments within the United Monarchie of Great Britaine, Ireland and the Islands Adjacent, with the Dissolved Monasteries Therein Contained* (London, 1631), p. 41.

[70] Weever, p. 51.

hollownesse of every bone, as well ribs as other, were filled up with solid lead. The skull with the lead in it doth weigh thirty pounds and six ounces … and is kept in a little chest in the said Church, neare to the place where the corps were found; there to bee showne to strangers as reliques of admiration. The rest of all the parts of his body are taken away by Gentlemen neare dwellers, or such as take delight in Antiquities. This I saw.[71]

Weever expresses a similar attitude in the aftermath of an excavation he attended with Robert Cotton in 1620, at an ancient Roman burial site in Radcliffe Field, Middlesex, in the Parish of Stepney.[72] He makes distinctions between antiquaries with a healthy admiration for the past, and mere treasure hunters. He condemns those who break into tombs looking for gold or jewels, calling them 'grave-rakers', and states that they are no better than the iconoclasts of the 1530s and 40s.[73]

Weever's early example set the standard for antiquarian enquiry and investigation and remained relevant for over two centuries, in part because of his opinions regarding souvenir hunting and grave robbing; but his book remained popular also because of his attitude toward literature. Specifically, Weever quotes from late Medieval poetry throughout his book. He especially quotes from Chaucer, (namely the Summoner's Tale and the Friar's Tale), and points out that Chaucer, by these narratives, had meant to criticise the corruption of the clergy. Weever also quotes from *The Vision of Piers Plowman* and from poems by Richard Rolle. As Graham Parry states, 'By linking poets and metrical chroniclers to the vigorous life of Medieval England that is evoked in his book, Weever does his best to make these writers attractive to an historically minded audience'.[74]

It is worth mentioning that during the mid to late nineteenth century antiquaries did at times cooperate with ghost hunters and 'psychical researchers' when it came to ghost legends concerning historical gravesites and other sites important to the lives of legendary persons.[75] In the later nineteenth century, ghost investigation and 'spiritualism' were considered to be forms of intellectual enquiry.[76] Séances, phantasmagoric performances, and 'psychical research' shared space in the antiquary's parlour along with his or her Wonder Cabinet and engravings. By the later nineteenth century the historiographer, the tomb excavator, the psychical researcher/spiritualist, and the

---

71 Weever, p. 30.
72 Weever, p. 30.
73 Weever, p. 51.
74 Graham Parry, *The Trophies of Time: English Antiquarians of the Seventeenth Century*. (Oxford, 1995), p. 198.
75 This point is made by Nicola Watson in *The Literary Tourist* (New York, 2006); although her subject matter deals mainly with authors' homes, and her discussion is largely about the Brontës and Jane Austen.
76 See P.G. Maxwell-Stuart, *Ghosts: A History of Phantoms, Ghouls, and Other Spirits of the Dead* (Stroud, 2006), p. 197.

curio collector could be the same person.[77] For the later Victorians, spiritualism sought to answer intellectual questions that other avenues did not; and that provided some common ground with the antiquary's work.[78]

Another mode of study considered important to antiquaries that is now dismissed as fiction is anatomic characterology, which caught on among educated groups both inside and outside universities around 1800. Anatomic characterology was a mode of study that sought to associate physical features of the body such as height, weight, eye and hair colour, skin colour, and the shape and proportion of the limbs and facial features with individual character and morals, and with stereotypical class, ethnic, or racial characteristics. Many antiquaries who engaged in disinterment and tomb research were anatomists or physicians who employed anatomic characterology as a means of validating presuppositions about class, race, gender, and individual character of the dead just as their colleagues did regarding the living. The most well-known aspect of this ersatz discipline is phrenology, a term used to describe the particular study of cerebral physiology. It was developed around 1800 by Franz Gall (b. 1758) and Johann Spurzheim (b. 1776), and it called for the examination of the human skull – namely, its bumps and ridges – to determine intellectual ability, talent, linguistic skills (such as eloquence or wit) and faculties of reason and sensibility.[79] The disinterment of historical figures provided excellent opportunities to examine the skulls of figures already determined by society to be regal or noble, to be heroes and geniuses, or, conversely, to be tyrants and villains.

Phrenology was used as an additional tool to verify and legitimise suppositions already held by those excavating tombs when they were faced with the corpses of the great or the notorious. It appeared to work well with the interpretive skills of the academic enquirer because it was believed to be a scientific principle that conveniently supported his conclusions in nearly every case. Phrenological publications such as *Essays on Phrenology, Or, an Inquiry into the System of Gall and Spurzheim* (1819), *The System of Phrenology* (1824), and *The Constitution of Man Considered in Relation to External Objects* (1828) are important nineteenth-century works that complemented the caracteriological and phrenological interpretations of corpses by antiquaries who

---

[77] See Deborah Blum, *Ghost Hunters: William James and the Search for Scientific Proof of Life After Death* (New York, 2006).

[78] This association of disinterment with hauntings is related only peripherally to Derrida's theory of *hauntology*, in which a culture is haunted by its past and its ideas, personages, and texts. These are ghostly remnants of the past. Disinterments seek to attach relevant contemporary value to the corpse, thereby elevating it from the status of remnant, or even revenant. Death fascination of the eighteenth and nineteenth centuries is thus distinct from *hauntology*. Haunting is produced by a troublesome preoccupation; fascination is driven by inquisitiveness and allure. Jacques Derrida, *Specters of Marx, the State of the Debt, the Work of Mourning, and the New International*, trans. Peggy Kamuf (New York, 1994), https://www.marxists.org/reference/subject/philosophy/works/fr/derrida2.htm.

[79] Sherrie Lynne Lyons, *Species, Serpents, Spirits, and Skulls: Science at the Margins in the Victorian Age* (New York, 2009), p. 54.

were anatomists. They made it possible for these scholars to see if their theories about the great or the notorious matched the *corporeal* testimony of history as to who was indeed a hero or a villain. In this sense the idea of a corpse as a text was seen to have a factual basis because the corpse's physical characteristics could be read literally. By the third quarter of the nineteenth century there were twenty-nine phrenological societies in Great Britain.[80]

Tourism was a persistent factor despite the antiquarian emphasis on academic enquiry. By the middle of the eighteenth century commemorative spaces containing celebrated burial sites like Westminster Abbey, the Tower of London, and The Church of the Holy Trinity in Stratford had become strongly linked with tourism, and this fact had a profound effect on how these spaces were experienced by visitors.[81] These buildings (or sets of buildings) were not merely repositories of the celebrated dead; they were places where 'greatness' itself was housed.[82] The connection of 'greatness' with the gravesite had been a common notion for centuries, and was an association most often made with the gravesites of saints and kings. In the eighteenth century religious pilgrimage no longer defined the 'greatness' of a burial site or its occupant, but reverence for the *locus* of an important burial remained linked to patriotism. The idea of 'greatness' became associated with figures of literature or history who were counted among the builders of the Empire. As Robert MacDonald states, 'a programme of conscious propaganda' during the eighteenth century caused London to be filled with tombs, public statues, monuments, and other forms of commemorative art depicting figures and scenes from history.[83] Those objects often contained texts, such as epigrams or epitaphs, but they also were seen *overall* as readable objects that expressed an appreciation of 'greatness'.

Many of these monuments were constructed in imitation of similar monuments in Italy and France. In his study of tourism before 1800, Aaron Santesso makes an important point: he states that the university graduate/tourist (such as a young man taking the Grand Tour of The Continent) was expected to engage with his surroundings and reconstruct them imaginatively. In doing so he was expected to develop his character and his appreciation for learning so that he could return home with a sense of intellectual power over history.[84] This is precisely the attitude taken by antiquarian scholars who sought to engage with sites of burial and the monuments that located them. Antiquaries like Richard Gough encouraged such engagement by providing locations, sketches, and descriptions of burial places in *Sepulchral Monuments of Great Britain* (1786–99). Gough demonstrated that visual materials were proper

---

[80] Lyons, p. 78.

[81] See Richard Jenkyns, *Westminster Abbey* (Cambridge, MA, 2005), pp. 112–13.

[82] See Watson, p. 26 for a discussion of Poets' Corner that employs this idea.

[83] Robert MacDonald, *The Language of Empire: Myths, Metaphors and Popular Imperialism, 1880–1918* (Manchester, 1994).

[84] Aaron Santesso, 'The Birth of the Birthplace: Bread Street and Literary Tourism Before Stratford', *English Literary History* 71, no. 2 (Summer 2004): 380 and 385.

objects of historical analysis and that they yielded a text of their own, contributing to a discrete narrative rather than serving as mere illustrative accompaniments to written texts.[85] Edward King expressed a similar sentiment in his book *Munimenta Antiqua, or Observations on Ancient Castles* (1799). Furthermore, William Nicolson's *English Historical Library* (1696) promoted the composition of a compete history of England, which drew heavily on antiquarian research.[86] The book encouraged the student of history to put together a 'body' of history by drawing upon a full range of sources rather than relying on printed text alone. In doing so he could achieve an imaginative reconstruction of the greatness of the past.

The rise in appreciation for tombs and monuments accompanies a cultural preoccupation with death that developed in the Georgian period and culminated in the Victorian period.[87] This preoccupation differed from the various forms of death fascination of the sixteenth through seventeenth centuries. Death fascination of the eighteenth through the nineteenth centuries is a varied phenomenon, as the ensuing chapters of this book will show; but sometimes unfortunate descriptive terms are used to describe it, such as a 'cult of death', a 'celebration of the macabre', or a 'love affair with melancholy'. Death fascination, especially over the course of its development between 1700 and 1900, cannot be described simply; moreover, the inclusion of the dead in the national rhetoric of patriotism over the course of those two centuries involves sentimentalism and anachronism, but surprisingly little melancholy. As Rosemary Sweet states, 'The move toward examining tombs and monuments critically, rather than simply as a means of inspiring melancholy thought and ancestral piety, was one of the important conceptual advances which antiquaries made in the course of the eighteenth century'.[88] In this sense the antiquarian objective was to establish the fact that visual materials were appropriate for historical analysis, and indeed to go further – to accept the dead themselves along with their tombs as contributors to historical narratives. This is the same type of attitude displayed by the designers of early to mid nineteenth-century public cemeteries who sought to take tombs and monuments out of castles and churchyards and combine memorial architecture with modern urban space.[89]

Alongside the architectural and historiographical developments of death fascination there occurred three extraordinary incidents of prodigious public mourning during the nineteenth century that reflected the desire to enfranchise the dead in a continuing rhetoric of national consciousness. These incidents connected that desire

---

[85] Rosemary Sweet, *Antiquaries: The Discovery of the Past in Eighteenth Century Britain* (London, 2004), p. 275.

[86] Sweet, p. 16.

[87] The Victorian cultural preoccupation with death waned during the Edwardian period (1901–10), and had changed significantly by the time of the accession of George V in 1910. See James Stevens Curl, *The Victorian Celebration of Death* (Stroud, 2000).

[88] Sweet, p. 273.

[89] Curl, pp. 69–108.

to the production of monuments that both celebrated and located the dead. These three events were: the death of Princess Charlotte Augusta in 1817, the death of the Duke of Wellington in 1852, and the death of the Royal Consort Prince Albert in 1861. These events related public identity in death to public status and urban space, as London was the setting of grand funerals for each of these public figures. These three funerals helped redefine remembrance within the context of public, yet normative, memorial observances. In his discussion of the outpouring of grief upon the death of Princess Charlotte Augusta, Stephen Behrendt states, 'The melodramatic structuring of reality had a calming effect, since the form of melodrama bore with it an assurance of an eventual rectification of perceived wrongs and a reinstatement of both a moral and a political or civic order that reasserted traditional values'.[90] Princess Charlotte Augusta's unexpected death in childbirth was so devastatingly tragic that the public consciousness constructed a complete discourse around it. That discourse unified the remembrance of a public figure with that of a private figure; Princess Charlotte Augusta stood as a deceased member of the royal family and as a martyred mother at the same time. The huge public outcry after her death reflected a cynical reaction on the part of many people to the public and private behaviour of her unpopular brothers, and it advanced the ideology of the melodramatic royal death in ways it had not been expressed before.[91]

The Duke of Wellington's death in 1852 produced a public reaction that was an odd mix of rationality and grief. The laudatory narrative of his death spoke to an idealised national identity, what Peter Sinnema calls 'a rather abstract but highly cherished set of "English" attributes'.[92] By paying tribute to a war hero, people, especially those of the upper and middle classes, celebrated Wellington's public and private persona – not because they knew him, but because they felt like they did. Thomas Carlyle's view on heroes in society encouraged much of this sentiment. Carlyle had attributed 'greatness' to many figures among the historical dead, such as Shakespeare, Oliver Cromwell, Henry V, and others. Wellington was a person to whom the issue of 'greatness' was attached while he was still living. His death produced an amplification of the concept for his benefit. His ornate monument in St Paul's Cathedral was breathtakingly lavish, and it featured a giant marble sarcophagus once intended for Henry VIII.[93] The vessel that bore Wellington in death carried with it associations of 'greatness' that

---

[90] Stephen Behrendt, *Royal Mourning and Regency Culture* (New York, 1997), p. 14.
[91] Behrendt, p. 30. A similar example of public consciousness that constructs a narrative around the death of a celebrated royal is the phenomenal global response to the death of Diana, Princess of Wales in 1997.
[92] Sinnema, p. 11.
[93] The sarcophagus had been made originally for Cardinal Wolsey; Henry VIII confiscated it along with other of the Cardinal's goods at Hampton Court Palace. The sarcophagus was never used, as the lavish tomb Henry VIII designed for himself was never completed.

his mourners associated with Henry VIII: formidable Imperial power,[94] irrepressible Protestantism, undeniable 'Englishness', and continuous relevance.

Prince Albert's death in 1861 underscored the acknowledgment of the royal dead as public and private figures. The nation mourned him as Prince Consort, and also as a husband and father. The sheer number of monuments that arose to Prince Albert in the years following his death contributed to the development of public attitudes toward greatness in death that informed antiquarian disinterment during the later nineteenth century. His tomb, of course, was the most significant monument. Queen Victoria established a new royal mausoleum by which she and Prince Albert could disassociate themselves from her Hanoverian ancestors. In designing the monument Victoria wished to associate herself and Albert with a time before the Hanoverians and the controversies that plagued her immediate ancestry: she chose a combination of Medieval and Early Modern styles, ranging from Romanesque for the architectural style to Raphaelesque for the figures, and neo-Gothic for the accents.[95] In creating a neo-Medieval monument Victoria wished to identify Albert as a chivalric figure in death. Statues of Albert after his death often featured him in Anglo-Saxon costume or a suit of armour; his figure thereby became an extension of the popular Medievalism for which the era was known. As Debra Mancoff explains, in the wake of the death of Prince Albert, '…the symbolic inference of the knight gained special currency … For the mid-Victorian advocate of chivalry, the Medieval knight was neither an historical entity nor a fictional character; he was a sign, functioning as a personification of an honorable and ancient code, kept alive in modern society and cultivated to signify the aspirations of contemporary British manhood.'[96]

In this manner the historical figures discussed in this book (as representatives of a large group of similar figures who underwent disinterment) could enjoy a double reputation; they were known for the events of their lifetimes, and for events that took place long after their deaths. In this way they could be made to fit somewhat neatly into contemporary ideals of Medievalism.

The stereotyping of the Tudor and Stuart eras during the eighteenth and also the nineteenth century also included the umbrella term 'Middle Ages', or, during the nineteenth century, 'Medieval'.[97] Defined variously and with great elasticity, a term like 'Medieval' could be used alongside equally elastic terms like 'Anglo-Saxon' or 'Gothic' to

---

[94] Henry VIII had proclaimed Britain to be an Empire in 1533. *Act in Restraint of Appeals*, 24 H8 c.12.

[95] Elizabeth Darby and Nicola Smith, *The Cult of the Prince Consort* (New Haven, CT, 1983), p. 24.

[96] Debra Mancoff, 'Albert the Good: Public Image and Private Iconography', *Biography* 15, no. 2 (Spring 1992): 144.

[97] The first recorded use of the term 'Medieval' occurred in 1817 by T. D. Fosbroke in *British Monachism*, 2nd edn, 2 vols. (London, 1817), vol. I, p. vi. The term 'Middle Ages' had been in use since the seventeenth century. See *OED Online*; access via University of Southern California, http://www.oed.com.libproxy1.usc.edu.

describe any phase of the entire period spanning 800–1600 CE and was sometimes even used to describe the mid-seventeenth century.[98] These terms were often used with what Rosemary Sweet calls 'an astonishing lack of precision', and the term 'Medieval' itself can be frustratingly arbitrary.[99] Some of the sources of this terminology appeared in late seventeenth-, eighteenth-, and nineteenth-century historical texts as the terminology developed. In his *English Historical Library* (1697),[100] William Nicolson argued for the composition of a 'complete history' of England, one that, as Rosemary Sweet observes, was meant to encourage the student of history to contextualise his sources within his own experiences.[101] She points out that there was a need for a comprehensive scholarly apparatus that would support the idea that history was defined not simply by a cataloguing of names, dates, and wars, but of other information and material that made an historical event or person worth remembering.[102] Gilbert Burnet's 1679 *History of the Reformation of the Church of England* was an important source that was reprinted many times over the course of the nineteenth century. Also, contemporary sources, such as Henry Hallam's *View of the State of Europe During the Middle Ages* (1818), Lingard's *History of England* (1819), and Thomas Babington Macaulay's *History of England* (1849–61) contributed to a growing fervour for patriotic expression of the past, and were reliable texts for antiquaries working in academia or pursuing their interests in private.[103] These studies encouraged the notion that the purpose of history was not necessarily to discover the past but to improve the present. Thousands of copies of these books were sold, and many scholars of history, both professional and amateur, developed the idea that the construction of a body of history included the actual bodies of the dead, and that memory proceeded from text but also from other, more literal forms of remembering. As an antiquarian interest, disinterment stood as a form of remembering that required the corpse of an historical figure to be placed in context with textual sources to form a larger *corpus* and a comprehensive system of reading that was both figurative and literal. Moreover, antiquaries demonstrated that a focus on smaller locations, such as counties, districts, and parishes, could produce the same effect as larger studies of history on a national level and produce a similarly viable *corpus*. Comprehensive ideas like these aided antiquaries in their defence against accusations that they were amateurs.[104]

---

[98] A full discussion of these somewhat elastic terms, their origins and usage can be found in Mandler, 'Revisiting the Olden Time', p. 29; also Ronald Hutton, *The Rise and Fall of Merry England: The Ritual Year 1400–1700* (Oxford, 1996); and Keith Thomas, *The Perception of the Past in Early Modern England* (London, 1983).

[99] Sweet, p. 238.

[100] William Nicolson, *The English Historical Library*, 3 vols. (London, 1697).

[101] Sweet, p. 16.

[102] Sweet, p. 16.

[103] Gilbert Burnet, *The History of the Reformation of the Church of England* (Oxford, 1865); also, Thomas Babington Macaulay, *History of England*, 3 vols. (London, 1849–61).

[104] Sweet, p. 4.

Other sources were literary or artistic. Poetry, plays, paintings, and novels compounded the effect produced by historical texts rather than competing with them. When poems about the Elizabethan defeat of the Spanish Armada, or about the Civil War, for example, accompanied traditional learning, those events were read in an alternative, but not necessarily secondary capacity. As Robert MacDonald states, verse added its own rhetorical weight to historical narrative, allowing people to enhance their understanding of the events and people of the past.[105] Rosemary Sweet notes that most antiquaries of the eighteenth century and also of the nineteenth, accepted the idea that literature, art, and historiography could and often did inform one another, and that they considered this understanding to be a progressive aspect of learning.[106] Novels were generally considered to be for women, but they were nevertheless a way for women to participate in the imagination of an historical discourse that reanimated figures of history in dramatic scenarios. Plays had a similar effect, and husbands who did not dare peep into their wives' novels often attended the theatre and had the same experience their wives had when they read. Paintings and statuary also encouraged the desire to 'fill in the details of history' with portraiture, busts, and large historical paintings of battles and treaties.[107] Roy Strong points out that the artists who developed the Gothic Picturesque movement – such as Benjamin West and Gavin Hamilton – were interested in two things: reproducing episodes from history in ways that complemented contemporary values, and depicting with as much accuracy as possible (as they defined it) locations important to the study of antiquity, such as churches, castles, abbeys, and tombs.[108] These artists did so in paintings of Henry VIII and his six wives, of Jane Grey, of Elizabeth I in procession. For an exhibition at the Royal Academy in 1776, Hamilton presented a grand painting of Mary Queen of Scots resigning her crown. Strong states that in the painting Hamilton attempted to recreate sixteenth-century Scotland 'with the same thoroughness that he bestowed on the worlds of Ancient Greece and Rome'.[109] Richard Westhall painted 'The Earl of Essex's First Interview with Queen Elizabeth' in 1789, and John Singleton Copley painted 'Charles I Demanding in the House of Commons the Five Impeached Members' in 1782. The paintings are very imaginative, and are based on a combination of various historical and literary accounts and the fantasies of the artists.

Such efforts found acceptance with Thomas Carlyle, who, in his widely influential book *On Heroes, Hero-Worship, and the Heroic in History* states that novels, reenactments, and paintings humanise the figures of British history. He was not speaking figuratively: Carlyle was an enthusiast of physiognomic interpretation and believed there was much value in the study of the faces of important historical persons. Carlyle believed that a person's inner character impressed itself on the features of his or her face; as Michael

---

[105] MacDonald, p. 59.

[106] Sweet, p. 135.

[107] MacDonald, p. 60.

[108] Roy Strong, *Recreating the Past: British History and the Victorian Painter* (London, 1978).

[109] Strong, p. 24.

Goldberg remarks in his biography of Carlyle, 'He never wavered in his adherence to this ancient belief in the ability to find moral and spiritual features reflected in the face and its expressions'.[110] Carlyle's influence was profound, and interest in physiognomy among antiquaries was widespread. It is not surprising that there was a strong tendency to gaze into the faces of the dead, not out of gruesome curiosity, as grave robbers and tourists did, but out of a desire for a continuous engagement with the past in which memory was an ongoing enterprise of construction and in which the character of the past was tied to current notions of the patriotic Self. The face of an historical figure's corpse could indeed function in a way similar to that of a portrait and confirm truths that were supposed about that person. The face of an historical corpse could even be compared with existing portraiture for the same verifying, 'legitimising' effect.[111]

Reading the dead is a manifold and continuous process between 1700 and 1900. Ideas about the concept change from one antiquary to the next, and no two disinterments are exactly alike. The examples in this book highlight several efforts that illustrate how politics, culture, literature, and folk belief affected the efforts to read the bodies of the dead. Disinterment during the years spanning the Georgian through the Victorian periods is not simply a macabre and voyeuristic exercise, although the following chapters certainly illustrate the fascination with death that was pervasive at the time. Disinterment between 1700 and 1900 seeks to normalise the state of decay, to enfranchise the dead in the world of the living and its immediate concerns. It gives voices to the dead, not so they can verify the existence of the afterlife, as saints are meant to; nor so they can warn humanity about coming wars or storms, or terrify the living, as ghosts and revenants are meant to. The voices of these dead speak constructively for the sake of the present. Giving voices to the dead is always a redundant and narcissistic practice by which humanity tells itself what it wants to hear. This book illustrates the extent to which antiquaries were willing to go to see how much of Britain's sense of itself lay deep down, waiting for its chance to surface and speak its narrative.

---

[110] Michael Goldberg, 'Introduction', in Thomas Carlyle, *On Heroes, Hero-Worship, and the Heroic in History*, ed. Michael K. Goldberg, Joel J. Brattin, and Mark Engel (Berkeley, 1993), p. xxxvi.
[111] Goldberg, p. xxxvi.

2

PRESUMPTIVE READINGS

King John

On 17 July 1797, Valentine Green, a renowned engraver and antiquary, made a survey of Worcester Cathedral. He intended to produce an addendum of sorts to his *History and Antiquities of the City and Suburbs of Worcester*, which he published in 1796.[1] In particular, he wished to locate the burial place of King John (1199–1216), which at the time was a subject of controversy. Although the sepulchral monument of King John stood prominently in the choir just before the high altar of the cathedral (Fig. 1), there was disagreement as to whether or not the sepulchre represented the location of King John's actual burial place. Green intended to show that upon the dismantling of King John's original tomb in 1540 the king's body was moved from Worcester's Lady Chapel to the location of the present monument in the choir.[2] Putative apocryphal accounts reported, variously, that the monument was cosmetic and that the erstwhile King's body had not been moved. Green did not agree.[3] Renovations undertaken at the cathedral in 1797 provided Green with the perfect opportunity to open the monument and see if King John was inside it. Green was anxious that his project be a success, for the question of the location of King John's corpse was quite literally a stone left unturned in the history of Worcester and its cathedral.

King John was no stranger to the subject of controversy in death. A large part of the controversy surrounding his posthumous legend is related directly to imaginative speculation and creative description of the events of his life and death. Most interestingly, much of this legend arose as the result of the development of King John as a character

---

[1] Valentine Green, *History and Antiquities of the City and Suburbs of Worcester* (London, 1796).

[2] The tomb was apparently dismantled but not destroyed. Green notes that John's effigy, and those of Saints Oswald and Wulfstan, 'seemeth to be as ancient as the time of Henry III, but the altar-tomb, on which it is placed, is of a modern fabric'. *History and Antiquities*, p. 176. The design of the altar tomb is similar to that of Prince Arthur, which stands nearby and is of early sixteenth century design. Green points to a scar on the floor of the Lady Chapel where he believes the original tomb stood. The shrines of Oswald and Wulfstan stood on either side of it.

[3] Green based his opinion on his own observations, on his knowledge of the work of John Leland, and on that of his fellow antiquaries William Stukeley, Browne Willis, Samuel Garbet (who was son of the educator Samuel Garbet), Richard Gough, and Treadway Nash. Dr Nash is responsible for the full excavation of the grave of Katherine Parr.

Fig. 1 Tomb of King John, Worcester Cathedral. Miniature figures of SS Oswald and Wulfstan flank his head, and a stylised lion is at his feet. Photo courtesy of Worcester Cathedral.

in literary texts. At first, his reputation as 'Bad King John' stemmed mostly from the chronicles, and then spread in a variety of imaginative but largely fictional directions. Ralph of Coggeshall and Raphael Holinshed depicted John as an unjust tyrant, his rule catastrophic. He was rumoured to be a man of uncontrollable lust and cruelty, who, at the last, requested to be buried in a monk's cowl in an effort to save his soul.[4] There was little, if any, substance to these rumours, but they persisted nonetheless. During the Reformation, John's reputation recovered to the extent that sixteenth-century reformers like John Bale, John Leland, and John Foxe saw King John's defiance of Pope Innocent III as a precursor to Henry VIII's 1533 defiance of Pope Clement VII; John's excommunication in 1209 was seen as persecution by Rome, and his death, long rumoured to be by poisoning in fulfilment of a prophecy, was seen as martyrdom.[5] Taking the

---

[4]   Raphael Holinshed, *Holinshed's Chronicles of England, Scotland, and Ireland* (1577). 6 vols. (London, 1807–8). Ralph of Coggeshall, *Chronicon Anglicanum, from BL Cotton Vespasian D. X.* Rolls Series, ed. J. Stevenson (London, 1875). See also D.A. Carpenter, 'Abbot Ralph of Coggeshall's Account of the Last Years of King Richard and the First Years of King John', *The English Historical Review* 113, no. 454 (November 1998): 1210–30; and also Antonia Gransden, *Historical Writing in England 500–1307* (New York, 1974), pp. 318 and 324–31.

[5]   See especially Carole Levin, *Propaganda in the English Reformation: Heroic and Villainous Images of King John* (New York, 1988). See also John Foxe, *Acts and Monuments. 12 Books*

example of earlier chroniclers who emphasised a connection between local events and institutions and the national stage,[6] John Bale journeyed to Worcester Cathedral to view King John's body when the king was disinterred in 1529, as the Lady Chapel underwent renovations. At that time the altar tomb of King John was refurbished, producing its early sixteenth-century style. Bale did not convert to Protestantism for several more years after this event;[7] he nevertheless composed a poem in commemoration of the opening of the tomb some twenty years later. The poem indicates Bale's earlier, and continuing, interest in King John's career and death, as it describes a regal corpse dressed in a gold vestment, with a crown on its head, and lying with a splendid sword. The poem reads: 'But yet adorned with a sword and a crown on his head/The right hand holding a fair rod and the left a sceptre/Next [to the body] came a golden vestment covered by a silk one/Spurs on his feet, a ring on his finger'.[8]

After Bale's conversion he praised King John in his 1539 play *Kynge Johan* and depicted him as a sacrificial lamb for proto-Protestant ideals. This sentiment was echoed (albeit more subtly) by the anonymous playwright of *The Troublesome Raigne of King John* in 1591.[9] Shakespeare presented King John as a tragic figure of hapless fate in *The Life and Death of King John* (1596?), but also as one who resented deeply the intrusions and interferences of Innocent III, the 'Italian priest' in Rome.[10] Later folklore of the mid-to-late nineteenth century claimed that King John haunted St Briavels Castle in Gloucestershire, and held him responsible for hauntings by his victims in King John's Castle in Limerick and in Rochester Castle.[11] Ballads and plays, namely those about Robin Hood, painted John as cruel and lustful, a slave to his vices, a Norman usurper persecuting the English.[12] Sometimes, however, King John was depicted as a

---

(London, 1570), Book IV.

[6] Jan Broadway, *'No Historie So Meete': Gentry Culture and the Development of Local History in Elizabethan and Stuart England* (Manchester, 2006), p. 14. The habit of monastic chroniclers of connecting events or persons in local histories to those of the national stage provided what Broadway calls 'a rich seam of material for later local historians'. Antiquaries of the Elizabethan and Stuart periods who used such material in this way were often members of the gentry whose frequent trips to and from London gave them opportunities to connect their political experiences in the capitol with their local histories. They had, as precedents, scholars like Bale who researched monasteries after the Dissolution.

[7] Bale claimed to have converted in 1533.

[8] Translated from the Latin by Thea Tomaini, lines 9–12. Poem appears in full below, see p. 34.

[9] John Bale, *Kynge Johan* (1539) ed. Peter Happe. *The Complete Plays of John Bale*, 2 vols. (Cambridge, 1985), vol. I, and Anonymous, *The Troublesome Raigne of King John* (London, 1591).

[10] William Shakespeare, *The Life and Death of King John*, in *The Norton Shakespeare, Second Edition*, ed. Stephen Greenblatt, et al. (New York, 2008).

[11] Richard Jones, *Haunted Britain and Ireland* (London, 2003), pp. 28, 38, and 62.

[12] In Green's day the best known of these were found in Joseph Ritson, *Robin Hood: A Collection of all the Ancient Poems, Songs and Ballads, Now Extant, Relative to that Celebrated English Outlaw: To Which are Prefixed Historical Anecdotes of his Life*. 2 vols. (London, 1795); and the popular but anonymous *An Excellent Ballad of King John and the Abbot of Canterbury. To the Tune of, The King and Lord Abbot* (Newcastle, c. 1711–69). Also well-known was Anthony

victim of circumstance who, despite his failures, was a forerunner of English resistance to Roman Catholicism and its influences. In this view John's excommunication and murder symbolised a Catholic disregard for the authority of the monarchy. Still, negative depictions of King John persisted in reprints and collections of old Robin Hood ballads (especially that of Joseph Ritson), and in performances and adaptations of Shakespeare's play. King John had been dead a long time, but his legacy was larger-than-life and compelling in its varietal interpretation. Unfortunately, however, King John's story was enthymematic, made up of more suppositions than facts, based on the expedient presumptions of those who constructed the wide-ranging narrative.

Valentine Green was intrigued by the posthumous legacy of his subject. Although he was not driven by John's reputation as a literary character, Green was well-read and deeply invested in the history and legends of Worcestershire. He believed that locating the burial place of King John was essential to the academic thoroughness of his survey; indeed, it begged a question of worthiness upon which he remarked:

> [John's original stone] was removed at the Reformation, for the evident purpose of perpetuating in the public mind the new policy of that important era. The influence of papal authority having been compelled to yield to regal supremacy, the image of that same king, whom two centuries before had been seen basely surrendering his dignity and his crown to that overwhelming tyranny, was now brought forward, and most appositely made the visible sign of that important part of the Reformation having taken full effect in the church of Worcester: but his corporeal remains, as if unworthy to assert a right so legitimate and just, were left to their repose in obscurity and neglect, and in so marked a manner, as at this time it remains a question with many, where they really are:– a question we shall endeavour to resolve.[13]

It was clear then, that the issue could only be resolved by opening the tomb. The endeavour represented one of the few times King John's life and death could be associated with facts. Green's fellow antiquary and poet Thomas Warton was in agreement that King John's burial space needed to be positively identified. He said, '… we think any unprejudiced reader of the above [i.e., Green's] narrative will draw the same conclusions'.[14] Green had considered opening the tomb as early as 1764, when he published his first draft of *Survey of the City of Worcester*,[15] a book that in 1796 was

---

Munday's *The Death of Robert, Earle of Huntington* (London, 1601). There are several others; see below.

[13] Green, *History and Antiquities*, p. 68.

[14] Thomas Warton, 'Remarks on Worcester Cathedral and the Churches of Eversham and Pershore', in Green, *History and Antiquities*, p. 177. Another colleague, Dr William Thomas, records his agreement with Green in his own 1736 survey of the Cathedral. William Thomas, *A Survey of the Cathedral Church of Worcester* (London, 1736), p. 176.

[15] Green, *Survey of the City of Worcester* (Worcester, 1764), p. 40. One of the reasons Green expanded this book into its larger and more comprehensive second edition is because he

revised and reissued to form the longer, more comprehensive *History and Antiquities*. In 1788, as he compiled sources for his expanded edition, he discussed the issue of the location of John's burial place with the Reverend Dr Andrew St John, who at the time was Dean of Worcester. Green's argument was convincing, and he was able to obtain the permission of St John to open the tomb at an appropriate time.[16] The appropriate time came on the occasion of renovations to the cathedral in 1797.[17] The tomb was to be inspected, and Green proposed that if the remains of King John were not inside or immediately under it, the monument could be moved to the location of John's original burial in the Lady Chapel. He wrote:

> ...if, upon examination, no vestige of sepulture should appear, its removal from thence to the Lady's Chapel, and there erecting it over the ancient grave in which King John's remains were supposed to lie, would be a measure fully sanctioned by propriety in respect of its appropriate designation, and in which portion of the cathedral it would also prove a befitting and dignified object.[18]

King John was the first of the Angevin kings to be buried in England. He stipulated in his will that he be buried at Worcester Cathedral, and his interment between Saints Oswald and Wulfstan indicated his devotion to St Wulfstan in particular.[19] Wulfstan, Bishop of Worcester, had been the last of the pre-Conquest English Bishops. John paid devotions at the tomb of St Wulfstan beginning in 1207, three and a half years after the translation of the saint's remains to Worcester in 1203. He visited Worcester Cathedral each year at Christmas until his own death in 1216. John's devotion to Wulfstan, and his desire to be buried next to the saint,[20] was contemporary with John's famous dispute with Innocent III, during which John was excommunicated and England was threatened with invasion from France. Although John's devotions at Worcester and his plan to be buried there were part of his effort to improve his image as an English king, it was his parents who first conceived of an agenda to attach English national

---

feared that his age at the time of publication of the first edition (he had been twenty-five) betrayed too much youthful indiscretion in his scholarship. By 1796 he was a member of the Society of Antiquaries and a renowned engraver in Britain and on the Continent.

[16] Green, *An Account of the Discovery of the Body of King John, in the Cathedral Church of Worcester, July 17th, 1797, from Authentic Communications; with Illustrations and Remarks* (London, 1797), p. 2.

[17] The Dean by that time was Dr Arthur Onslow – but not the same Arthur Onslow who was Speaker of the Commons between 1728 and 1761.

[18] Green, *Discovery*, p. 2.

[19] Graham Seel, *King John: An Underrated King* (London, 2012). In 1216 John was buried in the old Romanesque cathedral church, and then translated to a position between the two saints in 1232. See Ute Engel, *Worcester Cathedral: An Architectural History* (Chichester, 2007), p. 208.

[20] John was originally buried between Saint Wulfstan and Saint Oswald, a tenth-century Bishop of Worcester. Miniature effigies of these two saints flank the life-sized effigy of King John on the sixteenth-century monument.

identity to themselves via devotion to St Wulfstan. In 1158, Henry II and Eleanor of Aquitaine visited Worcester Cathedral and endowed their crowns to his shrine, vowing never to wear them again.[21] In 1540 iconoclasts destroyed the shrines of St Wulfstan and St Oswald but they did not destroy John's tomb; instead they improved it and moved it to the choir, near the high altar.[22] As Green suggested, if the body of King John still lay between the two saints in the Lady Chapel and not in or under the monument, the monument should be moved to its original location. Such a move would identify the burial place of John and also impart – or perhaps restore – a 'befitting and dignified' quality to the environment of the Lady Chapel that recalled the devotions of Henry II and Eleanor of Aquitaine. Although Green could appreciate the efforts of the sixteenth-century Reformers to bestow upon John a distinguished monument to emphasise his reinterpreted status as a proto-Protestant martyr, Green could also appreciate the restoration of King John's original wishes to be attached in death to the legacy of his parents and the residual holiness of the corpses of two saints. Even before the monument was opened Valentine Green was reading the tomb, its environs, and its purported inhabitant, preparing himself for revisions to the text of the corpse and the completion of its original message.

It did not take long for Green's theory of the location of King John's body to be confirmed. The stone coffin containing John's remains lay inside the sepulchral monument, less than twelve inches below the surface.[23] The stone slab on which the coffin had been laid was broken in two, likely as a result of its being moved from the Lady Chapel. The coffin was oddly shaped: it was narrower at the foot than at the top, with the spaces between the coffin's narrow end and the walls of the stone tomb filled in with rubbish.[24] The body of King John lay inside, in very poor condition – far different from what Bale described in his poem. The corpse bore marks of putrefaction, and the handfuls of maggot shells Green scooped from the coffin's interior suggested that the king had been embalmed inexpertly.[25] The body was clothed in a long robe, which once had been crimson damask, and was covered with a drapery that was thick with dust. The left hand once held a sword (as did the stone effigy of the sepulchral monument), but the sword was greatly mutilated, its parts, as Green reported, 'scattered

---

[21] See Ann Williams, *The English and the Norman Conquest* (Woodbridge, 1995). Interestingly, John's father, Henry II, compelled the monks at Glastonbury Abbey to excavate a grave in the Abbey's cemetery that, according to Welsh legend, contained the bones of King Arthur. Inside the grave was a coffin of hollowed oak, in which lay the skeletal remains of two individuals, one much taller than the other. A fragment of yellow hair was also found. By way of these artefacts Henry II sought to connect himself with the Arthurian legend and appropriate English history for the Angevins. See Inga Bryden, *Reinventing King Arthur: The Arthurian Legends in Victorian Culture* (Aldershot, 2005), p. 12.

[22] The church plate and other treasures were surrendered at this time.

[23] Green, *Discovery*, p. 2.

[24] Green, *Discovery*, p. 3.

[25] Green, *Discovery*, p. 3.

down the same side of the body'.[26] There were no spurs on the king's feet nor a ring on his finger.[27] It was clear that the tomb had been pilfered, the regal accoutrements stolen. The strangely shaped coffin included a round niche at the top specially designed to hold the head of the corpse in place. That was interesting in itself – but what gave Green pause was the appearance of the head. It was no longer wearing the crown suggested by the tomb effigy and recorded in Bale's poem; rather, it appeared to be covered with a hood that fastened just under the chin.

Moreover, King John's skull was detached from the body and was turned backwards, face-down.[28] Dr Sandford, 'an eminent surgeon of Worcester', described the arrangement of the remains as he examined them:

> The skull, instead of being placed with the face in the usual situation, presented the *foramen magnum*, the opening through which the spinal marrow passes down the vertebrae, turned upwards. The lower part of the *os frontis* was so much perished as to have become nearly of an even surface with the bottoms of the sockets of the eyes. The whole of the upper jaw was displaced from the skull and found near the right elbow.[29]

Neither Dr Sandford nor Valentine Green made observations as to why King John's head should be turned backwards, nor did Green make any connection between the positioning of the head and the small hood, except to mention an old legend about King John having been buried in a monk's cowl: '…on the skull in the coffin was found to be the celebrated monk's cowl, in which he is recorded to be buried, as a passport through the regions of purgatory'.[30] Green made a sketch of the corpse showing the position of the skull and the other aspects of its features and condition (Fig. 2). Not surprisingly, Green was not the only one who found the corpse's appearance to be intriguing. The excavation attracted a large crowd of onlookers – so large, in fact, that the multitude became unruly, forcing Green and the other members of the excavation party to close up the tomb sooner than they wished. Although Green was satisfied with the 'most judicious and accurate observation' they made, he was sorry to have to cut short the examination and interpretation of the tomb's contents.[31] He wrote, 'On the evening of Tuesday the 18th of July, the day after it had been taken down, the royal remains laid open to the view of some thousands of spectators, who crowded to the cathedral to see

---

[26] Green, *Discovery*, p. 3.
[27] The only thing that remained of the 'shoes' Bale saw were the fragments of leather boots that were almost completely disintegrated.
[28] Green, *Discovery*, p. 3.
[29] Green, *Discovery*, p. 3. Dr Sandford performed a complete examination of the body, detailing its condition from tip to toe; in fact, he noted that the toes on King John's right foot were in particularly good condition, as the nails were still visible (Green, *Discovery*, p. 4).
[30] Green, *Discovery*, p. 4.
[31] Green, *Discovery*, p. 8.

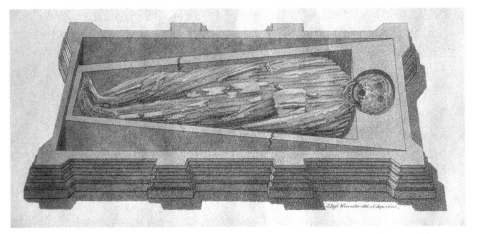

Fig. 2 Drawing of the corpse of King John by Valentine Green. The head of King John is placed face-down; the back of the cranium has collapsed, showing the eye sockets at the bottom of the coffin and the foramen magnum, *or hole by which the spinal cord connects to the brain. Photo reproduction courtesy of Worcester Cathedral.*

it, the tomb of King John was completely restored and finally closed.'[32] Although the tomb was closed, the issue of the state of King John's body was not. It left open several intriguing questions: under what circumstances had King John's head been turned backwards? What happened to the crown, ring, and spurs observed by Bale? Was the little hood in fact a monk's cowl? Did the turning of the head have anything to do with the hood? Green engaged in light speculation, but his account shows a resistance to letting his imagination run away with him. Although he was willing to interpret the corpse to a certain extent, he stopped himself from becoming too speculative. When it came to King John, such academic detachment was the exception rather than the rule.

Perhaps the single most descriptive term that can be used for King John's reign and posthumous legend is 'distrust'. The relationship between John and his barons degenerated in part because of his ruthlessness, but barons had followed ruthless, even cruel monarchs before, and they would do so again.[33] King John was suspicious of his barons, but he was hardly the first or the last king to be wary of his aristocracy. The distrust that occurred between King John and his barons was mutual, and was exacerbated by extenuating circumstances that seemed to validate the sentiment of all parties. The more John's barons distrusted him, the more jealous and clandestine he became; the more secretive John was, the more his vassals suspected him. King John would turn against one of his barons if the man became too powerful; an act like this

[32] Green, *Discovery*, p. 8.
[33] See C. Warren Hollister, 'King John and the Historians', *Journal of British Studies* 1, no. 1 (November 1961): 1–19.

would then cause other barons to desire more power in order to protect themselves from such threats.[34] The more King John defied Pope Innocent III the more the Pope pushed back. Pressure from the Pope caused John to become more defiant. The reign of King John was famous for these cycles of mistrust before it ended; but after John's death the chronicles of the thirteenth century added a new feature to the issue of mistrust in John's reign: the imaginative and speculative retelling of events that used the death of the king, indeed the *corpse* of the king, as the stimulus for the narrative.

As Graham Seel points out in his biography of King John,[35] the use of imaginative narrative in the chronicles was inextricably linked to the chronicles' validity and authority as texts. He states, 'To doubt the chronicles was to doubt the efficacy of the recordkeeping of the Medieval church. It was to maintain a continuous accusation that the Medieval church and its agenda worked against English autonomy.'[36] In this sense the chroniclers, especially Ralph of Coggeshall, Roger of Wendover, and Matthew Paris, composed and perpetuated narratives that reflected distrust for King John's personal history and reign in order to maintain the trustworthiness of the medium in which they worked. A.R. Braunmuller presents a similar view of the chronicles, saying that although the fantasy and invention are of a different type than that of history plays or Robin Hood legends, the degree of factuality is not higher in narratives found in the chronicles.[37] Interestingly, the narratives that emphasise a continued mistrust for King John do so by way of language that focuses on John's body, and in some cases, John's corpse.

Ralph of Coggeshall's account of John's reign is in part contemporary to it.[38] The early parts of Coggeshall's *Chronicum Anglicarum* are generally favourable to John, but as the *Chronicum* progresses, Coggeshall's disappointment with John's reign – and with John himself – becomes evident. Ultimately, Richard I becomes the hero in Coggeshall's narrative, as Coggeshall presents contrast after contrast of John with Richard. Some of those contrasts are political; but others focus on the body in life and in death. Richard the Lionheart was well over six feet tall, and tales of his virility and bravery on the battlefield were well recounted. He died fighting in the Limousin and lay interred at Fontevrault, with his formidable parents. Coggeshall's vivid descriptions and imaginative style presented a stark contrast: John was cowardly of constitution, an issue that attached itself to virility issues, and was lecherous but not virile. John did not tower over other men as Richard had, but stood several inches shorter, at five feet six inches. Death had not come gloriously on the battlefield, but pathetically after a surfeit of pears (or peaches, or eels, all of which were rumoured to have been poisoned). In death,

---

[34] Hollister, p. 15.

[35] Graham Seel, *King John: An Underrated King* (London, 2012).

[36] Seel, p. 5.

[37] A.R. Braunmuller, 'King John and Historiography', *English Literary History* 55, no. 2 (Summer 1988): 309–32.

[38] Ralph of Coggeshall, *Chronicum Anglicanum*, from *BL Cotton Vespasian D.X.*, ed. and repr. by J. Stevenson (London, 1875).

John lay apart from his mother, father, and brothers; instead, he wished to be buried between two English saints so that he might construct a truth out of presumption. Even in his grave John generated mistrust. Braunmuller calls this kind of narrative part of the 'positive public effects' of the chronicles.[39] In this sense, chroniclers sought to reconceptualise events and personages so that they cooperated with contemporary public sentiment. The process produces a *post hoc ergo propter hoc* situation, as D.A. Carpenter demonstrates in his discussion of Coggeshall's account of John's reign;[40] but Coggeshall and his readers would have seen these circular arguments as examples of the type of shrewdness necessary for a chronicler. Hollister also demonstrates that chroniclers habitually presented arguments that went in circles, especially when it came to King John: these arguments did the job of validating the authority of the chronicles and producing 'positive public effects'.[41]

As Seel notes, Roger of Wendover, who began his account of John's reign about ten years after the king's death, continued this trend of constructing a narrative of the (dead) body of King John.[42] The putative murder of Prince Arthur was at the forefront of this construction. Stories of Arthur's murder provided Wendover (and other chroniclers) with convenient allegories for the degradation of the Royal Body both physically and mystically. Wendover related other events, such as John's lust for his teenage wife, (or the wives of others)[43] and his killing of Maud de Briouze and her son by starvation;[44] he also related the tale of John's crushing to death of an archdeacon under a cope of lead and the threatening of papal emissaries with blinding and the slitting of their noses.[45] Much of the attitude of the chroniclers in their criticism of King John, therefore, is rooted in the horror of mutilation and/or corruption of the body. In each case, issues of the body in the text are attached to issues of mistrust, invalidation,

---

[39] Braunmuller, p. 310.

[40] D.A. Carpenter, 'Abbot Ralph of Coggeshall's Account of the Last Years of King Richard and the First Years of King John', *The English Historical Review* 113, no. 454 (November 1998): 1210–30.

[41] Hollister, pp. 1–19.

[42] Seel, p. 6.

[43] Such as that of Eustace de Vesci, one of John's barons. This story is disputed, but it fit the agenda of the chronicles for centuries. See William of Newburg, *Historia Rerum Anglorum: Chronicles of the Reigns of Stephen, Henry II, and Richard II*, ed. Richard Howlett. 4 vols, (London, 1884–9), vol. II, p. 521; and Matthew Paris, *Chronica Majora*. 3 vols. (London, 1852–4), vol. II, p. 559. See also Kate Norgate, *John Lackland,* for an example of the extent to which late Victorian histories continued to dramatise these episodes.

[44] Maud de Briouze was the wife of William de Briouze, a powerful baron of the Marshes. She is reported to have angered King John by refusing to send her son to court as a hostage during a dispute between her husband and the king regarding the purchase of lands in Leinster. She also openly doubted John's innocence in the death of Prince Arthur. For her defiance and her insinuations she and her son were starved to death in Corfe Castle in Dorset. See Thomas B. Costain, *The Conquering Family* (New York, 1962), pp. 260–2.

[45] The story of the cope of lead is found in Roger Wendover, *Chronica*, ed. H.O. Coxe. 5 vols. (London, 1831–44), vol. III, p. 229.

and physical corruption. John threatens to mutilate the royal body of Prince Arthur, who may in fact be the legitimate claimant to the throne; John defiles his own royal body by pursuing women with un-regal lust; and he corrupts the royal body further by gorging it with food, to the point of death. His defilement of the royal body reflects his disregard for Divine Right, for maternal dignity, for regal temperance and self-control. Moreover, these stories suggest that coming into proximity with John's defiled regal body is dangerous to the bodies of others: the corruption of John's body results in disfigurement, defilement, and death for those near him.

In the chronicle accounts, John's death after consuming a plate of poisoned food (or after eating a surfeit of food) speaks to the corruption of the internal workings of kingship that caused him to commit monstrous acts.[46] His bowels degrade in a grotesque deconstruction of the regal body. When Matthew Paris succeeded Wendover in 1235 he escalated the imaginative qualities of the narrative and, as Seel states, 'inserted speeches into the mouths of long-dead people', to embellish the existing symbolism of chronicled events and personages.[47] For example, Paris reports that upon hearing of the death of Hubert Walter, Archbishop of Canterbury (a man who had purportedly expressed doubt about John's ability to live up to his coronation oath), King John exclaimed, 'Now for the first time I am King of England!'[48] By using the ventriloquised voices of the dead, Paris produces a view of John that is removed from reality, but which is nonetheless practically unimpeachable because of the credibility of the genre. Concerning the story of the lead cope, Hollister, along with W. L. Warren, notes that Paris (following the lead of Wendover) is wrong about the identity of the man, and also about the year in which the purported event occurred.[49] Seel notes that the very *readability* of these tales, paired with the authority of the chronicles, accounted for the ease with which such stories were told, and retold over the ages.[50] Educated as he was, Valentine Green was familiar with these accounts and interpretations. It was apparent that the corpse of King John had been interfered with, as its appearance was drastically different from that described by Bale. The absence of the royal *accoutrements*

---

[46] Seel, p. 6.

[47] Seel, p. 6. Paris embellishes a story related by Wendover that the Archbishop added a provision to King John's coronation oath that admonished the king not to accept kingship unless he could truly commit to his coronation oath. In other words, Walter required the king to swear doubly: he was first to commit to his oath, and then to swear the oath itself. See Wendover, *Flowers of History*, in *Chronica*, ed. H.O. Coxe, 5 vols. (London, 1831–44), vol. II, p. 181, and below. See also Thea Cervone [Tomaini], *Sworn Bond in Tudor England* (Jefferson, NC, 2011), p. 140.

[48] Paris, p. 104.

[49] W.L. Warren, *King John* (London, 1961), p. 13. Wendover states that this event occurred in 1209 and that the victim was Geoffrey, Archdeacon of Norwich. This man was still alive in 1225. There is some evidence that the victim was a man named Geoffrey of Norwich who was the Justice of the Jews, but there is also evidence that he died in prison in 1212. Hollister, p. 3, n. 14.

[50] Seel, p. 6.

and the odd positioning of the head suggested theft and even desecration; and the signs of poor embalming and the presence of maggot shells suggested negligence. Despite Bale's account of a heroic and regal corpse, the body with which Green was faced read like the varied accounts of the chronicles: it was in disarray,[51] a jumble of ugly stories, a collection of untold or unfinished narratives inviting enthymematic suppositions as the corpse was read.

Bale's description of King John's corpse – the only posthumous description apart from Green's – is therefore anomalous from the standpoint of chronicled history. Bale does not record the poor embalming or insect infestation, nor does he record the destruction or removal of the royal regalia. He does not record interference with or desecration of the corpse. Those aspects of the corpse would have been apparent in 1529. If Bale saw them, he chose to overlook them, preferring instead to supply a description of King John that conformed to a revised legend: a text of the corpse that Bale composed himself. He writes:

> Epitaph on the Discovery at Worcester of The Most Illustrious John,
> King of the English.
>
> Enclosed in this stone is the famous King John
> Who once flourished while ruling the kingdom of England.
> No doubt he rests under this icy marble
> However much the hissing throng may claim otherwise.
> In the year of Christ 1529
> On that very day, which was the last of June
> Masons building another sepulchre
> (Where now, behold, he lies) found the body decayed
> But yet adorned with a sword and a crown on his head
> The right hand holding a fair rod and the left a sceptre
> Next [to the body] came a golden vestment covered by a silk one
> Spurs on his feet, a ring on his finger
> All of which to the few, indeed to many, and all manner of people
> Was exposed for two days and was visible [to all].
> Therefore whoever you are who reads this inscription
> Say, 'Omnipotent Father, look with favour on [your servant] John'.[52]

---

[51] Namely the lower mandible and parts of the right arm. The lower mandible and several teeth came loose when the head was detached and turned around (this is presumably also when the gilded crown was stolen). The bones of the right arm came loose when the sword that lay upon the arm was pried loose in an attempt to steal it. Due to its age, the sword merely came apart.

[52] Translation from the Latin by Thea Tomaini.

Although Bale witnessed the opening of King John's tomb in 1529, he did not compose the poem until two decades later, in the margin of his copy of Nicholas Trivet's *Annales Regum Angliae*.[53] By then Bale had earned (and lost) the patronage of Thomas Cromwell, Chief Minister of Henry VIII, and staunch iconoclast. Under Thomas Cromwell's patronage Bale's company performed his play *Kynge Johan* in September 1539;[54] at that same time Cromwell was commissioning iconoclastic missions to destroy the vestiges of Catholicism across Britain. Amid the whitewashing of murals and the smashing of stained glass windows in churches, monasteries, and priories, there occurred the systematic destruction of the tombs and shrines of saints; especially altar tombs that bore figural monuments. In January 1540, Cromwell's agents arrived at Worcester to dissolve its Benedictine priory, raid its cathedral's treasury, and destroy the shrines of St Oswald and St Wulfstan.[55] After the destruction of the shrines, the altar tomb of King John was moved from the Lady Chapel to the choir just below the high altar – a place of honour. They spared the figural monument.

This effort reflects the attitudes concerning the revision of John's reputation among reformers – namely, Bale. In Bale's play *Kynge Johan* John is lied to, manipulated, bullied, and eventually murdered by the villains Dissimulacyon, Sedycyon, and Pandulphus, all of whom represent the Catholic clergy and Papal forces. The villains are supported by other allegorical abettors: Privat Welth, a treacherous and greedy aristocrat, Clergye, a disobedient priest, and Cyvyle Order, an opportunistic lawyer. Bale lauds King John as the lone protector of the poor widow Ynglonde and her blind son Commynalte. Bale revises John's life and death, eliminating references to Prince Arthur and to John's military and political failures (he even avoids discussion of the Magna Carta). Bale prefers instead to focus on John's humiliation and martyrdom at the hands of the Roman Church, thereby revising John's legend in defiance of the chronicles. Bale, once a Carmelite historian himself, challenges the content and the academic and political

---

[53] Nicholas Trivet, *Annales Regum Angliae*. Parker Library, Corpus Christi College, Cambridge MS 152 fol. 48, marginal note by John Bale. J.H.P. Pafford argues persuasively that Bale must have transcribed the poem in the Trivet volume after his return from exile in 1548. Bale's letters from his exile period betray a Continental habit of placing a tick above the letter *u*. This tick also appears in Bale's autograph revision of *Kynge Johan* (1560?), but is absent from his handwriting in earlier pages of the play and from other samples of his earlier writing. See John Bale, *Kynge Johan*. HEH MS 128, Huntington Library, San Marino, CA; also J.H.P. Pafford, 'King John's Tomb in Worcester Cathedral', *Transactions of the Worcestershire Archaeological Society* 35, new series (1959): 58–60; see also W.T. Davies, 'A Bibliography of John Bale', *Oxford Bibliographic Society Proceedings and Papers*, vol. V, part iv (Oxford, 1940), and W.W. Greg, *English Literary Autographs* (Nendeln, Liechtenstein, 1968).

[54] Great Britain, Public Record Office, *Letters and Papers, Foreign and Domestic, of the Reign of Henry VIII*, ed. J. Gairdner and R.H. Brodie, 21 vols. (London, 1862–1910, repr. 1965–1976), vol. XIV, no. 2, item 782.

[55] The iconoclasts spared the tomb and figural monument of Arthur, Prince of Wales, presumably because he had been the brother of Henry VIII; nevertheless, a different group of iconoclasts vandalised Arthur's figural monument during the reign of Edward VI, by knocking off its head.

authority of the chronicles, and replaces those texts with his own dramatic revision of the same events.[56] Like his contemporary John Leland, Bale used his chronicling skills to defend Henrician politics and thereby attempt to exert control over England's past.[57] After the death of Kynge Johan by poisoning, the king returns from the dead as the figure Imperiall Majestie. Neither ghost nor revenant nor saint, Imperiall Majestie represents a spiritual archetype of kingship. He is regal authority personified via the king's mystical body.[58] Here, Bale revises the text of the king's dead body as Kynge Johan overcomes martyrdom in a pseudo-resurrection as a triumphant figure who is liberated not only from a victim's death and but also from the afterlife of a saint.

Accordingly, when sometime after 1546 Bale revisited his memory of the 1529 opening of King John's tomb, he revised the text of the corpse in a similar way. He notes the decay of the body, but mentions no extenuating descriptions regarding its condition.[59] Instead he focuses on its regality and its dignity, noting especially its splendid attire and accoutrements. Yet, even as Bale remembers his visit of nearly twenty years earlier, and writes the corpse of King John so as to echo the issues of his own play, he ironically mirrors the efforts of Ralph of Coggeshall and Roger of Wendover, who changed their minds about King John years after his death and revised their views of his kingship, and of his body, accordingly.

The efforts to revise the text of King John's corpse may have been pointed during the reigns of Henry VIII and Edward VI, but those efforts could not overwhelm centuries of tradition. The King John of the Elizabethan imagination is a complex figure, one who recalls reformist propaganda but who still carries a problematic legacy. That legacy remains inscribed onto King John's corrupt body.[60] Neither the anonymous author of

---

[56] Bale's other dramatic and polemical writings challenge the authority and validity of the thirteenth-century chroniclers on a variety of subjects. For Bale, the debauchery of the monastic orders argues against their reliability as historical witnesses. See Peter Happe, *John Bale* (New York, 1996); and Leslie Fairfield, *John Bale: Mythmaker for the English Reformation* (Indianapolis, 1976).

[57] Joseph M. Levine, *Humanism and History: Origins of Modern English Historiography* (Ithaca, NY, 1987), p. 80. In 1549 Bale published Leland's topographical and historical account of Henry VIII's realm, entitled *The Laboryouse Journey and Serche of John Leylande for Englandes Antiquities*. Jan Broadway calls the book 'the public manifesto for the development of local history and cartography'. Broadway, p. 27.

[58] For a full discussion of Imperiall Majestie, the roots of the character in the Medieval ghost tradition, and its symbolism as a figure for both Henry VIII and Elizabeth I, see Thea Cervone [Tomaini], 'The King's Phantom: Staging Majesty in Bale's *Kynge Johan*', *Studies in Medievalism* 17 (2009): 185–202. See also Ernest Kantorowicz, *The King's Two Bodies: A Study in Medieval Political Theology* (1957) (Princeton, NJ, 1997).

[59] There is no indication that Bale was untruthful in his recollection of the corpse's appearance. The purported desecrations and thefts described below likely happened after Bale left the cathedral but before the tomb was closed – a window of less than two days.

[60] For more comprehensive discussions of these and similar issues in Bale's *Kynge Johan*, *The Troublesome Raigne of King John* and Shakespeare's *The Life and Death of King John*, see Thea Cervone [Tomaini], *Sworn Bond*, pp. 134–67.

The Troublesome Raigne of King John nor William Shakespeare was directly familiar with Bale's work when they produced the era's two history plays about King John; but they were familiar with the work of Bale's protégé, John Foxe, who praised King John as a proto-Protestant figure who rightly defied the Pope.[61] They were also aware that King John's reputation had a varied and complex history, and that his reputation shifted uneasily between heroism and villainy. Elizabethan attitudes toward the chronicles, especially among the writers of history plays, were hardly conciliatory: Braunmuller explains that they did not likely suppose that the chronicles were – or were trying to be – objective records of past events or personages.[62] Even Raphael Holinshed, he notes, 'might have balked at the claim' that the chronicles were to be understood as genuine descriptions of the past.[63] For as much as Holinshed (and also Edward Hall) repeats stories from Wendover and Paris concerning King John's cruelty, lust, and cowardice, and for as much as Holinshed understood the power of the chronicle genre, he was aware that he was producing what Braunmuller calls 'a politically volatile text in the present'.[64] This awareness permeated the attitudes of playwrights who produced histories based in part on Holinshed's work – such as the author of *Troublesome Raigne* and Shakespeare – as they reworked the concepts and characters they found in his chronicle and, as Jonathan Price states, 'turned them just enough on their side so that an Elizabethan (and modern critic as well) may have wondered just which way he should evaluate John'.[65] The Elizabethan writers and audiences of history plays sustained a partial interest in what Price calls 'the provocative ambiguity' of King's John's death and posthumous legacy.[66]

In Shakespeare's *King John*, the abandonment of John by his barons focuses strongly on the corporeal aspects of desertion: after the barons swear allegiance to Lewis the Dauphin on the altar of St Edmund, Lewis partakes in the Eucharistic sacrament, by

---

[61] John Foxe, *The Unabridged Acts and Monuments Online* or *TAMO* (1570 edition) (HRI Online Publications, Sheffield, 2011), https://www.johnfoxe.org. Foxe was gentle with most of the salacious stories about King John. Regarding the death of Prince Arthur, Foxe writes: 'The same Arthur being thus taken in war, was brought before the Kyng at the castell of Falesie in Normandy: who beyng exhorted with many gentle words to leave the French kyng & to incline to his uncle, answered agayne stoutly and with great indignation: requiryng the kingdome of England with all the other dominions thereto belonging to be restored to hym as to the lawfull heyre of the crowne. By reason wherof he (provoking the Kings displeasure against him) was sent to the tower of Roane: where at length (whether by leaping into the ditch thinking to make his escape, or whether by some other privy hand, or by what chance els: it is not yet agreed upon in stories) he finished his lyfe. By occasion wherof, the foresayd Kyng Ihon was had after in great suspition: whether iustly or vniustly, the Lord knoweth.' (Book IV, p. 34.)

[62] Braunmuller, p. 321.

[63] Braunmuller, p. 321.

[64] Braunmuller, p. 321.

[65] Jonathan Price, '*King John* and Problematic Art', *Shakespeare Quarterly* 21, no. 1 (Winter, 1970): 26.

[66] Price, p. 26.

which he accepts their fealty.[67] By observing the Catholic rites of saint veneration and transubstantiation, John's enemies assert the mystical power of the consecrated body and align it with the authority of the Papacy. They then affirm their observance with an oath. This act displaces the kingly body, already corrupted by cruelty and failure, and prepares it for murder. Although King John's barons rediscover their loyalty, the damage is done. Like Bale's Kynge Johan and the king of *Troublesome Raigne*, Shakespeare's King John also succumbs to poison, but this issue is preceded by the corruption of the king's body in the form of weakness, inconstancy, and political impotence until he is nothing more than a statutory version of himself – a redundant, irrelevant text. He laments, 'I am a scribbled form, drawn with a pen/Upon a parchment, and against this fire/Do I shrink up'.[68] When images of the body such as this one converge with the visibility of performance, they produce what Braunmuller calls 'Shakespeare's unique vision of the body as text'.[69] In both plays King John's situation reduces him from regal status to that of a mere man, and then from a man to a mere shadow of a man, and finally to a mere corpse. The murder of King John obliterates him in both Elizabethan plays, and no resurrection figure follows his death. Both Shakespeare and the author of *Troublesome Raigne* inscribe utter defeat onto the body of King John. They depict a complete failure that produces a decay of his royal and human dignity from which John's physical body cannot recover. The death of the body follows. This interpretation differs from that of the chroniclers who inscribe textuality onto the body of John: in the chronicles, villainy (rather than failure) produces the corruption of John's royal and human dignity (and that of others), from which he cannot be saved. The death of the body follows. The Elizabethan history plays differ thus from Bale's: Bale's play inscribes victimhood onto the body of King John, which corrupts his human condition but not his regal dignity. Although the king's physical body cannot recover, his mystical body does, and Imperiall Majestie continues to produce text by chastising the play's villains and emphasising the eternal power of true kingship.[70] In all three cases, though, the catalyst for John's death is the same: external forces cause the decay of his living qualities, turning the king into a corpse before the fact. His death then validates the reality that has already been established.

Audience and playwright interest in such complexities was indeed partial. As Seel points out, despite efforts to 'rehabilitate' John during the middle part of the sixteenth century, that gesture proved to be only partly effective by the 1590s. In Anthony Munday's *Downfall of Robert, Earl of Huntington* (1597–8), Prince John pursues Matilda to her death, causing her father to call on the Virgin Mary to protect 'True

---

[67] V.ii.6. The events described actually take place offstage and are related as exposition by Salisbury.

[68] V.vii.32–3.

[69] Braunmuller, p. 319.

[70] In Bale's 1560 revision of *Kynge Johan*, Imperiall Majestie goes on to praise the recently crowned Elizabeth I for her continuing embodiment of these ideals.

English lords from such a Tyrant Lord'.[71] The John of *Look About You* is similarly temperamental and lecherous, pursuing Matilda with what Fred Jones calls 'the fury of a maddened beast'.[72] This is also true of seventeenth-century history plays about King John: Seel states that 'the salacious details of John's life and reign as they appeared in the chronicles and in the popular imagination proved too vivid to forget'.[73] When it comes to *Troublesome Raigne* and Shakespeare's *King John* the anti-Catholic and anti-sacramentalist sentiments of the plays guide the complex portrayal of King John. The rhetoric of Papal defiance is not as virulent as that of 'Bilious Bale', but it performs its function well, especially in the light of the theme of aristocratic disloyalty present in the plays. In both plays the betrayal of the barons is remedied when they learn of the double-cross planned by the Dauphin.[74] Their disloyalty, and John's defiance of the Pope, are part of a multifaceted whole message about Church and State, duty and conscience. This is not so in Jacobean history plays that do not emphasise these issues or that employ a strong anti-Catholic message, especially *King John and Matilda, A Tragedy*, by Robert Davenport (active 1623).[75] Drawing upon stories from Wendover, Paris, and Holinshed, and other stories from popular lore (such as Michael Drayton's poem *Matilda, the Faire and Chaste Daughter of Lord R. Fitzwater*),[76] the play tells the story of an aristocratic young woman pursued to her death by a lustful King John.[77] Matilda refuses King John's advances, and he murders her in a nunnery by giving her a poisoned left-hand glove. When Matilda's corpse is brought to King John, he turns to Hubert de Burgh[78] and says, 'Hubert, interpret this apparition'.[79] Hubert obeys, and reads the corpse as a text:

> HUBERT. Behold, sir.
> A sad-writ Tragedy, so feelingly
> Languaged, and cast; with such a crafty cruelty
> Contrived, and acted; that wild savages
> Wold weep to lay their ears to, and (admiring
> To see themselves outdone) they would conceive
> Their wildness mildness to this deed, and call

---

[71] Anthony Munday, *The Downfall of Robert, Earle of Huntington, Afterward Called Robin Hood of Merrie Sherwodde* (1597–8) (London, 1601), ll. 1217–18.

[72] Fred L. Jones, '*Look About You* and *The Disguises*', *PMLA* 44, no. 3 (September, 1929): 836–7.

[73] Seel, p. 6.

[74] *Troublesome Raigne*, II.xv.138, and *King John*, V.vi.49–57.

[75] Robert Davenport, *King John and Matilda, a Tragedy* (1623?) (London, 1662).

[76] Michael Drayton, *Matilda, the Faire and Chaste Daughter of Lord R. Fitzwater* (London, 1594). Drayton's poem is a source for Anthony Munday's two Robin Hood plays.

[77] The plot is rooted in stories of King John's persecution of Maud de Briouze.

[78] The character Hubert is based on the historical figure of Hubert de Burgh, First Earl of Kent (c. 1160–1243?) who also appears in *Troublesome Raigne* and Shakespeare's *King John*, as the dutiful but compassionate agent of the king who ultimately refuses to murder Prince Arthur.

[79] V.i.450.

> Men more than savage, themselves rational.
>
> …
>
> …Oh look here
> Look here, King John, and with a trembling eye
> Read your sad act, Matilda's tragedy.[80]

The Queen then taunts King John with a demand that he read the corpse of her daughter for himself and see his own commands, saying: 'O cruell king, go sate thy bloody eye/With thy blacke command, which there lyes executed'.[81] Young Bruce concurs. He says: 'King, go and read thy cruelty'.[82] This final scene of the play dramatises the suggestive narrative of the chronicles and literally asks the audience to read the body of Matilda as a tragedy wherein they will perceive King John's cruelty. The play is not merely a dramatisation of a popular legend about King John; it is a 'sad act' in and of itself, performed upon the body of Matilda by the lecherous John. The play unifies the narrative of the chronicles and popular lore about King John with its own dramatic mission and inscribes the legend of King John onto Matilda's corpse so that she herself becomes a narrative 'so feelingly languaged and cast'. Part of this effort is due to Davenport's imaginative storytelling; but part of it is rooted in a larger cultural context in which King John's body, whether in life, death, or afterlife, carries with it distinct textual associations. Davenport's play 'reads' corruption of the political and physical body, impotence both political and sexual (as John's nickname 'Softsword' suggests), along with mutilation and murder. The end of Davenport's play mimics the chronicles in that it demonstrates the consequences of Matilda's bearing of proximity to John's body: his cruelty becomes inscribed upon her corpse, and she becomes known to the history of King John by way of the corruption of her body.

There also persisted a pronounced interest in King John's role as a villain in plays about the Robin Hood legend. Although early Robin Hood ballads of the sixteenth century like *Here Begynneth a Geste of Robyn Hode*[83] and *A Lyttel Gest of Robin Hode*[84] set their action in the reign of Edward II, the Robin Hood tradition of the later sixteenth century sets the escapades of Robin and his band in the reign of Richard Lionheart, with Prince John functioning as a cruel and unwelcome substitute for his brother. Plays like *A Mery Geste of Robyn Hoode: And of His Lyfe* (1560, reprinted 1590)[85] associated Robin Hood strongly with the May Games, and thereby connected the Robin Hood legend with issues of English cultural identity. Other plays and poems combined the

---

[80] V.i.451–67.

[81] V.i.471–2.

[82] V.i.475.

[83] There are two versions, both with the same title, and both anonymous. The earlier of the two was published in London in 1506, and the later ballad was published in London in 1515.

[84] Richard Pynson, *A Little Gest of Robin Hode* (London, 1500).

[85] Anon., *A Mery Geste of Robyn Hoode: And of hys Life, with a Newe Playe for to Be Played in Maye Games Very Pleasaunt and Full of Pastime* (London, 1560, repr. 1590).

Robin Hood legend with issues of English political identity, like the play *Look About You* (1599/1600),[86] and the poem *Albion's England* (1586) by William Warner.[87] In these works the authors attach the legend of Robin Hood to political issues concerning the deference of rogue aristocrats to their king. These works were followed by *The Downfall of Robert, Earl of Huntingdon* and *The Death of Robert, Earl of Huntingdon* by Anthony Munday (1597–8),[88] plays that focus on the maintenance of political order and downplay the association of Robin Hood with the May Games.[89] Concerning both English cultural and political identity, the character of King John in these Robin Hood plays stands as an affront to Englishness, and is the cause of baronial disobedience rather than the victim of it. As Stephanie Barczewski notes, Elizabethan Robin Hood plays present an important juxtaposition of the King John legend with that of Robin Hood that serves to indict the judgments of bad princes and the liberties of bad aristocrats.[90]

As Barczewski states, although these considerations of King John's character differ from those of Shakespeare or *Troublesome Raigne*, they still represent a response, or perhaps a reaction to, the heroic depictions of King John earlier in the century by writers like Bale and Foxe. Henry VIII did not look favourably upon Robin Hood plays because they suggested the heroism of rogue aristocracy. This was especially true once the King's Great Matter became a delicate political situation.[91] By 1509 the city of Exeter had banned Robin Hood plays, and the Lord Warden of the Cinque Ports of Kent and Sussex followed in 1528;[92] in 1536 Sir Richard Morison condemned Robin Hood plays that often accompanied May Games or were performed at summer holy day celebrations because their 'lewdness and ribaldry' encouraged disobedience to one's superiors.[93] This is precisely where the legend of King John becomes convenient. Munday's plays are the first to place the Robin Hood legend in the reign of Richard the Lionheart, and in doing so the plays redirect the issue of baronial disloyalty. In the ballads, Robin rebels against the tyranny embodied by King Edward's administrators

---

[86] Anonymous, *A Pleasant Comedie, Called Look About You* (London, 1600).

[87] William Warner, *Albion's England* (London, 1586).

[88] Anthony Munday, *The Downfall of Robert, Earle of Huntington, Afterward Called Robin Hood of Merrie Sherwodde* (1597–8) (London, 1601); and *The Death of Robert, Earle of Huntington: Otherwise Called Robin Hood of Merrie Sherwodde: With the Lamentable Tragedie of Chaste Matilda, His Faire Maid Marian, Poysoned at Dunmowe by King Iohn* (London, 1601). *The Death of Robert, Earl of Huntingdon* contains contributions by Henry Chettle.

[89] See Stephanie Barczewski, *Myth and National Identity in Nineteenth-Century Britain: The Legends of King Arthur and Robin Hood* (Oxford, 2000), pp. 24–5; and Larissa Tracy, '"For Our Dere Ladyes Sake": Bringing the Outlaw in from the Forest – Robin Hood, Marian, and Normative National Identity', *Explorations in Renaissance Culture* 38 (Summer and Winter 2012): 35–66.

[90] Barczewski, p. 24–5.

[91] Barczewski, p. 24–5.

[92] Peter Stallybrass, 'Drunk With The Cup of Liberty', *The Violence of Representation: Literature and the History of Violence* (London, 1989), p. 24.

[93] Morison, p. xxx, in Barczewski, pp. 24–5.

and corrupt clergy in his absence.[94] In Munday's plays John (as Prince John) serves as a vehicle by which Robin Hood's defiance of regal authority is directed away from Richard Lionheart and toward a lesser (but nonetheless royal) figure.[95] Robin's rebelliousness to Prince John is seen as a gesture of loyalty and deference to the true aristocratic and royal dignity of Richard Lionheart. Moreover, Prince John is depicted as the enemy of English political and cultural identity: he is a Norman invader, a usurper of Divine Right who persecutes the Saxon nobles and their people. It did not matter (in Munday's work or in that of others) that John was the brother of Richard Lionheart; Richard's heroism as a Crusader made his legacy resistant to political criticism, and the efforts of Henry II to attach Englishness to himself and his sons were successful for Richard, Henry, and Geoffrey, but not John.[96] As a corrupt administrator John stands as an obstacle to the true fealty of a king's barons. These events precede John's failures as a king and function as prophetic warnings against regal tyranny.

In Munday's plays, John is a caricatured version of his depiction in the chronicles. He is temperamental, scheming, cowardly, and violent. In the second Robin Hood play by Munday (*The Death of Robert, Earl of Huntingdon*), Prince John pursues Matilda until she commits suicide: 'The guiltless feare not death', she says, drinking poison, 'Farewell, good friend/I praye thee be no trouble in my end'.[97] Stephen Knight points out that this union of political and cultural issues produces a variety of social meanings and therefore a variety of possibilities for the assessment of John's career.[98] By the early seventeenth century King John had become a character of frustrating elasticity: he could be made to represent Protestantism and English national strength, personal weakness and lack of moral fibre, regal and aristocratic dignity, political overreaching, martyrdom, predation, and self-destruction in just about any combination.[99] About sixteenth-century Robin Hood ballads and plays Knight states, 'Whatever history may say about Richard I's absenteeism and King John's shrewd management, the image held by Tudor historians from Major to Stowe was that King John was a thorough wastrel: to locate an outlaw then was implicitly to justify his extralegal actions'.[100] Although this statement rings true for the most part, the efforts of Bale and Foxe were not completely overlooked. By the beginning of the eighteenth century King John's posthumous reputation was more complex than ever.

By the time Valentine Green stared into the stone coffin at the remains of King John, the reputation of the long-dead king had undergone changes once again. These changes were the result of the revisiting of Henrician attitudes towards John's life,

---

[94] See Tracy, 'For Our Dere Ladyes Sake'.
[95] Stephen Knight, *Robin Hood: A Mythic Biography* (Ithaca, 2003), p. 53.
[96] This point is made in Shakespeare's play as he examines John's claim to the throne in comparison with that of his nephew Prince Arthur.
[97] Munday, *The Death of Robert, Earl of Huntington*, V.i.197–8.
[98] Knight, p. 63.
[99] Knight, p. 63.
[100] Knight, p. 63.

death, and corpse among many advocates of Protestantism in England. One important source whose take on history rivalled both the chronicles and the Elizabethan plays was a book by William Prynne. Its title says it all: *An Exact Chronological Vindication and Historical Demonstration of Our British, Roman, Saxon, Danish, Norman, English Kings' Supreme Ecclesiastical Jurisdiction Over All Prelates, Persons, Causes, Within Their Kingdoms and Dominions* (1666).[101] In Prynne's several introductions and prefaces, the book justifies monarchic ecclesiastical authority and argues against the Pope's authority over England's kings. Prynne states that from the very first year of King John's reign, his aim had been to protect England from Papal interference: '[action such as his defiance of Innocent III] was not to make him Judge of his Right, but merely to preserve it from the Popes and others invasions on it, by any clandestine machinations, or extraordinary means that might be used to interrupt or defraud him of it'.[102] John is credited with suspecting that the Pope would overstep his rights in England, and with taking steps to prevent such intrusion on England's rights. The book presents an implausible *post hoc ergo propter hoc* argument that recalls the efforts of Bale and Foxe, but which nonetheless argues against the depiction of King John in the ballads and plays. Prynne's methods of compiling sources were attractive to those with a budding interest in document collecting, even if Anthony Wood thought of him as old fashioned.[103] Prynne worked as a record keeper in the Tower under Charles II, where he used his antiquarian skills to sort through piles of old records that he describes as 'being interred in their own rubbish'.[104] Prynne compiled the records and published them with citations and commentaries to create a book that, although controversial, did not merely echo the chronicles but presented a new argument of its own.

There is no record of performances of Shakespeare's *King John* between 1700 and 1737, but after that date there seems to be a revival of the play. This mini-revival includes the much-altered 1745 adaptation of *King John* at Covent Garden by the actor, theatre manager, and Poet Laureate Colley Cibber.[105] Cibber, who did much to introduce sentimental comedy to the English stage, produced popular adaptations of Shakespearean plays that made the subject matter and the language more accessible to audiences than the Elizabethan style. Although Cibber's adaptations were derided by more traditional writers – namely Alexander Pope, with whom he had a longstanding

---

[101] William Prynne, *An Exact Chronological Vindication and Historical Demonstration of Our British, Roman, Saxon, Danish, Norman, English Kings' Supreme Ecclesiastical Jurisdiction Over All Prelates, Persons, Causes, Within Their Kingdoms and Dominions* (London, 1666).

[102] Prynne, p. 230.

[103] Anthony Wood, *Athenae Oxoniensis, an Exact History of all the Writers and Bishops Who Have Had Their Education in the University of Oxford*, 2 vols. (London, 1813), vol. I, p. lix.

[104] William Prynne, 'Letter to Sir Harbottle Grimston', 9 September 1661 (*Verulam MSS*), *Report on the Manuscripts of the Earl of Verulam, Preserved at Gorhambury* (London, 1906), p. 58.

[105] Cibber adapted several Shakespearean plays, but he was best known for his adaptation of *Richard III*. He played Richard on the stage many times before being replaced by a young David Garrick.

feud[106] – his plays were responsible for bringing bigger audiences to the Shakespearean stage. His staging of Shakespeare's *King John*, titled *Papal Tyranny in the Reign of King John*, was meant to capitalise on recent events, namely the 1743 outbreak of war between Britain and France, and the Jacobite Rising of 1745. Both Shakespeare's *King John* and Cibber's *Papal Tyranny* appealed to anti-Jacobite and anti-Catholic sentiment in audiences, and in the 1745 season *Papal Tyranny* was performed eleven times at Covent Garden (with Cibber as the villain Cardinal Pandulphus), while David Garrick performed *King John* at Drury Lane.[107] The major difference between Cibber's version of *King John* and Shakespeare's (apart from Cibber's changes in poetic language) is Cibber's emphasis on the Protestant and nationalistic messages of the play. As Braunmuller states, Shakespeare had been cautious with these issues, preferring to relegate them to secondary treatment in favour of a depiction of King John as a failure as a monarch and a man.[108] Although Shakespeare's anti-Catholicism is most apparent in *King John*, it is nonetheless depicted subtly compared to *Troublesome Raigne* or Bale's *Kynge Johan*. Shakespeare's patriotism is more apparent in other plays, like *Henry V*, rather than *King John*, and he avoids the kind of English nationalism depicted by Bale, but he also avoids the pro-Saxon nationalism of Munday's *Robin Hood* plays, in which Prince John is a thinly veiled Norman invader. Cibber wondered that Shakespeare 'should have taken no more Fire' at the 'flaming contest between his insolent Holiness and King John'.[109] It was what Cibber saw as Shakespeare's indifference that inspired him to depict King John 'with a resentment that justly might become an English monarch'.[110] Anti-Jacobean sentiment had audiences 'taking fire' at Catholicism and the French, and Cibber wanted so badly for his play to reflect that sentiment that he came out of retirement to stage it.

Shakespeare's *King John*, both in its traditional version and in adaptation, was produced in London in thirty-eight seasons between 1737 and 1823,[111] its popularity reflective of the same contemporary attitudes about British national identity that Cibber sought to tap into. Stephanie Barczewski states that national identity between the reigns of Queen Anne and Queen Victoria was something that people felt needed to be validated rather than developed. She says, 'National identity was something to be worried about by the nation-building Italians and Germans, or the revolution-plagued French…'[112] Britons of the eighteenth century acknowledged that national identity had developed in the past, but the prevalent attitude was that English national identity

---

[106] Pope's poem *The Dunciad* is in part a satirical portrait of Cibber.

[107] Braunmuller, p. 193.

[108] Braunmuller, p. 193.

[109] Colley Cibber, *The Dramatic Works of Colley Cibber, Esq.*, 5 vols. (London, 1767), vol. I, p. 240. See also Eugene Waith, 'King John and the Drama of History', in *King John and Henry VIII: Critical Essays*, ed. Francis Shirley (New York, 1988), p. 32.

[110] Cibber, p. 32.

[111] Braunmuller, p. 193.

[112] Barczewski, p. vi.

was firmly established and unquestionable.[113] Attitudes about King John as they relate to anti-Jacobism and anti-Catholicism of the eighteenth century follow this pattern. Theatre companies and their audiences looked to the sixteenth century to validate and provide assurance of their sentiments. Cibber was a Hanoverian supporter who had served the Earl of Devonshire upon William of Orange's invasion of England in 1688, and who was known to the court of George II upon his appointment as Poet Laureate. His audiences were attracted to these qualities as they were reflected in his work, just as they were attracted to his Whig politics. As Elizabeth Fay states, 'Whigs located a primitive democracy in the Medieval village and more particularly in pre-Norman medievalism, while the feudal system at large provided a contractual system that ensured individual liberties'.[114] In his *Reflections on the Revolution in France* (1793), Edmund Burke wrote:

> From the Magna Carta to the Declaration of Right, it had been the uniform policy of our constitution to claim and assert our liberties, as an entailed inheritance derived to us from our forefathers, and to be transmitted to our posterity; as an estate specifically belonging to the people of our kingdom without any reference to any more general or prior right.[115]

Britain's relationship with King John's legacy (uncomfortable as it might be) was part of a comprehensive relationship with the past. Via the high regard for Shakespeare (and his plays in adaptation) and via a deep respect for the past as it was imagined, King John's legacy symbolised defiance of both France and the Papacy.

Both Whigs and Tories used the literary and theatrical legends of King John as a template for national sentiment. Via the Robin Hood legend, King John's lechery, cruelty, greed, and gluttony could be used to argue in defence of Innocent III and John's barons. As Barczewski points out, 'Conservatives used the Medieval past to demonstrate the continuity and durability of Britain's political and social institutions'.[116] Britain's social and political institutions survived reigns such as that of King John, and their durability was the product of a long practical experience.[117] Elizabeth Fay also makes this point, saying, 'Tory authors and historians looked to the Medieval period for feudal paternalism and an interdependent community as a solution to economic crisis and class unrest... Conservative medievalism was concerned chiefly with chivalry and feudalism'.[118] In this sense King John became a convenient figure

---

[113] Barczewski, p. vi.

[114] Elizabeth Fay, *Romantic Medievalism: History and the Romantic Literary Ideal* (New York, 2002), p. 1.

[115] Edmund Burke, *Reflections on the Revolution in France and the First Letter on a Regicide Peace* (London, 1790), p. 47.

[116] Barczewski, p. 33.

[117] Barczewski, p. 33.

[118] Fay, pp. 1 and 3.

throughout the eighteenth and into the nineteenth century: through the emerging concept of medievalism King John symbolised both The Norman Yoke and Protestant autonomy. Regardless of one's politics, one could draw upon the legend of King John and cite an established 'Medieval' precedent for one's platform on national identity issues. As Barczewski states, 'The Middle Ages served as a battleground for the clash between competing visions of what the nation had been and what it should be. In this period, medievalism – and in particular the legends of King Arthur and Robin Hood – helped to create a past around which people could unite, but it also demonstrated just how difficult that unity could be to achieve in the present.'[119] Although achieving that unity could indeed be difficult, there did arise what Fay calls 'a varied revisionism' that drew upon established authorities: the precedent of the Henrician Reformation, the established authority of the Shakespearean stage, and the postmedieval legacy of the national heroes Robin Hood and Richard Lionheart. John's protracted legacy symbolised tyranny over liberty and an abuse of the feudal system, and indicated the values of the emerging concept of medievalism: a reverence for selective issues and figures of the Medieval and Early Modern past that were very often viewed through the values of the Tudor period.[120] Elizabeth Fay comments that this revisionist frame of mind creates a collapse into the Medieval, *per se*. As historical figures and events are viewed through 'an imprecise representation of the Medieval' (a term of convenience that often includes the sixteenth and early seventeenth centuries), they create what she calls 'an immediate ground for the modern, and it is in the modern that romanticism situates itself as an initiating moment'.[121] Historical personages and their legends are appropriated and romanticised so that they become accessible to contemporary attitudes. By this process, during the eighteenth century King John became a *Medievalist* figure, and more so, became what Tatiana String and Marcus Bull call a '*Tudorist*' figure. Both terms refer to a figure of the historical past that appears to communicate a preconceived set of terms reflecting values important to a scholar, student, or enthusiast in his or her own time.[122]

In 1795 Joseph Ritson published his collection of Robin Hood ballads. This collection also contributed to the grounding in modernism of the legend of King John. The book became a definitive edition of tales about Robin Hood – and King (Prince) John – for generations. Ritson, a firm supporter of republicanism and the revolution in France, issued his collection of Robin Hood ballads with an introduction instructing his readers to use the legend of Robin Hood as a means to express their political

[119] Barczewski, p. 35.

[120] For comprehensive discussions of this subject, see Kathleen Biddick, *The Shock of Medievalism* (Durham, NC, 1998); and R.J. Smith, *The Gothic Bequest: Medieval Institutions in British Thought 1688–1863* (Cambridge, 2002).

[121] Fay, pp. 8–9.

[122] For a comprehensive discussion of the term 'Tudorism', see *Tudorism: Historical Imagination and the Appropriation of the Sixteenth Century*, ed. Tatiana String and Marcus Bull (Oxford, 2011).

ideals.[123] Ritson wrote in his introduction that Robin Hood lived 'under a complicated tyranny', a phrase that was meant to promote republicanism by allying Robin Hood with the common people. The phrase was also meant to emphasise the villainy of Prince John and his agents as the symbols of monarchic and institutional tyranny instead of pointing to Richard Lionheart.[124] Prince John's role, although secondary to Ritson's concern, was important nonetheless: John was a more demonstrable historical figure than Robin Hood, and his political choices and regal politics had real and lasting consequences. As a former Jacobite, Ritson was sensitive to the complexities of patriotism and was aware that sometimes traitors were the very people who styled themselves as patriots. As Barczewski states, for Ritson, real patriots fought 'against those who were most eager to wave the flag and beat the war drum', and 'acted to overcome the oppression and tyranny they [the hawks] promoted'.[125] Robin Hood fits the description of the 'real patriot', while Prince John fits the description of the false flag-waver, whose recklessness puts the nation in danger. Here, Ritson's attitude focuses on John's hypocrisy as a Norman invader who used false patriotism to become an ersatz Englishman. Ironically, Ritson's omission of similar criticism for Richard Lionheart falls in line with the same omission by the chroniclers. John was more conveniently cowardly, cruel, and hypocritical.

It is even more ironic, perhaps, that criticism of antiquarian study from the Georgian through the early Victorian periods included the accusation that antiquarianism was too romantic, too fantasist, to constitute serious academic enquiry. Such criticism relied on stereotyped views of antiquaries listening to folk tales and digging up ephemera. That was not the case. The Anglican clergyman Thomas Percy is an important figure in the recovery and study of old ballads as legitimate works of literature and as important historical resources. His edition of ballads employed an important tactic: he attached class issues to his readings of the ballads in order to encourage contemporary scholars to extract useful social issues from them.[126] As Clare Simmons states, 'Percy's first contribution to the medievalist myth of the minstrel was to grant minstrels a kind of gentility that removed them from the populace yet placed them in a fixed relationship with the ruling classes, whose exploits in warfare their songs celebrated'.[127] Percy's depiction of the minstrel as a man who celebrated his king's power and glory was in stark contrast with Ritson's republicanism, but both collections of ballads emphasised the 'Norman Yoke' issue to which King John was firmly attached, and

---

[123] Joseph Ritson, *Robin Hood: A Collection of Poems, Songs, and Ballads* (London, 1795, repr. 1862); and Barczewski, p. 42.

[124] Ritson, p. xvi.

[125] Barczewski, p. 43.

[126] Percy actually continued the work of his uncle, also called Thomas Percy, who gave up the study of ballads because he considered it to be frivolous. Thomas Percy, *Reliques of Ancient English Poetry, Consisting of Old Heroic Ballads, Songs, and Other Pieces of our Earlier Poets (Chiefly of the Lyric Kind)*, 2 vols. (London, 1765).

[127] Clare Simmons, *Popular Medievalism in Romantic-Era Britain* (New York, 2011), p. 58.

both held Richard Lionheart as an exception to that rule, leaving John to stand alone as a tyrant and hypocrite. Ritson's literary antiquarianism was more concerned with historical authenticity (or the appearance of it) than Percy's, yet Percy's work did much to establish grounds for the authenticity of the oral tradition. As Valentine Green examined the corpse of King John, he was aware that in the present day King John was being used in politics, religion, folklore, and literature to put a face on the past. There was a world of legends, theories, and observations that attended Green's efforts to research the antiquities of Worcester Cathedral and its most famous corpse. When he opened the tomb he did so with a host of expectations; and those expectations led him to read the corpse in a manner dictated by several authoritative bodies whose influence reached back centuries. Those expectations also led him to make two significant mistakes when he viewed the body of King John. In short, he misread it.

The condition of King John's corpse was far different in 1797 than it had been (or purportedly had been) in 1529; Bale makes no mention of the position of the skull, nor does he mention a hood or cowl of any type. He does, in fact, mention a crown. Although he was writing from memory, Bale would surely have noted the odd position of the head, since it bears the earmarks of desecration. In any case, the crown, which Bale did mention, was missing, as were the spurs, sceptre, and ring. Whoever turned King John's head backward did so after Bale left the cathedral but before the king's body was reinterred. There is no record of an opening of the tomb between 1529 and 1797. Bale reports that the body of King John was on view for two days and attracted large groups of curious onlookers, during which time there may have been opportunities for thieves and souvenir hunters to pilfer objects from the coffin, especially small items such as the spurs and the ring. The sword appears to have broken into pieces as it was being wrenched from the king's arm. It is also likely that the person or people who stole the crown pulled off King John's head in order to remove the object, then placed the head back into the coffin carelessly, face-down. One thing is certain: the peculiar design of the coffin, that bore a cutout specifically meant to cradle the head, made it impossible for the head to have turned itself around as a consequence of the coffin being moved, or even dropped. The position of King John's head was no accident, and although carelessness is an acceptable explanation, there are others.

There are two other interesting explanations for the turned head that are connected to the area and that are rooted in King John's own time and in the centuries preceding. Andrew Reynolds discusses prone, or face-down burials,[128] during the Anglo-Saxon era, stating that the practice was long recognised as an indication of desecration or punishment, and that such desecration was often political.[129] The rite was widespread, but was commonly practised in the central South Midlands, and also in Gloucestershire and Worcestershire. The practice waned during the Anglo-Norman period, but its legend

[128] Only King John's head was turned backwards. In all likelihood it was either simply too difficult to turn the entire body around (at the risk of the corpse falling apart), or the vandals did not have time to turn the King's entire (but not whole) body over.

[129] Andrew Reynolds, *Anglo-Saxon Deviant Burial Customs* (Oxford, 2009), pp. 68–76.

persisted and was known among people in those areas. Although there is no general consensus on its specific use, Reynolds, and others, like M.L. Faull, point to an ancient tradition of prone burials being used as a political statement against foreign invaders.[130] In some cases prone burials were used as an expression of British survival. Faull states that early prone burials represent individuals who did not fit into society after the mixing of the Celtic and Anglo-Saxon cultures, or during the Roman occupation,[131] and V.I. Evison notes that in some areas, such as Norfolk, the practice could also mark an act of treachery or cowardice within a community.[132] Another possible explanation is that prone burials were sometimes used as a protection against witchcraft. Although most of the prone burials that correspond to this pattern are of women, men accused of sorcery could also be buried prone.[133] King John was never suspected of sorcery; but a long tradition held that Merlin, sorcerer to King Arthur, had prophesied the reign of King John, and had foretold of his wickedness. 'The Eleventh Prophecy of Merlin', as it was known, was part of *The Prophecy of Ambrosius Merlin Concerning the Seven Kings*, a twelfth-century poem attributed to John of Cornwall, which was based on Book VII of Geoffrey of Monmouth's *History of the Kings of Britain*.[134] This poem was used widely over the course of many centuries to attach persons and events to the legendary prophecies of Merlin.[135] It was used by John Bale as means of 'foretelling' events of the Reformation for propaganda purposes, but where he chose to praise King John, others interpreted the 'prophecy' in less flattering ways.[136] The Eleventh Prophecy was believed by many to refer to the reign of King John, who was symbolised by the figure of The Leopard, or The Lynx – a cruel and failing king.[137] The practice of prone burial as

---

[130] Reynolds, p. 68; M.L. Faull, 'British Survival in Anglo-Saxon Northumbria'. *Studies in Celtic Survival*, ed. L. Laing. *British Archaeological Reports* 37 (1977): 1–55.

[131] Faull, p. 9. A half century later the antiquary George Smith admired the ancient Britons for their ability to 'resist the inroads of Romish authority and maintain their independence'. George Smith, *The Religion of Ancient Britain: A Succinct Account of the Several Religious Systems which Have Obtained in this Island from the Earliest Ties to the Norman Conquest* (London, 1844), pp. 363, 364, and 368.

[132] V.I. Evison, 'Dover: Buckland Anglo-Saxon Cemetery', *English Heritage Archaeological Report* 3 (1987): 134.

[133] Faull, p. 9; also W. Matheson, 'Notes on Mary Macleod', *Transactions of the Gaelic Society of Inverness* 41 (1951): 11–25.

[134] Vatican Library MS: Codex Ottobonianus Latinus 1474, fols. 1r–4r. Transcribed by Carl Greith, in *Spicilegium Vaticanum* (Frauenfeld, 1838). See also Geoffrey of Monmouth, *Historia Regum Brittaniae, A Variant Version Edited from Manuscripts* (Cambridge, MA, 1951).

[135] See, for example, an edition of 1812: this edition includes the observations of Thomas Heywood. *The Life of Merlin Surnamed Ambrosius, his Prophecies and Predictions Interpreted* (Carmarthen, 1812).

[136] Bale's own bibliography identifies the poem as an important source in his work. John Bale, *Index Brittaniae Scriptorum*, ed, Reginald Poole and Mary Bateson (Oxford, 1902), p. 196.

[137] Rupert Taylor, *The Political Prophecy in England* (New York, 1911), pp. 16 and 112. See also Michael J. Curley, 'A New Edition of John of Cornwall's *Prophetia Merlini*'. *Speculum* 57, issue 2 (April 1982), 217–49. Reprints of and commentaries of the twelfth-century poem and/

a protection against sorcery was still in use up to the eighteenth century and was well known in Worcestershire.[138]

These studies about prone burials provide specific examples from targeted burial sites; but the practice of prone burials to 'mark' the foreign dead or the magical dead was widespread (albeit in uneven distribution), and it lasted well beyond the Anglo-Saxon period. S.J. Sherlock and M.G. Welsh point out, 'The Prone burial rite was evidently applied to a wide range of individuals, and probably for different reasons in each case. There was evidently a broad recognition of this highly distinctive mode of burial, however, and it seems likely that the overall motivation was to render the corpse safe to the living.'[139] Howard Williams also acknowledges that prone burial is subject to multiple interpretations between the eighth and eleventh centuries, but that those interpretations lend themselves toward punishment, sorcery, or a deliberate statement of disrespect that is particular to the community and people's relationship with the deceased.[140] Neither the monks of Worcester nor unwelcome visitors to the tomb site had anything to fear from King John's corpse; but if they believed that his burial between two saints amounted to a *de facto* sanctification of his remains that represented his desire to protect himself spiritually from his bad reputation, then the turning of his head would indeed be a formidable, if ultimately symbolic, statement – even (or especially) if God were the only witness to the act. As Reynolds states, prone burial was a very powerful rite that was enacted consciously by a burial party fully aware of its social meaning.[141] Because Green did not make anything other than a cursory mention of the position of the head, he missed an opportunity to draw upon a tradition that went back centuries in Worcester and its environs in which those seen as foreign invaders or usurpers, those suspected of treachery, or those connected to sorcery were buried face-down. Did the person or persons who stole the crown in 1529 replace the head backwards as a gesture of disrespect that stretched far back into cultural memory? Was the turning of the head an act of superstition? Was it an act of vandalism? Did the monks of Worcester turn the head themselves in a timely (if early) protest against John's defiance of the Papacy?[142] Green did not ask any of these questions, despite his interest in the cultural traditions of the area. Longstanding cultural traditions are very often loosely defined and have unclear roots or explanations, and yet generations of people observe them, even if those observances mean several different things at

---

or Geoffrey of Monmouth were available in the eighteenth century. For example: Edmund Curll, *The Rarities of Richmond: Being the Exact Descriptions of the Royal Hermitage and Merlin's Cave, with his Life and Prophecies* (London, 1736), pp. 87–8. For more discussion of political prophecy during Bale's lifetime see Keith Thomas, *Religion and the Decline of Magic* (New York, 1971), pp. 113–51, 389–434, and 615–30.

[138] Faull, p. 9, and Matheson, pp. 15–16.

[139] S.J. Sherlock and M.G. Welch, 'An Anglo-Saxon Cemetery at Norton, Cleveland'. *Council for British Archaeology Research Report* 82 (London, 1992), p. 75.

[140] Howard Williams, *Death and Memory in Early Medieval Britain* (Cambridge, 2006), p. 99.

[141] Reynolds, p. 69.

[142] In any case, John Bale had no involvement in the turning of the head or in any of the thefts.

once and even if they are transferred from region to region. Sometimes people observe ancient cultural traditions without knowing fully their history or meaning.

Even if Green understood these things (and with his interest in the antiquities of Worcestershire he had opportunities to research the subject) he chose to ignore this reading of the corpse. The reason is that he considered such speculation to be academically inappropriate. Green was not prone to believing stories. Although he understood the value of legends, he preferred to make conclusions that stood upon academic ground rather than to engage in speculations based on emotional response. He was especially sensitive to this issue when it came to King John. In a visit to Worcester Cathedral forty years before his examination of the tomb, Green was irked by the unfounded conjectures of a tour guide at the tomb of King John. In his Introduction to *History and Antiquities* Green writes:

The learning of a new lesson [about King John's burial] may, indeed, be found irksome to those officers of the church, who for a length of time past may have been in the habit of detailing the traditional errors of its former history, and with those ill-informed predecessors, I am persuaded, originated, among many others, the marvellous account I myself forty years ago heard a grave sexton retail, whilst he was shewing the tomb of King John ' – How that king had been poisoned by two monks, who had administered it to him in vessels like those they held in their hands (which are censers); that to avoid detection and punishment they swallowed poison themselves; and that the effects of the destructive draughts first appeared upon the backs of their own and the king's hands," the marks of which (where the jewels on the gloves of the king, and of the two bishops, Oswald and Wul[f]stan, had been set) he did not fail to point out to his wondering auditory, in solemn confirmation of his narrative ... Nor can there be a doubt, from a moral regard to truth, and a reverence of the place in which they are frequently called upon to render verbal accounts of various objects, and portions of the church, that the present officers will endeavour to supply the place of exploded fiction, by reports on which strangers who visit the cathedral may more safely depend, and by which its history, sufficiently abounding with real curiosity, may become better understood.[143]

Such was the purpose of his study: to provide visitors to Worcester Cathedral with more dependable information and to produce a more informed understanding than folklore or historical precedents for eighteenth-century studies of Anglo-Saxon or Romano-British burials could provide. Unfortunately, despite his best intentions, Green misread the corpse a second time – and this time he made a grave mistake.

Green did make a note concerning what appeared to be a small hood that fastened under the chin (Fig. 3). Green assumed that the hood was a monk's cowl. He theorised that the hood represented a desire of King John to be buried in a monk's cowl, saying, '...instead of a crown, a monk's cowl, used by the king's desire as a preservative against

---

[143] Green, *History and Antiquities*, pp. xvi–xvii.

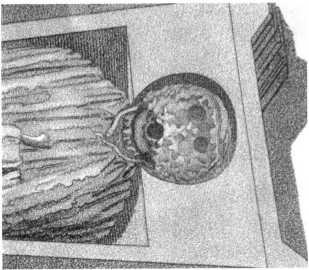

Fig. 3 Detail of the drawing by Green showing the chin strap of what he mistakenly identified as a monk's cowl. It is a crown cap or an arming cap for a crown or crowned helmet once placed on the corpse. The crown or helmet was stolen, probably in 1529. Photo reproduction courtesy of Worcester Cathedral.

evil spirits, was found upon his head'.[144] In making such a guess, Green drew upon a long-standing legend that King John had gone to his grave in a state of remorseful despair, and that he had made the request for a monk's cowl as he lay dying of poison. Here, Green chose to read the corpse according to centuries-old rumours and legends, source texts that still held strong because that reading validated a legend he felt could be supported by academic expertise. Such a legend was, for lack of a better phrase, more *historical*. Green claims that King John desired to be buried in a monk's cowl, but there is no real evidence for this wish. It is yet another story about King John, but it is one that Valentine Green chose to believe. Upon viewing the corpse, Green determined that the hood, a close-fitting cap that fastened under the chin, was the monk's cowl. According to a long-accepted legend it was supposed to be there, and upon receiving the apparent validation of this legend, Green interpreted it, thus:

> If the cowl of a monk was deemed by King John to be a helmet of salvation for him in a future state, we may conclude that the untenanted graves of two of the most celebrated saints of the monkish calendar [i.e., Oswald and Wulfstan] would be sought, as places of refuge, by those who had the power to secure them to themselves, for the repose of their mortal parts, unless they would either abandon or betray the avowed principles of their practical faith.[145]

Green was wrong. The crimson damask garment in which King John was buried is most likely a garment of unction, a coronation garment a king wore during the anointing

---

[144] Green, *Discovery*, p. 3.

[145] Green, *Discovery*, p. 3, and *History and Antiquities*, vol. I, p. 73.

with oil. It was not uncommon for kings to be buried in these coronation garments, and the fact that John is wearing one points to the probability, noted by D.A. Carpenter, that the fabric on John's head is an unction *coif*, or a cloth used during the anointing with oil.[146] However, the strap that fastens under the chin, and the close-fitting appearance of the 'hood' also associates it closely with an arming cap or a crown cap. Although kings were sometimes buried with unction *coifs*, they were also sometimes buried with crowned helmets; and underneath a crowned helmet the dead king would wear an arming cap just as he did on the battlefield. Even if he wore an actual crown, those dressing the king's body might still have placed on his head a close-fitting crown cap that fastened under the chin. The cap was all that was left after the crown (or crowned helmet) was stolen.[147]

Bale did not make this distinction in 1529 (if King John wore a crown or crowned helmet, Bale did not need to mention the cap underneath); but if King John had worn a monk's cowl, Bale would likely have mentioned it in his description of the king's clothing. In 1529 John Bale was still a Carmelite monk who wore a cowl similar in design to the one worn by the Benedictine monks of Worcester. A monk's cowl is a full garment that covers the head, shoulders, and entire upper half of the body – the 'bosom'. Bale would have known a cowl when he saw it. Instead, he describes the garment on the body as a *vestis*, which could mean 'vestment' (if Carpenter's assertion that John was buried in an unction garment is correct), or it could simply mean 'robe'. In 1529 the *vestis* was still gold, but by 1797 it was dusky brown and covered with a thick pall of dust. Green may not have been able to make the appropriate distinction between the garments of the upper and lower halves of the body. This fact, combined with the putative legend that John desired to be buried in a cowl, produced Green's misreading of the corpse. He took the opportunity to make critical remarks about John's presumption to cheat the fate of his soul, and about the Catholic doctrine of Purgatory.[148] Green meant that his remarks should lead to a discussion of theology and partisanship that was reflective of contemporary academic and political arguments concerning Catholic Emancipation and Tractarianism, and away from the rumours and legends of tour guide sextons.

Not everyone agreed with Green's assertion or appreciated his remarks about Catholicism. John Milner, a staunch Catholic, admirer of Gothic architecture, and antiquary, disagreed not only with Green's assertion, but also with his methods. In *The History, Civil and Ecclesiastical, and Survey of the Antiquities of Worcester* (1809), Milner attacked Green's claim that King John was buried in a monk's cowl. After viewing Green's sketch of King John's corpse, Milner concluded that the Protestant –

---

[146] D.A. Carpenter, *The Reign of Henry III* (1996) (London, 2006), p. 435.

[147] Engel, p. 209, and Mark Duffy, *Royal Tombs of Medieval England* (Stroud, 2003), p. 65.

[148] A secondary story holds that in 1529 the monks of Worcester removed the crown and dressed King John in a monk's cowl, but this story is apocryphal and is not true. The 1797 sketch of the corpse does not show a cowl and there is no record in Worcester's archives that record such an action by the monks.

and prejudiced – Green simply did not know what a proper monk's cowl looked like. He wrote:

> What a mass is here of ignorant and illiberal abuse, calculated to represent the piety of our ancestors as more stupid, and of a more immoral tendency, than the mythology of their pagan ancestors, and much less warranted or excusable than the sexton's tale of king John being poisoned by St. Oswald and St. Wulfstan... Mr. G. who writes so much about monk's cowls, proves himself not to know what a cowl is. He supposes it to be a mere hood, covering the skull. Upon due enquiry however, he will find it to be a large garment, which, particularly about the time in question, covered the whole, or almost the whole body... The said writer is here challenged to produce the record which he speaks of, as signifying that the said cowl was a 'passport through the regions of purgatory;' or instead of it, to bring forward the decree of any synod, or the writings of any divine or schoolman, imitating such an absurd dogma. The fact is, had this opinion been that of the age, as our writer says it was, we should not fail to find it in the Master of Sentences, and Sum. Of St. Thomas Aquinas, and other such works, written about this period and of course every corpse would have been buried in a monk's cowl, no less than King John's ... This writer [Green], before he spoke of the 'reverence and sanctification' which, he says, King John partook of from the place of his interment, and of 'the helmet of salvation, in a future state,' which he describes him as wearing, ought to have examined what were the real sentiments of the age concerning the state of the deceased monarch's soul.[149]

The offence, in Milner's eyes, is not only based on Green's uninformed assertion, but in the presumptions of the onlookers who crowded Worcester Cathedral to see the body of King John a decade earlier. Ignorant of what a monk's cowl looked like, and prejudiced against Catholicism, Green, his readers, and the curious tourists at the cathedral read the text of the corpse not for what it actually said, but for what they expected it to say based on what earlier erroneous and prejudiced texts had said. In Milner's view, Green was no better than the tour guides he despised or the propagandists of the Reformation. Milner intended that his book, a rival antiquarian study written from a Catholic point of view, correct this misinformation. Twenty-six years later, another antiquary, John Britton, commented on Milner's attack of Green's assessment with a twinge of sarcasm: he states that Milner claims Green 'is never satisfied of repeating his calumnies on the subject of King John's funeral'.[150]

Valentine Green died in 1813, before nineteenth-century writers and scholars would amplify the notion of the Norman Yoke in works such as *Ivanhoe* by Sir Walter Scott

---

[149] John Milner, *The History, Civil and Ecclesiastical, and Survey of the Antiquities of Winchester*, 2 vols. (London, 1809), vol. I, p. 240.

[150] John Britton, *The History and Antiquities of the Cathedral Church of Worcester* (London, 1835), p. 17.

(1820) and dramatic and poetic adaptations of the novel that followed.[151] As Graham Seel states, in the wake of England's victories over France and amid the stereotype of the Anglo-Saxons as heroic, many nineteenth-century historians chose to overlook the hyperbole and fabrications of the Medieval chroniclers in favour of a general view that the chroniclers were well-informed about their subjects.[152] For historians such as William Stubbs, King John had no redeeming features whatsoever.[153] C. Warren Hollister's assessment of nineteenth-century scholarship on King John is similar: John was often depicted as monstrous, fraudulent, and depraved, even if many historians did concede that the qualities that identified John as a failure and a tyrant caused him to stand up to Papal oppression.[154] The nineteenth-century Arthurian revival stems largely from the issue of Anglo-Saxon heroism, especially as it is connected to the re-envisioning of the Robin Hood legend and continued interest in the life and career of King John. Inga Bryden's study of Victorian Arthurianism attributes much of the roots of the concept to 'antiquarian groundwork'[155] that includes Thomas Bulfinch's commentary on the Robin Hood legend,[156] and renewed antiquarian interest in William Prynne's method of collecting documents: in 1867 a copy of Prynne's book sold for £155.[157] Nineteenth-century nationalist sentiment, says Bryden, was expressed in an epic form that proceeded from a meticulous (re)construction of an imagined past.[158] That reconstruction relied in part upon the meticulous *deconstruction* of the past undertaken by antiquaries like Green in the eighteenth century. Even if Green was mistaken in his reading of the corpse of King John, his efforts are nonetheless important to the development of a material view of the past that is connected directly to the textual view of the past. Still, John wavers, as he ever does, between hero and villain; even when he is the corpse at the centre of a *corpus* he is a wretched figure, whose fate is determined by powers outside his control.

---

[151] To name a few: Sir Walter Scott, *Ivanhoe* (1820), ed. Graham Tulloch (Edinburgh, 1998). Anonymous. *Ivanhoe; Or, The Knight Templar: Adapted from the Novel of that Name* (London, 1820); A. Bunn, *Ivanhoe; Or, The Jew of York: A New Grand Chivalric Play* (Birmingham, 1820); and W.T. Moncrieff, *Ivanhoe! Or, The Jewess; A Chivalric Play* (London, 1820).

[152] Seel, pp. 6–7.

[153] William Stubbs, *Historical Introductions to the Rolls Series*, ed. A. Hassall (New York, 1902), pp. 239, 442–3, and 487.

[154] Hollister, p. 2 and 7.

[155] Inga Bryden, *Reinventing Arthur: The Arthurian Legends in Victorian Culture* (Aldershot, 2005), p. 2.

[156] Thomas Bulfinch, *Bulfinch's Mythology: The Age of Fable, The Age of Chivalry, and Legends of Charlemagne* (1855) (New York, 1991).

[157] Willis and Sotheran (Corporate Authors), *A Catalogue of Superior Second-Hand Books, Ancient and Modern, Comprising Works in Most Branches of Literature and Offered at Very Low Prices for Ready Money*. New Series, vol. XXV, no. xxxv (London, 1867).

[158] Bryden, pp. 1–2.

3

THE TEXT IN NEGLECT

Katherine de Valois

In 1778 the Percy vault in St Nicholas' Chapel, Westminster Abbey, was under renovation not long after the interment of the Duchess of Northumberland. As the vault was expanded beneath an impressive figural monument already installed in the chapel, the Dean of Westminster proposed that an additional coffin be placed into the vault. It was the coffin of the dowager Queen Katherine de Valois, daughter of Charles VI of France and Isabeau of Bavaria. She was the widow of Henry V and also of Owen Tudor, and she was consequently the mother of Henry VI and grandmother of Henry VII. She was the progenitrix of two English kings from two dynasties. And she had lain in a broken and delapidated coffin on the floor of Westminster Abbey, her mummified corpse exposed and displayed as a tourist attraction, for 276 years. After nearly three centuries she was laid to rest in a vault meant for someone else and named for a family that was not hers. Even so, this place of interment would not be her final one; 100 years later she would be disinterred again. Dean Stanley, by permission of Queen Victoria, would supervise the final interment of Katherine de Valois in a simple vault in the upper chantry of the chapel of Henry V. The bizarre story of the fate of Katherine de Valois' corpse beggars belief. How could it be that the body of a queen be displaced and exposed in such a way? What, if any, meaning can be inferred by such neglect and exploitation? Some answers to these questions are found by way of a manifold theory of reading concerning Katherine's exposed corpse. Her corpse, from the time of its first disinterment in 1503 to its final interment in 1887, is the 'thing' around which historical and literary narrative revolves. Those narratives, however, are not consistent but are revised several times over the decades before being brought to a halt by Katherine's final interment. This continual revision of the text of the corpse is due to the appearance of the character Princess Katherine in Shakespeare's play *Henry V* (1599),[1] to the emergence and growth of antiquarian interest in the royal tombs of Westminster, and to the employment of Katherine's historical and literary legacy in popular literature and historical texts. The text of the corpse is thus revised because of, rather than in spite of, its visibility, since its physical presence provides a material connection to one of Shakespeare's greatest plays and one of English history's greatest heroes. Interestingly, this connection to Henry V is achieved via the

---

[1] William Shakespeare, *Henry V, The Norton Shakespeare, Second Edition*, ed. Stephen Greenblatt et al. (New York, 2008).

exposed corpse of his widow. The material presence of Katherine's corpse enhances and complicates the culture of Henry V's tomb. It represents an example of the adaptation of public memory concerning the past and its dead, as tourists, scholars, and politicians consider and reconsider the career of Henry V by way of an examination of the corpse of Katherine de Valois.

Henry V died of dysentery at Vincennes on 31 August 1422. His funeral at Westminster Abbey was of unprecedented extravagance and it featured a display of both the English and French standards at a royal funeral for the first and only time.[2] The site of Henry V's tomb in its own chapel, with its wooden figural monument bearing a silver head and hands, attracted throngs of people eager to associate the grandeur of his burial with the successes of his reign. His saddle, helmet, and shield were displayed for all to see. By the time his widow Katherine de Valois died in 1437 Henry's legacy had changed, affected ironically by developments in his wife's personal circumstances. Katherine had married the Welsh nobleman Owen Tudor seven years after her husband's death, and the marriage was attended by controversy. In 1428, the year before Katherine remarried, Parliament passed a law forbidding dowager queens from remarrying without the king's permission. When she left court in 1429, she did so in the company of Owen Tudor and allegedly married him without the sanction of her son, Henry VI.[3] Despite what some at court saw as his mother's defiance of the law, Henry VI acknowledged the marriage by knighting his stepfather and giving titles to his two half-brothers. Katherine died in 1437, and because of her remarriage she was buried in the Lady Chapel of Westminster Abbey rather than near or next to Henry V.

The years following Katherine's death were kind neither to Owen Tudor nor to Henry VI. Owen Tudor was charged with violation of the remarriage statute and although he acquitted himself in court, he was arrested and imprisoned briefly, first at Newgate Prison and then at Windsor Castle. He was captured while leading Lancastrian forces in the Battle of Mortimer's Cross and beheaded at Hereford in 1461 (despite his connection to the royal family he was given no reprieve). The reign of Henry VI was marred by the continuing wars between the houses of York and Lancaster, by the loss of his throne, his unstable mental state, and the second loss of his kingdom, which led to his death (purported by some to be murder) in 1471. After his death a budding cult grew up around Henry VI by those who saw him as a martyr for the Lancastrian cause. The tomb of the erstwhile king at St George's Chapel, Windsor, became a site of pilgrimage for those seeking intercession for cases of adversity (and headache). Henry VII encouraged this cult and became a devotee, mostly out of political expediency.

---

[2] John Field, *Kingdom, Power, and Glory: A Historical Guide to Westminster Abbey* (London, 1996), p. 53.

[3] Before she left court with Owen Tudor, Katherine petitioned for a marriage to Edmund Beaufort, Duke of Somerset. Her petition was rejected by her son's regents (both brothers of Henry V). Somerset subsequently married Margaret Beauchamp of Bletsoe and became the other grandfather of Henry VII.

He intended that his predecessor be canonised, an act that would grant the newly established Tudor dynasty and its Lancastrian ancestors unimpeachable validity.

For a short time Henry VII sought to be buried at Windsor, next to Henry VI; but after consideration he decided to demolish the existing Lady Chapel at Westminster Abbey and build a new one. The new Lady Chapel was meant to be a showcase for the relics of the venerated (and, as Henry VII hoped, soon-to-be-canonised) Henry VI and attract pilgrims from far and wide. The Chapel would also serve as a future repository for the descendants of Henry VII and Elizabeth of York. Pilgrims at the new Lady Chapel were expected not only to observe the contextual relationship between the Tudors and their adopted patron saint; they were expected to derive an experience from it that was both politically and spiritually genuine. Henry VII expected for his corpse, as it lay in the tomb he proposed for himself and his queen, to communicate spiritually in real time with that of the canonised Henry VI.[4] He expected the same for the future kings of his dynasty. In this sense the pilgrimage site and saint's tomb would be permanently and physically linked to the family of Henry VII: the corpses themselves would be communicative via the sanctity of the saint's body and the miracles that proceeded from it. This milieu was meant to form a narrative of the Tudor dynasty.[5] Together the Tudors would compose an authoritative and sanctified historical/ecclesiastical text that depicted their Divine Right. Moreover, this authoritative text would be continually performative, since pilgrimage sites, especially tombs, are constructed to produce a repeated experience of visitation. Commemoration and remembrance at the site are intended to be continual, renewed by the visitation of pilgrims and commemoration by clergy at appropriate times of the year.[6] The repeated experience causes the venerated body of the interred saint to become a figure of a kinetic and dynamic present; despite the fact that the person is no longer living, the venerated corpse nonetheless performs, rather than merely symbolises, wholeness. In fact, the venerated corpse performs wholeness precisely *because* it is no longer living. This unimpeachable text iterating the validity of the Tudors was intended by Henry VII to be a repository of public memory.[7] 'Writing' the memory of the Tudors in this way would protect his legacy and preserve his victory at Bosworth in the face of possible future insurgencies. The corpses themselves would re-contextualise the historical narrative.[8]

Work on the new Lady Chapel began in 1502, beginning along the outside of the lowest section of the walls of the old Lady Chapel. At that time the body of Katherine

---

[4] This type of spiritual communication at the burial site was presumed to take place among saints and those buried in their immediate vicinity. See Barbara Meyer-Hochstetler, 'The First Tomb of Henry VII of England', *The Art Bulletin* 58, no. 3 (1976): 364–5.

[5] Meyer-Hochstetler, pp. 364–5.

[6] Elizabeth Valdez del Alamo and Carol Pendergast, eds., *Memory and the Medieval Tomb* (Aldershot, 2000), p. 5.

[7] Meyer-Hochstetler, pp. 362–4.

[8] Valdez del Alamo and Pendergast, p. 6.

de Valois was removed from its existing tomb and placed into a temporary one.[9] Henry VII made a provision in his will for the translation of his grandmother's remains from her original tomb (which was described as being in poor condition as early as 1460) to a new tomb in the improved Lady Chapel once the body of Henry VI was translated. He writes:

> … And forasmoche as we have received oure solempne coronacion and holie inunccion, within our monastery of Westminster, and that within the same monasterie is the common sepultre of the kings of this Reame … and specially the body of our graunt dame of right noble memorie Queen Kateryne, wif to King Henry the Vth and doughter to King Charles of France, and that we by the grace of God purpose right shortely to translate into the same the bodie and reliques of our uncle of blyssed memorie King Henry the Vith.[10]

Upon her disinterment Katherine became a central figure in the king's planning and construction of the Lady Chapel. Her presence in the new Lady Chapel was meant to be part of its contextual performance of memory and legitimacy for the Tudors. Through her sepulchral monument Henry VII intended to demonstrate his dynastic legitimacy.[11] In his will Henry VII links his ancestry through Katherine de Valois to Henry VI and Henry V rather than to his natural grandfather Owen Tudor. In doing so, Henry VII intended to associate himself with the victories of Henry V in France and with the English claim to the French throne. He could also associate himself with Henry V's supposed descent from Louis IX of France. The king's lineage by Owen Tudor could not offer him these things.[12] As the new Lady Chapel was constructed, a new tomb for Henry VI was built in a lavish gothic 'grille' style, and the Chapel, with its distinctive fan-vault ceilings, rose around that central focal point. As it was, Henry VI was not canonised and his remains were not translated from Windsor. Henry VII's petition to several popes (accompanied by a catalogue account of miracles at the Windsor tomb)[13] went unanswered, and when Henry VII died in 1508 his son Henry VIII continued construction of the Westminster 'grille' tomb with the objective of putting his own parents into it.[14]

---

[9] Tim Tatton-Brown and Richard Mortimer, eds., *Westminster Abbey: The Lady Chapel of Henry VII* (Woodbridge, 2003), p. 63.

[10] Great Britain, Public Record Office, *Will of Henry VII*, E 23/3.

[11] Tatton-Brown and Mortimer, p. 196.

[12] Tatton-Brown and Mortimer, p. 63.

[13] BL MS Royal 13 C. viii.

[14] The completion of the tomb included reclining figural monuments of Henry VII and Elizabeth of York. Henry VII had desired a standing figural monument of himself holding the circlet he purportedly took from the helmet of Richard III at Bosworth. Henry VIII continued to campaign for sainthood for Henry VI early in his reign, but changes in his ecclesiastical policies of the 1530s and 1540s ended his interest in canonisation for his great-uncle.

Between the translation of Katherine de Valois to her temporary tomb in 1502 and the chapel's completion in 1509 there is little indication of the location of Katherine's coffin. For at least part of that time she lay in the temporary vault reserved for her; but at some point her coffin was removed from that location and placed next to the tomb of Henry V. The wooden coffin was in a horribly dilapidated state. The side boards were loose and barely held together at the joints, and the lid no longer fit snugly atop it. Worse, the upper half of the lid had disintegrated almost completely, exposing Katherine's mummified remains from the head to the chest. There appears to have been an effort (or the beginnings of one) to reinter Katherine de Valois near Henry V, either near the massive tomb itself or above it in the upper chantry where there was an altar. In any case, this did not happen. For reasons still unknown, if ever there were any, Katherine's coffin remained on the floor near her first husband's monument until 1787.

The text of the new Lady Chapel was interrupted by extenuating circumstances: without canonisation for Henry VI there would be no communication among the dead for the sake of the living. The chapel could still stand as a symbol of dynastic continuity and power, but it could only do so figuratively: without the sanctified body of a saint the dynamics of real communication with or via the dead could not take place. Moreover, one of the central figures of the new chapel – Katherine – was not buried in it and lay uncommemorated in an open coffin. The fate of Queen Katherine's corpse, from its unattended condition to its disturbingly convenient placement, interrupts the narrative represented by a queen's body that commemorative sacred space was meant to communicate. Like the tombs of all royals, that of a queen establishes the interactive process of memory. Her tomb, especially if it includes a figural monument, is meant to establish a kinetic relationship with the visitor that constructs part of a larger narrative of dynastic power and legitimacy, especially concerning her ability to produce a future king.[15] As Elizabeth del Alamo and Carol Pendergast discuss in their volume on Medieval tombs, a queen's tomb is an acknowledgment of the sacredness of her body.[16] Figural monuments especially depict the queen's body in a state of wholeness and often in the prime of life, to emphasise her role as the producer of the next king. As Lisa Hilton states, in life a queen was subject to a cultural process in which 'the regular and ordinary limitations of the physical body were ritualised and reinterpreted for her sole benefit, to keep her distinct from other women ... Private acts such as prayer, eating, and sleeping were ritualised into constant affirmations of power'.[17]

This constant ritualism continues to define a queen's body after her death. Like her husband, a queen continues to be viewed as a powerful and sacred extension of the

---

[15] Valdez del Alamo and Pendergast, pp. 3–5. Even childless queens can enjoy this status, as they draw the privileges of the Davidic elect from the bodies of their husbands. Even in death they retain this privilege, evidenced by the burial of queens next to their husbands and depicted in figural monuments. This funerary depiction is meant in part to emphasise the derivation of a queen's elect status via her husband's body (Valdez del Alamo and Pendergast, pp. 5–7).

[16] Valdez del Alamo and Pendergast, pp. 3–5.

[17] Lisa Hilton, *Queens Consort: England's Medieval Queens* (London, 2008), p. 7.

body royal and the body politic after death, so that the mundane physical act of dying and decomposing is ritualised into an affirmation of royal power. For most people, death and decomposition represent a deprivation of identity. Because a queen is sacred, however, she receives an enhancement of her identity upon her death. This is partly due to the fact that kings and queens do not enter unmarked graves before being removed to a charnel house some years later. Royalty, the nobility, and the priestly elite represent the few members of Medieval society to retain identity in death. Moreover, queens were especially connected to the memorialism of the dead by way of their singular responsibility to affirm and sanctify their dynasties via patronage of monastic houses.[18] They were expected to found and maintain monastic and other religious houses whose main purpose was to offer prayers for the royal dead. The more royal tombs contained in a monastic house, the more power (both terrestrial and mystical) that house would have. This was especially true if one or more of the royal dead were canonised. Part of Katherine's role in death, therefore, was to function as a symbol of ongoing queenly patronage for the monks of Westminster. There was a chantry dedicated to Henry V; Henry VI was the focus of a cult that aspired to sainthood; and Henry VII established one of the grandest chapels in Europe. The corpse of Katherine de Valois was supposed to be the focus of all these things.

In this construction there is no more important symbol than the tomb effigy, for it perpetuates a memory of the queen's body in a state of ideal wholeness, generation, power, and identity in the past and in real time.[19] Dead queens are not formerly generative and powerful; they are *continually* generative and powerful. The mnemonic agenda of the royal tomb does more than simply locate the corpse in a sacred space, such as a cathedral, abbey, or chapel. It produces what Valdez del Alamo and Pendergast call a '*simulacrum*' by which visitors read the signs of the tomb and reconstruct the identity and life force of the queen *phantasmically*.[20] They call this resulting phenomenon 'the power of effective response'.[21] In Katherine's case the 'effective response' is severely damaged by the exposure of her corpse and its placement on the floor near Henry V's tomb. The exposed corpse recontextualises the royal burial and humanises it to a

---

[18] Hilton, p. 9.

[19] Philip Lindley, in his article about Katherine de Valois, suggests that her wooden effigy in Westminster Abbey may not be a funeral effigy, as is commonly supposed, but a tomb effigy. If this is true, then there may be established a correlation between the abuse of Katherine's corpse and the neglect of her effigy. Furthermore, there may also be established a correlation between the relocation of the effigy to the upper chantry of the Henry V chapel and the translation of Katherine's remains to the same location. See Philip Lindley, 'The Funeral and Tomb Effigies of Queen Katharine of Valois and King Henry V', *Journal of the British Archaeological Association* 160 (2007): 165–77.

[20] Valdez del Alamo and Pendergast quote Aquinas on the principle of *phantasmata* (p. 3); their larger point about mnemonic technique and Medieval tombs is based largely on the work of Mary Carruthers, *The Book of Memory* (Cambridge, 1990); and Frances Yates, *The Art of Memory* (Chicago, 1966).

[21] Valdez del Alamo and Pendergast, p. 5.

degree unanticipated by the memorial strategy of Medieval tomb making. It halts the ability of the queen's body to perform the mental constructs essential to the creation and maintenance of the images (*phantasmata*)[22] that guarantee a proper reading of the queen's body. As Valdez del Alamo and Pendergast point out, 'Medieval memorial strategies capitalised on the potent combination of visual, liturgical and physical elements in a sacred space; these could produce a heightened aesthetic, or synaesthetic, experience which directed memory paths'.[23] If these paths are clear, tomb narrative establishes the sacred dead as members of a living community, who are continually participant and permanently relevant. This is why kings are so eager to be located in the direct physical proximity of the tombs and relics of saints. In the case of Katherine de Valois, her exposed corpse affects adversely these aspects of memorial strategy. The corpse becomes an unwelcome intruder into the land of the living and risks no longer being associated with aesthetic, phantasmic experience. The corpse functions as a text in its own right, replacing the text of the tomb and its signs, and visitors are able to read signs directly from the body.[24] This situation is exacerbated in Katherine's case, as her original tomb was physically demolished, leaving no text to argue with that of her corpse. Her exposed queenly corpse proclaims its fallibility, its loss of generative power and identity, its loss of legitimacy and direct association with her descendants. This situation causes visitors of all types to make presumptive phantasmic associations about what the corpse, in their estimation, is trying to communicate. Presumption becomes arbitrary and charged with emotion.

Katherine de Valois' presence, for better or for worse, came to provide a context limited to her relationship with her first husband and her subsequent personal life. For the first ninety-seven years that she lay in her half-open coffin few people viewed her corpse, as tourism at Westminster Abbey did not have much momentum before 1600. The monks of Westminster and their administrative body certainly knew she was there, and there is no doubt that much of the London aristocracy knew as well, since they married, buried, and visited the tombs of their own relatives in the same Abbey church. It is certain that Henry VIII knew about the state of his great-grandmother's corpse and it is a mystery as to why he did nothing about it, since it was he that finished the reconstruction of the Lady Chapel (the altar was finally installed in 1512) and oversaw the investiture of the tomb of his parents. Henry VIII was also aware that iconoclasts, upon ransacking Westminster in 1546, broke into the Henry V tomb and stole the silver head and hands and gilt plates of the figural monument of Henry V.[25] As they

---

[22] Valdez del Alamo and Pendergast, p. 3.

[23] Valdez del Alamo and Pendergast, p. 5.

[24] The exception is that of the canonised saint; and in that case the presumption of incorruptibility argues against a reading of the corpse as a mundane object in a state of decomposition. Reading a canonised corpse in such a way argues against the authoritative ecclesiastical text of hagiography – a dangerous reading in Medieval Europe.

[25] A separate theory of the corpse is required to discuss the implications of the destruction of Henry V's monument. Because they were iconoclasts, the men rejected the phantasmic

pried the silver head and hands from the figure and carried away their booty in triumph
they could not have missed the open coffin of Katherine de Valois with her desiccated
corpse inside. An illustration of 1677, in a view through the gates from the west front
of the tomb, shows the coffin lying just as it had in 1546: to the right of Henry V's
monument (Fig. 4).[26] The iconoclasts were practically on top of it. Neither Edward VI,
nor Mary I, nor Elizabeth I made a gesture toward reinterment of their great-great-
grandmother in subsequent years. Why was there no effort to rebury their ancestor?
Why did the deans of Westminster fail to insist upon it? Why was Katherine not at the
very least placed into the nearest crypt at the earliest convenience? In any event, these
things did not happen, and when Shakespeare staged his play *Henry V* in 1599, arguably
his most successful play to that point, his audiences attended the play just over a mile
away from where Katherine's corpse lay exposed to the air.

Shakespeare most likely knew of Westminster Abbey's oddest resident corpse. John
Stow, in his 1598 book *Survey of London* (a book Shakespeare knew) included Katherine
de Valois in her present state among his list of kings and queens buried at Westminster.
After he lists Henry V he adds:

> *Katherin* his wife was buried in the old Lady Chapel, 1438. But her corps being taken
> vp in the raign of *Henry* the 7. When a new foundation was to be laid, she was neuer
> since buried, but remayneth aboue ground in a coffin of boordes behinde the East end
> of the Presbyterie.[27]

Tourism at Westminster Abbey circa 1600 was not as profuse as it would become in the
following century, but people still toured the Abbey Church to see the royal tombs and
the wooden effigies of kings and queens on display. For an extra charge the sexton could
be convinced to show a visitor some particulars, such as the saddle, helmet, and shield
of Henry V, which hung in the chantry above his tomb. Shakespeare's audience were
familiar with this practice, and they also knew that the perks of friendship or relation
might garner one special access to these artifacts. In 1613 Thomas Middleton made
reference to the issue in *A Chaste Maid in Cheapside*; devoid of a weapon for a duel, the
collegiate Tim brags that he can get one easily enough. He says, 'If need be, I can send for
conquering metal ne'er lost day yet; 'tis but at Westminster. I am acquainted with him that

---

connection between the tomb and the corpse. If they accepted the dead king's body as a
descriptor of Divine Right (and they probably did), they did not extend the same acceptance
to the figure. For them, the figure was idolatrous, a false text, a pretension to and intrusion
upon scripture, from which the principle of Divine Right extended. Moreover, they did not
likely see the corpse as a sacred text in and of itself because doing so supported the theology
of sainthood. They had no intention of 'reading' the body in that way.

[26] Francis Sandford, *A Genealogical Historie of the Kings of England, and Monarchs of Great
Britain* (London, 1677), p. 281.

[27] John Stow, 'The Citie of Westminster', in *A Survey of London, by John Stow: Reprinted from the
Text of 1603* (1908), pp. 97–124, www.british-history.ac.uk/report.aspx?compid=60057.

Fig. 4 Engraving by Francis Sandford of the tomb and chantry of Henry V in 1677. The coffin of Katherine de Valois can be seen to the right of the tomb, on the floor. Photo reproduction courtesy of the Huntington Library, San Marino, CA.

keeps the monuments; I can borrow Harry the Fifth's sword. 'Twill serve us both to watch with.'[28] In the same vein, visitors could also be shown the coffin of Queen Katherine lying very near these *accoutrements*. There is no evidence that visitation to Westminster Abbey to see the tomb of Henry V increased during the staging of Shakespeare's play; but it is certain that many audience members who saw his play (or Middleton's) knew the state of the corpse of Henry V's Queen and perhaps even paid to see it.

It is certain, though, that the rise in tourism at Westminster Abbey between 1600 and 1700, especially the rise in visits to Henry V's tomb and chantry, is connected to public perceptions of the characters in Shakespeare's play. These perceptions are based on adaptations of historical or traditional depictions of the figures of Henry V and Katherine de Valois that admit dramatic characterisations from the play into existing historical narratives. As Richard Dutton points out, much of the muddling of historical persons with their respective stage characters during the Elizabethan/Jacobean eras is due to the fact that the traditional chronicle format, which had been known for centuries, was obsolete by the end of the sixteenth century.[29] This is especially true in the case of Henry V. A generation before Shakespeare, Henry VIII attempted to associate himself with Henry V concerning his French campaigns, and later Elizabeth I stimulated the national memory of Henry V for the purposes of her own military endeavours. For decades the legend of Henry V enjoyed a surge in interest, and for many people the 1587 reprint of Holinshed's *Chronicles* was an insufficient narrative. The rising popularity of historical plays in the 1580s and 1590s, including the anonymous *The Famous Victories of Henry V,* Marlowe's *Edward II*, and Shakespeare's *Henriad, Richard II, Richard III*, and also *King John*,[30] left audiences desirous for more emotionally driven portrayals than the chronicles provided.[31] Dutton says, 'The sheer plasticity of romance allows for a range of reference that a stricter adherence to the laws of history would preclude; and the generic elasticity of these forms allows kings to carry concerns from the council or the battlefield into the courting of fair maidens, or (often in disguise) conversations with commoners'.[32] Shakespeare's play fits its hero Henry V into this framework successfully; and that success extends to the portrayal of Katherine de Valois.

The play introduces Princess Katherine by way of a view that draws upon posthumous attitudes about her marriage to Owen Tudor, many of which were based on popular cynical interpretations of Holinshed and other chroniclers. Shakespeare's acknowledgment of these attitudes, and his greatest departure from the chronicles,

[28] Thomas Middleton, *A Chaste Maid in Cheapside* (1613), in *English Renaissance Drama, A Norton Anthology*, ed. David Bevington et al. (New York, 2002).

[29] Richard Dutton, '"Methinks the Truth Should Live from Age to Age": The Dating and Contexts of *Henry V*', *Huntington Library Quarterly* 68, no. 1–2 (March 2005): 173.

[30] Also including, but not limited to, Marlowe's *Edward II* and *Massacre at Paris*, Heywood's *Edward IV*, Heyward's *Life and Reign of Henry IIII*, and the anonymous *Troublesome Raigne of King John* and *Famous Victories of Henry Vth*, for example.

[31] Dutton, p. 175.

[32] Dutton, p. 175.

appears via his desire to present Princess Katherine as a comic figure. Some of the
basest comedy in the play stems from III.iv, a scene that pretends to depict English
lessons for Princess Katherine, but which fills the theatre with vulgar but accidental
sexual puns from the mouth of the French princess; notably, 'Foh! Le foot et le coun!'[33]
Shakespeare winks at Holinshed's condemnatory view of Katherine, but in doing
so he also expands it with extraordinary cynicism and a desire to lampoon both the
Princess and the chronicle. Holinshed had been dismissive of Katherine's relationship
with Owen Tudor, citing the dowager Queen's apparent inability to control her sexual
appetites. He writes:

> This woman, after the death of king Henrie the fift hir husband, Katharine mother
> to king Henrie maried Owen Teuther. Being yoong and lustie, following more hir
> owne wanton appetite than fréendlie counsell, and regarding more priuate affection
> than prince-like honour, tooke to husband priuilie a galant gentleman and a right
> beautifull person, indued with manie goodlie gifts both of bodie & mind, called
> Owen Teuther, a man descended of the noble linage and ancient line of Cadwallader
> last king of the Britains.[34]

In *Henry V* this 'wanton appetite' driven by 'private affection' is depicted via an accidental
exploration of sexual puns. Unbeknownst to her, Princess Katherine's genuine desire
to seek love translates poorly and taints her legend with vulgarity. Here, Shakespeare's
manipulation of Katherine's legend as it was perceived in Holinshed's *Chronicle* speaks
explicitly to her posthumous legend as it developed in a popular sense. The desiccated
corpse, no doubt imagined by many in the year of the play's debut, stands as a symbol
of poor translation: of language, of culture, of burial place. The fact that Shakespeare's
portrayal is comic is tantalisingly macabre. Is the audience, via an ironic form of
'effective response', expected to gawk and point?

  Holinshed had been cryptic about the romantic relationship between Henry V and
Katherine de Valois, stating that when Isabeau of Bavaria brought her daughter with
her to Mante she did so '...onelie to the intent that the king of England beholding hir
excellent beautie, should be so inflamed and rapt in hir loue, that he to obteine hir to his
wife, should the sooner agrée to a gentle peace and louing concord'.[35] Her plan evidently
worked; for Holinshed reports that '...a certeine sparke of burning loue was kindled
in the kings heart by the sight of the ladie Katharine'.[36] Shakespeare makes much of
passages like these, perhaps understanding that audiences were interested in the type of
'elasticity' they produced, as Dutton theorises. Dutton states that many playwrights of
the Elizabethan/Jacobean eras relished interweaving what he calls 'respectable history'

33 III.iv.51.
34 Raphael Holinshed, *Chronicles of Englande, Scotlande, & Irelande*... 6 vols. (London, 1587), vol.
    VI, p. 615.
35 Holinshed, vol. VI, p. 569.
36 Holinshed, vol. VI, p. 569.

with ballads, rumours, and myths.[37] In the case of *Henry V* Shakespeare is able to use Holinshed's *Chronicle* in conjunction with popular tales of Katherine's nobility, beauty, and fine manners. The same woman who seemingly cannot control her sexual appetites to the extent that they flood from her accidentally and comically in III.iv is also the woman who values true love to the extent that she uses charming amorous restraint to assure herself that Henry V will love and cherish her in V.ii. Although she at times pretends not to understand Henry's profuse declaration of love ('I cannot tell vat is dat'[38]), she soon understands his intention well enough. Despite Holinshed's image of Katherine as an embarrassment to the Lancastrians, and John Stow's bland reference to her as a leftover object pushed into a corner, Shakespeare's play does in fact add 'plasticity' to Katherine's legend.

As tourism and antiquarian interest in Westminster Abbey grew between 1600 and 1700 the connections between Shakespeare's historical plays and their characters were further interlaced and became even more elastic than they had ever been.[39] One early example of the seventeenth century comes from Hugh Holland, a contemporary of Edmund Spenser, Ben Jonson, and Sir Philip Sidney. A great admirer of Shakespeare, Holland contributed a laudatory sonnet to the First Folio containing a poignant reference to Shakespeare's own corpse, saying, 'That corpse, that coffin now bestick those bays[40]/Which crowned him poet first, then poets' king'.[41] Holland also wrote laudatory verses about Katherine de Valois and Owen Tudor in his epic poem *Pancharis* (1603). The poem depicts the courtship between Katherine and her second husband in overwrought romantic terms that at once praise and lament Tudor's courtship of the dowager Queen. In the poem, Katherine's grief for Henry V is profound but soon the goddess Venus interferes and causes Katherine to fall in love with Owen Tudor.[42] Owen Tudor appears in the poem as a classic Elizabethan/Jacobean lover, appealing to his beloved in the manner of a sonneteer. As Holland narrates, he wonders how such a well-born beauty and honourable widow could love a man like Tudor, but says the answer to such a question is known only to the gods.[43] Venus' influence renders Katherine unable to resist Tudor's love in favour of the emotional detachment of public

---

[37] Dutton, p. 177.

[38] V.ii.178.

[39] Even Shakespeare himself was subject to this elasticity. By 1700 his image was thoroughly mythologised and bore little if any resemblance in character (or appearance) to who he actually was.

[40] Meaning, that the bays of the poet's laurel wreath now turn to sticking thorns, similar to Christ's crown of thorns.

[41] Hugh Holland, 'Upon the Lines and Life of the Famous Scenic Poet, Master William Shakespeare', *Mr William Shakespeare's Comedies, Histories & Tragedies, Published According to the True Originall Copies* (London, 1623), p. 11, ll. 7–8. (Facsimile courtesy of the Huntington Library, San Marino, CA.)

[42] Hugh Holland, *Pancharis* (1603), repr. in *Illustrations of Old English Literature*, ed. J. Payne Collier. 2 vols. (London, 1866), vol. II, p. 33.

[43] Holland, *Pancharis*, p. 33.

respectability. As she succumbs to Tudor's courtship, Katherine accepts his love in conjunction with her grief for Henry V; she states that although she is to be Tudor's private wife, she will always be Henry's public widow:

> As unto him, so for his onely sake
> I will remaine no lesse true to my selfe
> For Henries wife and widow will I die.
> Honours, vaine pleasures, transitory pelfe
> I force not of such gaudes a whit, not I
> Yet doth this trash the minds of many tempt
> To loves delights, from whose vile tyranny
> Princes, no more then other, are exempt.[44]

Holland attaches a dedicatory letter to Sir Robert Cotton in the prefatory pages to *Pancharis*. In the letter he states that he intends to '...doe so much right to that dead Lady sometimes our soveraigne Queene and mistresse'[45] with his verse, but he knew that little right was being done to Katherine in the material world.

Cotton's contemporary and fellow antiquary John Weever was also interested in Westminster's tombs and funerary monuments. During the first thirty years of the seventeenth century Weever travelled extensively throughout Britain and Ireland cataloguing funeral monuments and epitaphs. In 1631 he published his huge, nine-hundred-page tome *Ancient Funerall Monuments Within the United Monarchie of Great Britaine, Ireland and the Islands Adjacent, with the Dissolved Monasteries Therein Contained*. The book laid out the meticulous observation and examination of artifacts combined with the subjective observations on interments for which later antiquary interest in funerary monuments would be known. In the case of Katherine de Valois, Weever addresses the mythmaking that was connected to the recent desire on behalf of the public and the stage to add drama to the old stories of the chronicles, namely Holinshed. Weever first describes the formidable tomb of Henry V, long since defaced by iconoclasts, as having been constructed as an extension of Katherine's devotion to her dead husband: '...upon whose tomb Katherine his wife caused a royal posture to be laid, covered all over with silver plate gilded ... all which, (at the suppression, which the battering rams of destruccion, as maister Speed saith, did sound almost in every church) were sacrilegiously broken off...'[46] He then describes the exposed body of Katherine lying in its coffin next to the tomb. Citing long-told but unfounded rumours that Henry V forbade Katherine from giving birth to their

---

[44] Holland, *Pancharis*, p. 40.
[45] Holland, *Pancharis*, p. 55. Collier attaches Holland's letter to Cotton to the end of the poem in his reprint of *Pancharis*.
[46] John Weever, *Ancient Funerall Monuments, Within the United Monarchie of Great Britaine, Ireland, and the Islands Adjacent, with the Dissolved Monasteries Therein Contained* (London, 1631), p. 475.

son at Windsor Castle, Weever notes the popular connection between the Queen's putative defiance of the regal authority of her husband to her poor state of non-interment. He observes:

> Here lieth Katherine, queene of England, wife to aforesaid King Henry the fifth, in a chest or coffin, with a loose cover to be seene and handled of any that will much desire it, and that by her owne appointment (as he that sheweth the Tombes will tell you by tradition) in regard of her disobedience to her husband for being delivered of her Sonne Henry the sixth at Windsore, the place which he forbade. But the truth is that she being first buried in our Ladies Chappell here in this Church, her corps were taken up; when as Henry the seventh laid the foundation of that admirable structure his Chappell royall, which have ever since so remained, and never reburied.[47]

The sexton's assistants/tour guides at Westminster Abbey in Weever's day used a dubious legend (passed down to them through many generations of Westminster scholars and popular lore) to explain the presence of Katherine's exposed corpse. According to this legend, Katherine gave birth to Henry VI at Windsor even though Henry V forbade it (he didn't); and she provided Henry V with a lavish figural monument to atone for this transgression (she didn't); she then appointed herself to be exposed after death as a further act of atonement for her illegitimate marriage to Owen Tudor (it wasn't).[48] The story is one of extraordinary dramatic energy that appears to be sourced in a combination of interpretations of the chronicles and London's urban folklore. In this case the sexton's assistant/tour guide cited by Weever connects the dramatic and romanticised sentiment about the fate of Katherine's body to her idealised romance with Henry V and to her subsequent moral failings as an ideal dowager. The desecration of the former king's figural monument is then seen as a metaphor for his wife's betrayal of his royal authority and dignity. As the corpse is viewed by tourists and curiosity-seekers (who have paid extra to see it), they are able to read the double tragedy of betrayal and desecration in the shocking condition of the corpse, especially as it is framed by the vandalised figural monument. Weever's discussion of the corpse challenges this mythmaking, but offers little in its stead. All he knows is what anyone knows: that upon the demolition of the Lady Chapel Queen Katherine was disinterred, placed next to her former husband, and simply never reburied. Weever did not provide a detailed description of the coffin's contents; that was left to later antiquaries and tourists, who, using Weever's book as a guide, pursued their own interests in funerary antiquarianism and curiosity-seeking.

---

[47] Weever, p. 475.

[48] There is no statute either in 1428 or 1430 forbidding the marriage of Katherine de Valois and Owen Tudor. Any problem that did exist likely arose from restrictions placed upon Welshmen, barring them from citizenship in England. In any case, Tudor was awarded a special exception ('*sicut verus anglius*' – as though he were a true English subject). See S.B. Chrimes, *Henry VII* (New Haven, CT, 1999), p. 5, n.1, and pp. 6–7.

The example of the diarist Samuel Pepys stands out in this regard. On 23 February 1668/9, which was the occasion of his thirty-sixth birthday, Pepys, a naval administrator and MP under Charles II and James II, spent the morning at the office.[49] He returned home, ate lunch, and then took his wife and daughters to Westminster Abbey for a tour of the royal tombs. The Abbey church was crowded with worshippers and tourists, as it was Shrove Tuesday, and so Pepys (who was a bit of a spendthrift) hired a private tour guide for his own small party. From this guide he procured a special favour, for an extra fee: he asked to kiss the corpse of Katherine de Valois. Pepys relates the experience in his own words with all the excitement of a tourist on a special outing for his birthday:

> …here we did see, by particular favour, the body of Queen Katherine of Valois; and I had the upper part of her body in my hands, and I did kiss her mouth, reflecting upon it that I did kiss a Queen, and that this was my birth-day, thirty-six years old, that I did first kiss a Queen. But here this man, who seems to understand well, tells me that the saying is not true that says she was never buried, for she was buried; only, when Henry the Seventh built his chapel, it was taken up and laid in this wooden coffin; but I did there see that, in it, the body was buried in a leaden one, which remains under the body to this day.[50]

Pepys apparently had a secret wish (what we might today call a 'bucket list' wish) to kiss a queen during his lifetime. In Katherine de Valois he saw his opportunity and, forgoing the macabre aspect of the undertaking, fulfilled his wish.[51] Pepys also dabbled in literature and book collecting, splurging for a complete volume of Shakespeare's plays (among many other books)[52] and seeing several seventeenth-century stage adaptations of Shakespearean plays, most of which he disliked.[53]

---

[49] Samuel Pepys, 'Entry for 23 February 1668–9', *The Diary of Samuel Pepys*, ed. Henry B. Wheatley (London, 1893), www.gutenberg.org (full text).

[50] 23 February 1668/9. Pepys observed that the corpse lay in a leaden coffin. Katherine's wooden coffin was placed inside a larger lead one as a temporary measure and removed at a later time (see Fig. 5).

[51] Pepys' disregard of the ghoulish nature of his desire is rooted in various aspects of his lifestyle and culture. Pepys' attitude toward corpses is average for the time, as is evidenced by his diary entries. He watches with great political satisfaction and emotional detachment the hanging of the disinterred bodies of Cromwell, Ireton, and Bradshaw on 30 January 1660/61; and on 11 April 1661 the married Pepys and one of his mistresses court each other by riding playfully underneath the body of a hanged man left to rot upon Shooter's Hill. During a 27 February 1662/63 visit to a 'Chyrurgeons hall', he observes the bodies of hanged men in various states of dissection. His moment of pseudo-academic anatomical interest at the surgeon's hall identifies Pepys as an amateur scholar, which he was.

[52] 7 July 1664. It was probably one of two 'Third Folio' issues of 1663/64. Pepys Library, *Catalogue of the Pepys Library at Magdalene College, Cambridge* (Woodbridge, 2004), p. 265, item 2635.

[53] On 11 September 1661 he sees *Twelfth Night*, but has 'no pleasure at all in it'; on 29 September 1662 he sees *A Midsummer Night's Dream*, which he calls 'the most insipid ridiculous play that ever I saw in my life'; on 9 April 1667 he sees *The Taming of the Shrew* but calls it 'a mean play';

Pepys' desire to choose Katherine de Valois as the queen to kiss on his birthday is thus linked in part to his bibliophilic interests. In embracing the dead queen, Pepys does not merely reach into the coffin to pull out the corpse of Katherine de Valois; he reaches into the play *Henry V* to pull out the character of Princess Katherine. Although his kiss might be seen as an acknowledgment of the dignity of the queenly body in death, it is more likely that his actions forgo such a political reading of the body in favour of a literary reading of the corpse. This reading requires him to overlook the actual queenly body in front of him in favor of a phantasmic image of the charming, accessible character found in Shakespeare's play. Pepys does not record the reaction of his wife and daughters to his action, nor does he record the response of the tour guide, except to note that the man took the opportunity to dispel another popular myth that Katherine was never buried at all. Perhaps the man did so to diffuse an uncomfortable moment. Pepys dramatises the emotional connection to Shakespeare's character Princess Katherine and empowers that connection beyond what would occur if a living queen or a properly buried dead queen were present in Katherine's stead. Had Pepys intended to read the queenly body in the traditional manner, he would have hesitated to touch or kiss it at all, just as he would have hesitated to steal a kiss from Katherine of Braganza, wife of Charles II. As Lisa Hilton states, 'The macabre eroticism of [the Pepys incident] says a good deal about Samuel's own tendencies, but it also recalls that Catherine … was a queen whose sexuality, both sanctified and transgressive, had dominated not just her own life but that of the royal dynasty of England'.[54] The sexualising of a queen's body with a stolen kiss or touch is taboo whether the queen is living or dead.

In the years following the Restoration of the Monarchy, Shakespeare's plays enjoyed a surge in popularity that further contributed to the tendency of his admirers to view the historical persons of his plays as dramatic characters. Moreover, there were apocryphal dramatisations of the plays, along with poetic and novelised reimaginings of Shakespeare's characters and their historical legends. Among these was *Queen Catharine, Or, The Ruines of Love*, by Mary Pix (1698).[55] This melodrama makes the most of the legend of Katherine's 'forbidden love' with Owen Tudor and turns their 'secret' marriage into a fatal romance. In one telling scene, Catharine stages a mock funeral for herself. She invites the friends she has left to view her body as though she were dead while she, still sentient, can perceive their grief. She asks them to share her suffering and sympathise with her as they view her living body as a corpse. She says:

> Friends, I've none, if thou pretend'st to ought
> Be gone and leave me: Leave me to earth and

---

and on 7 November 1667 he sees *The Tempest*, which he says is good, but 'of no great wit'. In fairness to Pepys, these plays were sometimes performed as musical or operatic adaptations and bore little resemblance or quality to the plays as they appeared in the First Folio.

54 Hilton, p. 321.
55 Mary Pix, *Queen Catharine, or the Ruines of Love* (London, 1698).

> Deep despair; death and destruction are the
> Only friends I chuse
> Here I will fall; strow me
> With herbs and flowers, then weep
> About me as if I were dead: perhaps I may
> Grow senseless.[56]

Pix presents the ersatz funeral as a living tableau of the actual events that took place regularly in Westminster Abbey when people viewed Catherine's corpse and imagined her life, love, and heartbreak. The scene associates the dramatic context of Katherine's corpse with the dramatisation of the queenly body of the character Catharine as she imagines her fate. Interestingly, the novel presupposes the reader's knowledge of, and relationship to, Shakespeare's Princess Katherine. Pix's novel invites the reader to re-imagine Shakespeare's Princess Katherine outside the text of the play; the reader is then invited to sympathise with Catharine's perception of being observed in death. It is an affective emotional experience for Pix's reader. The issue of affective emotional experience for apocryphal character development and dramatic interpretation is unsurprising to the twenty-first-century scholar, as it describes the phenomenon of 'fan fiction' to which contemporary popular entertainment is subjected. Literary fantasies like that of Mary Pix recontextualise the queenly body in death to the extent that it is secularised and removed from its traditional connection to the Davidic elect, to dynastic political clout, and to the maintenance of monastic houses as monuments to aristocratic power. As a dramatised apocryphal text, the queenly body is available to the imagination in ways the traditional reading of the queenly body forbids. She becomes a mother, a lover, and a corpse whose experiences are accessible to affected readers. Any reader of Pix's book could have gone to Westminster Abbey and paid a tour guide to show him or her the corpse so he or she could partake in the bizarre funerary reenactment for which the character Catharine appeals to those who love her – or to those who imagine they do. That same reader could go so far as to add this imaginative interpretation of Pix's Catharine to his or her existing affected response to Shakespeare's Princess Katherine, and develop a personalised, enhanced affective response to the character. This is precisely the aim and accomplishment of 'fan fiction', here in its Early Modern phase. It demonstrates the development of dramatic and literary ideas in accordance with changes in the public sentiment for historical figures in the late seventeenth and early eighteenth centuries.

During the eighteenth century there continued to be published poems and novels dramatising Katherine's love life. Shakespeare's *Henry V* continued to be performed as well, especially as France was renewed as an enemy during the latter half of the century. During that time the tomb of Henry V became a bigger tourist draw

---

[56] Pix, p. 50.

than it had ever been, and so did the exposed skeleton of his wife.[57] Specifically, the advent of antiquarian interest in cataloguing tombs and other points of interest in Britain's churches caused Katherine's corpse to acquire new significance; but in this case she came to be viewed as a readable catalogue item. Before the eighteenth century, antiquarianism was controversial to the extent that it was associated strongly with tomb-robbing and pilfering for the purposes of maintaining odd collections of ephemera.[58] But after 1700 attitudes began to change, and antiquarianism eventually lost much of that stereotype. The eighteenth-century antiquaries who professed interest in the tombs of Westminster saw themselves as scholars serving the needs of public memory. These efforts coincided with the desire of the aristocracy to fill Westminster's Abbey Church with as many figural monuments as possible, in an effort to document and memorialise their ancestries as exhaustively as possible. Here, antiquarianism and memorialism cooperate in their focus on remembrance and the way monuments describe relationships between the living and the dead. Between 1538 and 1700 that relationship was cautionary at best and antagonistic at worst; but after 1700 monuments, and especially the lavish ones at Westminster, celebrated the positive sentiments of remembering.[59] Tourism attended to both aristocratic and antiquarian energies; eighteenth-century sepulchral monuments, especially those created by Roubilliac, Scheemakers, Rysbrack, and others, generated tourist interest in their unique beauty,[60] and visitors to places like Westminster Abbey were keen on carrying a catalogue of the tombs as a guide.[61] Descriptive catalogues of sepulchral monuments invited visitors to read the past as an advertisement of contemporary values: *because* of their grand sepulchral monuments the great aristocratic dynasties of Britain validated ideas of English political, cultural, and ecclesiastical superiority. Westminster's architectural grandeur did the same for ideals promoting London as the city at the centre of the world. Eighteenth-century tourists were well aware that tombs and monuments at Westminster advertised patriotic ideals.[62]

[57] The tension that led to the Napoleonic Wars created what Orr calls 'a many-sided romanticism' that included neo-chivalry, neo-monarchism, and a renewed, modernised interest in queenship as an exemplary form of womanhood. Henry V, both the historical figure and the Shakespearean character, was important to this issue—and therefore, so was Katherine de Valois. Clarissa Campbell Orr, *Queenship in Britain 1660–1837* (Manchester, 2002), p. 6.

[58] Rosemary Sweet, *Antiquaries: The Discovery of the Past in Eighteenth Century Britain* (London, 2004), p. 4; also Philippa Levine, *The Amateur and the Professional: Antiquaries, Historians, and Archaeologists in Victorian England 1838–1886* (Cambridge, 1986), pp. 2–3.

[59] See Orr, pp. 6–7.

[60] See David Bindman and Malcolm Baker, *Roubilliac and the Eighteenth-Century Monument* (New Haven, CT, 1995); also John Field, *Kingdom, Power, and Glory: A Historical Guide to Westminster Abbey* (London, 1996); and Richard Jenkyns, *Westminster Abbey* (Cambridge, MA, 2005).

[61] See Orr, p. 4.

[62] See Nicola Watson, *The Literary Tourist* (New York, 2006).

Taking his cue from John Weever, Henry Keepe (d.1688) catalogued Katherine's corpse in *Monumenta Westmonasteriensa* in 1683.[63] Although he could not resist the temptation to mention the legends surrounding Katherine's disinterment, he downplayed the dramatic elements of the story and coupled his description of the corpse with cautionary language about its purported accessibility:

> On the south side of this tomb [Henry V] is a wooden chest or coffin, wherein part of the skeleton and perched body of Katherine Valois Qu. (from the waste [sic] upwards) is to be seen; of whom many fabulous stories are reported for her lying here: But the truth is, that when Henry VII caused the old Chappel of our Lady (at the entrance whereof this Queen was interred) to be pulled down the Workmen finding her coffin among others to be well-nigh perished and decayed. What remained of her body was taken thence. And placed in this Capsula nigh her husband, where it hath continued ever since: which is not frequently shewn to any, but is an especial favour by some of the chief Officers of the Church.[64]

Keepe's history of Westminster Abbey remained a popular guide book well into the eighteenth century. It is interesting that only fourteen years after Pepys paid a bit extra to kiss the queen, Keepe is cautiously tactful on the subject of seeing the corpse up close. His attitude may have to do with not offending his patron, Henry Howard, Earl of Arundel,[65] but it is also likely attributed to his view of himself as a scholar rather than a seeker of curiosity. The tomb of Henry V still bore the scars of iconoclasm, and his accoutrements still hung near the tomb. Those things warrant more of Keepe's energy as memorial symbols. Even so, his commentary provides instruction to the visitor concerning how Katherine's corpse is to be 'read': not as an illustration of legend or as a dramatic or romantic depiction, but as a document – however peculiar – of Britain's royal history. The texts of 'fabulous stories' can suffice for a simpler but nonacademic context. For the next generation of antiquaries (indicated by the following group of examples) the academic validation of peculiar objects and documents was important to expand what they considered to be parochial and canonical academic ideas about what constituted 'proper' objects to document.

Jodocus Crull (d. 1713/14), a German scholar who graduated from Cambridge and was later admitted to the Royal College of Physicians, took much interest in history, topography, and antiquity. He had an especial interest in Westminster's sepulchral monuments, and in 1711 he produced *The Antiquities of St Peter's, Containing the Inscriptions and Epitaphs Upon the Tombs and Gravestones.*[66] Like his predecessor Keepe,

---

[63] Henry Keepe, *Monumenta Westmonasteriensa, Or, An Historical Account of the Original, Increase, and Present State of St Peter's, Or, The Abbey Church of Westminster* (London, 1683).

[64] Keepe, pp. 155–6.

[65] Keepe, p. A2.

[66] Jodocus Crull, *The Antiquities of St Peters, Containing the Inscriptions and Epitaphs Upon the Tombs and Gravestones* (London, 1711).

Crull is meticulous, cataloguing the tombs and monuments with deep appreciation for their historical significance and reserving much of his personal judgment regarding the legends surrounding the tombs' occupants. About Katherine he says:

> … part of her skeleton is still to be seen in a wooden chest, standing on the south-side of her husband's monument. Many stories have been raised concerning her lying here in so mean a posture, but the most probable opinion is that this Lady being interr'd formerly at the entrance of the old chapel of Our Lady when King Henry VII caused that to be pull'd down, her coffin being found much decay'd, the remainders of her body were enclos'd in this chest and placed in this small chapel near her husband …[67]

Like Keepe, Crull is concerned with describing the location of the coffin in context of the tomb of Henry V. Although he mentions the exposure of the corpse he offers little more than mention of the fact. He prefers, as Keepe does, to forgo an interpretive reading of the corpse, insisting instead upon a use of the corpse as a documentary, rather than descriptive, text. He notes that stories and opinions exist, but does not recount them. Crull moves quickly to a full reprinting, in Latin and in English, of the long epitaph (purportedly by Skelton) that had been copied on a plaque two centuries before and that now stood against the wall. If anything is going to speak for the corpse, Crull prefers that it be the appropriately literary epitaph, which accomplishes its task in the traditional manner. Crull's full reprinting of the epitaph in two languages points to his desire for the descriptive language of the tomb to be preserved in its traditions, and enhanced, but not defined, by its aberrances. This is the same attitude with which the great museum collections of the eighteenth and nineteenth centuries were built.

John Dart (d.1730) sought to create a guidebook of his own for Westminster in 1723.[68] Keepe's book was a ready resource (as was Weever's). Dart was intrigued by the story of Katherine's corpse, but perhaps a bit too much; as he sought entrance to the Henry V chantry he crossed the line from inquisitive antiquary to curious tourist. Wanting to view the chantry, he is told that the iron gates are locked and that the key has been lost for many years. He reports, '…I could not satisfy my curiosity in this respect, being informed that a sacrist, some years since dying suddenly in the night, the key was lost, and the choir have never since had one made to it'.[69] Undeterred, Dart obtains a ladder (he does not state how) to climb over the gates and wall at the end of the staircase leading to the upper chantry. He notes that the chapel is covered with a layer of dust so thick that the colours of Henry V's shield are obscured. Upon investigating the turrets leading down on either side he reports that the steps are 'buried in dust'.[70] By 1723, then, the chantry had been locked for many years; although

---

[67] Crull, p. 187.
[68] John Dart, *Westmonasterium, Or, the History and Antiquities of the Abbey Church of St Peters, Westminster* (London, 1723).
[69] Dart, p. 45.
[70] Dart, p. 63.

Katherine's coffin and part of her corpse could be seen through the iron gate, it appears that even if Dart had been able to obtain the special permission suggested by Keepe it would not have been possible to view the queen up close. Dart catalogues the corpse of Katherine de Valois with a blandness that suggests disappointment: 'Item 87: Henry V and a view of the skeleton'.[71] It is perhaps this attitude toward his work that caused an antiquary of better reputation such as Richard Gough to be dismissive of Dart's career; he called Dart's book 'pompous' and 'inaccurate'.[72]

James Ralph provided a rare example of emotional commentary in 1734. In *A Critical Review of the Publicke Buildings, Statues, and Ornaments In and About London and Westminster* he writes, 'I think nothing can be a greater violation of decency … than to expose [the queen's] reliques in so licentious a manner and make a shew of what once commanded respect and adoration'.[73] Ralph's outburst is an anomaly among eighteenth-century Westminster surveys and guidebooks that mention Katherine's corpse. The vast majority of the others display a rather stoic academic detachment. David Henry, for example, in his famous guide to Westminster Abbey,[74] avoids any mention of stories or legends but only states that Katherine's remains lie

> enclosed in an old wooden chest … Queen Katherine herself received an honourable burial in the Chapel of Henry III (the old Lady Chapel) but when her grandson pulled down that to build his own, her body was taken up, the bones whereof were firmly united, and thinly covered with flesh, but the coffin being decayed was put into a wooden chest and moved to a place where it is now to be seen.[75]

These few examples illustrate the attempts to detach antiquarian study from urban legends, folklore, literature, and popular tourism. Some tourists, namely those who had antiquarian interests, sought to intellectualise their journeys and their interests by using such guide books on their walks and tours. In this sense Katherine's body underwent two alternative readings during the eighteenth century, both of which reflect progressive, albeit different ideas about historical remembrance.

By 1778 Katherine de Valois had lain next to Henry V for two hundred and seventy-six years. At that time a series of circumstances emerged that allowed Katherine to receive a traditional tomb space even if that burial was not to be permanent. The Percy vault was being expanded and renovated just over a year after the interment of the

---

71 Dart, p. 72.
72 Richard Gough, *British Topography Or, An Historical Account of What Has Been Done for Illustrating the Topographical Antiquities of Great Britain and Ireland*, 2 vols. (London, 1753), vol. I, p. 763.
73 James Ralph, *A Critical Review of the Publicke Buildings, Statues, and Ornaments in and about London and Westminster* (London, 1734), p. 86.
74 David Henry, *An Historical Account of the Curiosities of London, in Three Parts*, 3 vols. (London, 1753), vol. III, p. 91.
75 Henry, p. 91.

Duchess of Northumberland. During that renovation Dean Thomas made the decision to reinter Katherine de Valois for the first time since 1502. The gates to the Henry V tomb and chantry remained locked, but it appears that by 1778 the problem of a lost or unavailable key was resolved. Either the old key had been found or a new one was made, and Katherine's exposed corpse was removed from the Henry V tomb and interred with the descendants of Henry V's Lancastrian relations. There is no indication as to why the decision to reinter Katherine took as long as it did, and there is especially no definitive sentiment that Dean Thomas, or any previous Dean, was waiting to reinter Katherine with a set of appropriate relations. The placement of Katherine next to the tomb of Henry V had always been considered to be a temporary measure, the remedy for which the brief loss of the key to the gates seems an insufficient explanation. There was too little tourism between 1502 and 1669 for the exposed corpse to have been such a big draw as to dissuade the Abbey's administrators from reburying Katherine; and the increased tourism between 1669 and 1778 did not bring in so much money as to dissuade the administrators on those grounds, either. Moreover, sometime between 1683 and 1723 the key to the Henry V tomb was lost, and so even if tourists wanted to see more of the erstwhile queen than they could by peering through the gates, it was impossible to do so (provided the sexton was telling Dart the truth). At some point a new key was procured, but there is no clear indication of a relationship between the procurement of a new key and the burial of Katherine in the Percy vault. Perhaps it was for the best; for once the corpse was accessible again it appears that the adolescent scholars of Westminster began having fun with it. Richard Gough, in his book *Sepulchral Monuments in Great Britain* (1796) reports, 'Of late years the Westminster scholars amused themselves with tearing [Katherine's corpse] to pieces'.[76] Of all the issues surrounding the exposure of Katherine's corpse, the inaction of the Abbey's administrators for so many years concerning the matter is most puzzling. Still, no one explanation satisfies the reason for reburying Katherine in 1778 other than convenience of circumstances. In any case, Katherine was given a new coffin and a new tomb space in St Nicholas' Chapel, not far from either her original burial place in the Lady Chapel, or from the Henry V chapel.[77]

The legacy of Katherine's posthumous exposure found a place in nineteenth-century monument and tomb guides to Westminster Abbey, most of which reprint or summarise either Weever's entry or that of Stow. Because Katherine was no longer visible there was less concern about describing the coffin's placement or contents in

---

[76] Richard Gough, *Sepulchral Monuments in Great Britain*, 2 vols. (London, 1796), vol. II, p. 115. It should be noted that these are the same students who developed a tradition of carving their names into the coronation chair over the course of the centuries.

[77] In 1786 the royal funeral effigies (including Katherine's) were catalogued and sketched by John Carter. The effigies were kept in the upper chantry of the Henry V tomb, where Carter complained that they 'lie neglected, and mouldering into dust'. Reprinted, along with Carter's drawings, in Jocelyn Perkins, *Westminster Abbey, its Worship and Ornaments* (Oxford, 1940), vol. II, p. 142.

antiquarian studies of Westminster's monuments. With no 'readable' text of the corpse and no individual monument for her, little commentary on Katherine's burial space was needed. Still, there were those who commented on the issue as an historical matter, and although the vast majority of historians avoided a discussion of Katherine's long disinterment (except to mention that it happened), Agnes Strickland chose to engage in a reading of the corpse long after it had been put into its vault. In her multi-volume work *Lives of the Queens of England* (1844) she provides a unique example of commentary on royal life, death, and interment. She interprets royal biography in conjunction with traditional rumours and legends, her views on that person's literary legacy, and her own personal moral judgment. Strickland's scholarship in *Lives* is affected by her strong emotional investment in the personage behind the biography. Although she does not openly fictionalise in her melodramatic interpretations of people and events like historical novelists and dramatists of the nineteenth century do, her work is nonetheless informed by the practice.

Forgoing Weever's or Stow's detached descriptions of the corpse and its location, Strickland relates the story of the exposure of Katherine's corpse with much drama and a nod toward legends rejected by other (mostly male) scholars. She does not, for example, attribute the disinterment of Katherine to the renovations that took place under Henry VII, but attributes the disinterment to the reign of Henry VIII, whom she calls Henry VII's 'ungracious descendant'.[78] She claims incorrectly that Katherine's corpse was deliberately shown as a curiosity because it had been found to be in an excellent state of preservation upon its removal.[79] She mentions the Pepys incident as an example of the way Katherine 'was shown for the extra charge of two-pence to the curious in such horrors'.[80] She continues, stating that the 'same disgusting traffic was carried on' through the reign of George III, at which time Katherine was finally 'sheltered from public view in some nook of the vaults of Westminster Abbey'.[81] Strickland respectfully presumes Dean Thomas to have been ignorant of the desecration of the royal bones, a presumption that is most unlikely in the light of the long list of deans before him, none of which could have been ignorant of the fact.[82] Although Strickland's work is not representative of mainstream history writing of the time, it nonetheless points to a continued reading of the corpse three quarters of a century after Katherine's reinterment. This reading displaces the language of antiquarianism and replaces it with some of the melodramatic language found in poems, novels, and plays romanticising historical figures. Strickland is imaginative without crossing the line into fiction, but she nonetheless asks her reader to envision, with feeling, the corpse and its condition. This is very similar to the attitude of Mary Pix in her depiction of Katherine's fantasy ersatz funeral.

---

[78] Agnes and Elizabeth Strickland, *Lives of the Queens of England*, 3 vols. (London, 1844), vol. III, p. 176.
[79] Strickland, p. 176.
[80] Strickland, p. 176.
[81] Strickland, p. 177.
[82] Strickland, p. 177.

Strickland's attitude is far different from that of Sir George Gilbert Scott, who surveyed Westminster Abbey from 1849–78 and recommended moving Katherine a second time. In 1877, the Percy vault was opened on the occasion of the funeral of Lord Henry Percy on 7 December. Soon after, in 1878, Scott wrote a letter to the Dean and Chapter of Westminster advising that Katherine be translated to the Chantry of Henry V:

> ...the removal under the immediate direction of the Dean of the remains of Queen Catherine of Valois from their late resting place in the Percy vault to a monument on the site of the ancient Altar in the Chantry of her husband Henry V is historically if not architecturally important. The ancient altar slab, which had been used as a part of the paving of this chantry now forms the top of the monument.[83] The space in the floor from which the slab has been removed should be repaired with tiles made to correspond with the ancient tile paving forming the main portion of the floor.[84]

Without mentioning any legend or rumour, and without mentioning Katherine's long disinterment, Scott emphasises the importance of a permanent tomb space for her. Aware that sepulchral monuments invite historical, genealogical, and architectural readings whose relevance extends beyond the immediacy of the burial space, Scott acknowledges that Katherine's long journey towards a permanent burial is not over. The text of the corpse is incomplete. It does not describe royal burial in a truthful or appropriate way. Moreover, Scott notes that there is architectural significance to consider. Despite the existence of or location of a monument the placement of the corpse must nonetheless correspond to it. Although most burials in Westminster's vaults were near but not directly under their monuments, it was still necessary to provide a correspondent *locus* for the corpse. It would not be fitting to place a monument in the Henry V chantry without moving the corpse itself. The corpse and the monument must describe each other; together they contribute to the architectural integrity of Westminster Abbey (just as they are presumed to do in any monastic space dedicated to aristocratic or royal burial). In this way the reading of Katherine's corpse returned as closely as it ever had to its fifteenth-century context. Scott's recommendation reflects the fact that the corpses of Westminster Abbey are as much a part of its architectural significance as the monuments. Cooperation between the two produces an appropriate description of aristocracy and monarchy in death, and Katherine de Valois was the prime example of the consequence of that loss of reciprocal descriptive language. Visitors and family members do not merely read the monuments; they read the entire structure of the Abbey church and its mission. Scott's argument for the architectural importance of the translation of Katherine's remains modernises and secularises a

---

[83] In 1539 Reformers removed the altar slab and used it to pave the floor. The new construction would return the slab to its former location and replace it with new floor tiles.

[84] Sir George Gilbert Scott, 'Letter to the Dean and Chapter of Westminster', 4 March, 1878, repr. in Arthur Penrhyn Stanley, *Historical Memorials of Westminster Abbey*, 2 vols. (Philadelphia, 1899), vol. I, p. 106.

much older idea of the royal burial space as spiritually communicative and ritualised. It speaks to a sense of completeness and coherence that reflects upon the stability and power of Britain's ideals. It is, in short, a Victorian idea.

Ideas about queens changed profoundly after the accession of Victoria. More popular than her Hanoverian relatives, Victoria, along with her husband Prince Albert, presented the public with a carefully constructed image of wholesome family life. As John Reed states, art, literature, and history of the nineteenth century sought to place women into stereotypes that conformed to Victoria's image of a queen as virtuous, maternal, and cohesive, as a woman who held both her dynasty and the family unit together.[85] These types of changes reflect an aversion to the eighteenth-century image of the 'bluestocking', or Learned Lady, which in the nineteenth century was replaced with an image of domesticity, motherhood, and submissiveness. At the same time, however, this image identified women, and especially aristocratic or royal women, as powerful social forces, as dignified emblems of the nation's greatness.[86] Changes in reference to Katherine's corpse, toward an adapted sentimentalism and away from cataloguing, follows this pattern.

Although Katherine's 1778 reburial located her in the aristocratic vault of a family whose pedigree complemented that of her regal husband and grandson, the internment was seen by Scott as insufficient, incomplete, and unregal. His recommendation to the Dean and Chapter was met with approval – Dean Stanley expressed the sentiment that it was unsuitable that royal remains should be interred in 'an obscure vault, unknown, unrecorded even in the register of the Abbey'.[87] Scott's recommendation was followed by an appeal to Queen Victoria herself for funds to pay for the new burial space and locate Katherine's corpse in the immediate vicinity of her husband.[88] For his own part, Dean Stanley, a respected antiquary in his own right, took a sympathetic view of Katherine's posthumous history. In his own survey of Westminster Abbey (in which he oversees several royal and noble disinterments) he makes note of the Pepys incident as a literary testimonial to the poor treatment of Katherine's corpse. He frames the story with some regrettable details:

> Queen Catherine, after her second marriage with Owen Tudor, sank into almost total
> oblivion. On her death her remains were placed in the Abbey, but only in a rude tomb in

---

[85] John Reed, *Victorian Conventions* (Columbus, OH, 1975), p. 77.

[86] Reed, p. 34.

[87] Arthur Penrhyn Stanley, 'On the Depositions of the Remains of Katherine de Valois, Queen of Henry V, in Westminster Abbey', *Archaeologia* 46 (January 1881): 292. Stanley considered the Georgian vault to be inappropriate for a French princess. It is startling that the Abbey's own register evidently did not record the interment.

[88] This construction almost completely overlooks Katherine's marriage to Owen Tudor. Tudor's image still faltered occasionally in critical historiographical studies of the time, and most of the language surrounding Katherine's life, death, and (re)burial presumes Henry V to be her authentic spouse.

the Lady Chapel beyond, in a badly apparelled state. There the coffin lay for many years. It was, on the destruction of that Chapel by her grandson, placed on the right side of her royal husband, wrapt in a sheet of lead taken from the roof, and in it from the waist upwards was exposed to the visitors of the Abbey; and so it continued to be seen...[89]

Katherine's permanent tomb is one whose composition and placement discourage visibility. Indeed, when her remains were translated in 1878, the process, as described by Dean Stanley and D.C. Bell,[90] was one marked by its reverence and carefulness. Its very quietness is apparent in Dean Stanley's recollection of the event, which he published in *Archaeologia*, a journal for antiquarian scholars:

> Early on Saturday, the 8th of December 1877 [the day after Lord Percy's funeral], the Dean, Canon Farrar, and Mr Doyne Bell met in the chapel of St Nicholas; the Percy vault was opened and a portion of the wall of separation was removed, so as to allow a coffin to pass through the wall. This wall was found to be of the thickness of one brick instead of three ... so that the opening was made with great facility. Through this aperture there was visible the chest containing the remains of the Queen. It was lying on the south side, close to the south wall...[91]

The wood of the coffin had rotted almost completely through because of the dampness of the vault, and the group were concerned that moving the coffin would cause it to disintegrate completely; but the bottom of the coffin was sound, and with great care it was lifted out of the vault. Stanley continues:

> This operation took some time, and required extreme caution, as the space was very limited, the openings were narrow, and it was necessary that the chest should be kept in a horizontal position in consequence of its rotten condition ... The rotten pieces of wood were gradually and gently lifted off, together with the one large piece to which a leaden inscription was attached, and the remains of Queen Katherine were then exposed to view.[92]

D.C. Bell then examined the corpse meticulously and respectfully. As Stanley notes, the upper part of the body 'was much disturbed, and several portions are missing', with only half the skull and a few ribs remaining.[93] The schoolboys of Westminster had apparently vandalised the corpse to a great extent, producing a

[89] Arthur Penrhyn Stanley, *Historical Memorials of Westminster Abbey*, 2 vols. (Philadelphia, PA, 1899), vol. I, pp. 186–7.

[90] D.C. Bell is also the man who supervised the excavation of the grave of Anne Boleyn in the Chapel of St Peter ad Vincula at the Tower of London two years earlier.

[91] Stanley, 'Depositions', p. 287.

[92] Stanley, p. 288.

[93] Stanley, p. 289.

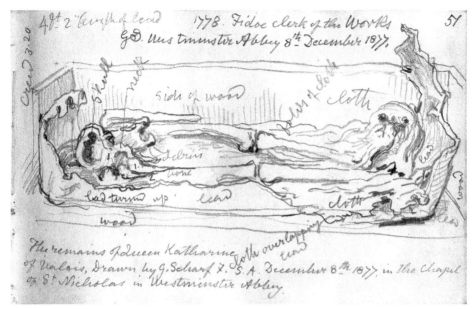

Fig. 5 Drawing by Sir George Scharf of the remains of Katherine de Valois in 1877. The remains are in almost complete disarray, with the pelvic bone at the top of the dilapidated coffin, the skull near it, and the legs extending to the right. Photo reproduction courtesy of the National Portrait Gallery Archive, London.

syncopated effect: Katherine's story was patchwork, and now her corpse, literally in pieces, narrated that story. The lower half of the body was in better condition: wrapped in several layers of cerecloth, the legs still retained their musculature and skin. After measuring the body, Bell determined that Katherine de Valois had been five feet six to five feet seven inches in height – very tall for a woman of the fifteenth century.[94] George Scharf made a sketch of the remains (Fig. 5), after which they were returned to the coffin and brought up to the chantry. Mr Bell records the event as being of a thoughtful and reverential nature:

> It was a striking and impressive scene, which I shall ever remember, and which at the time it was impossible to view without some feeling of emotion. The daylight had quite faded, and we were alone in the darkened Abbey … Mr George Scharf and myself followed [the workmen], no one else was present, and we seemed unconsciously and silently to fall into a sort of processional order. I remarked to him, 'we are attending the Queen's third funeral'. Not a word was said as we passed slowly round the ambulatory in the darkness.[95]

---

[94] Stanley, 'Depositions', p. 290.
[95] Stanley, 'Depositions', p. 290.

Fig. 6 The monument of Katherine de Valois as it appears today, as part of the altar in the upper chantry of Henry V. Photo courtesy of Westminster Abbey.

After the coffin was lowered into the tomb and the slab put in its place, an epitaph was erected. It is a very simple one, stating only that underneath the altar lies Katherine de Valois, daughter of Charles VI, King of France, wife of Henry V, mother of Henry VI, grandmother of Henry VII (Fig. 6). The epitaph ends with the dates of her birth and death. The location of the tomb in the upper chantry, with a simple epitaph, all but deprives Katherine's burial place of the conspicuous visibility of other royal tombs, even that of her husband. There is little opportunity to construct a text of the body, and little material by which to make such a construction in any case. The placement of the body is similar to what it had been in centuries past: she is near Henry V, amid his shield, helmet, and accoutrements; but the context is completely different. It silences past readings of the corpse and replaces them with precious few words and no figural image. It supplants the desire to construct an imaginative narrative of her life or her death.

Still, in his overview of the translation of the remains, Stanley introduces Katherine de Valois to his readers as 'The Kate of Shakespeare'.[96] Even as he remarks that the simplicity of the burial is a dignified and welcome contrast from her former state, he

---

[96] Stanley, 'Depositions', p. 202.

adds nonetheless that the context of the tomb's location encourages the imagination concerning national pride and due reverence to royalty:

> Here she rests in the midst of the royal sepulchres; yet, in conformity with the obscurity into which she fell, withdrawn from them, after vicissitudes in death equal to her vicissitudes in life, midway between the older Plantagenets and the later Tudors – the missing link which unites the earlier and the later history of England together.[97]

As the Dean of Westminster, Stanley had a greater responsibility than others to ensure than the interments and monuments of the Abbey reflected public ideals. His quiet reverence and careful recording of the event is decidedly, albeit unofficially, ceremonial – so much so that Mr Bell remarked upon it – and it indicates Stanley's professional focus on the combined scientific and sociological approach toward excavation and posthumous examination for which antiquaries of the late nineteenth century were known. It replaces a syncopated narrative of the corpse with a pseudo- epideictic one; it is a rhetoric of ceremony indicated by few words and a silent procession, but it speaks volumes.

The final interment of Katherine de Valois references Victorian funerary ideals that connect the traditional socio-cultural discourse with the dead with political ideals of Victorian public mourning. The death of Prince Albert in 1861 redefined the tradition of public mourning, secularising and personalising it to produce a complex ideal of citizenship that revolved around the capacity of the individual to mourn a royal figure and communicate that patriotic sentiment to the state.[98] In this sense Stanley's sympathetic attitude and Bell's reverent, impromptu funeral procession represent the effort by a great many in public service to translate individual affection to civic sentiment, to give personal meaning to political events, and to share these emotions with the historical and the literary dead, creating what Esther Schor calls 'the enduring membership of the dead in the body politic'.[99] The staging of this moment for Katherine de Valois indicates a culmination of the diachronic triangular relationship between her life, her death, and her legacy, in which her corpse is translated uncomfortably from materiality to melodrama and back again before it finally comes to rest in a private and a quiet place.

---

[97] Stanley, 'Depositions', p. 293.
[98] For a full discussion of this issue, see James Stevens Curl, *The Victorian Celebration of Death* (Gloucestershire, 2000); Elizabeth Darby and Nicola Smith, *The Cult of the Prince Consort* (New Haven, CT, 1983), and Esther Schor, *Bearing the Dead: The British Culture of Mourning from the Enlightenment to Victoria* (Princeton, NJ, 1994).
[99] Schor, p. 198.

4

APPROPRIATED MEANINGS

Thomas Becket

On 23 January 1888, a skeleton was discovered in the crypt of Canterbury Cathedral. The bones were that of a tall man, over six feet, and the skull was crushed. Rumours swirled immediately that the body was that of Thomas Becket.[1] Sceptics dismissed the rumours, stating that history demonstrated clearly that the bones of Becket had been burned in 1538 by the agents of Henry VIII. Their scepticism was met with a chorus of dissent, mainly from Catholics, claiming that the burning of Becket's bones had itself been a rumour, and that the monks of Canterbury Cathedral had hidden Becket's bones in advance of Thomas Cromwell's arrival to oversee the dismantling of the Becket shrine. The contents of the shrine had not been Becket's, they said, but were switched with those of a long-dead monk. What followed was a controversy in print involving newspapers, academic journals, and personal letters that addressed issues of religious toleration, historical memory, and scientific investigation. As scholars and churchmen wrote to and about each other they faced the possibility that one of the most defining events of the Reformation was not a matter of historical fact, but of legend. If such a thing were true, how could Britain be sure that the Reformation was remembered correctly? Those who believed that the bones were Becket's argued that the Reformation was not in fact, remembered correctly. If *that* was true, how confident could the Church of England be that history had been written by the victors? Many who supported Catholic Emancipation or who supported non-conformism argued that it had not. Writing in 1921, J.H. Pollen recalled the controversy, saying, 'Every right-minded Englishman desired to know what became of the relics of Becket'.[2]

---

[1]   In his study of the controversy John Butler attempts to determine whether the bones were indeed those of Becket. He also examines other theories that Becket's bones lie buried in other parts of the cathedral and traces the history of these controversies into the late twentieth century. My discussion of this issue does not consider whether the bones were Becket's or whether any 'switched-body' theories are true. My study revolves around antiquarian interest and the implications of 'reading' the skeleton for ecclesiastical and political purposes in 1888. See John Butler, *The Quest for Becket's Bones: The Mystery of the Relics of St Thomas Becket of Canterbury* (New Haven, CT, 1995).

[2]   J.H. Pollen, 'Henry VIII and St Thomas Becket, Part I', *The Month* CXXXVII (February 1921): 119–28; and 'Part II', CXXXVII (April 1921): 324–33.

The bones were discovered while the crypt of Canterbury Cathedral was being assessed for improvements. Specifically, the investigation into the crypt was meant to find the easternmost boundaries of an eleventh-century Norman church.[3] The excavation of the bones was commissioned by the Dean and Chapter, and overseen by three clergymen who took great interest in the antiquity of Canterbury and its churches, two of whom were canons of the Cathedral: Rev. C.F. Routledge, who authored several guidebooks of churches in Canterbury;[4] Rev. W.A. Scott-Robinson, who researched the Medieval history of Kent and also of Canterbury Cathedral,[5] and Rev. J.B. Sheppard, who edited collections of Medieval letters and records in Canterbury and who had researched materials on Becket.[6] John Butler describes the site of excavation:

> The bones were contained in a coffin buried just below the surface in the eastern crypt between the westernmost two of the three Purbeck marble pillars in the central aisle. Immediately to the east of this place (that is between the two easternmost of the three pillars) a hollowed-out space was found, extending to about three feet beneath the surface, filled with rubble. It was in this place that Becket's body had been buried for fifty years from 1170 to 1220; and the committee thought that the hollowed-out space was probably the actual grave in which the marble coffin had lain. Two long, thin steps of Purbeck marble were also uncovered nearby, which the committee identified as those leading to the altar where the tomb had stood until its destruction in 1538. The coffin containing the bones was therefore lying in a place most intimately associated with Becket – a mere few feet away from the site of his erstwhile tomb, and almost exactly beneath the place in the Trinity Chapel above where his shrine had once stood.[7]

A 'reading' of the site was taking place.[8] The site of excavation documented the story of Becket's interments in the crypt and in the location of the former shrine above it, reflecting the well-known narrative of Becket's hagiographic legend: after his initial interment in 1170 Becket's body was moved around Easter 1171. At that time there were rumours that enemies of the martyr intended to steal his body, and so Becket's corpse

---

3 Butler, p. 35.
4 For example, C.F. Routledge and Thomas Field, *Canterbury Official Guide to the Cathedral Church* (Canterbury, 1897).
5 Mention of his publications is found in 'Proceedings at Meetings of the Royal Archaeological Institute: Annual Meeting at Canterbury, July 20–27, 1875'. *The Archaeological Journal* 32: 495.
6 *Materials for the History of Thomas Becket, Archbishop of Canterbury*, ed. J.B. Sheppard and J.C. Robertson, 7 vols. (London, 1875–85).
7 Butler, p. 35. Routledge, Sheppard, and Robertson published their findings in 'The Crypt of Canterbury Cathedral', *Archaeologia Cantiana* 18 (1889): 253–6.
8 The idea that an archaeological/excavation site is a text, that it provides a narrative for itself and that it can be connected to literary analysis and theory, is examined in Philip Schwyzer, *Archaeologies of English Renaissance Literature* (Oxford, 2007), John Hines, *Voices in the Past: English Literature and Archaeology* (Cambridge, 2004), and Jennifer Wallace, *Digging in the Dirt: The Archaeological Imagination* (London, 2004).

was removed from its marble tomb and placed in a wooden coffin behind the altar of St Mary of the Undercroft.[9] Fifty years later Becket was translated by Archbishop Steven Langton. The disinterment was attended by Henry III, and the appearance of the king drew such large crowds that free wine was distributed to keep them happy. The monks placed Becket's bones into an adorned wooden chest, which they fastened with iron nails and then laid into a casket covered with gold and precious stones.[10] The bones remained at that site until 1538, when the shrine was destroyed.

The grave discovered in 1888 generated mystery because no one's bones, much less Becket's, were supposed to be there. The three churchmen/antiquaries, whose interests included studies in theology, history, archaeology, and architecture, found themselves faced with a provocative series of interpretations of the site.[11] The site suggested a revised version of Becket's legend, a narrative from which important facts threatened to be missing. In a cautious acknowledgment of this gap, the clergymen immediately turned their attention to the contents of the coffin. The bones were not laid in the coffin in the regular manner, but were bunched together in the upper portion of the coffin, and were mingled with debris.[12] The coffin itself (if it could be called that) was so narrow that it could not accommodate the body of a grown man.[13] When the bones were laid out they appeared to be those of a very tall man, and the skull bore several holes, as though the man's head had been subjected to severe blows. The dead man, whoever he was, had clearly been moved from his original burial place, and reburied with haste, in a makeshift ossuary, or bone-box.

A 'reading' of the corpse was taking shape, albeit one of great conjecture because of expectations and suppositions about the dead man's identity. These suppositions had the effect of *auxesis*: the creation of hyperbole by the deliberate rearranging of the elements of an existing text. In this sense, the 'auxetic' arrangement of the bones is meant to create – or recreate – the narrative of a saint's body. Arranging bones in this way and for this purpose had a precedent in the false narratives of the Medieval relic trade and fraudulent pilgrimage sites. One such deception that was known to antiquarian circles in the nineteenth century was that of St Cuthbert. In 1827 James Raine, an antiquary and the librarian of Durham Cathedral, excavated the shrine of St Cuthbert in Durham Cathedral and concluded that the story of incorruptibility of the saint's body was not true. Raine demonstrated that the body of St Cuthbert had decomposed and fallen

---

[9] James Craigie, 'Materials for the History of Archbishop Thomas Becket', *Chronicles and Memorials of Great Britain and Ireland During the Middle Ages*, 99 vols., vol. LXVII, no. 4 (London, 1879), p. 427.

[10] William Stubbs, ed., 'The Historical Works of Gervase of Canterbury', *Chronicles and Memorials of Great Britain and Ireland During the Middle Ages*, vol. LVVIII, no. 1 (London, 1879–80), p. 71.

[11] None of the three were present when the coffin was raised, and it is not known how much time elapsed between the uncovering of the coffin and the attendance of the three overseers of the project.

[12] Arthur James Mason, *What Became of the Bones of St Thomas?* (Cambridge, 1920), p. 174.

[13] Mason, p. 181. Apparently, one of the workmen lay down in the coffin to determine this fact.

apart during the first eleven years after his death in 698, and that the dry bones had been taken out of the coffin, arranged, and then swaddled together and covered in an allover fabric so the body appeared coherent and uncorrupted.[14] Interestingly, the eye sockets bore a foreign substance that was meant to suggest intact eyeballs beneath the cloth that covered the face. When Raine tested the material, it crumbled between his finger and thumb.[15] He says that the tale of the incorruptibility of the saint's body was 'invented for interested purposes in a superstitious age'.[16] In short, the body's parts had been arranged to produce a hyperbolic narrative.

When a corpse is unidentified it can only be 'read' according to what its immediate physical signs communicate. The 'narrative' of the corpse is interrupted, as the suppositions of the viewer are constrained by the gravesite and its proximate environs, and by the limitations of the corpse itself. When the identity of a corpse is known or suspected, the viewer brings a host of texts to the viewing of the body in its grave: genealogy, history, legend, myth, literature, scripture, and hagiography. In such a case the corpse does not speak entirely for itself; it functions as a page upon which the viewer's suppositions are inscribed. In the case of the Canterbury bones there was an immediate temptation to inscribe existing texts onto the corpse – arranging the bones and the elements of the narrative – to construct a hyperbolic supposition. Such a temptation was made greater considering that Becket's corpse already had a functioning narrative attached to it. Becket's body had been read as a hagiographic text during his two translations, as the corpse was inspected for incorruption and signs of miracle. Archbishop Langton had anticipated as much when he reportedly withheld a few small bones to distribute to other churches and important clergy.[17] Were there now any bones missing from the unidentified tall man in the crypt? There were – but whether it was because they had been collected by Archbishop Langton or because they had simply turned to dust could not be known. Those present at the discovery of the bones were well aware that this corpse had controversy written all over it.

The onset of the Oxford Movement from 1778–1829 contributed to the development of medievalism during that time. In addition to the well-known increase in neo-Gothic architecture and the rise of pre-Raphaelite art at the time, there is also a close connection with renewed interest in Medieval texts. Many Medieval Latin works that spanned the Anglo-Saxon period to the thirteenth century were translated; and

---

[14] James Raine, *Saint Cuthbert: With an Account of the State in which His Remains Were Found upon the Opening of His Tomb in Durham Cathedral in the Year MDCCCXXVII* (Durham, 1828), p. 227.

[15] Raine, p. 214.

[16] Raine, p. 227; see also R.D. Townsend, 'Hagiography in England in the Nineteenth Century: A Study in Literary, Historiographical, and Theological Developments'. Unpublished D. Phil. Thesis. Oxford, 1981, p. 187; repr. in Stephen Bann, *The Clothing of Clio* (Cambridge, 1984), p. 2.

[17] Craigie, p. 427.

among these, fifteen volumes were devoted to Thomas Becket. They include: Robert of Gloucester's thirteenth-century *Life and Martyrdom of Thomas Becket* in 1845,[18] and *The Life and Letters of Archbishop Thomas à Becket* by the Rev. John Giles.[19] James Craigie Robertson produced *Materials for the History of Thomas Becket,* a seven-volume work published between 1875 and 1885,[20] and William Holden Hutton treated the Becket legend with reverence in *S[aint] Thomas of Canterbury, His Life and Fame from the Contemporary Biographers and Chroniclers* in 1889;[21] Edwin Abbot did the same in *St Thomas of Canterbury: His Death and Miracles* in 1898.[22] The great antiquary and Dean of Westminster Arthur Penrhyn Stanley published *Historical Memorials of Canterbury Cathedral* in 1888 as a companion to his exhaustive catalogue of memorials and monuments in Westminster Abbey, which records many translations, disinterments, and reburials. The centrepiece entry of the Canterbury volume was, of course, the story of the Becket shrine.[23]

Moreover, there is a host of plays and poems written about Becket during the nineteenth century – sympathetic works that present melodramatic defences of Becket's martyrdom, and attacks on Henry VIII's tyranny. To name a few: 'The Murder of Thomas Becket', a dramatic narrative of Becket's murder, appeared in *The Manchester Times* in 1865,[24] and *St Thomas of Canterbury, A Dramatic Poem*, written in iambic pentameter by Aubrey de Vere, appeared in 1876.[25] Douglas Jerrold's play *Thomas à Becket: A Historical Play in Five Acts* was presented in 1829,[26] and was followed in 1840 by *Thomas à Becket: A Dramatic Chronicle in Five Acts* by George Darley.[27] Alfred Lord Tennyson staged his celebrated play *Becket* in 1884.[28] Sermons on Becket also became popular, such as one by Archbishop Henry E. Manning, a Roman Catholic convert and Cardinal-Archbishop of Westminster. The sermon, which was reprinted in the *London Daily News* in 1868, appeals for funds to restore the Church of St Thomas of Canterbury in Rome. Manning cites Becket among the

---

[18] Robert of Gloucester, *fl.* 1260–1300. *The Life and Martyrdom of Thomas Becket, Archbishop of Canterbury, from the Series of Lives and Legends Now Proved to Have Been Composed by Robert of Gloucester*, ed. and trans. William Henry Black (London, 1845).

[19] John Giles, *The Life and Letters of Archbishop Thomas à Becket*, 2 vols. (London, 1846).

[20] J. B. Sheppard and James Craigie Robertson, *Materials for the History of Thomas Becket, Archbishop of Canterbury*, ed. James Craigie Robertson (London, 1875–85).

[21] William Holden Hutton, *S. Thomas of Canterbury, an Account of his Life and Fame from the Contemporary Biographers and Other Chroniclers* (London, 1889).

[22] Edwin Abbott, *St Thomas of Canterbury: His Death and Miracles* (London, 1898).

[23] Arthur Penrhyn Stanley, *Historical Memorials of Canterbury: The Landing of Augustine, The Murder of Becket, Edward the Black Prince, Becket's Shrine* (London, 1888).

[24] Anonymous, 'The Murder of Thomas Becket', *Manchester Times*, Saturday, 30 September, 1865.

[25] Aubrey de Vere, *St Thomas of Canterbury, a Dramatic Poem* (London, 1876).

[26] Douglas William Jerrold, *Thomas à Becket: A Historical Play in Five Acts*. As Played at the Surrey Theatre (London, 1829).

[27] George Darley, *Thomas à Becket: A Dramatic Chronicle in Five Acts* (London, 1840).

[28] Alfred, Lord Tennyson, *Becket* (London, 1884).

chiefest of Catholic martyrs and says that 'the pages of English history have been unfortunately perverted on the subject'.[29]

About the same time, S.R. Maitland, a Church of England controversialist who was no stranger to debate, challenged the academic authority of John Foxe's *Book of Martyrs* in a series of essays and letters published as a response to a major edition of Foxe's book that appeared between 1837 and 1841.[30] Maitland's views were harsh: Foxe was a propagandist, not a historian, and Foxe had resorted to mythmaking to promote his cause. Foxe's harsh treatment of Becket had laid much of the groundwork for stereotyping about the Reformation and its legacy; now Maitland, a conformist member of the Church of England, intended to challenge that legacy. Maitland's attack on Foxe's work suggested that if Henry VIII was indeed the vainglorious, oversexed tyrant Catholics claimed him to be, then the Reformation could in fact be rooted in mythmaking. This supposition threatened to produce an uncomfortable development of English historical memory that many scholars, politicians, and clergymen were unprepared to accept.

Although the discovery of the Canterbury skeleton occurred over forty years after Maitland's attack on Foxe, the find encouraged a revisitation of questions about the history of the Church of England, about the persistence of English Catholicism, and about the construction of national memory concerning the Reformation. Some – especially the people cited below who were quick to take the debate to journals and newspapers – felt that the history of the 'Tudor Church' was being compromised by those who represented (or defended) factions of English Catholicism, and who were eager to identify the bones as Becket's. Their concerns notwithstanding, it was difficult for them, as it is for scholars today, to determine just what the term 'Tudor Church' meant. Patrick Collinson, in his analysis of the subject, argues that the 'Tudor Church' was certainly not one thing; in fact, if it was anything at all, it was a continuous reappraisal of English Catholicism.[31] Even so, it was several churches at various times and all at once. Henry VIII did not see eye to eye with the most ardent reformers, such as John Frith and Simon Fish; nor did he support William Tyndale's translation of the New Testament. The king suspected even those who worked for the Crown, such as John Leland, and those who enjoyed patronage at the highest levels, like John Bale, whose patron was Thomas Cromwell – who himself fell out of favour with

---

[29] Henry Manning, Cardinal-Archbishop of Westminster, 'Archbishop Manning on St Thomas à Becket', *London Daily News*, Thursday 3 September, 1868, issue 6970.

[30] *The Acts and Monuments of John Foxe: A New and Complete Edition: With a Preliminary Dissertation by the Rev. George Townsend*, ed. Stephen Reed Cattley, 8 vols. (London, 1837–41). Also, S.R. Maitland, *Six Letters on Foxe's Acts and Monuments* (London, 1837), and *Essays on Subjects Connected with the Reformation in England* (1849) (London, 1899).

[31] Patrick Collinson, 'Through Several Glasses Darkly: Historical and Sectarian Perceptions of the Tudor Church', in *Tudorism: Historical Imagination and the Appropriation of the Sixteenth Century*, ed. Tatiana String and Marcus Bull (Oxford, 2011), p. 98.

the king and was executed in 1540.[32] Elizabeth's relationship to the 'Tudor Church' during her father's reign was completely different from her relationship to the same 'Church' during the reign of her brother, Edward VI. During the sixteenth century terms like 'Protestant', 'Recusant', 'Reformed', and 'Puritan' were yet to take on the meanings that they held in the 1880s. Eamon Duffy points out in *The Stripping of the Altars* that terms like the 'Tudor clergy', or the 'Tudor laity' are poorly defined at best and unusable at worst.[33] Similarly, Greg Walker argues in *Persuasive Fictions: Faction, Faith, and Political Culture in the Reign of Henry VIII* that there is no one definition of 'faction' that satisfies the entire Tudor period.[34] The 'Dissolution', a term to which the destruction of Becket's tomb can be assigned, is actually several Dissolutions. Such terms became conflated and overused over the course of the later seventeenth century in histories like Gilbert Burnet's *History of the Reformation of the Church of England* (1679), a text that was reprinted well into the nineteenth century.[35] Burnet politicised the Reformation period, playing down theology in favour of speculation about the individual allegiances and motives of figures like Wolsey, Cromwell, and More. He also focused on the personal histories of the king's marriages. Histories that followed, such as the work of Richard Fiddes[36] and of Agnes and Elizabeth Strickland,[37] responded to Burnet's agenda in defence of what Andrew Starkie calls 'high church historical tradition'.[38] In defending such traditionalism, books like these relied very heavily on convenient, stereotypical terms, like 'Dissolution', 'Recusant', and 'Reformation'. These studies produced a dialogue constructed of problematic terms and references that nevertheless were presumed to be self-explanatory by authors and readers alike. Through the reprinting and academic distribution of texts like these, such terms came into continuous use, and 'The Tudor Era' became grossly oversimplified. Sometimes the reign of Mary I was included in definitions of the 'Tudor Church' and sometimes it was not. Terms like 'Marian Counterreform' are less than helpful, and the term 'conformism' in regards to any part of the sixteenth century is a term that is frustratingly fluid. As Collinson remarks, 'We know about the awkward squads, Papists and Puritans. But inarticulate conformity has no history.'[39] The nineteenth-century idea of the 'Tudor

---

[32] Collinson, p. 98.

[33] Eamon Duffy, 'Introduction', *The Stripping of the Altars* (New Haven, CT, 1992).

[34] Greg Walker, 'Introduction', *Persuasive Fictions: Faction, Faith, and Political Culture in the Reign of Henry VIII* (London, 1996).

[35] Gilbert Burnet, *History of the Reformation of the Church of England* (1679) (Oxford, 1865).

[36] Richard Fiddes, *The Life of Cardinal Wolsey* (London, 1724). Another, earlier work to which Burnet's book was compared was Nicholas Sander, *The Rise and Growth of the Anglican Schism* (London, 1877). Sander's book also enjoyed a long publishing history well into the Victorian era.

[37] Agnes and Elizabeth Strickland, *Lives of the Queens of England from the Norman Conquest*, 12 vols. (London, 1840–4).

[38] Andrew Starkie, 'Henry VIII in History: Gilbert Burnet's *History of the Reformation* (v.1), 1679', in *Henry VIII and History*, ed. Thomas Betteridge and Thomas S. Freeman (Farnham, 2012).

[39] Collinson, p. 100.

Church' lumps together a host of terms, thereby creating a convenient, but troublesome terminology. The scholars who weighed in on the controversy in the months following the discovery of the Canterbury skeleton accepted that Becket had been appropriated by the 'Tudor Church' and was reinterpreted as a 'Tudor figure', one whose disinterment and destruction satisfied the goals of Thomas Cromwell's iconoclastic agenda. This fact presented scholars with a precedent that allowed Becket to be appropriated in death a second time to become a '*Tudorist*' figure in the same vein as King John had among those who interpreted his legend.[40] In response to such an idea, some clergy and historians of the Church of England developed a reactionary and stereotyped view of 'The Reformation' that was far more nineteenth-century than sixteenth-century in its attitude. They saw 'The Reformation' as a sensible development of the Protestant religion that was hardly revolutionary, never fantastical, wholly English, and completely antithetical to Catholicism.[41] This view reflected Imperialist ideals about the superiority of the English Church and State over that of the Catholic Church specifically, and over that of world religion in general. It reinforced the stereotype of the Anglican constitution as practical, rational, and emotionally detached. Patrick Collinson explains the attitude: it was 'the way we do things in England'.[42]

History dictated that Becket's bones had been burned after the destruction of his shrine at Canterbury Cathedral in 1538. Indeed, the destruction of the Becket shrine was part of a larger campaign against the erstwhile archbishop by Henry VIII. Anxious to destroy the cult of Becket and channel its energies toward devotion to the Royal Supremacy, Henry VIII banned the veneration of Thomas Becket and sought to erase him from English history and memory. Destroying the shrine was only part of the process, however; Henry VIII and his Chief Minister, Thomas Cromwell, devised a complete regimen for the forgetting of Thomas Becket. The so-called 'Becket ban' of 1538 forbade pilgrimages to Canterbury, images of Becket, and plays depicting his martyrdom. It was a tall order: since his death the memory of Thomas Becket had been thoroughly incorporated into English historical identity. Now the king sought to interrupt that memory, and he demanded that England literally forget the Archbishop.

The process of forgetting was swift and severe. A formal citation was exhibited at the Becket shrine in Canterbury, followed by the sentence: the shrine was to be destroyed, its treasures turned over to the Crown, the bones burned and the ashes scattered. The dismantling of Becket's shrine and tomb took over a week, from the third to the eleventh of September 1538. The jewels and precious metals were pried from the shrine (a ruby given by Louis VII of France in 1179 was made into a thumb ring for Henry VIII).[43] Finally, the iron box containing the bones was opened and the remains of the Archbishop were burned in a pyre, the ashes scattered to the wind in front of a crowd of onlookers. This process was important: as Philip Schwyzer points

[40] String and Bull, pp. 1–5; and Collinson, pp. 98–101.
[41] Collinson, p. 101.
[42] Collinson, p. 101.
[43] Anne Duggan, *Thomas Becket* (London, 2004), p. 239.

out, saints represent channels of communication between the dead and the living. The destruction of Becket's body in particular was meant to emphasise his very *deadness* – it was a defiance of the belief that saints' bones had an enduring life-force.[44] It assured that Becket was merely a corpse, and that he could not communicate rebelliousness to the English faithful.

The king's proclamation of 1538[45] called for an end to the veneration of Becket's physical body, but it also referred to an end to the veneration of images of his body both in life and in death. Paintings, stained glass windows, statuary, and any other depiction of Becket, especially of his murder, were banned. In the wake of the destruction of the shrine, many seals, including those of the Archbishops of Canterbury and the city of Canterbury, replaced depictions of Becket's martyrdom with other imagery. Hubert Walter (1193–1205) had been the first to use a depiction of Becket's murder on his seal, and this tradition continued (with some exceptions) until the tenure of John Morton (1486–1500).[46] In the same year as the Becket ban and destruction of the shrine, Thomas Cranmer changed his seal, which also bore the image of Becket's murder. He introduced a new seal bearing the image of the crucifix, thereby replacing Becket's corpse with the body of the dying Christ. The city of Canterbury also issued a new seal that year, replacing the image of Becket's murder with the arms of the city. Other clergy, cities and towns, and fraternal organisations followed suit.[47] Seals do not merely contain text, they *are* texts in their own right and are meant to be read in their entirety: words, symbols, and figures together. The widespread replication and distribution of seals denotes their ability to proclaim truth, validity, and legality where words alone do not suffice. The whole text of the seal validates the alphabetic text of the document to which it is attached. For centuries the image depicting Becket's murder validated documentary text for much of the nation. Revised seals invalidated the venerated body in death, thereby reducing the status of Becket's body to that of a mundane corpse. Cranmer's new seal of 1538 contributed to the overall effort to appropriate the body ecclesiastical from the Roman church to the king.

The 1538 Injunctions were followed by a proclamation of 16 November of that same year[48] that was meant to clarify them by way of stemming the tide of progressive

---

[44] See Schwyzer, p. 110–11.

[45] *Tudor Royal Proclamations*, no. 186, 16 November, 1538, in Hughes, P.L. and Larkin, J.F., eds., *Tudor Royal Proclamations* (New Haven, CT, 1964).

[46] See W.G. Birch, *Catalogue of Seals in the Department of Manuscripts in the British Museum*, 2 vols. (London, 1887), for a list of the eleven archbishops who used images of Becket's martyrdom on their seals, with corresponding images and descriptions.

[47] One fifteenth-century seal for English merchants in the Low Countries bore an image of Becket's soul floating over a ship. The town of Arbroath, Angus, along with its Abbey, also had images of Becket's martyrdom depicted on their seals. Great Britain, Public Record Office, *A Guide to British Medieval Seals*, ed. P.D. Harvey and Andrew McGuiness (London, 1996), Seal nos. 156, 436, and 740, pp. 94 and 111. Langdon Praemonstratensian Abbey in Kent depicted Becket's martyrdom as well. Roger Ellis, *Catalogue of Seals in the Public Record Office*, 2 vols. (London, 1986), vol. I, item M453, p. 48.

[48] *Tudor Royal Proclamations*, no. 186, in Hughes and Larkin.

reforms. The last two sections (out of ten) attacked the prevalence of 'superstitions and idolatries' remaining in the realm. Henry VIII and his ministers undermined the traditional version of the Becket story by presenting an account unflattering to Becket, blaming him for instigating the altercation that resulted in his death. They then declared that Thomas Becket no longer be called a saint but rather be considered 'to have been a rebel and traitor to his prince'.[49] Becket was charged with offences against the crown, including treason and rebellion, for having defied his king (Henry II, but also Henry VIII, by implication).[50] G.R. Elton, in his discussion of Thomas Cromwell's revision of the Becket legend, states that Cromwell devised an explanation for Becket's death that stemmed from Becket's resistance of 'wholesome laws established against the enormities of the clergy'.[51] This explanation held Becket responsible, albeit posthumously, for violating laws of both the past and the present.

An amusingly dubious but nonetheless compelling story arose from Cromwell's efforts. According to the story (first chronicled and likely invented by Chrysostom Henriquez in the seventeenth century), Becket was accused posthumously of disturbing the realm and was called upon to defend himself from beyond the grave. If he failed to appear (either materially or spectrally) within thirty days, judgment would be given against him. The thirty days came and went. Becket did not appear in court, and the king went ahead with the dissolution of the Canterbury shrine. The story's macabre suggestiveness and the popularity of David Wilkins' *Concilia Magnae Brittaniae et Hiberniae* (1737),[52] in which the most well-known version of the story is told, made the legend of Becket's posthumous trial popular among Catholics who wished to remember Henry VIII as an irrational tyrant rather than a Protestant hero. The story was also popular among eighteenth- and nineteenth-century nonconformists, reflecting an eagerness to interpret narratives of the dead with sentimentalism and theatricality for political purposes. For the most part, historiographers who held faculty positions at Britain's universities did not believe the tale. For example, Henry Jenkyns dismisses the story in *The Remains of Thomas Cranmer*, and Charles Le Bas Webb ridicules it in *The Life of Thomas Cranmer*.[53] Archbishop Manning, however, did believe it – or at least

---

[49] *Tudor Royal Proclamations*, no. 186, in Hughes and Larkin.

[50] G.R. Elton, *Policy and Police: The Enforcement of the Reformation in the Age of Thomas Cromwell* (Cambridge, 1972), p. 257, n.1; see also Helen Parish, *Monks, Miracles, and Magic: Reformation Representations of the Medieval Church* (New York, 2005), p. 96.

[51] Elton, p. 257; and Hughes and Larkin, *Tudor Royal Proclamations*, vol. I, pp. 275–6.

[52] David Wilkins, *Concilia Magnae Brittaniae et Hiberniae*, 3 vols. (London, 1737), vol. III, pp. 835–6: 'Sanctum citandum in regio concilio esse, ubi ejus causa juridice erat decidenda, ut eam vel defenderet, vel defendi cerneter, sub poena, quod contra illum per contumaciam procederetur'. [They will proceed with their sentence (i.e., that Becket's shrine is to be broken up and the proceeds given to the king) unless he can either defend himself or have someone else defend him]. Henriquez is responsible for overinterpreting the language of the phrase in the Papal Bull, but Wilkins is guilty of encouraging Henriquez's interpretation and repeating the story.

[53] Henry Jenkyns, *The Remains of Thomas Cranmer*, 4 vols. (Oxford, 1833), vol. I, p. 262; and Charles Le Bas Webb, *The Life of Thomas Cranmer*, 2 vols. (New York, 1833), vol. II, p. 275.

he chose to for political purposes. He references the story in his sermon on Thomas Becket of 1868, saying, '[the posthumous trial] was an inglorious page in the history of England when the Saint and Martyr à Becket was summoned before a secret tribunal to be accused of high treason; and it was a page of ignominy in our history, which is not forgotten, only to be recited in order to be deplored'.[54] D.R. Woolf suggests that some form of judicial procedure did indeed take place. He cites a letter from Thomas Knight, writing from Valencia, to Thomas Cromwell, in which he reports that everyone wanting news from England wishes to know about what has become of 'the Saint of Canterbury'.[55] Knight refers to the involvement of Thomas Wriothesley (who in 1538 was Henry VIII's ambassador in Brussels) in the matter, saying, '...but Mr. Wriothesley, who played a part in that play had before sufficiently instructed me [while Knight was in Bruges] to answer such questions'.[56] Even if such a 'trial' were purely *pro forma* (whether enacted physically in a court of law or merely described in a legal document), it would still signal an important connection between the dead body of a saint and the law: that the two are continuously communicative and relative to one another until the law determines otherwise. Peter Roberts suggests, however, that the 'trial' was part of an actual stage drama rather than court theatrics. He discusses the possibility of a lost Becket play in his study of the Becket cult and drama.[57] Either of these is possible, or perhaps even both; nevertheless, they point to an important relationship between Becket's corpse, iconoclasm, and dramatic narratives.

Much of the credence for the story is found among amateur historians and Catholic apologists, many of whom misinterpreted (or chose to interpret differently) the language of the Papal Bull excommunicating Henry VIII and condemning the destruction of the Becket shrine, which read:

For being not satisfied with the blood of several living prelates and worthy men, he [Henry VIII] hath insulted over the dead, and such as former ages have for their sanctity canonised: witness its immanities against the sepulchre and shrine of Thomas late Archbishop of Canterbury, whose bones (by which were many Miracles wrought in England) he disturbed, and caused the relics of his dead body to be taken up, and

---

[54] Henry Edward Manning, Lord Archbishop of Westminster. 'Archbishop Manning on St Thomas à Becket', repr. in Henry Edward, *Sermons on Ecclesiastical Subjects*, 2 vols. (New York, 1872), vol. I, p. 438.

[55] D.R. Woolf, 'The Power of the Past: History, Ritual, and Political Authority in Tudor England', in *Political Thought and the Tudor Commonwealth: Deep Structure, Discourse, and Disguise*, ed. Paul Fideler and T.F. Mayer (London, 1992), p. 42, n. 24; Thomas Knight, 'Letter to Thomas Cromwell, 5 October 1538'. Public Record Office, Calendar of Letters and Papers, Foreign and Domestic, of the Reign of Henry VIII, vol. XIII, ii, p. 542.

[56] Knight, 'Letter to Thomas Cromwell'. His instructions from Wriothesley are apparently to avoid answering such questions; or to give a diplomatic and vague response.

[57] Peter Roberts, 'Politics, Drama, and the Cult of Thomas Becket', in *Pilgrimage: The English Experience from Becket to Bunyan*, ed. Colin Morris and Peter Roberts (Cambridge, 2002), p. 216.

(to the greater aggravation of his barbarous impiety) caused him to be condemned for a son of Rebellion, and his said bones to be burned, and the ashes thereof to be thrown into the Air.[58]

Condemning Becket publicly as a 'son of rebellion' does not amount to trying him posthumously, much less demanding the appearance of the dead man (or even that of a representative) in court. Still, the symbolism of the story was telling: for nineteenth-century scholars and churchmen wrestling with the legacy of the Reformation and the identity of the Canterbury bones, the tale acknowledged that Becket was a formidable *physical* force in death – a continually relevant corpse that defied royal authority, and to whom dramatic narrative was connected.

By the nineteenth century, Becket's reputation was embedded in centuries of hagiography. As Rachel Koopmans explains, the endurance of medieval saints' tales and legends requires a wide social circle in which the narrative of the hagiography's miracle stories can move freely and develop.[59] It requires both oral and written texts in various forms, and by various media – including the saint him or herself by way of intercessions and miracles performed. In short, the development of a saint's legend requires a 'conversational web'.[60] She says, 'These conversations were the generators of cultic communities, groups of people feeling a strong attachment to a saint and believing in his or her power in the world'.[61] The theological and doctrinal controversies of the nineteenth century generated a rival conversational web that threatened to redefine 'The Reformation' as one of England's greatest historical moments.

The revised legacy of Becket was meant to conform to a view of English identity devised and promoted by Henry VIII and Thomas Cromwell. As champions of anti-papist and nationalist thought the king and his Chief Minister had the shrine destroyed and the bones burned in an act of defence of the true English faith. The suppression of the cult, the destruction of the shrine, and the burning of the bones communicated a patriotic purpose. Three hundred and fifty years later, that purpose was threatened. The bones, if they were Becket's, stood to return Canterbury Cathedral to the status of a pilgrimage site. If that were to happen, the Church of England could be wrestled away from its Anglicised identity, and relegated to that of a subordinate to its Continental neighbours – and to the Vatican. The situation was tenuous –and it was exacerbated when, as if on cue, a miracle was reported in the crypt. A man from Margate came to the crypt with his young son, who had failing eyesight. The man asked to see the bones to find out if they could help his son, as he had visited

---

[58] Pope Paull III, Bull of Excommunication, 16 January 1538/9, repr. in R.W. Heinze, *The Proclamations of the Tudor Kings* (Cambridge, 1976), p. 10.

[59] Rachel Koopmans, *Wonderful to Relate: Miracle Stories and Miracle Collecting in High Medieval England* (Philadelphia, PA, 2011), p. 15.

[60] Koopmans, p. 17.

[61] Koopmans, pp. 17 and 26.

all the local doctors in vain.[62] Rumours circulated immediately that the boy had been healed; and those who were anxious for a positive identification of the bones pointed out that Becket's legend included many stories of restored eyesight. They pointed in particular to Eilward, a blind pauper whose sight was restored after praying to Becket, and whose story was memorable enough to warrant a thirteenth-century glass panel in the Cathedral.[63] As Rachel Koopmans points out, the miracle stories of saints are incredibly durable, especially when they are localised, as in a city like Canterbury, and when they employ repetitive imagery, as in the healing of the blind. Such elements become folkloric very quickly, establishing themselves as communal narratives and defying quantification.[64] When such stories stem from a respected source, like Benedict of Peterborough, who compiled miracle stories about Becket in the aftermath of his death, an authoritative text is produced. The miracle story of the blind boy of Margate produced a communal phenomenon that had the power to restore the 'narrative voice' of Becket's sanctified remains and validate the texts of the hagiographers hundreds of years later. The Canterbury skeleton threatened to reveal a hidden text that stood to renew the validity of saints' tales and invalidate the authoritative text of the Becket ban. John Butler states that this situation and its many complexities 'helps explain the speed with which the debate about the identity of the bones ensued, the intensity with which it was prosecuted, and the form it took'.[65] The ensuing debate in scholarly journals and newspapers represents a struggle for dominance over the text of English historical memory.

The debate was ignited by the examination of the bones. Soon after the bones were discovered they were presented to W. Pugin Thornton, a physician, phrenologist, member of the Royal College of Surgeons, and a practising Catholic. Dr Thornton conducted a forensic examination of the corpse and concluded that the bones were those of Becket.[66] He arranged the bones on a board 'in anatomical order',[67] fitted the bones of the crushed skull together on modeller's clay, and photographed it (Fig. 7). He determined that no bones were missing with the exception of some of the smaller foot and hand bones. There were five teeth, described as being in very good condition. The skull was crushed, but it could not be determined whether swords had made the fractures. Thornton estimates the height of the man at six feet two inches, and his age at forty to fifty-five years old, statistics that were consistent with Becket's height and age at the time of his death. He associates the hearty condition of the bones with a strong

---

[62] Agnes Holland, *Letter to Miss Lisa Rawlinson*, 10 February, 1888; repr. in James Arthur Mason, *What Became of the Bones of St Thomas?* (Cambridge, 1920), p. 179.

[63] Koopmans, p. 9.

[64] Koopmans, p. 15.

[65] Butler, p. 44.

[66] W. Pugin Thornton, 'Surgical Report on a Skeleton Found in the Crypt of Canterbury Cathedral', *Archaeologia Cantiana* 18 (1889): p. 258; Thornton later re-published his findings with more commentary in *Becket's Bones* (Canterbury, 1901).

[67] Thornton, 'Surgical Report', p. 258.

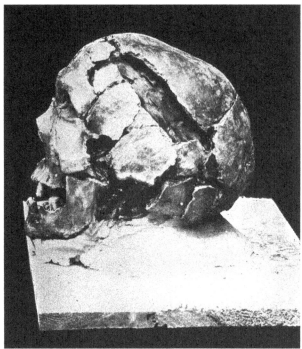

Fig. 7 Photograph by Dr W. Pugin Thornton of the unidentified skull at the centre of the Becket controversy in 1888. Reproduced in What Became of the Bones of St Thomas? *By George Mason (Cambridge, 1920). Photo reproduction courtesy of the Huntington Library, San Marino, California.*

physical constitution (incorrectly), saying, 'The bones of the body and limbs have the idea of great strength. The rough places on the bones, where the muscles were inserted, especially on the arm and leg bones, were larger and rougher than is usually met with skeletons'.[68] As most people today know, bone size or circumference is not linked to a strong or muscular build; but those connections were made in 1888. Thornton's desire to connect the physical constitution of the bones with the physical characteristics of Becket represents an effort to inscribe existing hagiographic text upon the corpse. Thornton 'reads' a connection between the size and height of the Canterbury bones and the vital statistics of Becket in a manner consistent with the way he reads hagiographic text. In doing so Thornton encourages the corpse to 'speak' its identity in a manner that validates his research, reflexively. Thornton is unconcerned that doing so represents a redundant and narcissistic practice; in fact, Thornton, and others who remarked that the bones 'looked' like those of Becket, expected the corpse to confirm its own identity by 'speaking' for itself. Thornton then compared the statistics of 'Becket's bones' to those of Henry VIII in 1538: six foot three, of heavy or sturdy build, and forty-seven years old. Interestingly, the body of Henry VIII was the preferable model in this scenario rather than that of Henry II, since the issues of the Reformation concerning memory and Becket's legend were the focus of the narrative of the bones.

---

[68] Thornton, 'Surgical Report', p. 258.

Dr Thornton performed a phrenological examination on the skull, 'reading' its bumps, brow, and overall shape to determine the character of the dead man. He concluded, '... the breadth of the brow would give large perceptive qualities; the rising appearance of the fore part of the skull would show much intellect; the flat appearance at the centre of the head would denote worldliness; and the immense volume of skull at the back indomitable energy'.[69] Dr Thornton did as many Victorian physicians did who studied the anatomy of the body for its purported intellectual or racial properties: he applied presumptions he already held to the physical condition of the body. Because the skeleton was unidentified and not buried with clothing or accoutrements, 'reading' the bones for information about the deceased could only yield so much for the nineteenth- century physician: age, gender, mode of death, and the general physical condition of the person at the time of death. In applying to the skeleton attributes of Becket's persona and physical constitution that he already knew (or thought he knew), Dr Thornton inscribed text derived from history, legend, and hagiography onto the corpse. In doing so Thornton established a dialogue between the corpse of Becket and the body of Henry VIII; he then 'read' the compilation of sources he constructed and determined that his suppositions were correct. The skeleton told Thornton what he wanted to hear: that it was a formidable match for the physical build and headstrong constitution of Henry VIII, and that English Catholicism was neither outwitted nor 'out-manned' by the Church of England.

This method of 'reading' the corpse is rooted in the ersatz discipline of anatomic caracteriology (also called physiognomy), the nineteenth-century pseudoscience that interpreted personality, gender, and racial attributes through physical characteristics.[70] Phrenology is a facet of this discipline. According to physiognomic standards, Thornton's examination of the bones made sense. He pitted Becket's body against that of Henry VIII regarding height (a very important factor in anatomic caracteriology), strength of conviction, robustness, and authoritative bearing. Both men had been larger than life, and via Thornton's 'reading' they remained matched in a struggle for mastery over the body ecclesiastical in death. It did not matter that Thornton was participating in a system of fiction-making, creating a dialogue of character traits that revolved around two men who never knew each other; nor did it matter that neither Becket's body, nor that of Henry VIII, were actually analysed.[71] Thornton had a precedent. The idea that Becket's physical constitution and that of the Royal Body were competitive goes all the way back to the time of Henry II, as is demonstrated by the work of J.F. Davis.[72] This idea was reinterpreted in 1538 to substitute Henry VIII as the royal rival

---

[69] Thornton, 'Surgical Report', p. 259.

[70] See Introduction.

[71] There is not now, nor has there ever been, any solid evidence pointing to the identification of the bones either as those of Thomas Becket, or any other person. The bones of Henry VIII had been located by 1888 after years of obscurity, but they had not been fully disinterred and examined forensically.

[72] J.F. Davis, 'Lollards, Reformers, and St Thomas of Canterbury', *University of Birmingham Historical Journal* 9 (1963): 13.

to Becket's ecclesiastical power. In this construction, Henry's imposing (and virile) physique embodied the living Protestant faith – the newly born Church of England – which for Reformers provided a stark contrast to the desiccated bones of Becket in their shrine.[73] By 1538 Henry VIII was the proud father of a male heir, and as Supreme Head of the Church he presented himself as an alternative to the celibate, childless clergy. Even though Henry VIII was not physically present when Becket's bones were burned, the contrast between the two bodies was observed by the crowd, and by the chroniclers.[74] Of course, by 1888 the desiccated bones of Henry VIII rested deep beneath St George's Chapel at Windsor, but that also did not matter to Thornton. The Royal Body presented a continuing physical challenge to the sturdy bones of the Canterbury vault. Moreover, Thornton's reading suggested contemporary relevance: although Queen Victoria was a woman, she was the embodiment of the strength and persistence of English Protestantism. The 'empire' established by the 1534 Act in Restraint of Appeals was now hers; and her physical character was, both figuratively and literally, larger than life. Thornton's analysis of the bones suggested that they also could not compete with the formidable character of the Royal Body in Victoria.

Soon after the publication of Dr Thornton's findings in *Archaeologia Cantiana*, correspondence among academics, theologians, and interested amateurs began to appear in various publications. Interestingly, many of the letters and articles are anonymous. Anonymous letters and articles on academic, political, or religious subjects were common in the nineteenth century, reflecting an interest in modesty for the general sake of one's career or family reputation; but in this case the anonymity of many of the letters suggests a desire to distance or extract oneself from an argument that was so tenuous it threatened to become embarrassing. It was important to stake a claim upon historical memory and 'own' the Reformation, but the letter writers knew that the subject was rooted in a long tradition of fiction-making that first canonised the murdered Archbishop, then eradicated the hagiographic text of St Thomas Becket, and then replaced that text with the rhetoric of Imperial Protestantism. Expressing one's opinion on the subject was tempting but risky, and the anonymity of many of the letters and articles provide their authors with opportunities for confidence in their opinions.

As M. Beazeley wrote in *The Morning Post* on 28 January 1888, 'The theory is put forward that at the time of the burning of the bones of Thomas à Becket in the reign of Henry VIII … a portion of them may have been secured and buried'.[75] Such a theory had been whispered among Catholics for centuries as part of a 'switched-body' theory, but the discovery of the bones now provided an opportunity for this long-standing rumour to become part of a dialogue validated by text. Arguments, theories, and rumours, no matter how questionable, gain authority and validity when they are textualised as print media. M. Beazeley was one of several scholars who collected his

---

[73]   Davis, pp. 13–15.
[74]   Davis, pp. 13–15.
[75]   M. Beazeley 'Letter to the Editor', *The Morning Post*, 28 January 1888, repr. in M. Beazeley, *The Canterbury Bones* (London, 1913), pp. 5–6.

correspondence on the Canterbury bones, combined them with his written opinions on the subject, and then published them as a book to establish their academic authority (the three clergymen who oversaw the excavation of the bones, and Dr Thornton, also did this).[76] The printing of letters written to a newspaper or in a journal establishes a dialogue, and then the publication of a scholarly book on the subject validates the dialogue as scientific, professional, and worthy of formal investigation.

One anonymous correspondent wrote to *The Bristol Mercury and Daily Post* on 1 February 1888, that the condition of the skull was proof that the bones were those of Becket. He is confident that they will soon be replaced in the coffin in which they were found and returned to the crypt fully identified, an act that will lead to the full restoration of the Becket shrine.[77] His attitude is echoed in the optimistic pronouncements of J. Morris, who wrote on 3 February 1888 to *The Morning Post* that because of the condition of the skull the remains 'have practically been proved to be those of Thomas Becket'.[78] Later that year an anonymous letter entitled 'Thomas à Becket's Remains' in *The York Herald* expressed a similar sentiment.[79] On 24 March 1888, however, H.W.B. wrote to *The Graphic* that the bones did not appear to be those of Becket because they did not correspond with a sixteenth-century engraving purportedly showing the bones that was held by the British Library (Fig. 8). He suggests that investigators draw their attention to:

> ... a very curious old engraving of the shrine and bones of the saint as they appeared in the reign of Henry VIII ... it was copied from an ancient drawing in a manuscript preserved in the Cotton Library, which would appear to have been made at the time that the shrine was being destroyed, or shortly after. It shows ... the little iron chest containing the skull and bones of the saint, with the piece of cranium, which was struck off at the martyrdom rejoined to the skull. Now it will be at once noticed that these remains do not indicate anything like a perfect skeleton, but only a skull, two shoulder-blades, and two arm or leg bones and if this was all that was preserved, in the Shrine, it is certainly difficult to reconcile the idea that the skeleton recently discovered at Canterbury was really that of St Thomas à Becket.[80]

---

[76] M. Beazeley, *The Canterbury Bones* (London, 1913).

[77] Anonymous, 'Thomas a Becket', *The Bristol Mercury and Daily Post*, Wednesday, 1 February, 1888, issue 12393.

[78] J. Morris, 'Letter to *The Morning Post*' (London), 3 February, 1888. Another letter on 2 February expressed a similar sentiment.

[79] Anonymous, 'Thomas Becket's Remains', *The York Herald*, Saturday 11 August, 1888, issue 11606, p. 5.

[80] H.W.B. 'The Shrine and Bones of St Thomas à Becket', *The Graphic* (London), Saturday 24 March, 1888, issue 956. The original engraving is in BL MS Cotton Tiberius E. viii. 278v, is copied in William Dugdale, *Monasticon Anglicanum* (1655), 3 vols. (London, 1846), vol. I, p. 84, and is reprinted in facsimile with commentary in Arthur Penrhyn Stanley, *Historical Memorials of Canterbury Cathedral, Second American Edition* (New York, 1888), pp. 267–8. The engraving does not actually show the bones; but rather shows the lid of the box onto which

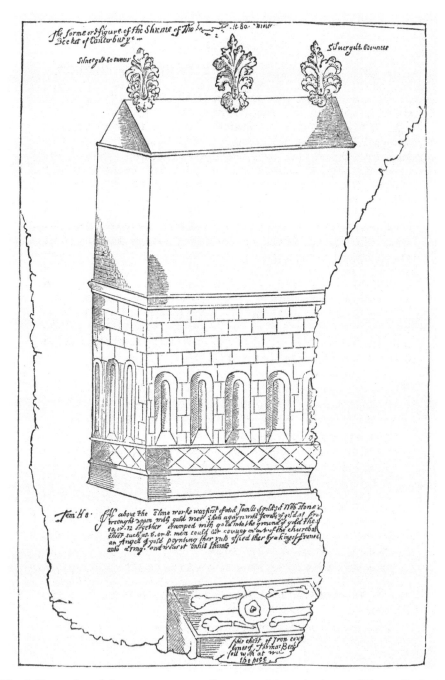

Fig. 8 Engraving of the ossuary purportedly extracted from the shrine of Thomas Becket by
the agents of Henry VIII in 1538. The drawing does not actually show the bones, but rather
an artistic representation of the bones on the lid of the ossuary. Photo reproduction courtesy
of the Huntington Library, San Marino, California.

These representative examples (there are many, most of which assert short pronouncements similar to this type) demonstrate the interest of many academics, churchmen, and armchair enthusiasts in a dialogue on revisionist history. Were Catholics, in their quick acceptance of the validity of the bones, the revisionists? Or was it the Church of England and its insistence upon the permanence of the iconoclasm of the 'Tudor Church' that produced the revisionist rhetoric? Not all were impressed by such drama; a correspondent named 'Father Morris' wrote several letters to *The Times* dismissing the idea that the bones were Becket's.[81] He claimed that after double-checking various manuscripts in the British Museum he could maintain the status-quo position that the bones were burned in 1538. His point was simple: regardless of the appearance of the bones at Canterbury, the texts describing the bones in the British Museum should take precedence. The manuscripts may not be scientific, but they were emblems of systematic proper study and correct research.

At least one correspondent was offended by the disinterment altogether. His letter to *The Times* reads:

> The Dean and Chapter and Mr Austin do not seem to have been aware that the unlawful removal of remains from consecrated ground ... is not only a misdemeanour at common law, but a statutory offense. Further it should be borne in mind that the act has been done, not by a sacrilegious layman, but by the connivance and sanction of one of the most important ecclesiastical bodies in the kingdom – the Dean and Chapter of Canterbury.[82]

The letter is signed, 'An Englishman'. To him, the whole business of taking bodies out of consecrated ground for identification and examination is anathema, whether the corpse 'speaks' to sainthood or not. The incident reeks of connivance and self-interest on all sides; and moreover, as he points out, it is against the law. 'An Englishman' suggests that the investigation into the bones is neither ecclesiastical nor political, but *merely* antiquarian, in the sense that the term 'antiquary' is here used as a polite term for 'amateur'. He accuses the Dean and Chapter of Canterbury, an authoritative body with the power to give sanction, of having acted in response to mere antiquarian interest. 'An Englishman' fears that macabre specimen-hunting – akin to grave robbing – is masquerading as a convenient hybrid of history and science. Taking picks and shovels to the floors and walls of a consecrated church amounts to chipping away at the moral centre around which Christian burial revolves.

After the bones were returned to their crypt on 10 February 1888 the dialogue continued for years afterward, as the fate of the Becket site remained a subject of concern: A correspondent calling himself 'Arkasden' [sic] (referring to his postmark)

---

an artistic representation of the bones was either carved or painted. The view of the box is limited, as MS Cotton Tiberius E viii was damaged by the Cotton Library Fire in 1731.

[81] Father Morris. 'Letter to the Editor', *The London Times*, Friday 10 February, 1888.

[82] 'An Englishman', Letter to *The Times of London*, 20 February, 1888.

shows much impatience with the desire to proclaim the bones to be Becket's after one cursory forensic examination. Demanding that a more reliable standard be used than that of conviction or opinion, he refutes the claims of identification of the bones with accepted historical text. Citing the sixteenth-century account by the Windsor Herald, which had been published in recent years by the Camden Society, 'Arkasden' quotes the text:

> September 1538 – At Austen's Abbey at Canterbury was suppressed and the shrine and goodes taken to the Kynge's treasury... and the bones of St Thomas of Canterbury were brent in the same church by my Lord Crumwell. They found his head whole with the bones which had a wound in the skull.[83]

He also cites Stow's *Annales*, which states that the bones were indeed burnt under the auspices of Thomas Cromwell.[84] 'Arkasden's' method of presenting evidence, and the overall tone of his letter, reflects a confident reliance on published material that was accepted by the authoritative bodies of academia, Parliament, and the Church of England. Opinions, suspicions, and conspiratorial theories of switched bodies and hidden truths were not authoritative texts. For 'Arkasden' and those who shared his viewpoint, the narrative of Becket's body ends with the authoritative text describing the 1538 destruction of the shrine. The bones, along with the legend of Becket's sanctified body, were destroyed, and that destruction was recorded by an authoritative source and published. 'Arkasden's' acceptance of the chronicler's account of the burning of the bones recalls other accounts of the burning of texts like Bibles and forbidden books during the Henrician period. When a heretical or banned book was burnt, the memory of that text was meant to be eradicated, its legacy literally going up in smoke. Such was the power of Thomas Cromwell's enforcement of Henry VIII's policies. Although there was certainly no consensus as to the effectiveness of the events of the Dissolution in 1538, 'Arkasden' chooses to accept the authority of the long-published work of the *Windsor Herald*. The account of the burning of Becket's bones is true because it was chronicled; and that chronicle has been accepted as an official account by Church, State, and academia. 'Arkasden's' is a staunch, uncompromising, and undeniably imperialist attitude; and yet it is common among those who were comfortable with the idea that the 'Tudor Church' had been a single, clearly defined entity of definitive action and permanent reform. 'Arkasden's' attitude is also unapologetically hypocritical: it validates the revisionist work of Henrician, Edwardian, and Elizabethan chroniclers and polemicists (such as Edward Hall, John Bale, and John Foxe) because their work was informed by Protestantism and nationalism and was therefore, in his mind, true.

---

[83] Arkasden, 'Letter to the Editor', *The Standard* (London), Saturday 17 October, 1896, issue 22558, p. 2; also Charles Wriothesley, *A Chronicle of England During the Reigns of the Tudors*, 2 vols. (London, 1875–7,), vol. I, p. 86.

[84] John Stow, *Annales, or a General Chronicle of England* (1580) (London, 1631), p. 576.

Responding to 'Arkasden's' letter two days later, a correspondent named G.I.H. writes:

> As the son of a former curate, some fifty years back, I well remember an entry in one of the old registers, stating that the skull, or some portion of Becket's remains, were enclosed in a silver casket and reburied in that church [Church of All Hallows-By-The-Tower, Barking], which is one of the oldest in London. The registers no doubt exist still, and a reference to them might add somewhat to your correspondent's information.[85]

The perspective of G.I.H. is that of many who held a less staunch attitude than 'Arkasden': established historical texts, especially those written during the tenure of the notorious revisionists and propagandists Leland, Bale, and Foxe, are not sufficient to explain the recent events at Canterbury Cathedral. G.I.H. wishes to draw human experience and the authority of individual memory away from published texts and towards an open dialogue. His letter provokes a response from 'Arkasden', just over a week later. Having investigated the claim, 'Arkasden' says: 'I wrote to the Vicar of All Hallows, Barking, and have received a courteous reply, saying what I expected to be the case, that, there is no foundation for the statement'.[86] 'Arkasden' determines that G.I.H. must be misremembering another legend pertaining to another saint or other historical figure.[87] After mentioning the letter he received from the Vicar, 'Arkasden' immediately returns the scope of the discussion to evidence that can be supported by published texts. He says he has not found any such record in the Transactions of the London and Middlesex Archaeological Society (a respected antiquarian publication) 'or in any life of the Bishop'.[88] 'Arkasden' is unimpressed by the idea that established texts can or should be overwritten by memory – as proof he cites the fact that the Vicar of All Hallows did not remember the event mentioned by G.I.H. in any case.

Interestingly, some of the most fascinating correspondence comes not from academics or churchmen with antiquarian interests, but from a rank amateur on the subject who happened to be a young woman whose interest was piqued by the discovery of the bones. Miss Agnes Holland was the adult daughter of the Rev. Francis J. Holland, who was present at the opening of the crypt and who was a canon of Canterbury Cathedral. Miss Holland visited the site and viewed the bones for herself, after which she reported her observations and opinions in several letters to a friend, Miss Lisa Rawlinson, daughter of the Rev. George Rawlinson, who was also a canon of the Cathedral.[89] After viewing the reconstructed skull she writes, 'The fracture begins on the top and extends all down the left side, and it was on the left side and shoulder that the blow

---

[85] G.I.H., 'Letter to the Editor', *The Standard* (London), Monday 19 October, 1896, issue 22559, p. 4.

[86] 'Arkasden', 'Letter to the Editor', *The Standard* (London), Tuesday 27 October, 1896; issue 22566, p. 2.

[87] There was also a legend that the heart of Richard the Lionheart was buried in that church.

[88] 'Letter', 27 October, 1896, p. 2.

[89] Miss Holland's letters to Miss Rawlinson are reprinted in Mason, pp. 175–7.

was struck. The corona is not cut off, but that may have been only the tradition if this really is St Thomas of Canterbury'.[90] Here, Miss Holland is willing to accept the idea that an identification based on the presumed state of the bones may not be factual, but may rely on legend. She is willing to concede that the chroniclers, hagiographers, and artists who wrote about and depicted Becket's murder over and over again may have gotten an important detail of the corpse wrong: that the corona of the skull was cut off. As she engaged the clergymen overseeing the project in conversation about the bones, she found disagreement and scepticism among them. H.G. Austin, surveyor of the Cathedral, was convinced that the bones were Becket's based on his assessment of the condition of the bones and on his interpretation of Wordsworth's edition of the chronicle of Nicholas Harpsfield, Archdeacon of Canterbury under Mary I. Austin cited Harpsfield's account that the bones of Becket were secreted away and buried by the monks of the cathedral in 1538, switching the body of the archbishop with that of a simple monk, who had died centuries earlier.[91] Miss Holland records the disagreement of Rev. Sheppard with Mr Austin's assertion:

> Dr Shepherd [sic] says, 'piff-paff, all rubbish', and scouts the bare notion. But he is evidently at daggers drawn with Austin … he goes on to assert, which maddens Austin, that the skull has been fractured within the last fortnight, implying that Austin did it himself.[92]

Dr Sheppard's rejection of Nicholas Harpsfield's account was common. There were many scholars, both amateur and professional, who determined that Harpsfield's account was either misrecorded or misread by later readers.[93] In either case, those who rejected the Marian account accused those sympathetic to Catholicism of wishing the disputed information into verity. Here, Dr Sheppard accuses Mr Austin of trying to force verity onto the bones by writing martyrdom onto them – and smashing the skull himself. He was no doubt irritated by the fact that Mr Austin was delighted by the miracle story of the blind boy from Margate.[94]

Agnes Holland tries to keep an open mind as she considers the information that comes to her, respecting each person's opinion but soon finding herself overwhelmed and disappointed at the direction taken by the emotional dialogue. She says, 'I do not know what to think about it all, and find myself always agreeing with the last person, which is very weak, of course…I suppose no Roman Catholic would think of allowing us to

---

[90] Agnes Holland, *Letter to Miss Lisa Rawlinson*, 24 January, 1888, repr. in Mason, p. 175.

[91] This was a common story, one that had been circulating among the locals in Canterbury in several versions since 1538, and one for which there is no evidence.

[92] Holland, *Letter to Miss Lisa Rawlinson*, 24 January, 1888; in Mason, p. 176.

[93] Arthur Mason addresses this controversy in his book. Mason believes that Harpsfield's account was incorrectly copied by 'Ro. Ba.', who 'misread the manuscript'. As a result, Mason condemns Harpsfield's account as 'worthless'. Mason, p. 139.

[94] Holland, *Letter to Miss Lisa Rawlinson*, 10 February, 1888; in Mason, p. 179.

find such a treasure'.[95] It would seem that one thing Miss Holland did take away from the events of January and February 1888 is that the party that lay claim to the discovery of the bones was just as important as the identity of the bones themselves. In that sense her supposition is riddled with speculation: did Catholics know of a secret burial place for Becket's bones? And if they did, would they ever allow representatives of the Church of England to find it? What form would such interference in the excavation take? And if the bones were discovered accidentally, would Catholics reject the identification of the bones as Becket's in order to deny Protestants the satisfaction of making such a monumental discovery? In frustration she laments, 'I wish the newspapers had not taken it up'.[96] Ultimately, Miss Holland made up her own mind, and determined that the bones were not those of Becket. Still, she and her mother made a pall of silk and lace to lay over the bones, although she admits, '…we did not let any one know that we had made it'.[97] When the bones were finally replaced in the coffin on 10 February 1888 Agnes Holland was present alongside her father to record the event. The silk pall was placed over the bones, and inside the coffin was placed a glass bottle containing a photograph of the skull and an account of the finding. Anticipating that another disinterment of the bones would be forthcoming, they turned the gravesite into a sort of time capsule.[98] It contained the tantalisingly unidentified bones, a record of the investigation into the remains, and also a respectful nod at the possibility that one of the most controversial and consequential churchmen in English history – and possibly a saint – lay buried there.

The investigating committee issued several official-sounding pronouncements stating that it could not be proven that the bones were Becket's, nor could it be shown whose bones they were, in any case. The corpse was reinterred as a document in and of itself. After having been read and interpreted – albeit variously – the corpse became a record, part of the history of Canterbury Cathedral and part of the narrative of religious toleration in England. For all its closure, however, the reburial of the Canterbury bones was hardly definitive. In reburying the bones the committee knew they were bringing only a temporary silence to the dialogue about the fate of Becket's corpse. The written report of the excavation that was enclosed in the coffin anticipated a later disinterment of the bones and a continued discussion of the subject of their identification. The text of the report represented the investigative committee's acknowledgment of an ongoing dialogue about national memory and the narrative of the Reformation that would continue long after they themselves were dead and buried. It was an acknowledgment that the legacy of 'Tudor England' was putative. Once again, Thomas Becket was frustratingly silent, having refused, in the face of demands from church, state, and academia, to speak for himself.

---

[95] Holland, *Letter to Miss Lisa Rawlinson*, 4 February, 1888; in Mason, p. 176.
[96] Holland, *Letter to Miss Lisa Rawlinson*, 4 February, 1888; in Mason, p. 176.
[97] Holland, *Letter to Miss Lisa Rawlinson*, 4 February, 1888; in Mason, p. 176.
[98] The bones were, in fact, reexamined during the twentieth century. No conclusive identification was made. As John Butler shows in the final chapter of his book, there were further enquiries into the switched-body theory of Becket's burial place as late as the 1990s.

5

FICTIONS AND FANTASIES

Henry VIII and Anne Boleyn

Much of death fascination of the nineteenth century employs the subject of romantic love as a central point around which the peculiar, tragic beauty of death revolves. One needs only to consider the work of major authors of the period such as Charles Dickens, Bram Stoker, Mary Shelley, and Edgar Allan Poe; and artists such as Dante Gabriel Rossetti, John Everett Millais, and John William Waterhouse to find examples of love and death placed together in an eerie tandem. Ill-fated, star-crossed pairs of lovers appeared steadily in literature and art throughout the nineteenth century, and their stories were extremely popular with audiences who found a forbidding, yet irresistible attraction to the idea of love-and-death, and to the particular idea that death can loom over a pair of lovers like a black cloud from the moment of their meeting.[1] For the most part, such lovers-in-death are fictional; but novels, poems, and plays about historical figures, especially figures of the Tudor era, also draw upon this notion. They accompany melodramatic narratives that, although they presume to be historical in scope, are imaginative and sensational rather than academic. They include inventive retellings about Elizabeth I and her ill-fated love for Essex and Raleigh, or Jane Grey and her doomed love for Dudley, as if death were an essential part of what had brought them together. Some of the most compelling examples of such work tell the fateful story of Henry VIII and Anne Boleyn. As characters in this multi-genre narrative of fatal attraction, their story is unique because the corpses of both Henry and Anne were disinterred during the nineteenth century. Unlike characters in a novel or poem, the physical bodies of these lovers were exhumed, viewed, and analysed according to the academic standards of the day. This facet of their story allows for a unique theory of reading when it comes to Henry and Anne. One might imagine the beloved in death (Poe's Annabel Lee); one might even imagine the revenant lover (Stoker's Lucy Westenra) or the lover as living corpse (Dickens' Miss Havisham); but the narratives concerning Henry VIII and Anne Boleyn are exceptional because they depict love and death in a disturbingly literal way. These narratives are also attended by two myths of the corpse that are related directly to their respective disinterments: namely, that Anne

---

[1] Shakespeare's *Romeo and Juliet* is the archetype for this pattern, but the idea is also sourced in the Petrarchan tradition and in Arthurian Romances; hence the attractiveness of the pattern to proponents of nineteenth-century medievalism.

Boleyn was buried with her head tucked under her arm, and that the corpse of Henry VIII exploded after his burial. These legends are attended by two minor corpse myths: that Anne Boleyn had a sixth finger on her left hand, and that Mary Tudor exhumed the bones of her father Henry VIII and had them burned secretly. As it was, none of these myths were true, but they invited readings of both corpses as corrupt texts, as interrupted narratives deprived of wholeness.

The key factor that sets apart the story of Henry VIII and Anne Boleyn from other pairs of lovers is the presumption of authenticity. As John Kucich states in his discussion of the work of Charles Dickens, the love-and-death paradigm represents a desire to connect absence and loss with real experience; romantic expressions of the terrifying reality of death ground the concept in social conventions and observances, allowing people to relish death for its own sake and indulge in what they see as an authentic emotional experience.[2] Sarah Tarlow also discusses this idea, saying that by the nineteenth century, the identification of the Self with a unique physical body caused people to see the human individual as being at the centre of a web of relationships that produced authentic emotional experiences. Upon his or her death, a person remains unique and distinguished from other people because his or her emotional experiences in life can be understood in a broad historical and cultural context. This is true of the private grief response in the cases of kinship deaths, and it is true of the public grief response of royal or other celebrated deaths.[3] Disinterment adds to this experience because it is immediately material, and also because the pseudo-archaeological methods of exhumation and meticulous recording by diligent antiquaries present it as a constructive and affirmative part of the whole process of death and the whole cycle of history. Such wholeness complements romantic narratives and becomes relevant to the public (and in particular to the middle-class reader) because 'historical' concepts of espousal, sex, motherhood, and masculinity in the story of Henry and Anne can be linked to ideals the Victorians held in their own time. The result is a compelling irony: authenticity is combined with fiction-making to create an emotional experience that disturbs and satisfies at the same time. This experience, of course, meant different things to different people, and the construction of a whole narrative of death is but one of the many peculiarities that discourages a generalisation of nineteenth-century culture in the present-day academic profession. Still, for the majority of people at the time there was a focus on connecting romantic emotions to the inevitability of death – from the reassessment of cemetery design across Britain, to lavish funeral processions for even the poorest in society, to the enormous market in mourning clothes, jewellery, and accessories.[4] Narratives, both literary and historical, that imagined Henry and

---

[2] John Kucich, 'Death Worship Among the Victorians: The Old Curiosity Shop', *PMLA* 95, no. 1 (January 1980): 58–9.

[3] Tarlow, 'Wormie Clay and Blessed Sleep: Death and Disgust in Later Historic Britain', in *The Familiar Past?* ed. Sarah Tarlow and Susie West (London, 2002), pp. 192–3.

[4] For discussions of cemetery design, material culture, and funerary customs among the working and middle classes see James Walvin, 'Dust to Dust: Celebrations of Death in

Anne to be ill-fated lovers, were combined with the popular culture of death and with pseudo-archaeological narratives to produce a fascinatingly new way to think about love and death and the legacy of the grave.

Part of the uncanny appeal of the story of Henry and Anne has to do with an attraction to the violence of the Tudor period, and especially to the practice of beheading. The sixteenth century is strongly associated with violent deaths by execution: people burned at the stake, dismembered, or drawn and quartered. Beheading, however, stands out as the signature mode of death for the period because it was suffered by so many of those who were closest to royal power. As Billie Melman states in her discussion of the sensationalist view of Tudor execution during the eighteenth and also the nineteenth centuries, beheading produced a peculiar excitement in popular culture.[5] The horror of the act of beheading is accompanied by its startling swiftness – at least in the stereotyped view – and its function as the ultimate act of silencing produces a combination of allure and revulsion.[6] Much of the nineteenth-century view on beheading developed in the wake of the guillotine executions in France between 1793 and 1794, after which the legacy of the clumsy English axe and block (that often required several strokes to remove the head) were replaced with newly developed ideas about the efficient power of the state to silence its enemies.[7] In this context, Anne Boleyn emerged as a figure of liminality, whose death bridged the distant Tudor past with more recent events: she had been executed with swift efficiency with a sword in the French manner, and she had been buried along with her head. Unlike the execution of her archenemy Thomas More, there was no axe, no pike on a bridge or gate for public display, and there was a complete interment in a royal chapel.[8] For the nineteenth century, Anne's death provided an important distinction between the 'brutal' Tudor past and the 'civilised' present, for which public violence, and namely beheading, had been redefined in recent memory.[9] Moreover, after the guillotine deaths of *La Terreur*, violence at the hands of the state became known as something for which the state itself was responsible: execution might be presented as a form of justice on behalf of the state, but the state

---

Victorian England', *Historical Reflections* 9, no. 3 (Fall 1982): 353–71, and James Stevens Curl, *The Victorian Celebration of Death* (Stroud, 2001).

[5] Billie Melman, 'The Pleasure of Tudor Horror: Popular Histories, Modernity, and Sensationalism in the Long Nineteenth Century', in *Tudorism: Historical Imagination and the Appropriation of the Sixteenth Century*, ed. Tatiana String and Marcus Bull (Oxford, 2011).

[6] Melman, p. 55.

[7] Regina Janes, 'Beheadings', in *Death and Representation*, ed. Sarah Webster Goodwin and Elisabeth Bronfen (Baltimore, 1993), p. 242; and also *Losing Our Heads: Beheadings in Literature and Culture* (New York, 2005).

[8] Thomas More's body was buried in the chapel of St Peter ad Vincula, while his head (after it had stood on a pike for a month, and once it had been retrieved and kept as a relic by his daughter Margaret Roper) was finally buried in the Roper vault of St Dunstan's Church, Canterbury. Although both the head and body eventually received interment on sacred ground, they are not together, and so the narrative of the corpse remains interrupted.

[9] Janes, *Losing Our Heads*, pp. 242–3.

also bore the burden of having to justify its actions.[10] These changes in attitudes toward state-sanctioned violence, and particularly in the practice of beheading, encouraged a view of Anne Boleyn as a figure whose death represented nineteenth-century views about execution rather than sixteenth-century ones. The nostalgia for the horror of Tudor execution was combined with reverence for the purported civility of the current age;[11] Anne's death was seen as considerably more efficient and less gruesome than that of Margaret Pole or Mary, Queen of Scots;[12] and Henry VIII was seen as a powerful and merciless Head of State who remained saddled with the unmet obligation to justify his wife's murder.

The corpse myths attendant upon the story of Henry and Anne reflect these appropriations of historical figures and events, and demonstrate the eagerness of many scholars to include in their historical writing tales for which there was little, if any, empirical evidence. Narratives of the king's death that were popular during the nineteenth century (the most dramatic of which was by Agnes Strickland in her biography of Anne)[13] depict a bloated, friendless tyrant who, having died alone in 1547, was brought to his funeral in an immense coffin. In one version of the story, the king's corpulent body burst open upon its arrival at Syon Abbey. His blood spilled from the coffin and was lapped up by an eagerly waiting dog. This event was said to be foretold by one Friar Peto, a Franciscan of Greenwich who made the prophecy years earlier as part of a sermon protesting the king's divorce from Katherine of Aragon. George Aungier noted it in his nineteenth-century history of Syon Abbey as a longstanding legend of the place, but assured his readers that the events were 'misconstrued'.[14] Narratives of Anne's execution are also thick with rumours and legends, most of which are heavily romanticised: one states that as she stood on the scaffold, Anne looked around for Henry's men riding onto Tower Green to grant a last-minute reprieve; another claimed that the executioner, in a moment of compassion, removed his shoes so that Anne would not hear him approaching.[15] By far the most pervasive rumour was that after her

---

[10] Janes, *Losing Our Heads*, p. 243.

[11] Melman, p. 55.

[12] Further distinctions can be made between Anne's death and the deaths of Margaret Pole and Mary, Queen of Scots on the specific grounds of the love-and-death paradigm. Henry and Anne were lovers and then spouses, whereas Henry's relationship with Margaret Pole was not a personal one; moreover, Elizabeth I had a familial, non-sexual relationship with her cousin, rather than a relationship based on espousal.

[13] Agnes Strickland, *Lives of the Queens of England*, 3 vols. (London, 1857), vol. III, p. 255.

[14] George Aungier, *History and Antiquities of Syon Monastery* (London, 1840), pp. 91–2. In the seventeenth century Gilbert Burnet had related the story; but he did so as a cynical rebuke of critics of Henry VIII and the Reformation (namely Nicholas Sanders). Gilbert Burnet, *The History of the Reformation of the Church of England* (1679) (Oxford, 1865). Book II, p. 151.

[15] Neither of these rumours can be traced farther back than the late eighteenth century. They are rooted in various combinations of folk narratives associated with ghost legends and tourism at the Tower of London, Hever Castle, and Blickling Hall. See Thea Cervone [Tomaini], 'Tucked Beneath Her Arm: Culture, Ideology, and Fantasy in the Curious

death, Anne was placed by her own ladies in a rude and hastily acquired arrow box, with her head tucked under her arm.[16] The image is both gruesome and poignant, and it pairs the tragic event of Anne's execution with an act of compassion and nurturing.

The duality associated with Anne's corpse myth is a major factor in how she was depicted during the nineteenth century. It stems from the dualities of her life and causes them to become portentous, as they are made to reflect on her death. In novels, dramas, and histories there are two headless Anne Boleyns: the one, a sacrificial figure, a woman in love with and in danger from her tyrannical husband. Devoted to her progressive faith, she becomes the progenitrix of a great Protestant tradition. Before she can perform her duties as mother to the infant Elizabeth I, her relationship with her child is literally severed. The other headless Anne is a predatory vixen, an intrusive, adulterous figure whose affront to male power threatens the Crown and the Church. The voice of the mistress, of the usurper Queen, and of the female evangelist is depicted as destructive. It must be interrupted by the ultimate act of silencing: beheading. These characterisations do not speak to ideas of empowerment; in the nineteenth century both characterisations describe two forms of tragic failure in the feminine character. The duality of Anne's character epitomises what John Reed calls 'the Victorian taste for mingling saintly and sinful femininity',[17] and yet this epitome is only fully realised when Anne is depicted or imagined in death.

Often Anne is depicted as a sort of *femme fatale*, her death directly associated with and proceeding from her sexuality. Moreover, the accusation of witchcraft attached to Anne's treason charges gives her literary and cultural persona the air of enchantment, of a magical sexuality that seduces and emasculates royal power. As Rebecca Stott notes in her discussion of the Victorian *femme fatale*, 'the public were challenged and discomposed by a series of widely publicised trials, divorces, and general muck-raking, a chronicle of scandal-mongering, which suggested a new mode of discourse...'[18] The image of Anne as a sexually aggressive woman destined for ruin fits into this discourse, especially since she had been the 'other woman' in one of the most legendary divorces in history. The *positionality*[19] of such a woman locates her on the outside of normative space and behaviour;[20] she invades normative space in the family group and home – more so if the family group and home is Royal. Part of the particular appeal of Anne Boleyn is that even in death her *positionality* remains tantalisingly exotic: her location in the chancel of the Chapel of St Peter ad Vincula is outside normative burial space – not because it is a place of privilege, but because it is a place of traumatic memory. Buried only a few yards from the place of her execution in an arrow box, with

Legend of Anne Boleyn', in *Heads Will Roll: Decapitation in Medieval Literature and Culture*, ed. Larissa Tracy and Jeff Massey (Leiden, 2012), pp. 289–310.

[16] Cervone [Tomaini], 'Tucked', pp. 289–310.

[17] John Reed, *Victorian Conventions* (Columbus, OH, 1975), p. 75.

[18] Rebecca Stott, *The Fabrication of the Late Victorian Femme Fatale* (London, 1992), p. 14.

[19] The word is coined by Stott.

[20] Stott, pp. 37–8.

her severed head purportedly tucked under her arm, Anne represents a woman whose Otherness confines her to the fringe of death celebration but whose seductive appeal makes her corpse unforgettable. This idea is exemplified in plays like George Boker's *Anne Boleyn, a Tragedy* (1850).[21] Just before she ascends the scaffold, Anne addresses her own head as though it were already separated from her shoulders, as though it were independent from the rest of her persona. She says,

> Alas, poor head, thou'lt roll
> In a brief time amid this scaffold's dust;
> As thou in life didst not deserve a crown,
> So by thy doom is justice satisfied,
> And her great beam repoised.[22]

Anne turns her own head into a fetish object, a provocative and unsettling expression of her vanity that is emblematic of what Robert Tracy calls the 'physical, metaphysical/ supernatural and sexual fear' present in literature of the *femme fatale* during the Victorian period.[23] Here, anxieties about female sexuality, independence, and a lingering uncanny attraction to a woman beautiful in death are projected onto Anne's head specifically. Despite the fact that her head is still attached to her body, the audience is invited to imagine its impending severance. The head promises to be a gruesome object, but eventually one that is cradled in the arms of its possessor – Anne herself. This connection between sexuality and death recalls that which is found in *Carmilla* (1872), by J. Sheridan Le Fanu or *Jewel of the Seven Stars* by Bram Stoker (1903); not in that Anne is a sexualised revenant, but that in death she is a figure of sexual transgression and is both the object and subject of sexuality.[24]

Interestingly, this idea is at the core of perhaps the largest paradox of nineteenth-century death fascination: as Robert Tracy points out, a person might talk endlessly and exhaustively about death, funerals, tombs, memorials, and corpses, but one could not be so open about sex and sexuality – unless one cloaked it with death.[25] As Michael

---

[21] George H. Boker, *Anne Boleyn, A Tragedy* (Philadelphia, 1850).

[22] Boker, Scene VI, p. 224.

[23] Robert Tracy, 'Loving You All Ways: Vamps, Vampires, Necrophiles, and Necrofilles in Nineteenth-Century Fiction', *Sex and Death in Victorian Literature*, ed. Regina Barreca (Indianapolis, IN, 1990).

[24] Anne is neither a vampire nor a reanimated corpse; but there is a strong ghost tradition that combines death and assertive or even aggressive sexuality in women. In this sense, Anne is a part of what Elisabeth Bronfen calls 'the feminine diabolic': an association of feminine identity and sexuality with sorcery, faerie magic, Satanism, and ghost lore (Elisabeth Bronfen, 'Dialogue with the Dead: The Deceased Beloved as Muse', in *Sex and Death in Victorian Literature*, ed. Regina Barreca (Bloomington, IN, 1990), p. 69). In addition to Stoker and Le Fanu, ghost stories by many nineteenth-century authors (such as Edgar Allan Poe and Henry James) also make these associations.

[25] Tracy, 'Loving You All Ways', p. 33.

Wheeler states, 'Like the deathbed, then, the grave is a site of conflicting ideas. It is a site of strong and often confused emotions, not least because the mourner will naturally meditate on his or her own "end" as well as that of the departed.'[26] Readers of novels, plays, and even histories that construct such a heroic and also erotic mystique of death position themselves as mourners for the character that is depicted. For most people the grave also functions as a site of purification, of cleansing, as the corruption of the flesh is absorbed into the earth;[27] but in the case of Anne Boleyn, her headlessness has a negative effect on this purity and consigns her to a permanent Otherness even among the dead. This Otherness keeps her on the fringes even of the culture of the dead – similar to other uncanny figures found in the literature and drama of the time, which are also associated with noble or aristocratic bodies in death. These are vampires, such as the aforementioned Carmilla (who is really Mircalla, Countess Karnstein), ghosts, such as Elizabeth Gaskell's Miss Maud Furnivall, and upper-class women, such as Edgar Allan Poe's Madeline Usher,[28] who, although they are still living, take on the appearance of corpses in a psychic preparation for their inevitable deaths.

As a combination of an accused figure and a martyred figure Anne symbolises sexuality and victimhood, both of which were qualities applied to the cultural/literary paradigm of the dead mother. In most Victorian discourses on the subject (especially novels), sexuality and the female body in death are unified in narratives of the death of a mother by illness or in childbirth. As Jill Matus states, such novels were often exploratory, 'constructing multiple and contesting versions of womanhood and female sexuality', and searching out places where liminality was lurking.[29] In Anne's case this liminality is found in the narrative of her beheading. It is especially apparent in *Windsor Castle* (1843), a novel by W. Harrison Ainsworth. In the novel, Anne is depicted as a woman whose inability to control her capacity for true love results in her betrayal. Villainy is assigned to Katherine of Aragon, who is portrayed by Ainsworth as the king's aging, vindictive wife in a fantasy of open confrontation between the two women. Katherine growls:

'I denounce you before heaven, and invoke its wrath upon your head. Night and day I will pray that you may be brought to shame...'
    'Take her from me Henry!' cried Anne faintly, 'her violence affrights me'.

---

[26] Michael Wheeler, *Heaven, Hell, and the Victorians* (Cambridge, 1994), p. 55.
[27] Wheeler, p. 57.
[28] Sheridan Le Fanu, *Carmilla*, ed. Cathleen Costello Sullivan (Syracuse, NY, 2013); Elizabeth Gaskell, 'The Old Nurse's Story', in *The Phantom Coach: A Connoisseur's Collection of Victorian Ghost Stories*, ed. Michael Sims (New York, 2014); and Edgar Allan Poe, 'The Fall of the House of Usher,' in *The Fall of the House of Usher and Other Writings*, ed. David Galloway (London, 2011).
[29] Jill Matus, *Unstable Bodies: Victorian Representations of Sexuality and Maternity* (Manchester, 1995), p. 4.

'No, you shall stay', said Katherine, grasping her arm and detaining her, 'You shall hear your doom ... the crown unjustly placed upon your brow will fall to the ground, and it will bring the head with it ... Look me in the face, minion – you cannot – you dare not!'

'Oh, Henry!' sobbed Anne.[30]

Although Anne is depicted as an intrusive figure of sexual licence, she is also depicted as a victim of fate; and yet, she is made accountable for her own loss of control. Jill Matus notes that novels of this type produce a discourse that is itself an unstable body of representations.[31] She states that such imaginative texts mobilise fantasies but that they do so without legislating action.[32] In this sense Anne's case is again unique. The disinterment of an iconic figure, a figure almost more legendary than real, to whom there is a corpse myth attached, is an action legislated by fantasy. The publication of novels like Ainsworth's did not provoke the exhumation of Anne's body in 1878; but the entire culture of remembrance that held Anne up as a complex and liminal figure, one who literally generated the Elizabethan era, did contribute to interest in the condition of her corpse. There was a desire to connect materially with the body, and to read it for signs of martyrdom, nurturing motherhood, Tudor greatness, and poetic justice.

There is much of the 'primordial mother' figure in Anne Boleyn as well. It is an idea that stems largely from Lacanian ideas about the relationship between motherhood, death, and sexual fantasy.[33] Anne's death represents the denial of her right to motherhood by her tyrannical husband, and it also represents nature's denial of those same rights for a different reason: because of her sexual transgression and outspokenness. In either case she is cut off from her role as a lifegiver and a nurturer; and yet her beheading, when contextualised within the scope of the survival of the Tudor dynasty, provides her daughter Elizabeth with the motivation to survive and realise her own greatness. Elizabeth becomes the icon of a golden past, an emblem of England's own greatness, but she does so because of, and not in spite of, her mother's death. Anne's status as dead Queen Mother is at the very core of Imperial ideas of nationhood rooted in deep memory. Because of the macabre drama of beheading, Anne's memory represents an elemental trauma that lies behind the successes and triumphs of the Elizabethan era. Indeed, as Elisabeth Bronfen points out, the death of the mother in this sense exposes much of the nervousness of Imperial thought: Imperialism fears threats to its stability and longevity from enemies foreign and domestic.[34] The destruction of beauty via the decapitation of the nourishing body reveals a past that is vulnerable and in danger of ineffective and interrupted remembrance. It threatens to expose the fear of castration

---

[30] W. Harrison Ainsworth, *Windsor Castle* (London, 1843), pp. 18–19.

[31] Matus, p. 5.

[32] Matus, p. 7.

[33] Jacques Lacan, *Feminine Sexuality*, ed. Juliet Mitchell and Jacqueline Rose (New York, 1985), esp. p. 157.

[34] Bronfen, pp. 60–1.

and impotence present in the masculine qualities of aggression and dominance for which Imperialism is known.[35] A presumed knowledge of the elemental trauma of beheading lies beneath the glorification of an era that produced English Protestantism, victory over Spain, and the career of Shakespeare. The figurehead of that trauma lies beneath the Chapel of St Peter ad Vincula. Anne's legacy was inextricably linked to the fantasy that she lay in her arrow box with her head tucked under her arm. When she was disinterred in 1878, many people were interested in finding out if the romantic legend was true; they were interested in knowing whether they were remembering her, and the era she generated, correctly.

Ironically, the deep memory of Anne can never be fully reconstructed because she cannot be fully re-membered. Her severance from her daughter, from the Henrician court and the Reformation, are permanent because of the act of silencing that beheading represents, and because of the impossibility of reattachment of the head. As the lifegiver and emotional head of her family, the mother can never be replaced once she is taken away.[36] As Barbara Thaden states in *The Maternal Voice in Victorian Fiction*, the dead mother in Victorian fiction and culture is a figure of speechlessness combined with the inability to act. She is completely removed from influence over her child, eclipsed by her husband and his (inevitable) new wife.[37] Anne fits neatly into this stereotype in that she is certainly eclipsed by Henry VIII and a succession of wives; but also in the sense that the facet of her voice that stands to exert the most influence over her daughter – the voice of Protestantism – is silenced by the king's more traditionalist attitude.[38] In this construction, Elizabeth becomes a figure who overcomes the absence of her mother and the powerlessness associated with it. She builds a power structure that acknowledges the weakness of her condition, but also overcomes it with the voice of Supreme Governor of the Church of England. For many who wrote about and fantasised about Anne, she was the ideal prototypical Protestant whose death represented a 'cutting off' of progressivism before the reluctant and fickle-hearted monarch was ready to accept it. Melodramatic accounts of Anne's alleged last words reflect this sentiment. An 1817 guidebook of the Tower of London provides the most dramatic example: on the scaffold Anne is alleged to have called out, 'O Father! O Creator, thou who are the way, the truth, and the life, thou knowest that I have not

---

[35] The issue is further complicated by the fact that during the latter half of the nineteenth century the British Empire was headed by Victoria: a woman who exalted in her role as a nourishing mother of nine children.

[36] This idea is essentially Derridean. The mother's head is only partly phallic because it is not a prosthesis, as a shoe or a glove is, but it does function in part as a 'woman's penis' because it is where a woman's emotions and voice are located, as a locus for the performativity of the fetish object, the truth-of-the-taking-place. See Jacques Derrida, *The Truth in Painting*, trans. Geoff Bennington and Ian McLeod (Chicago, 1987).

[37] Barbara Thaden, *The Maternal Voice in Victorian Fiction: Rewriting the Patriarchal Family* (New York, 1997), p. 17.

[38] Although Elizabeth did enjoy the influence of Katherine Parr some years later, her fourth stepmother provided the voice of a mentor rather than that of a substitute mother.

deserved this death!'[39] In *Anne Boleyn, A Dramatic Poem*, by H.H. Milman (1872) Anne goes to her execution with a final affirmation of the Royal Supremacy, a sign that she understands the concept better than her husband, who has abandoned her for another woman. She cries, 'Now God Bless the King/And make His Gospel shine throughout the land!'[40]

There was never anything but rumour to support the idea that Anne was buried with her head tucked under her arm. There are several accounts of Anne's execution, and although they have minor variations they share one glaring omission: none of them describe the positioning of Anne's body in the arrow box.[41] Physical inspection of the corpse was the only way to determine if the story (or any other corpse myth about Anne) was true, and in 1876 the opportunity presented itself to make such observations. D.C. Bell, Secretary to Her Majesty's Privy Purse and avid antiquary, spent much of his leisure time researching the deaths, burials, and sepulchral monuments of the sovereigns of England.[42] He visited their places of interment and made sketches of the locations where he pursued his interest. He eventually set his sights on the Chapel of St Peter ad Vincula at the Tower of London, where he was disturbed to find that the graves of Anne Boleyn and Katherine Howard, who he calls 'the two unhappy Queens', did not have proper grave markers and that the general condition of the chapel was poor.[43] He collected several supporters, among them Dudley Fitzgerald, Lord de Ros; Sir Charles Yorke, Constable of the Tower; and Colonel Milman, resident Governor of the Tower,[44] and then presented to Queen Victoria a plan by which the chapel would be architecturally restored to its Tudor design. The plan would include the inspection

---

[39] *An Improved History and Description of the Tower of London* (London, 1817), p. 14. These 'last words' are heavily embellished from Anne's brief scaffold speech, in which she only hints at such ideas.

[40] H.H. Milman, *Anne Boleyn, A Dramatic Poem* (London, 1872), p. 168. Anne's 'last words', as depicted in the poem, are based very loosely on the actual speech she gave at the scaffold, of which there are several very similar versions. See Great Britain, Public Record Office, *Calendar of Letters and Papers, Foreign and Domestic* (London, 1888, impr. 1965), vol. X, item 911; Samuel Bentley, *Excerpta Historica* (London, 1833),pp. 261–5; p. 264; and Edward Hall, *Hall's Chronicle* (London, 1809), p. 819.

[41] Great Britain, Public Record Office, *Letters and Papers*, X. 461. Two principal versions come from accounts by an Imperial witness and a [possibly] Venetian diplomat. These accounts are also translated into French and Portuguese with minor variations. See X. 911 and Bentley, pp. 261–5. It is true that Anne was buried in an elm arrow box, but it is not true that the box represents a further insult to her dignity by the king. The responsibility for measuring Anne for a coffin fell to William Kingston, Lieutenant of the Tower. Overwhelmed by his duties, Kingston neglected to hang the scaffold with the black draperies appropriate for someone of Anne's social rank, and he also forgot to have her measured for a coffin. See Hester Chapman, *Anne Boleyn* (London, 1974), p. 223.

[42] D.C. Bell, *Notices of the Historic Persons Buried in the Chapel of St Peter ad Vincula* (London, 1877), p. vii.

[43] Bell, p. vii.

[44] Bell, p. 10.

of the graves in the chancel, a scientific examination of the bones, and a record made of the project, which Bell would compose himself.

The excavation took place on 9 November 1876.[45] If Mr Bell and his team expected to find Anne Boleyn laid out neatly in a supine position, much less with her head tucked under her arm, they were disappointed. Anne's grave was in close proximity to those of various people, some of whom were also victims of Tudor execution; but it was also positioned near the graves of others who had lived within the Tower walls or in the immediate neighbourhood over the course of the centuries. With time, the older bones had been pushed aside to accommodate new burials. As the various wood and lead coffins in the chancel decomposed, they displaced the bones of other burials next to and below them, and buckled the paving stones above them. Fragments of Anne's arrow box survived, but the bones inside it were shoved into a heap at what once was the top of the box. Mr Bell delved into the Chapel's records of the burials and discovered that over a century before, in 1750, a woman named Hannah Beresford was interred in a lead coffin near Anne's gravesite. Anne's arrow box had decayed, leaving a hollowed space around it, and the gravedigger had manually pushed Anne's remains into the top corner of the space to make room for Mrs Beresford.

The bones were handed over to Dr Frederick J. Mouat, who removed them to the Queen's House at the Tower. There he made a caracteriological and phrenological examination of the bones, reading them for signs confirming the historical accounts and medical records he was familiar with, and affirming preconceived notions he had about the physical and intellectual superiority of the aristocracy. In his memorandum,[46] Dr Mouat reports that in life Anne bore the features of a superior aristocratic character, which in any case he had expected. He says, 'The bones of the head indicate a well-formed round skull, with an intellectual forehead, straight orbital ridge, large eyes, oval face, and a rather square full chin ... the forehead straight and ample, denoting considerable intelligence'.[47] He pronounced her height at no more than five feet, three inches, and reported that her limbs were duly proportional – all qualities associated with nobility and intellect.[48] Dr Mouat noted that, true to legend, her neck 'was indeed slender'[49] (if such a thing can be said about skeletal vertebrae). His observation recalled an account reported by William Kingston, Lieutenant of the Tower, just before Anne's death in 1536. Kingston claimed that Anne had joked morbidly that her execution

---

[45] Present on 9 November 1876 were the Rt Hon. Gerard Noel, 1st Commissioner of Her Majesty's Works, A.B. Mitford, Secretary to the Commissioners of Her Majesty's Works, Col. G. Bryan Milman, C.B., resident Governor of the Tower, the Hon. Spenser Ponsonby Fane, C.B., Comptroller in the Lord Chamberlain's Department, Dr Frederick J. Mouat, FRCS, Local Government Inspector and Physician, and the aforementioned Mr D.C. Bell. Bell, p. 19.

[46] Dr Mouat's memorandum is recorded and published by D.C. Bell.

[47] Bell, pp. 26–7. Dr Mouat did not find any evidence of consanguinity.

[48] Bell, p. 26.

[49] Bell, p. 21.

would be an easy one, because she had a 'lytle neck'.[50] This story was of great use to Thomas Cromwell, the king's Chief Minister. As one of Anne's archenemies, Cromwell was interested in depicting Anne as emotionally unstable and inappropriately glib about her coming death. The alleged comment about Anne's 'lytle neck' was long repeated, and although it was supported by no facts, by 1876 it had worked its way into many biographies and novelisations of Anne's life, as part of her corpse myth. Dr Mouat also inspected Anne's hands, looking for the purported extra finger or phalangial deformity alleged, as Bell notes, 'in [George] Wyatt's *Life*'.[51] He found no deformities, and certainly no extra finger. Dr Mouat's mention of the slenderness of the neck and the 'very perfect' condition of the little finger of Anne's left hand[52] demonstrates the effect even a minor corpse myth can have on an educated, professional person when he or she reads a corpse with a canon of texts in mind. Even if he had not read all the applicable texts (and as a physician, it is very doubtful that he read novels or the melodramatic histories of the Strickland sisters), he did bring with him to the examination an intellect informed in part by popular acceptance of these myths of the corpse. He therefore inspected the neck and left hand and reported on the verity of the myths.

Dr Mouat and Mr Bell interpreted the obvious slenderness of skeletal vertebrae as evidence complementary to the corpse myth they knew. They could, if they chose, imagine a half-mad *femme fatale* clutching ominously at her little neck; in this case the text of the corpse complimented the myth. It was not so with the little finger. The text of the corpse did not correlate with the text of the myth. It did not permit the anatomist and the antiquary to imagine an enchantress whose long sleeves covered the witch's mark on her left hand.[53] The biggest corpse myth, however, remained unresolved: without knowing the original placement of the bones, it was impossible for Bell or his team to determine whether Anne had been buried with her head tucked under her arm. The corpse did not offer up any of the hyperbolic elements that had been associated with it for centuries. Ironically, that fact allowed the macabre, yet romantic legend to remain accessible to the imagination and to appear in subsequent novels, poems, songs,

---

[50] William Kingston, *Letter to Thomas Cromwell*, 19 May, 1536. MS Cotton Otho C x 223; also *Letters and Papers*, item 910.

[51] Bell, p. 28; and George Wyatt, *Extracts from the Life of the Virtuous, Christian and Renowned Queen Anne Boleyn* (1605) (London), 1817, p. 4.

[52] Bell, p. 28.

[53] There was, of course, no way Dr Mouat could inspect the corpse for Anne's purported third nipple. This legend appeared as a result of rumours from various sources. Those rumours became associated with other myths about Anne (particularly the corpse myths); eventually those rumours worked their way into legitimate sources, namely anatomical and physiological texts. For a discussion of how this myth became a false medical 'fact', see Thea Tomaini, 'Reconstructive Texts of the Queenly Body: The Posthumous Legend of Anne Boleyn'. Conference Paper. 2015 Southeast Medievalist Association (SEMA) Conference in Little Rock, AR, United States. Available at the author's page on www.academia.edu. For a discussion of how rumours and folklore develop within Early Modern Society, see Adam Fox, *Oral and Literate Culture in England* (Oxford, 2000).

and folklore for the next hundred years at least.[54] Ultimately, the facts had enough of a humanising effect to warrant a respectful reinterment for Anne, in a new lead coffin, in the original location of the grave, with a new stone marking the spot.

As the man responsible for Anne's death, Henry VIII became associated in many texts with a combination of cruelty and sexuality that gave his marriage to Anne a portentous quality. Of all the English monarchs up to the nineteenth century, Henry VIII was the one who acquired the strongest connection between the public and private aspects of his life. Learning about Henry VIII was, for most people, only partly about learning the history of the Reformation and the developments in ecclesiastical policy and factional politics that proceeded from it. It was also about his personal life, his six marriages, his personal habits, and his appearance. Much of the connection between the public and private spheres revolved around a reading of the king's royal body as a testament to excess: his obesity, his sexual appetites, his obsession with producing a male heir, the decline of his physical health, and his death. In the nineteenth century, these issues of the royal body had much to do with ideals of manliness common to Victorian society. As Stephen Garton states, the 'helpmate ideal' dictated that upon marriage a woman was absorbed into her husband's life, her own body defined by his through her ability to provide him children.[55] Through her marriage a woman became an integral part of a man's complete self-realisation, her influence crucial to his means for achieving ideal manhood, with all its connotations of chivalry, self-control, and patriarchal authority.[56] A wife was the means by which the male self was made; the king may rule according to Divine authority, but the queen makes him relevant via the royal succession. This principle of nineteenth-century gender theory appeared to the public in an inverted form: that of Queen Victoria, who, although she was monarch, was absorbed almost completely into Prince Albert's identity. She channelled her sexual energies toward the production of heirs and her personal energies toward support of her husband. When Albert died in 1861, Victoria devoted those same energies to his memory, transforming her role of 'helpmeet' into that of chief mourner. Although the connection was not literal, the implications of this inversion of the 'helpmeet' ideal were not lost on those who considered the life and body of Henry VIII in relation to contemporary values. Where Victoria succeeded, Henry appeared to fail. As a man who was unable to find an ideal spouse and helpmate, someone to regulate the king's body with the production of heirs, Henry VIII was unable to maintain control over his royal body. He was depicted as a man overwhelmed by insatiable and unhealthy appetites for food, sex, and violence.[57]

---

[54] See Cervone [Tomaini], 'Tucked Beneath Her Arm', pp. 289–310.
[55] Stephen Garton, 'The Scales of Suffering: Love, Death, and Victorian Masculinity', *Social History* 27, no. 1 (January 2002): 47.
[56] Garton, p. 47.
[57] Queen Victoria's plump figure was seen less as evidence of indulgence and more as a sign of domesticity and nurturing motherhood.

Such meditations upon the body of Henry VIII were pervasive during the nineteenth century. In her discussion of the 1536-7 Holbein portrait of Henry VIII, Tatiana String notes that the painting was copied dozens of times over the course of the late eighteenth, and then the nineteenth centuries (there are over eighty copies of the Holbein portrait in the National Portrait Gallery that were painted during the period 1700–1900, and at least forty-two depictions of Henry VIII and/or his queens painted between 1781 and 1900).[58] The portrait allowed viewers to 'read' the body of the king and familiarise themselves with signs indicating what String calls 'Henry-ness'.[59] These signs defined the royal body as massive, impervious to defiance both figuratively and literally (not only because of Henry's wide stance and imposing girth but because of the phallic authority suggested by his prominent codpiece).[60] String says, 'And, thanks to the availability of a readily recognisable portrayal, myth and memory could be poured into the king's massive frame, in the process revivifying him to become an actor in later imagined scenes of Tudor history...'[61] The king's body became a phallogocentric text to be read via the copied paintings and via his portrayals in the same novels, dramas, and histories that depicted either Anne or another one of his six wives. In historical text, Burnet's *History of the Reformation* (1679) made connections between the king's imposing physicality and the need for strong authority over the succession, the Church of England, and Parliament.[62] Such connections, says Andrew Starkie, remained relevant, and were key to the ongoing popularity of Burnet's *History* over the years: in 1679, when the book was published, the nation was wrestling with the idea of excluding the Duke of York (later James II) from the succession because of his Catholicism, and was thereby experiencing a crisis of succession. A hundred years later, the book's issues reflected the crisis succession of the Hanoverians that lasted through to the coronation of Victoria; and although there was no crisis of succession after the death of Prince Albert in 1861, Victoria's extreme reaction to her husband's death, followed by years of profuse national mourning, pointed to a crisis of isolation and vulnerability for the monarch. Because it was reprinted over such a long course of time, Burnet's *History* provided grounds for comparison between the reign of Henry VIII and contemporary issues that periodically renewed themselves.[63]

An important part of the construction of the text of the body of Henry VIII has to do with the connection between his insatiable lust and death. This is a royal body that

---

[58] Tatiana String, 'Myth and Memory in Representations of Henry VIII, 1509–2009', in *Tudorism: Historical Imagination and the Appropriation of the Sixteenth Century*, ed. Tatiana C. String and Marcus Bull (Oxford, 2011), p. 201, and Roy Strong, *And When Did You Last See Your Father? The Victorian Painter and British History* (London, 1978), p. 160.

[59] String, p. 201.

[60] String, p. 205.

[61] String, p. 201.

[62] Andrew Starkie, 'Henry VIII in History: Gilbert Burnet's History of the Reformation vol. I (1679)', in *Henry VIII and History*, ed. Thomas Betteridge and Thomas Freeman (Farnham, 2012), p. 153.

[63] Starkie, p. 162.

produces corpses – specifically, beheaded corpses – that stem directly from the king's concupiscent desires. Moreover, Henry's is a royal body that is read via the corpses it produces. Mark Rankin discusses this facet of the royal body, saying, 'Henry VIII reached the eighteenth century as a figure, physically and politically, of concentrated power – partly the result of effective work of Thomas Cromwell and his propagandists and partly the result of the memory of many beheadings. This was the Henry whom Geoffrey Hill has called "this king of bloody trunks".'[64] This image defines Henry's body through the acts of acquiring and then destroying the bodies of Anne Boleyn and others, especially those who were beheaded.[65] Two early plays figured prominently in generating later textual associations of the body of Henry VIII with the bodies produced by his actions: Samuel Rowley's *When You See Me You Know Me, Or, The Famous Chronicle Historie of Henry The Eight* (1605), and Nicholas Rowe's 1709 edition of Shakespeare's *Henry VIII*. In both plays the king's cruelty is attributed to a deficiency in masculinity caused by his inability to produce a male heir; unsatisfied by his divorce, he compensates further for this deficiency by destroying the body of Anne Boleyn. Cooperating with this depiction were histories like David Hume's *History of England Under the House of Tudor* (1759). Hume depicts Henry VIII as a slave to his humours, the possessor of a dysfunctional, imbalanced body that inflicts death upon others, namely Anne.[66] Jonathan Swift was shockingly harsh in his view of the king's royal body as a generator of corpses. In his marginal notes to his copy of Herbert of Cherbury's *Life and Raigne of Henry VIII* (1649) he wishes that the king's own corpse will be transformed by desecration into a text meant to be read by future monarchs about the consequences of tyranny:

> And I wish he had been Flead [flayed], his skin stuffed and hanged on a gibbet, his bulky guts and flesh left to be devoured by birds and beasts for a warning to his successors for ever. Amen.[67]

Swift imagined Henry's corpse functioning literally as a record of the grotesque consequences of obsession, sex, and tyranny. He was not the only one. In 1855, Henry William Herbert wrote of the death of Anne Boleyn in *Memoirs of Henry VIII*: 'A beautiful contrast of this [Anne's execution] to the brutal, bloated tyrant,

---

[64] Mark Rankin, *Henry VIII and His Afterlives: Literature, Politics, Art*, ed. Mark Rankin, Christopher Highley, and John N. King (Cambridge, 2009), p. 115; also Geoffrey Hill, *A Treatise of Civil Power* (New Haven, CT, 2008).

[65] Especially Thomas More, and eventually Thomas Cromwell himself. Rankin, p. 115.

[66] Judith Richards, 'Unblushing Falsehood: The Strickland Sisters and the Domestic History of Henry VIII', in *Henry VIII and History*, ed. Thomas Betteridge and Thomas Freeman (Farnham, 2012), p. 165.

[67] Jonathan Swift, 'Marginal Note in Herbert of Cherbury's *Life and Raigne of Henry VIII* (1649)', *Miscellaneous and Autobiographical Pieces, Fragments, and Marginalia*, ed. Herbert Davis Oxford (London, 1959), pp. 246–51.

waiting on his eager horse ... until the dull roar of the culverin, booming down the wind, should tell him that the lovely form, which had so often slept softly on his bosom, was now a mutilated mass of gory clay'.[68] Such images of Henry's living body juxtapose his grotesque appearance in life with Anne's grotesque appearance in death. This juxtaposition produces striking images of a king whose royal body, decayed by vice, bloated, and rotting from the inside (because of gluttony, ill-humour, and ulcerated sores on his legs) is a veritable living corpse years before his actual death. In histories of the Tudor period and dramatic interpretations of history that use such images, the king's body becomes a secondary text of signs to be read independently of the language of the printed book. In this set of signs, the phallogocentrism is inverted: it revolves around the impotence, rather than the sexual potency, of the royal subject.

After the king's death, a corpse myth became associated with him: it held that Henry's destructive energies finally destroyed the royal body from the inside out, and that his corpse literally exploded. There are two versions of the myth.[69] The first references a prophecy made by father Peto, a Franciscan of Greenwich, who, during a sermon protesting the king's divorce from Katherine of Aragon, predicted that dogs would lap the king's blood as they had the Biblical tyrant Ahab.[70] Burnet's *History of the Reformation* repeated the well-known story, as did Agnes Strickland, in her biography of Anne Boleyn in *Lives of the Queens of England* (1854). These books and others like them aided the absorption of the story into the historical canon.[71] A second version of the myth stemmed from the accidental rediscovery of the king's remains in 1813 and again in 1888. The second version of the myth purported that the king's corpse exploded in the vault after its interment.

After he died, the body of Henry VIII was autopsied (by the medical standards of the day) and embalmed. It was then prepared for transport to Syon Abbey, where it was to lie in state.[72] During the transportation of the remains, the king's very large coffin was jostled about in the carriage for some time, action that probably weakened

---

[68] Henry William Herbert, *Memoirs of Henry VIII* (New York, 1855), pp. 365–6.

[69] Both versions of the myth are rooted in folklore and even today are spread via word of mouth (such as by tour guides) or on the Internet as part of Tudor 'fan sites', where they function as unsubstantiated retellings. The most concrete record of the myth is found on the website for the College of St George's Chapel itself. The site posts the document, 'Henry VIII's Final Resting Place: Background Notes', that refers to various aspects of the Chapel, including facts and stories about Henry VIII's burial, will, disinterment, and the placement of the current grave marker that identifies all the occupants of the vault. URL: www.stgeorges-windsor.org/assets/files/LearningResources/Background NotesHenryVIII.pdf

[70] I Kings 20:19.

[71] See Adam Fox, *Oral and Literate Culture in England*, for how rumours, sayings and omens, and folklore become attached to, and legitimized by, textual sources.

[72] Robert Hutchinson, *The Last Days of Henry VIII: Conspiracies, Treason, and Heresy at the Court of the Dying Tyrant* (New York, 2005), pp. 221–32.

the coffin's lead seams. At some point the coffin was dropped upon its arrival at Syon's church, for its large size and great weight made the object unwieldy. When the coffin was dropped onto the floor of the church, bodily fluid, such as that which was left after the embalming, leaked out onto the church floor. The next morning men arrived to solder the coffin's split seam. According to Agnes Strickland, they witnessed an eerie sight: here, she quotes 'a contemporary document' that she fails to identify, in which an unidentified 'woman of the sixteenth century' alleges the following:[73]

> In the morning came plumbers to solder the coffin under whose feet was suddenly seen a dog creeping and licking up the king's blood. If you ask me how I know this, I answer William Greville,[74] who could scarcely drive away the dog, told me and so did the plumber also.[75]

By the nineteenth century the story had acquired the qualities of folklore. As the story was distributed around the country and passed down from generation to generation over the course of three centuries, it was cobbled together from differing second and third hand reports of the incident.[76] The subsequent retellings of the story incorporated various aspects of the legend of Henry VIII's grotesque living and dead body into it. Ultimately, the dropping of the coffin onto the floor of Syon Abbey's church was forsaken in favour of a claim that the king's body had exploded *inside* the coffin, and that the explosion of the body had caused the seam in the lead to burst. Because the myth was supported by a prophecy, it acquired and retained strength among those who interpreted the story as divine retribution against Henry for his cruelties and vices. Father Peto's sermon had condemned Anne Boleyn as a Jezebel figure, and compared

---

[73] Strickland, vol. III, p. 255.

[74] The 'William Greville' of the unidentified woman's story is probably either Sir William Greville, who was a Judge of the Court of Common Please during the reign of Henry VIII, or his son William. Neither Strickland nor her source identifies the man completely, and there is no evidence that the conversation took place, since Strickland does not identify the 'document' in which it appears.

[75] Strickland, vol. III, p. 255.

[76] See Fox, *Oral and Literate Culture in England*, for a comprehensive discussion of the various ways in which this phenomenon takes place. Here, Strickland quotes a document for which she gives no source, and attributes it to a woman who cites, as her own (unsubstantiated) proof of the story, a man with an influential name – Greville. Throughout Fox's book he notes that dropping the names of influential persons into rumours and stories was key to taking the story to a higher level of credibility, and a way to assure that the story made its way into text. Once a story becomes a written (especially published) text, it has greater credibility. Owen Davies makes this same point about ghost stories in his book *The Haunted: A Social History of Ghosts* (New York, 2007). This point is also made by researchers of folk tales, such as Anthony D. Hippisley Coxe, *Haunted Britain* (London, 1973), and Christina Hole, *English Folklore* (London, 1940). To observe the practice, see T.M. Jarvis, *Accredited Ghost Stories* (London, 1823), and Catherine Crowe, *The Night Side of Nature, Or, Ghosts and Ghost-Seers*, 2 vols. (London, 1848).

Henry VIII to Ahab. Popular interpretation of Father Peto's prophecy was tantalisingly portentous: Henry VIII had destroyed the body of the church, allowing his seductive wife to slaughter the prophets of the true church (namely Thomas More) and replace them with the false prophets of Protestantism. The king had dissolved the monasteries, a slight that the monks at Syon Abbey took personally. He had bullied the body of Parliament to press his ecclesiastical policies into legislation. He had lusted for the body of Anne Boleyn, and the product of this lust had produced the Princess Elizabeth, an illegitimate heir who displaced the succession of the Princess Mary who, in a further insult, was declared illegitimate by her father. When he could satisfy his lusts no longer, Henry VIII destroyed the body of Anne Boleyn and imposed the taint of illegitimacy upon the Princess Elizabeth. Henry VIII had redefined the royal bodies of his Tudor wives and daughters via desecration, by violating the way queens validated the royal body of the king and its authority to sustain itself by way of succession. As a result, Divine Providence, the very power that brought Henry VIII to the throne, exacted its revenge upon his body. Putrefying and wracked with sin, the king's corpse exploded, violating the sanctity of the church at Syon with an unholy display of blood, pus, and fat both inside and outside the coffin. The explosion was accompanied by a horrific stench.

The implications of the legend are very telling – they make direct correlations between the primal human fear of rotting corpses and the deep psychosocial fear of corruption in government. The story associates the explosion of the corpse with images of bombast (a tempting near-homonym with *bomb-blast*), grotesqueness, irrationality, blood, and guts. As it was, no such explosion took place, nor was one possible. The king had been embalmed before there was any chance for his corpse to bloat. The fat he bore was under the skin, and any pus on the body, such as that which oozed from his ulcerated leg sores, had ceased to flow when he expired. Any liquid leaking from the coffin was merely residual body fluid (and not necessarily blood) that had collected in the bottom of the coffin – not uncommon for a sixteenth-century royal burial.

The story of Henry VIII's exploding corpse provided a lurid backdrop for the excavation of the king's grave in his vault at St George's Chapel, Windsor in 1813. The many decades of public disappointment with the Hanoverians was at its peak when the remains of Henry VIII were reexamined. People were not slow to make comparisons between the heavy Hanoverian princes and dukes and the obesity of Henry VIII. Many also noted that the succession was decidedly less than clear. Workmen cutting a passage under the choir to a new mausoleum accidentally broke through a brick wall and discovered four royal coffins: those of Charles I,[77] Henry VIII, Jane Seymour, and an infant child of Queen Anne.[78] When the vault was excavated several days after its discovery, George III (who was enjoying a period of lucidity) and the Prince Regent

---

[77] For a discussion of the examination of Charles I's remains see Chapter 8.

[78] Sir Henry Halford, *An Account of What Appeared on Opening the Coffin of King Charles the First ... on the first of April, MDCCCXIII ...* (London, 1813), pp. 6–7.

were on hand, as was Sir Henry Halford, physician to the king and the man who recorded the account of the excavation.[79] Several others were also present.[80] The coffin bearing the body of Henry VIII was much larger than the others, and it was not in good condition. Halford reports:

> The larger [coffin], supposed on good grounds to contain the remains of King Henry VIII, measured six feet ten inches in length, and had been enclosed in an elm [coffin] of two inches in thickness; but this was decayed and lay in small fragments near it. The leaden coffin appeared to have been beaten in by violence about the middle and a considerable opening of it exposed a mere skeleton of the king. Some beard remained on the chin but there was nothing to discriminate the personage contained in it.[81]

Halford does not record the width of the king's coffin, but the living measurements of Henry VIII at the time of his death included a waist measuring fifty-four inches and a weight of nearly four hundred pounds.[82] It was therefore at least twice the width and depth of a coffin for a man of average size. The outside of the coffin suggested an imposing, formidable figure in death; and yet when Halford peered inside he could not help but notice that the body was completely skeletonised. It had shrunk to the proportions that made all people equal – that of skeletal remains. It had not exploded, nor had its presence posed any threat of defilement to its surroundings; rather, the king's body shrank away from its environment, appearing as a poignant epilogue to the text of the corpse that dominated the narrative of the royal body. In fact, the royal corpse could scarcely be read for signs of identification; only by the fragments of beard and by the presumption of its once-huge size could the identity of the occupant of the coffin be discerned. That fact alone presented a quiet alternative text to the bold language of the novels, plays, poems, and paintings in which the king appeared. Those works emphasised the boisterous royal body, identifiable instantly by its bulk, stance, and quintessential ginger beard.

It would appear, in fact, that any violent bursting that occurred in the vicinity of the king's corpse had come from the outside. Halford theorised that the 'violence' done to the coffin was due to the urgency with which Charles I had been buried in 1649. King Charles was indeed buried hastily, amid a constant worry either that supporters of Oliver Cromwell would try to do violence to his corpse or that royalists would attempt to steal parts of it for veneration as relics.[83] Halford guessed that the coffin of Charles I, as it was lowered with ropes, was dropped onto Henry VIII's coffin. This is unlikely, mainly because the coffin of Henry VIII rested on wooden trestles; if the coffin of

---

[79] Halford, pp. 6–7.
[80] They were: the Duke of Cumberland, Count Munster, the Dean of Windsor, Benjamin Charles Stevenson, Esq., and several workmen.
[81] Halford, p. 10.
[82] Hutchinson cites a weight of approximately 28 stone, or 392 lbs. Hutchinson, pp. 17 and 142.
[83] See Chapter 8.

Charles I were dropped with enough force to damage the coffin below it, it would have knocked Henry's coffin off the trestles.[84] However, another incident that occurred during the 1649 interment of Charles I better explains the poor appearance of Henry's coffin. A foot soldier assisting with the interment was caught stealing mementos from the coffin of Henry VIII.[85] The man cut away part of the huge velvet pall that covered the coffin, and, according to Isaac, the sexton's assistant, 'wimbled a hole through the said coffin that was largest [i.e., that of Henry VIII], probably fancying that there was something well worth his adventure'.[86] When searched, the foot soldier was found to have hidden a bone on his person, and he confessed that he intended to make a knife out of it. The bone was confiscated and returned to the coffin. The hole bored by the foot soldier could not have been very small; otherwise he would not have been able to probe for a good-sized bone and extract it.[87] Environmental changes in the crypt would have caused the wood of the coffin to rot and disintegrate from the place from where it had been borne through, and those same environmental changes would have caused the lead envelope (which also had a hole in it) to decay and collapse. What may have appeared to Halford as a coffin 'beaten in with violence' simply represented an accumulation of these factors. Nevertheless, Halford's record reveals his attempt to read the corpse and its immediate surroundings in a certain way. He associated the appearance of the coffin with violence; specifically, that it had been 'beaten in'. He chooses that descriptive term over 'caved in', or 'collapsed', as he drew upon the association of Henry VIII with ruthless acts of cruelty and violence made continuously in historical and literary texts, and works of art.

In 1888 the Prince of Wales, Albert Edward (later Edward VII), had the vault opened so that a few relics of Charles I collected in 1649 could be returned to his coffin. A hole was made in the floor of St George's chapel for this purpose, and when a light was lowered into the vault, the observers noted that the coffin of Henry VIII was in a state of utter dilapidation. Among them was architect and artist A.Y. Nutt, Surveyor to the Deans and Canons of St George's. Nutt sketched the vault (Fig. 9) and recorded his experience of the event:

> The King's skull, with its very broad frontal, his thigh bones, ribs and other portions of the skeleton are exposed to view as the lead has been extensively ripped open, apparently, to judge by the fractured edges, owing to the action of internal forces outward.[88]

---

[84] Hutchinson, pp. 229 and 272.
[85] Anthony Wood, *Athenae Oxoniensis*, vol. II (London, 1721), p. 703, and Hutchinson, p. 270.
[86] Wood, p. 703, and Hutchinson, p. 270.
[87] The bone was either the radius or the ulna of the left arm. The foot soldier bored the hole from the coffin's right-hand side as he stood between it and the coffin of Jane Seymour. The space between Henry's coffin and that of Charles I was too small to accommodate a grown man.
[88] A.Y. Nutt, quoted in *Henry VIII's Final Resting Place: Background Notes* (Addendum to Halford's Account). Chapter Archives of St George's Chapel, Windsor Castle, www.stgeorges-windsor.org.

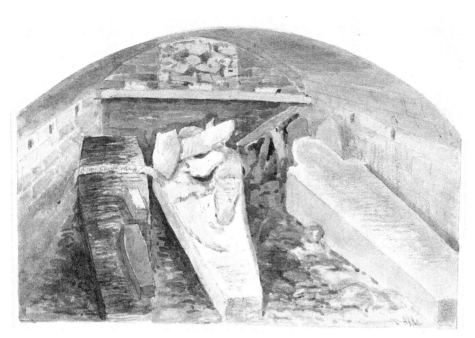

Fig. 9 Drawing by A.Y. Nutt of the vault containing the damaged coffin of Henry VIII (centre). To the right is the coffin of Jane Seymour; and to the left is the coffin of Charles I, atop which rests the coffin of an infant child of Queen Anne. Photo reproduction courtesy of the Chapter Archives of St George's Chapel, Windsor Castle.

Although Nutt was evidently aware of the investigation into the vault seventy-five years earlier, he does not appear to be familiar with Halford's account, for he neither refers to the speculation that the coffin was 'beaten in', nor does he relate the story of the vandalising foot soldier. Instead, his speculation is based on the presumption that the body must have exploded after burial. Nutt theorises that the natural process of decay had produced sufficient gases to cause the lead envelope to burst after the coffin was already in the crypt. Interestingly, despite the fact that he was not a scholar, Nutt's observation is informed by an academic attitude more common in 1888 than in 1813; namely, that if indeed the king's corpse had exploded, as legend had it, then the explosion was due to the natural accumulation of gases in the lead envelope and not Providential retribution. This rewriting of the corpse myth employs an equalising factor similar to that presumed by Halford's account of 1813: it humanises the royal body. In 1888, however, the rewriting of the corpse myth reduces the royal body to the status of artefact, a specimen for scientific voyeurism. Even so, Nutt's speculation about the myth was not true; since the king had been embalmed after his death, his body cavity was empty and was therefore unable to produce the gases necessary for the abdomen to burst. Even if it had, such a bursting of the abdomen and release of the gases would not have been enough for the lead envelope to blow out. In the seventy-five years since the last opening of the vault in 1813, changes in temperature and humidity caused the existing break in the lead of the coffin to fracture and peel outward. Still, Nutt employed a bit of academic licence to make one further observation: he mentions that the king's skull had a 'broad frontal', a clear phrenological reference to the intelligence and capacity for leadership that a king was supposed to have. Even as he reduces the language of the royal body to scientific terms, he nonetheless employs the popular science of the day to rescue the king's body and its legend from the mundane status of mere corpse. This is a corpse, and maybe an exploded one; but it is a royal body nonetheless.

The Tudors, namely Henry VIII and his most notorious second wife, provide so much drama that they developed a broad cultural appeal in the centuries after their deaths. This appeal extends to other figures of their time and to figures attached to their time, so that the comprehensive Tudor and Stuart periods become associated with dramatic energy that proceeds from these two central figures. In a celebrated lecture, David Starkey proclaims the Tudors to be 'soap', and indeed they are.[89] Their family relationships and the very human causes for their behaviours make them relatable. Their motives seem, or are made to seem, to derive from the same emotions that drive everyday people. This idea forms what Jill Matus refers to as a connection between cultural and biological connections to figures of the past. Where Henry and Anne are concerned, this connection is sexualised to a very high degree and attached to nineteenth-century attitudes toward masculinity and motherhood. But such an idea is not without its complications: Anne's sexuality cannot be grounded completely in the biology of motherhood as it relates to queenship, because the stability of her sexuality, and therefore her humanity, is interrupted by the issues of incest and witchcraft. Her dramatic death by beheading leaves the body in a permanent state of horrifying disfigurement. Similarly, Henry's sexuality cannot be grounded completely in the biology of virility. The stability of his sexuality and also of his humanity is interrupted by the issues of obesity and cruelty. Both figures are thereby made monstrous. The use of melodramatic depiction in conjunction with the corpse myths of Henry and Anne points to a desire to humanise the royal bodies in death, to draw them closer to the emotional experiences of the living; to look at the horror of Tudor violence and tyranny through the lens of the sentimental reader, who sees, by design, a complicated narrative of the corpse.

[89] David Starkey, 'The Tudors: Famous for Five Centuries'. Lecture delivered at the Colston Research Symposium on 'Tudorism', University of Bristol, 6 December, 2008, in String and Bull, eds., p. 266.

6

INVESTIGATIONS AND REVISIONS

Katherine Parr

In the spring of 1782, a group of women made their way across the Cotswolds to Sudeley Castle, where the fifteenth-century castle lay in ruins against the backdrop of the rolling hills. Their visit was antiquarian in interest and was inspired by the recently published *New History of Gloucestershire* by Samuel Rudder.[1] Their attention was drawn to the chapel, long out of use and scarcely with any roof left (Fig. 10). Rudder's book lamented its sad state: 'There is nothing remaining of the church but the shell or outer walls (by which it appears to have been a neat building, adorned with battlements and pinnacles all round) except a small aile, called the chapel, where divine service is performed once a fortnight'.[2] Observing a large block of alabaster against the north wall of the chapel, they speculated that the block marked the location of an old sepulchral monument – a monument that was catalogued in Rudder's book. Upon closer inspection they found they were right; and after enlisting the help of some local men to dig, they found, barely two feet below the surface, a lead envelope inscribed with the name of Katherine Parr, the sixth and last wife of Henry VIII, who had died two centuries earlier, in 1548.[3] It was exactly what they were looking for.

Rudder's *New History of Gloucestershire* was a massive book of over eight hundred folio pages. It was also expensive, at two and a half guineas – but well worth the cost to anyone with antiquarian interest in local history.[4] It catalogued exhaustively the natural history of the area, its important buildings and residences, its historical and cultural artefacts, and its churches, monuments, and tombs. Rudder's *New History* provided a detailed description of Sudeley Castle and its grounds. Despite the fact that it lay in ruins, the castle was still beautiful, still architecturally significant, and still historically

---

[1] Samuel Rudder, *A New History of Gloucestershire, Comprising the Topography, Antiquities, Curiosities, Produce, Trade, and Manufactures of that County* (Cirencester, 1779).

[2] Rudder, p. 719.

[3] The inscription on the lead envelope read: 'Here lyeth queen Katherine Wife to Kynge Henry the VIII and Wife of Thomas Lord Sudly high Admy of Englond and ynkle to Kynge Edward the VI'. repr. in Treadway Nash, 'Observations on the time of Death and Place of Burial of Queen Katherine Parr', *Archaeologia: Or, Miscellaneous Tracts Relating to Antiquity*, vol. IX (London, 1789), p. 1.

[4] J. Parsloe, 'The First Issue of Samuel Rudder's *The History and Antiquities of Gloucester*', *Transactions of the British and Gloucestershire Archaeological Society* 117 (Gloucestershire, 1999).

Fig. 10 Engraving by Samuel Rudder of Sudeley Castle in ruins in 1779. The Chapel
containing the tomb of Katherine Parr is off to the right. Photo reproduction courtesy of the
Huntington Library, San Marino, California.

important. Royalist troops had quartered there during the Civil War before Oliver
Cromwell ordered the castle to be 'slighted', or wrecked, so that it would be unusable
for further royalist occupation. A century before those events, the castle had been the
home of Thomas Seymour during his marriage to Katherine Parr, and it was also at that
time home to the young Elizabeth I and Lady Jane Grey. Upon her death, Katherine
Parr had received the first recorded Protestant funeral in English history, and she was
subsequently buried at Sudeley.

From the engraving in Rudder's book the antiquaries were able to direct their
attention toward the north wall of the chapel where Katherine's grave was likely to be
located. The diggers opened the ground not far from the wall and uncovered the lead
envelope. They cut first the lead and then the cerecloth beneath it, and exposed the
stunningly well-preserved face of Katherine Parr. The flesh of her face was firm to the
touch, its features intact, and her eyes open and astonishingly lifelike.[5] An inspection
of one of her hands produced a similar observation: the flesh was firm, the nails intact,
and the skin of a brownish colour.[6] Instead of wearing the knotted shroud in which
most people of the Tudor period were buried, Katherine wore an embroidered gown.

---

[5]   Nash, p. 3. Nash transcribes the findings of the first group, but the original record of their
      excavation is lost.
[6]   Nash, p. 3.

The sight was alarming to the party (as was the odour emanating from the cerecloth), and they ordered the workmen to rebury the body immediately.[7] Four years later in 1786, the Reverend Treadway Nash, an antiquary of substantial reputation, obtained permission from Lord Rivers, then-owner of the castle, to visit the site for a follow-up excavation.[8] He arrived at Sudeley on 14 October in the company of the Hon. John Sommers Cocks and Mr John Skipp, both of whom also had antiquarian interests in the history of Gloucestershire that had been piqued at least in part by the publication of Rudder's book. They were aware of the events of the previous excavation, but their expectations of seeing the uncorrupted face of Henry VIII's last Queen were met with disappointment. The lead envelope containing the body had not been resealed properly, and the skull of Katherine Parr had decayed substantially. Nash recorded his inspection of the corpse for a new journal named *Archaeologia*, a publication dedicated to antiquarian interests in Britain:

> Upon opening the ground, and heaving up the lead, we found the face totally decayed; the teeth, which were sound, had fallen out of their sockets. The body I believe, is perfect; as it has never been opened, we thought it indelicate and indecent to uncover it; but observing the left hand to lie at a small distance from the body we took off the cerecloth, and found the hands and nails perfect, but of a brownish colour...The Queen must have been low of stature; as the lead that enclosed her corpse was just five feet four inches long.[9]

Rev. Nash made a sketch of the body (Fig. 11);[10] he also transcribed the inscription on the lead envelope, and then the grave was closed up again.

The discovery of the corpse of Katherine Parr bears greatly upon the subject of the queenly body and its connection to eighteenth-century values. Katherine Parr lived in a time when queenship in England underwent monumental changes: Henry VIII redefined queenship via the fact of his multiple marriages, as he changed his mind serially about the criteria by which a queen was deemed rightful, her children legitimate. He supported his personal requirements in marriage with modifications of the royal prerogative, which was in turn supported by ecclesiastical policy and legislation. His efforts to annul his marriage with Katherine of Aragon and delegitimise his daughter Mary were exhaustive and ultimately successful, and although Anne Boleyn and her daughter were at first legitimated they too were soon delegitimised; however these

---

[7]   See S.H. Burke, *The Men and Women of the English Reformation, from the Days of Wolsey to the Death of Cranmer*, 2 vols. (New York, 1872), vol. I, p. 223.

[8]   Nash, p. 3. Hubert S. Burke records that in 1784, between the first disinterment and Nash's excavation, a farmer named Lucas (or perhaps Locust) opened the grave and reported the body to be in a condition similar to that described by the first group. He reburied the body in its lead envelope, but neither he nor the first party sealed the top of it completely.

[9]   Nash, p. 3.

[10] Nash, p. 1.

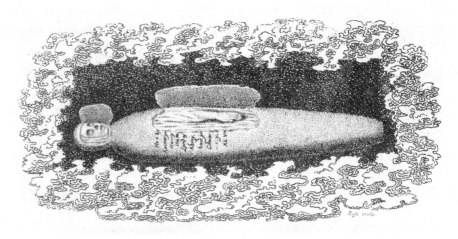

Fig. 11 Drawing by Rev. Treadway Nash of the corpse of Katherine Parr as it looked when he opened the grave on 14 October 1782. Note the cut to the side of the cerecloth so her left hand could be viewed. Photo reproduction courtesy of the Huntington Library, San Marino, California.

changes took place under a different set of circumstances and criteria from those of the king's first marriage. The king was dissatisfied with his fourth wife, Anne of Cleves,[11] and was able to divorce her more quickly and easily than he had Katherine of Aragon. Katherine Howard went to the block on charges of treason and adultery that did not need to be bolstered with the additional charges of incest and witchcraft that followed Anne Boleyn to the scaffold. By the time Katherine Parr became Queen she knew that the role of queen consort was profoundly different than it had ever been in England, and she understood that with the accession of her step-daughter Elizabeth there could very well be more changes to come. In Katherine Parr's tenure as Queen Consort, the extent to which a queen lived up to her role depended less on her ability to reflect the long-standing traditions of the Plantagenet queens and their focus on dynastic continuity and wide-ranging familial alliances, and more on the particular whims of the king and his unique relationship to the royal prerogative.

When she is crowned, a queen consort is consecrated and her body deemed sacred – although not to the extent of her husband. Divine Right does not extend to her, but rather through her to her first male heir.[12] Possessed of a sacred body, a Medieval queen

---

[11] Henry's third wife, Jane Seymour, died in childbirth after giving birth to Edward VI.

[12] If a woman is monarch, as in the case of Mary Tudor or Elizabeth I, there is no queen consort and Divine Right extends through the body of the monarch exclusively. A female monarch is therefore in a unique position of being both monarch and consort. She is, essentially, married to herself – despite the presence of her husband. John Knox is one polemicist of the sixteenth century who noted this issue and railed against it as a hermaphroditic abomination in *The First Blast of the Trumpet Against the Monstrous Regiment of Women* (London, 1558).

was associated with the Virgin Mary because of her connection to Divine Right and the Davidic Elect through her son. Lisa Hilton points out that this fact argues against the stereotype of Medieval and Early Modern queens as mere property '… for they amounted to more than a catalogue of their lands, movables, treasures and allies. Nor can they be dismissed as mere breeding machines for the patristic monarchy.'[13] Because of the privilege granted to her through her inclusion among the Davidic Elect, the Medieval queen was a figure of elite political authority in her own right. She could bring a suit in court and preside over legal cases, make ecclesiastical appointments, and even raise armies.[14] England was not subject to Salic law, as France was, and so English queens held exceptional status, as a king could make his claim to the throne through his mother or grandmother. Henry VIII's own father, Henry VII, had done just this, making his claim in part through his mother, Margaret Beaufort, and his grandmother, Katherine de Valois.[15] A queen's alliances, wealth, and political clout made her formidable in her own right; and her *friendship* with the king, both in the public and private sense, gave her exclusive privilege and authority. It is no surprise that the game of chess acquired the figure of the Queen during the later Middle Ages. Rare was the contest of political intrigue that could be won without her.[16] Katherine Parr was not crowned queen (nor were any of Henry VIII's consorts after Anne Boleyn); but her body was nonetheless set apart from those of all other women because of her duty to produce a legitimate heir to the throne (whether she ultimately did so or not).

The association of the queen with the Virgin Mary had disappeared by the time Katherine married Henry VIII in 1543, but the inclusion of the queen in the Davidic Elect persisted and Katherine married the king, her third husband, expecting to produce an heir. She expected to live her role as consort apart from Catholic tradition, and she directed the sacredness of her body toward her mission to advance Protestantism in the king's court. Katherine had held reformist views from the time of her first marriage, and perhaps before; her beliefs were partly rooted in her humanist education, but she took her attitude toward humanism away from the model represented by Erasmus and toward a more progressive view.[17] Influenced by Miles Coverdale, who later became her almoner, she supported the Bible in English and arguments against Purgatory, and she welcomed the king's ban on pilgrimages and indulgences.[18] Katherine was aware that transmitting her beliefs to the king was dangerous, however. Her life in the king's household was accompanied by the constant reminder that Anne Boleyn had failed in a similar effort to promote progressive beliefs and had suffered total annihilation as a result: Anne's intellectualism was replaced in political rhetoric and popular lore with an

---

[13] Lisa Hilton, *Queens Consort: England's Medieval Queens* (London, 2008), p. 3.
[14] Hilton, p. 4.
[15] Hilton, pp. 6–7.
[16] For a history of the chess queen, see Marilyn Yalom, *The Birth of the Chess Queen: A History* (New York, 2005).
[17] Elizabeth Norton, *Catherine Parr* (Stroud, 2010), pp. 121–2.
[18] Norton, pp. 121–2.

obsessive focus on her sexuality. Her queenly body was demystified by sexual scandal, de-sanctified by witch paranoia, and then destroyed by execution. Because of these and other factors, Katherine accompanied her progressivism with a cautious manner. Her friendship with the martyr Anne Askew nearly cost Katherine her life, but when she heard her rooms were to be searched, she cleared all suspect books and materials from the rooms; and when she was questioned by the king her answers were orthodox and uncontroversial, her demeanour submissive and deferential. She did not wish to suffer the same fate as either Anne Askew or Anne Boleyn.

After the death of Henry VIII in 1547, Katherine Parr secretly married Sir Thomas Seymour, brother of Jane Seymour, Henry VIII's third wife. She had intended to marry Seymour years earlier, but had deferred to the king's wishes when Henry took interest in her. Katherine died the following year at Sudeley Castle, Seymour's home, on 5 September 1548, of puerperal fever after giving birth to her only daughter, Mary. Her funeral, which took place two days later, was the first recorded Protestant funeral in England. By 1779 the particulars of the funeral had become obscure, but Samuel Rudder learned the details via antiquarian research. He found the account of the funeral in a manuscript held by the Herald's College of Arms called *A Book of Buryalls of Trew Noble Persons*.[19] Rudder reprinted the account in the *New History of Gloucestershire* alongside his description of Sudeley Castle and its chapel. For a sixteenth-century funeral of a dowager queen consort, the funeral is strikingly simple. The queen was wrapped in cerecloth and encased in a lead envelope, and then was brought out to the chapel a mere two days after her death. The procession was on a much smaller scale than other funerals of its type, with only members of Katherine's own household taking part: there were gentlemen, squires, knights and yeomen, ladies and gentlewomen, walking either two by two or three by three.[20] Lady Jane Grey was chief mourner. The chapel was hung with black draperies and scutcheons bearing the king's arms and also Seymour's, alongside Katherine's own arms. There were cushioned stools for the mourners to sit on, but very few tapers – only two, which stood on either side of the lead envelope during the service. At the service psalms were sung and three lessons were read. The mourners placed alms into the alms-box, after which Katherine's almoner, Miles Coverdale, delivered the sermon. In his sermon, Coverdale admonished the mourners against the belief that their alms benefited the dead in any way, and he instructed them to believe that they only benefitted the poor to whom they were donated. The record reads: 'he toke a occasion to declare unto the people how that thei shulle none there thinke Seye nor spread abrode that the offering wch was there don was don any thing to prffyt the deade but ffor the poore onlye'.[21] Coverdale also instructed the mourners not to attach any significance to the tapers flanking the corpse, as they had no benefit to the dead but were there for an honorific purpose only: 'And also the lights wch were

---

[19] College of Arms MS R20 and RR21C.
[20] College of Arms MS R20 and RR21C, reprinted in Rudder, pp. 719–20.
[21] College of Arms MS R20 and RR21C, reprinted in Rudder, pp. 719–20.

carried & stode abowte the corps were for the honor of the parson & for none other entente nor purpose'.[22]

After Coverdale's sermon, the mourners retired to dinner and then disbanded as Katherine was buried. The entire funeral 'was don in a mornynge',[23] extraordinarily quick in terms of the average Early Modern funeral of a dowager queen. The funeral of Jane Seymour,[24] in contrast, had involved much more ceremony and was more lavish concerning the use of tapers, draperies and images, the number of mourners, and prayers for the dead. After her death on 24 October 1537, Jane lay in state for seven days, then her body proceeded first to Hampton Court's Chapel Royal where a service was held, and after that her body was taken to St George's Chapel at Windsor Castle for a second service before she was interred there on 12 November. The simplicity of Katherine's funeral indicated a clear agenda: she (along with Coverdale and chief members of her household) intended that the funeral represent Protestant innovation. The funeral was meant to reflect progressivism and modernity, and it was meant to stand apart from Henry VIII's stubborn attachment to traditionalism. Despite his research, Rudder's comments on Katherine's funeral record betrays the relative values he held for funerary practices. Katherine's funeral was radically simplified for a sixteenth-century queen consort; and yet, Rudder remarks that she was buried 'with much funeral pomp'.[25] Rudder reads the record of the funeral (which he also reprints in his volume)[26] in a completely different manner that did those who made the original record. It is not surprising that subsequent readers of his book and excavators of Katherine's grave engaged in a similar type of relativism.

The facts of Katherine's life, religious faith, and death were interpreted with a great deal of licence two hundred years later. To many, Katherine's progressivism reflected eighteenth-century ideals of Protestantism in relation to queenship. The antiquary George Ballard's brief biography of Katherine in *Memoirs of Several Ladies of Great Britain* (1752) is an example of the type of enhancement to which her memory was subjected. Ballard writes that Katherine was a forerunner of Protestantism, and credits her posthumously with the ability to detect the course of English Protestantism outside the scope of her lifetime. He depicts Katherine as a patroness of reformed religion, overlooking the fact that in her own time her views were considered aberrant and potentially treasonous. About her book *The Lamentation of a Sinner* he says,

> In it she acknowledges with great sincerity the sinful course of her life for many years, in which she, relying on external performances, such as fasts and pilgrimages was all that while a stranger to the internal and true power of religion, which she came afterwards

---

[22] College of Arms MS R20 and RR21C, reprinted in Rudder, pp. 719–20.

[23] College of Arms MS R20 and RR21C, reprinted in Rudder, pp. 719–20.

[24] Jane Seymour was the only one of Henry VIII's six wives to receive a *queen's* funeral, although Katherine of Aragon and Katherine Parr did receive *royal* funerals.

[25] Rudder, p. 719.

[26] Rudder, pp. 719–20.

to feel by the study of the scripture, and that calling upon God for the assistance of the Holy Spirit by whose direction they were written.[27]

Ballard's Katherine Parr is influenced directly by the Holy Spirit. She is concerned not only for her husband's spiritual wellbeing, but also for that of the nation. John Strype does something similar in his 1751 portrayal of Katherine. He depicts her as a woman ahead of her time, someone whose legacy was relevant from age to age and who was therefore unbound by Tudor ideals of womanhood. He cites an anecdote about her childhood, which he attributes to a friend who collects quotes[28] (a common eighteenth-century pastime): 'When her mother used sometimes to call her to Work, she would say, "my Hands are ordained to touch Crowns and Sceptres, not Needles and Spindles"'.[29] As a child, Katherine in Strype's narrative is endowed with the prescient knowledge that she is destined for a royal purpose. Here, Strype employs apocryphal legends about Katherine in a similar way that Rudder employs the narrative of her funeral: both men interpret her Protestantism retroactively so that her life and beliefs reflect and validate contemporary values.

As Clarissa Campbell Orr discusses, eighteenth-century queens consort and aristocratic ladies were associated with intellectualism and scholarly interests – at least those of the sort that were acceptable for women at that time.[30] The women who went searching for Katherine's long-lost grave in 1782 were self-taught antiquaries, and perhaps thought themselves to be bluestockings. They and many others like them were attracted to the legacy of intellectualism and scholarship with which Katherine had become associated. Despite the fact that Katherine's education was not extensive in Latin and Greek, biographers like Ballard and Strype (as well as later biographers like Agnes and Elizabeth Strickland) nonetheless depicted Katherine as the academic equal of Margaret Roper.[31] By the late eighteenth century Katherine's intellectual circle of well-educated, Protestant women[32] was legendary, and although the members of the the circle met with extreme caution and discretion, it was remembered in the eighteenth century in the context of contemporary values: as a salon. In this context, Katherine Parr symbolised the ideal eighteenth-century intellectual, aristocratic woman: the leader of a salon, educated in humanism, defiantly Protestant, devoted to

---

[27] George Ballard, *Memoirs of Several Ladies of Great Britain, Who Have Been Celebrated for their Writings or Skill in the Learned Languages, Arts, and Sciences* (Oxford, 1752), p. 85.

[28] A 'Doctor Sampson of London'.

[29] John Strype, *Ecclesiastical Memorials*, 3 vols. (London, 1751), vol. I, p. 132.

[30] *Queenship in Britain 1660–1837*, ed. Clarissa Campell Orr (Manchester, 2002), p. 10.

[31] C. Fenno Hoffman, 'Catherine Parr as a Woman of Letters', *Huntington Library Quarterly* 23, no. 4 (August 1960): 350–1.

[32] The group included Anne Stanhope, Countess of Hertford, Mary Howard, Duchess of Richmond, and Catherine Willoughby, Duchess of Suffolk. Others acquainted with or related to Katherine Parr who may have been members of her circle were Lady Denny, Lady Fitzwilliams, Katherine's sister Anne Parr, her cousin Lady Lane, and Lady Tyrwhitt, another relative. All held strong reformist beliefs. See Norton, pp. 132 and 146.

her husband's intellectual and religious development, and patriotic. This last quality is especially important in the light of eighteenth-century militarism. At the time of Katherine's disinterment, France was again an enemy, and the party of female antiquaries who discovered her body – and also their successor, Rev. Nash – were well acquainted with the fact that Katherine had been made Regent General while Henry VIII campaigned against the French in 1544.[33] They were familiar with the association of Katherine's loyalty to the king with dedication to monarchy in general. Nash himself made reference to the idea that Katherine's discussions with the king were directed at monarchic, as well as personal self-improvement:

> … She could not help arguing sometimes with the King: a thing he could never bear, especially in matters of religion, in which he thought every one should conform to his ideas and deemed it the highest presumption that Kate, as he called her, should turn Doctor and pretend to instruct him.[34]

Another important quality attributed to the ideally intellectual aristocratic woman was prudence. As Clarissa Campbell Orr states, the eighteenth-century woman of the salons was expected to accept the neo-Platonic ideal of the woman as 'the object of unconsummated adoration' in a way different from the way the *honnette femme* of the sixteenth century had done.[35] The Tudor model was one of domestic harmony, submissiveness, and sacred motherhood, and it was qualified by standards of Christian virtue that did not take education or intellectualism into account.[36] On these terms Katherine Parr, in her own time, stood out as an aberrant figure threatening disobedience and subversion; her intellectual qualities marked her as a 'froward' wife and potential heretic and traitor if she failed to be careful about her activities and associations. In the eighteenth century she was lauded as a woman acknowledged for her capacity for modernity because of those very same qualities. As Orr states, eighteenth-century intellectuals wished to respect a woman's essentially feminine and maternal qualities, but they also wished to add a neo-Platonic recognition of a woman's intellectual, as well as moral, capacities.[37] To do otherwise was to place an archaic focus on sexual matters and domestic priorities. Yet, there was pressure on such women to display sobriety and prudence. They were expected to be, as Orr states, 'morally serious', shunning balls, masquerades, the theatre, card games, gambling, and gossip.[38] They were also expected to shun conspicuous consumption and spend their time and money in a tasteful manner. Orr notes that due to expansions of the physical and conceptual boundaries of the English court in the eighteenth, and then

---

[33] Norton, p. 109.
[34] Nash, p. 6.
[35] Orr, p. 9.
[36] Orr, p. 9.
[37] Orr, p. 9.
[38] Orr, p. 39.

in the nineteenth centuries,[39] private retirement became important to the London-based aristocracy. Katherine Parr's retirement to the country after the king's death appealed to eighteenth-century aristocratic values that stressed the moral uprightness of a withdrawal to country life. In this sense, Katherine could be seen as someone who scorned the fashion, gossip, and idle games of the Tudor court. Again, such an image is based on an ideal: Thomas Seymour, Lord Rivers, and the Chandos family conducted public business and engaged in wide-ranging family politics from Sudeley. Samuel Rudder himself accepts this notion when he translates Katherine's Latin epitaph (composed by Dr Parkhurst, one of her chaplains) into comfortable English couplets of iambic pentameter:

> In this new tomb the royal Katherine lies,
> Flower of her sex, renowned, great and wise,
> A wife by every nuptial virtue known,
> And faithful partner once of Henry's throne;
> To Seymour next her plighted hand she yields,
> (Seymour, who Neptune's trident justly wields)
> From him a beauteous daughter blest her arms,
> An infant copy of her parents' charms.
> When seven short days this tender flower had bloom'd,
> Heaven in its wrath the mother's soul resum'd;
> Great Katherine's merit in our grief appears,
> While fair Britannia dews her cheek with tears;
> Our loyal breasts with rising sighs are torn,
> With saints she triumphs, we with mortals mourn.[40]

The ideal is tailored to fit the image of Katherine as a stoic Protestant dowager of the Imperial period rather than of her own time. Rudder goes one step further and uses iambic pentameter to connect the age of Henry VIII to the milieu of Shakespeare, and thus doubly emphasise the significance of Katherine's queenship. He knew the connections were peripheral at best: Elizabeth I was in her teens upon the death

---

[39] The court in Katherine Parr's time was for the most part limited to those who were in close physical or conceptual proximity to the king's body and/or the imperial power base, i.e., the aristocrats and political figures that inhabited London or who were related to the king. The late eighteenth/early nineteenth century court was larger and incorporated much more of London and its environs than before. More members of the aristocracy became urbanised, building townhouses and patronising galleries, theatres, and public locations in which one could see and be seen on a large scale. Buckingham Palace boasted the largest room in London because the Duke needed it. The court of the middle to late nineteenth century had an even longer reach. There were even more places in London in which the court could establish and assert itself, and the 'London Season' of the late Victorian era seemed to appropriate nearly all of London's fashionable districts for this purpose. See David Starkey, *The English Court* (London, 1987).

[40] Rudder, p. 720.

Fig. 12 Engraving by William Camden Edwards of Katherine Parr, after Hans Holbein the Younger; early nineteenth century. The engraving is highly interpretive, reproducing little of the sense of the older painting and showing Katherine as a nineteenth-century ideal of Protestant sobriety. Reproduction courtesy of the National Portrait Gallery, London.

Fig. 13 Anonymous portrait of Katherine Parr, oil on panel, late sixteenth century. Katherine is dressed in a lavishly embroidered scarlet gown, and her fingernails are buffed to a shine. Reproduction courtesy of the National Portrait Gallery, London.

of Katherine Parr, and Shakespeare had not yet been born; but Rudder chooses to telescope figures and events of the Tudor era together to construct a convenient Golden Age that complements his present time. Others did so as well: one of the best examples of the eagerness to associate Katherine Parr with late eighteenth-century (and early nineteenth-century) public virtues by telescoping her lifetime with those of influential persons of the Elizabethan/Jacobean era is an engraving of the early nineteenth century by William Camden Edwards (1777–1855) (Fig. 12). The engraving is loosely based on a sixteenth-century engraving by Hans Holbein the Younger. Edwards modifies the earlier engraving to create an image of Katherine as a Protestant heroine of the Puritan age as he imagines it. Gone are the lavish gown and jewels Katherine preferred in everyday dress; the engraving supplies a simple black dress and black and white headdress in a reimagined Puritan style. Here Katherine is remembered as an almost completely different person: someone who did not enjoy fine clothes or entertainments, who did not make conspicuous display or keep ill company. The serene-faced woman of the engraving is not the Katherine Parr who likely supported the dangerously outspoken Anne Askew, or who wore magnificent jewels daily, or who, in her most well-known portrait, wears her fingernails buffed to a shine (Fig. 13).

The group of ladies who went looking for Katherine in 1782 were likely familiar with George Ballard's book of biographies. Indeed, some of them may have owned a copy; Ballard was a fellow antiquary of Gloucestershire (Chipping Camden, about ten miles from Sudeley), and of the 400 subscribers to *Memoirs of Severall Ladies of Great Britain*, 143 were women. By the time the lead envelope was opened, the group of women already had an image of Katherine Parr in their minds, conceived from a combination of Tudor portraiture, biography, and, by way of things like Rudder's transcription of Katherine's epitaph in iambic pentameter, literature – as it refers to eighteenth-century Shakespeareanism. The ladies were prepared for a reading of the corpse that they hoped would validate their presumptions and expectations. What they got was a stunning visual affirmation of those presumptions: Katherine Parr's nearly uncorrupted face looked directly at them, eyes open, golden brown hair curling delicately around the face and neck.[41] The unique state of the corpse provided the women with a text of historical memory that came so close to their expectations it was uncanny: she appeared to be looking at them across the ages, validating their presumptions about who she had been and what she represented. As a well-embalmed and nearly uncorrupted corpse she did not appear dessicated or mummified, and she therefore did not communicate the same sense of exotic archaism that corpses inevitably communicate. The ladies who saw Katherine that day were able to read in her face the legacy of the sixteenth-century 'Protestant ladies' salon' as they imagined it: vibrant, innovative, indomitable.

The effect did not last long, however, for exposure to the air made the corpse turn colour almost immediately, and decomposition began straightaway.[42] Still, for the few moments

---

[41] Nash, p. 1.
[42] Nash, p. 3.

in which Katherine's face appeared strikingly lifelike, it reminded the ladies of the well-known belief that even in death a queen was viewed as a powerful and sacred extension of the body politic.[43] The entire culture that revolved around the body of a queen called for the ordinary functionalities of her physical body to be ritualised and reinterpreted for her sole benefit. This fact kept the queen distinct from all other women except saints and the Virgin herself, and established what Hilton calls 'her unique symbolic status', which amounted to a constant affirmation of power.[44] In 1782 that power was not the same as it had been in 1548. By the Georgian period, queenship had undergone significant changes (especially after 1660); namely, the sanctity of the monarchy had been reinterpreted into an idealised model of neo-Platonic philanthropy and respectability rather than piety.[45] When the female antiquaries looked into Katherine's (nearly) uncorrupted face, they saw the respectable coherence and neo-Platonic steadfastness and control they expected to see. They also watched that phenomenal text correct and revise itself before their eyes. Within minutes the colour of the face changed and the eyes dimmed, as the exposure to fresh air corrupted the remains of Katherine Parr's latent resoluteness.[46] That physical change was accompanied by the persistent intrusion of a horrible stench. The revised text of the corpse of Katherine Parr corrected the presumptions of the present and reminded those who were there that their connection to the past was not reciprocal. A contemporary age may have strong connections to the past, but at best the past has only marginal connections to the future. The text of the corpse revised itself in a refusal to acknowledge a connection to the eighteenth century that had never been intended by Katherine Parr herself.[47] If the antiquaries desired validation for their presumptions about Katherine via the corpse, they were denied the opportunity to do so with literality. They returned the body to its grave and left the site.

An incursion (or perhaps invasion) of the grave by a local farmer named Lucas (also called Locust) is recorded by Agnes Strickland in her biography of Katherine

---

[43] Hilton, p. 7.
[44] Hilton, p. 7.
[45] Orr, p. 2.
[46] Nash, p. 3.
[47] There were many examples of people who did in fact consider how (and by what means) their corpses would be viewed in the future. In Catholic Europe the practice of examining corpses for signs of incorruptibility continued; and the clerical elite, especially Popes, counted on these inspections for the canonisations they expected. Moreover, some orders of monks in Italy and France mummified their dead and displayed them in catacombs. In England John Donne imagined the disinterments of himself and his beloved in his poems *The Relic* and *The Funeral*. In both poems he expresses concern for the appearance of the corpses and how they will be interpreted by others. Moreover, the revenant tradition continued in both Britain and on the Continent; it held that those suffering a 'bad death' (such as before confessing their sins) would return to display their putrefying corpses to the community as a warning against dying in a state of sin. See *Death in England: An Illustrated History*, ed. Peter C. Jupp and Clare Gittings (New Brusnwick, NJ, 1999), Peter Marshall, *Beliefs and the Dead in Reformation England* (Oxford, 2002), Keith Thomas, *Religion and the Decline of Magic* (New York, 1971), and Robert Bartlett, *Why Can the Dead Do Such Great Things?* (Princeton, NJ, 2015).

Parr in *Lives of the Queens of England* (1844).[48] Writing two generations after the event and with the dramatic flair for which she is known, Strickland betrays an attitude reflecting her priority of class-consciousness over academic thoroughness. Drawing upon rumour, and after telescoping and combining events, and citing a third-hand account, she writes:

> The repose of the buried queen was again rudely violated by ruffian hands, in the Spring of 1784,[49] when the royal remains were taken out of the coffin, and thrown on a heap of rubbish, and exposed to public view. An ancient woman who was present on that occasion, assured my friend Miss Jane Porter, some years afterwards, that the remains of costly burial clothes were on the body, not a shroud but a dress, as if in life; shoes were on the feet, which were very small, and all her proportions extremely delicate; and she particularly noticed that traces of beauty were still perceptible in the countenance, of which the features were at that time perfect, but by exposure to the air, and other injurious treatment, the process of decay rapidly commenced. Through the interference of the vicar, the body was re-interred.[50]

The ancient woman (if she existed) is a convenient figure for Strickland. What she saw, or at least what she reported to the novelist Jane Porter (who was a friend of Strickland's), corresponds with Strickland's mid-nineteenth-century expectations about queenship and womanhood. Strickland's reading of Katherine Parr's corpse promotes the ideals of femininity expected of Victorian aristocratic women: the deceased queen is a figure of petite delicacy, dressed with an extravagance appropriate to her class and station. Here, the ancient woman's report – in whatever original form it was given (such as a letter or personal communication) – is translated by Jane Porter and then by Agnes Strickland into the language of Victorian values. The most important thing about this translation is that unlike the female antiquaries, neither Miss Porter nor Miss Strickland has seen the original source text represented by Katherine Parr's corpse. A communication of language and of meaning is made without firsthand knowledge of the original source. This aspect of Strickland's interpretation of the second disinterment is evident in inclusion of the detail (provided by Porter) that the Ancient Woman looked for traces of Katherine's original youth and beauty in her decayed face. By the middle of the nineteenth century queenship was linked strongly to ideals of femininity

---

[48] Nash makes quick mention and no analysis of this event.

[49] Discrepancies between Strickland's account and Nash's suggest that Strickland is wrong about the date of 1784 and may be referring to a later disinterment of the body (see below). She also may be over-dramatising. In any case, Nash does not record that the body was in a state of disarray or dishevelment but that the body was almost wholly encased in the lead envelope, with the exception of the face and left hand. In a secondary reference to the event, Strickland simply states that Lucas and his party looked at the body and returned it to the ground. Strickland, *Lives of the Queens of England* (London, 1840–4), vol. V, p. 140.

[50] Strickland, vol. V, p. 140.

and motherhood as exemplified in Queen Victoria, who seemed to reflect strength, delicacy, authority, and submission all at once to those who admired her. In this sense, Katherine's body is 'rudely violated by ruffian hands' that probe the aristocratic body too closely. The 'ruffians' are corrected by the vicar, who demands that the body be returned to its place of rest. In Strickland's hands Katherine's body becomes a text of utter propaganda involving each of the three estates in antagonism with the others.

The Rev. Treadway Nash encountered a different situation – indeed, a different text – when he excavated the gravesite in 1786, four years after the first disinterment.[51] He approached the site with academic reserve and treated the corpse like an historic document. He perceived the very *deadness* of the Tudor age in Katherine's face, because she was by then partly skeletonised and appeared to be more of an artefact than a person. Yet, when it came to the rest of her body, Rev. Nash perceived her remaining regal dignity. He observed her left hand through the cut in the lead envelope that had been made four years earlier, but he did not open the rest of the envelope to observe her body. To do so, he said, would have been indecent, disrespectful to the sanctity of the royal body, in life and in death.[52] In her body, clad as it was in an embroidered gown, Nash saw an extension of the king's body and the splendour of the Henrician court. He did not wish to violate it. Instead he assumed the body to be 'perfect',[53] sketched those parts of the corpse that were visible, or readable, to him, and left the rest unread. Nash's presumption of meaning is telling in his use of the word 'perfect' to describe the corpse. Based on his sketch and his detailed description of the body (which shows the corpse wrapped in its cerecloth with only the face and left hand exposed) Katherine's physical state does not reflect perfection – at least not in the present-day sense. Her eyes, having dried up since the first disinterment and exposure to the air, had sunk into their sockets and the cartilage of her nose had disappeared almost completely. Her lips had shrivelled considerably, exposing the few teeth that still clung to the jawbone. Her left hand is described by Nash as being 'of a brownish colour' – obviously desiccated and far from a lifelike state.[54] By using the word 'perfect' to describe the parts of the body he felt unworthy to see, Nash effectively summarises the rest of the text of the corpse and presumes its meaning. He reverently presumes the past – and namely the Tudor era – to be a time long past but yet preserved in an excellent state, corrupted only slightly by time but with its dignity intact. In this sense, memory is made to serve presumption, causing Nash to attempt to remember a text he has not read. He does so for the sake of the larger sense of memory for that text. The text with which he is faced is hidden beneath the cerecloth; but it is supported by hundreds of other texts that laud the sixteenth century as a well-preserved Golden Age. For Nash this means that reading the original text is unnecessary, even if he risks error by not reading it. Katherine's corpse represents a presumptive *Ur*-text that has been

---

[51] Nash mentions the 1784 opening of the grave but does not provide detailed comments. He does not report that the body was in a desecrated condition.
[52] Nash, p. 3.
[53] Nash, p. 3.
[54] Nash, p. 3.

complicated by analysis, criticism, and adaptation. Before the initial discovery of her body in 1782, Katherine Parr's corpse had last been read by the chief architects of her funeral: Miles Coverdale and Lady Jane Grey. They approved of her burial in an embroidered gown rather than a shroud, and they constructed the simplicity and innovation of a first-ever English Protestant funeral around that spectacularisation of the queenly body. They had to have been aware of the contrast of the lavish presentation of the corpse and the simplicity of the funeral service; and they were certainly aware of the complexity of her dowager status, especially since she had borne a child, but not by the king. They were aware that she was a controversial, but innovative figure. If anything can be presumed, it is that they understood that they lived in a time marked by complexity, controversy, and change. Nash avoids discussion of this idea in favour of a more stereotyped view of the Tudor era via the same body. Nash communicates to the subscribers of *Archaeologia*, nearly all of whom are fellow antiquaries, that the unseen corpse is 'perfect' because his presumptions about Tudor regality and English Protestantism are idealised. As an original source – a text in its own right, the corpse is unimpeachable *because* it has not been read rather than in spite of that fact.

With perhaps more care than in 1784, Katherine Parr was once again returned to her grave. However, in an addendum to his record of 1786, Rev. Nash reports that six years later Katherine's body was once again disinterred, this time with much rough handling and very little respect. He writes, 'At the commencement of the year 1792, the remains of the Queen were again exhumed by a set of bacchanalians, when outrages so disgraceful were perpetrated, that a veil must be drawn over them'.[55] Once again Nash accepts the mystique of the royal body and refuses to describe that which he deems unfit to be seen, whether by himself or others. He literally veils the body with a pall of deference. Strickland is also vague on the issue of what occurred in 1792,[56] but it is apparent that grave robbers pilfered various body parts, particularly teeth, fingers, and hair, and sold them as souvenirs. It also seems that the unnamed men charged curiosity seekers a nominal amount to view the body, and for a further sum allowed them to take away other tokens, such as parts of the dress or adornments on the corpse. When the men were finished (or when they were forced to stop), it appears that they simply threw the body back into the ground, upside-down and without placing it properly within the cerecloth. In the end, the embroidered dress and shoes were gone, and Katherine's body was reduced to a pile of bones, lying in a heap. The souvenir hunters read the body as a text of commodity, a record of the glories of the Tudor age and a veritable catalogue of the value of its parts and accoutrements. They saw, quite literally, a pricing list for teeth, locks of hair, finger bones, and pieces of a queen's dress. That pricing list was applied to a ready market for collectors and the curious, some of whom had likely never read a word by or about Katherine Parr, but who were eager to have a piece of the age of Henry VIII. Scenes like this were greatly feared by late eighteenth-century antiquaries

---

[55] Nash, p. 41.
[56] Strickland is wrong about the date; she claims the event occurred in 1784.

who struggled against the stereotypes of tomb robbers and dealers in macabre ephemera that were often foisted upon them by 'serious' academics. In the 1790s antiquarianism was not yet associated with the exotic dignities of Egyptology and the competitive peculiarities of collecting, as it would be a half century or more later; in 1792, Nash and his contemporaries still fought against cartoonish images of antiquaries poring endlessly over epitaphs in old churches and nicking valuable manuscripts from others' libraries.[57]

A fourth and final disinterment for Katherine Parr occurred in 1817, one which, twenty years after the disgrace of the desecration of her grave, was conducted with an antiquarian interest similar to Nash's.[58] This examination of the corpse precedes the final interment of the bones. It is recorded in a mid-nineteenth-century guidebook for Sudeley Castle, which states, 'In July 1817, another examination took place, which had more the plea of antiquarian research to justify it. Nothing more remained in the coffin but a confused heap of bones, and a small portion of the hair.'[59] The fact that the skull remained is remarkable, but perhaps not as remarkable as its presentation. Because the corpse lay in the bare ground, set apart from what remained of the cerecloth, seeds and shoots grew among the bones. One branch of ivy had wound around the dome of the skull several times in a circlet, forming a natural coronet around the temples – a simple parenthetical element that inserts new, albeit non-essential meaning into the text of the corpse. The scene is dramatised by Strickland in her reference to the event. She calls the ivy wreath 'a green sepulchral coronet',[60] and suggests (or perhaps insists) that nature itself replaced the identifying markers of regality that were stolen from the queen's body. This time the corpse was interred definitively, by Rev. I.J. Lates, rector of Sudeley, who, '...with a view to the better preservation of the few remains, and to secure them as much as possible from future indecent disturbance, caused the coffin to be removed from the open grave in the ruined chapel, into a fine stone vault, in which are deposited the remains of George, 6th Lord Chandos, in the small chapel adjoining, and which was then very carefully and securely closed.'[61] There was little, if anything, left of the text of the corpse, and what remained was an account of defilement no one wanted to read. Only one textual note remained: the ivy circlet, whose presence indicated the words 'queen' and 'crown', words that were once proclaimed by the corpse, but which now could only be inserted parenthetically: (queen); (crown).

Despite the interment of Katherine's remains into a secure vault, there was an opportunity for one more hand to reach into the grave and withdraw a keepsake artefact, one which, many years later, was sent to Agnes Strickland for inspection. Strickland writes, 'A lock of hair which was taken from the head of Queen Catherine Parr, after it had lain in the dust and darkness of the grave for nearly two centuries and

---

[57] See the front cover illustration of this book for an aquatint depicting this stereotype.
[58] J. Okell, *A Brief Historical Account of the Castle and Manor of Sudeley, Gloucestershire, Including Curious and Interesting Particulars Relative to Queen Katherine Parr* (Tewkesbury, 1844).
[59] *A Brief Historical Account*, p. 42.
[60] Strickland, p. 224.
[61] *A Brief Historical Account*, p. 42.

a half was kindly sent for my inspection by Mrs Constable Maxwell. It was one of the most exquisite quality and colour, exactly resembling threads of burnished gold in its hue; it was very fine, and with an inclination to curl naturally.'[62] The adoption of such a romantic notion by Strickland just a few sentences after her condemnation of the pilfering of the grave in 1792 is striking. Despite the insistence by the Strickland sisters that their work was thorough and academic, Agnes Strickland's attitude in particular is informed by the romance of artistic and literary depictions of the Tudor era. Her language is dramatic, and her descriptions of historical figures are like portrayals of characters in a novel. One novel of the type whose style is reflected in Strickland's work is *Henry VIII and His Court; Or, Catherine Parr, A Novel in Two Volumes* (1865).[63] It depicts the marriage of Henry VIII and Katherine Parr with typical melodrama. In one scene, Katherine placates an enraged Henry, who has drawn up an arrest warrant for her on a charge of heresy:

> ...and as the King's hand stroked her cheek it was as though death was just then touching her, never again to release her ... She busied herself about him with officious haste; she put her arm tenderly on his shoulder and supported him; and properly arranged for him the gold chain which had slipped out of place on his doublet and playfully plaited the lace ruff which was about his neck.[64]

The distinctions between Strickland's 'history' and novels of this type (of which there were many) could indeed be slim; and similar sentiments were found in artistic depictions of Katherine during the Victorian era (Figs. 12 and 14). In contrast with eighteenth-century depictions of Katherine, these novels and artistic renderings show a vulnerable figure whose constitution is linked strongly to her feelings of love. Katherine's reinterpreted femininity is also found ironically in the decidedly masculine profession of Victorian architectural design. When Sir George Gilbert Scott was enlisted to restore the ruined St Mary's Chapel at Sudeley Castle in 1855, he drew upon romantic notions of the Tudor ideal to design the neo-Gothic chapel that exists today.[65]

Sudeley Castle's fifteenth-century design was enhanced by sixteenth-century additions made by Thomas Seymour when he acquired the castle upon the death of Henry VIII in 1547. The castle was heavily damaged during the Civil War and was uninhabitable until 1837, when it was purchased from the Chandos family by John and

---

[62] Strickland, p. 225.

[63] L. Mühlbach, *Henry VIII and His Court; Or, Catharine Parr: A Historical Novel in Two Volumes*, 2 vols., trans. Rev. H.N. Pierce (Mobile, AL, 1865), vol. II, p. 142.

[64] Mühlbach, pp. 116–17.

[65] Scott, a famed Gothic Revival architect, also designed the stable block at Sudeley. He is responsible for much of the neo-Gothic renovation in public and sacred spaces in Britain, namely parts of Westminster Abbey. He supervised the final interment of Katherine de Valois and designed her tomb in the Henry V chantry at Westminster Abbey. He is also the architect of the Albert Memorial.

Fig. 14 Engraving by William Henry Mote of Katherine Parr, mid-nineteenth century. This imaginative portrait depicts Katherine as a highly romanticised figure, and as more vulnerable than she appears in sixteenth-century portraits. Reproduction courtesy of the National Portrait Gallery, London.

William Dent. Upon purchasing the ruined castle, the Dents began restoring it, and together with the architect Harvey Eginton they conceived a veritable 'Tudor makeover' for Sudeley. The original parts of the castle were redesigned with a neo-Tudor design, which was enhanced with neo-Gothic flourish. The architectural design of Sudeley was therefore made to conform to the Victorian imagination about the era of Henry VIII. The castle's Medieval history and its Civil War history were downplayed architecturally so that Sudeley would stand in the Cotswolds as a living tribute to the Tudor era specifically. Moreover, the Dents purchased a large amount of Tudor furnishings, works of art, and ephemera from the famous sale at the Strawberry Hill home of noted antiquary and collector Horace Walpole in 1842.[66] The Dents literally overwrought Sudeley with *Tudorism*,[67] inside and out. That effort extended to St Mary's Chapel. Scott constructed a chapel that was not only meant to enhance the castle's reimagined

---

[66] Walpole's Strawberry Hill house was itself an eighteenth-century neo-Gothic confection made up of various elements of Gothic cathedral designs. It became the literary model for Dr Frankenstein's castle in Mary Shelley's *Frankenstein*. The catalogue for the 1842 sale is now held by the Lewis Walpole Library, Yale University.

[67] For the coinage of this term, see *Tudorism: Historical Imagination and the Appropriation of the Sixteenth Century*, ed. Tatiana String and Marcus Bull (Oxford, 2011).

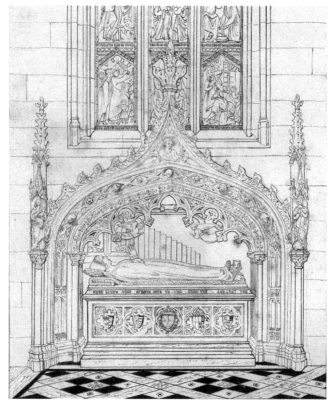

Fig. 15 Plan for the tomb of Katherine Parr by George Gilbert Scott, mid-nineteenth century. The plan reflects Scott's talent for neo-Gothic architecture and design. Photo reproduction courtesy of Sudeley Castle Archives.

Tudor identity, but was also meant to announce and extol the presence of Katherine Parr as Sudeley's most famous (albeit deceased) resident. The restoration of the chapel was completed in 1863, with a new tomb for Katherine Parr as the crowning element of the interior design. Scott designed a neo-Gothic canopy tomb that referenced various aspects of typical Gothic tomb designs in Britain and on the Continent, but with more flourish and with a more delicate, almost lacy construction than that found in genuine Gothic tomb design (Figs. 15 and 16). In a word, the tomb was *ladylike*, with its marble canopy pointing to the graceful strength that a queen in the middle part of the nineteenth century was expected to have. Upon its completion in 1863, the tomb was topped with a recumbent marble figure of Katherine by John Birnie Philip. The figure is much like other artistic depictions of Katherine that show her dressed simply, in a reimagined 'Tudor' style more akin to Victorian tastes in style than to the actual Tudor dress in which she was buried.

Fig. 16 The tomb of Katherine Parr, Sudeley Castle, Gloucestershire. The figural monument is depicted wearing clothes of a later period and of a more plain style than those favoured by Katherine. Photo reproduction courtesy of Sudeley Castle Archives.

The figural monument does more than reimagine Katherine's virtue in relation to her style of clothing and her demeanour; it reimagines the body itself. It restores the sense of wholeness that was apparent at the first excavation and that was completely destroyed by the time of the last disinterment. It reproduces the facial features, plump skin, and articulate limbs not only of the person who once lived (as all figural monuments of the dead do), but also of the figure who once *died*. The legacy of Katherine's well-preserved condition upon the grave's first excavation is informed by a reading of the restorative sense of the tomb figure. The figure presents the visitor to the tomb with a replacement text for that of the body, which can no longer be read. This new text seeks to reproduce the old one and congratulates itself for its accomplishment, albeit its success is quite limited. The new text of the body is impervious to the progression of time, but it seeks to be impervious to the past as well. It overwrites the text of the body of Katherine Parr. Sepulchral monuments perform remembrance, not only for the legacy of the person buried within the tomb, but for his or her actual body – the visitor is invited to remember the deceased in a state of wholeness. In addition to being an exercise in remembrance, Katherine's Victorian tomb also represents an act of forgetting. With its unfortunate, desecrated remains locked away in the Chandos vault nearby, the figural monument replaces the corpse – and the narrative of its desecration – with a nineteenth-century narrative of an aristocratic tomb as a proclamation of wealth, power, and indomitability. The new tomb locates the text of the corpse in the narrative of Victorian neo-Gothic architectural design. It parallels the continuous rewriting of Katherine's life in the two and half centuries after her death that casts her variously as a defiant Reformer, a bluestocking, a Puritanical matron, or a vulnerable woman in love.

John Birnie Philip adds to this act of forgetting with the finality of the figural monument. It is another text imposed upon the body, not merely changing but *forgetting* the earlier, more authentic text because that text no longer functions as a satisfactory agent of national memory. Today, the tourist narrative at Sudeley Castle is one of poignant remembrance. It revolves almost exclusively around the death, burial, and interment of Katherine Parr as a sort of romantic tragedy spanning life and death; most tourists visiting Sudeley are there to see the tomb and hear the story of Katherine's postponed marriage to Seymour, the birth of her longed-for child, her untimely death, and her unfortunate disinterments. But in the mid-nineteenth century, Katherine's *post mortem* narrative was problematised by suspicions about antiquarian motives and stories of horrific desecrations. The text of her corpse was corrupted even as it was probed for authenticity. The situation required the permanence of a deliberately constructed sepulchral memory whose primary task was the performance of forgetting. At the time, the newly renovated chapel and tomb spoke to the concerted effort by traditionalists to direct the narrative of a hybrid Tudor/Victorian monarchic power, dynastic continuity, and Anglo-Protestant supremacy into the future.

7

A SURFEIT OF INTERPRETATIONS

William Shakespeare

No one dares disturb the grave of William Shakespeare. There is, after all, a curse upon those who would violate the bones that lay under the chancel of the Church of the Holy Trinity in Stratford-upon-Avon. On that subject Shakespeare made himself perfectly clear:

> Good friend, for Jesus' sake forbear
> To dig the dust enclosed here.
> Blessed be the man that spares these stones,
> And cursed be he that moves my bones.[1]

Despite such a warning, some admirers of Shakespeare during the eighteenth century and continuing into the nineteenth, expressed dissatisfaction with his gravesite at the Church of the Holy Trinity. They also expressed dissatisfaction with his burial location at Stratford, and with his memorial, including the lines of the epitaph on the grave and the bust that hangs on the wall above it. Periodically, that dissatisfaction developed into a proposal to forgo the curse and move Shakespeare to the more 'fitting' burial space of Poets' Corner in Westminster Abbey, where he would lie near Chaucer, Spenser, Jonson, and Dryden. For this idea there was a precedent: William Basse expressed the sentiment very early on. In his elegy 'On the Death of William Shakespeare' (before 1623), Basse implores Spenser and Chaucer to make room for Shakespeare in Westminster Abbey by volunteering their own bones for removal:

> Renowned Spenser, lie a thought more nigh
> To learned Chaucer and rare Beaumont, lie
> A little nearer Spenser, to make room
> For Shakespeare in your threefold, fourfold tomb.[2]

[1] Gravesite epitaph of William Shakespeare. Church of the Holy Trinity, Stratford-upon-Avon, United Kingdom.

[2] The poem was attributed to John Donne for many years, but is now identified as Basse's. It is printed variously, but most recently, in Brandon Centerwall, 'Who Wrote Basse's Elegy on Shakespeare?' *Shakespeare Survey* 59 (2006): 267–84.

Ben Jonson held the opposite opinion, answering Basse's view in his dedicatory poem to Shakespeare (which was printed in the First Folio of 1623), and arguing that Westminster Abbey's famous dead would overshadow Shakespeare:

> My Shakespeare, rise; I will not lodge thee by
> Chaucer or Spenser, or bid Beaumont lie
> A little further to make thee a room:
> Thou art a monument without a tomb.[3]

For many, it was not enough that Jonson should make such a statement, nor was it enough that Shakespeare's sonnets (especially 18, 55, 71, and 81) appeared to support his apparent assertion that his work should be his best monument. Shakespeare's burial place, its location at Stratford, and the issue of whether Shakespeare's tomb was a fitting monument to his memory, continued to fuel discussion among authors, scholars, and actors. During the eighteenth, and continuing into the nineteenth century, a continuous expression of dissatisfaction with Shakespeare's burial place produced discussions about death, memory, nobility, empire, and even scientific inquiry. Dissatisfied with the way Shakespeare was being remembered, yet unable (or unwilling) to move his body, some of his admirers over the course of the period 1700–1900 reimagined and reinterpreted Shakespeare's death and burial. Their varied efforts are reflected in the construction of Shakespeare's 1740 monument in Westminster Abbey, in the so-called *bardolatry* generated by the Bicentenary Jubilee, in literary and artistic appropriations of the dead playwright's persona, and even in phrenology and natural history. Their intention was to reproduce and re-experience Shakespeare's death and burial in a manner that would produce for them a sense of completion, and would validate a sense of national identity, of *Englishness,* with which they felt comfortable.

This dissatisfaction begins in a rather unassuming place: a simple slab on the Chancel floor of the Church of the Holy Trinity, with a short epitaph written upon it. Many who visited the grave in the two and a half centuries after Shakespeare's death simply refused to associate the simplicity of the verses with Shakespeare's literary genius. They dismissed the quatrain as mere doggerel, assuming in many cases that the epitaph was not written by Shakespeare at all, but by a poet of lesser talent. Desiring for the epitaph to reveal hidden truths about a man of which they knew little, many tourists, scholars, and lovers of the theatre refused to take the epitaph at face value: as an appeal to the churchwardens not to remove to the charnel house the bones of a

---

[3] ll. 6–9. Interestingly, Jonson himself was not buried in Poets' Corner, but elsewhere in Westminster Abbey; legend has it that he felt himself inferior to the other poets buried in the South Transept. Whatever his reason, it was not good enough for his own admirers. During the eighteenth century, a monument to Jonson was erected in Poets' Corner (designed by Gibbs and executed by Rysbrack). Rather than moving his remains, as Chaucer's admirers had done, Jonson's admirers erected a monument where they thought he should be interred within the same church. In that sense, Jonson is 'twice buried' in Westminster.

titleholder who had provided for the chancel in which he was buried.[4] In his study of Early Modern epitaph writing, Scott Newstok addresses this issue. He writes, 'Such disappointment arises from the apparently shallow sincerity of the epitaph's limited charge of preventing [Shakespeare's] bones from being moved to the charnel house; readers yearn for a more profound sincerity, a "deeper" meaning that would somehow be satisfied by a penetrating analysis of the two couplets'.[5] During the period 1700–1900, there were several published efforts that argued that the Shakespeare epitaph held some kind of encrypted message that, when decoded, would reveal the deepest secrets of Shakespeare's personal and professional lives. Among them are *The Tomb of Shakespeare, A Vision*, by John G. Cooper (1755); *Shakespeare's Bones* by Clement Ingleby (1883); *Is It Shakespeare's Confession? The Cryptogram in His Epitaph* by Herbert Janvrin Brown (1887); *The Take of the Shakespeare Epitaph* by Edward Clark (1888); and *William Shakespeare, of Stratford-on-Avon, His Epitaph Unearthed* by Scott Surtees (1888). Such readings and interpretations of the epitaph have more to do with the desires and sensibilities of the authors of these books than with those of Shakespeare; still, they reveal a resistance to letting the matter rest. These authors all communicate the same message: if they could not disturb the bones to find the truth, they felt they could (and indeed *should*) decode the epitaph to 'get a better look' at the man under the floor. It is a textual, figurative effort to resolve unfinished business, an effort that parallels and mimics disinterments where the body is viewed and interpreted literally.

Admirers of Shakespeare possess, as Stephen Orgel puts it, 'a fairly special notion of drama', which arises as the result of the admirer's cumulative understanding of Shakespeare through the study and performance of his work.[6] This notion produces the idea that Shakespearean drama is exclusive and exceptional. One effect of this Shakespearean exceptionalism is that the admirer, whether he or she is an actor, scholar, or aficionado, imagines him or herself to be in a sort of collaboration with Shakespeare. This sense of collaboration indicates an imagined interactive relationship with Shakespeare both on and off the stage.[7] It allows the enthusiast – the *bardolater*, to use an eighteenth-century term[8] – to feel entitled to a shared understanding of Shakespeare's body of work, and in this case, of his body in death. The enthusiast seeks to validate his or her admiration of Shakespeare's life and work by reimagining the playwright's death, and in doing so attempts to establish a theatre of remembrance in which Shakespeare's life is performed continuously as a drama in and of itself. In this construction the performance of memory is not centred on the stage, but rather in the town of Stratford, where even to this day tourist imagination performs memory in the actual burial place. Westminster Abbey becomes a second (albeit not always secondary)

---

[4] Schwyzer, *Archaeologies of English Renaissance Literature*, p. 119.
[5] Scott Newstok, *Quoting Death in Early Modern England* (New York, 2009), p. 163.
[6] Stephen Orgel, *Imagining Shakespeare* (New York, 2003), p. 9.
[7] Orgel, p. 9.
[8] In the twenty-first century such admirers might be called 'super fans', or 'Shakespeare geeks'.

place of reenactment via the visual sign of a lavish monument as an ersatz location of Shakespeare's body. Both forms of theatricality seek to redefine the burial space and replace dissatisfaction with comfort.

These forms of theatricality create fictions of the dead. Attitudes toward commemoration that develop into reimagination generate a host of fictions regarding the relationships between the living and the dead, between public and private spaces, between sacred and secular spaces, and between history and fantasy. Sentimentalism is at the heart of these fictions. Shakespeare's lifetime, in particular the Elizabethan years, is heavily sentimentalised – even to the extent that it overshadows the reign of James I, who was monarch for the most successful years of Shakespeare's career, and who was his patron. As an icon of the Elizabethan period, Shakespeare himself is sentimentalised into fiction, even in death. This fantasist energy causes the language of memory, indeed the text of remembrance, to be inscribed upon Shakespeare's body in addition to the *corpus* of his work. As his admirers reimagine and reenact his death and burial, Shakespeare's body of work is overwritten onto his actual body. In this way the collaborative relationship between Shakespeare, his work, and those who wish to remember him is preserved; Shakespeare is marked as belonging to those who remember him, and his very body is appropriated as an agent of English thought and culture. With the playwright's body objectified in this way, Shakespeare in death becomes an object of fetish even though his body cannot be seen. Marjorie Garber argues that the fetishism of Shakespeare's life and work stems from a desire to return to an original sense of text and performance, to become close to the Bard as never before, and to renew that desire and repeat the effort continuously.[9] The fetishism of Shakespeare's body in death goes one step further: it relies upon a fascination with death to renew the desire to return to an original or perhaps genuine sense of his *person*. In this sense, Shakespeare can be 'known' by revisiting, either literally or imaginatively, the locus of his body, and the admirer can return to a place to which he or she has never been.[10]

By the eighteenth century, Stratford-upon-Avon was the centre of literary tourism in Britain, and its popularity was due largely to those who returned time and time again, trying to 'find Shakespeare' in the town. Londoners who made the trip to Stratford were charmed by its quaintness and quiet streets; they imagined the Bard composing masterpieces on the banks of the Avon; they paid to see New Place, and the Birthplace; and they bought, often with tongue in cheek, souvenirs made from the wood of the fabled mulberry tree. But the Church of the Holy Trinity was hardly as impressive as Westminster Abbey, and Shakespeare's gravesite could not compete with the monuments in that magnificent holy place. The reality of Stratford did not always agree with what Aaron Santesso calls the 'tourist's conception' of a cultural

---

[9] Marjorie Garber, 'Shakespeare as Fetish', *Shakespeare Quarterly* 41, no. 2 (Summer 1990): 243.

[10] Garber's argument is rooted in Freudian theory. Garber, p. 243; see also Sigmund Freud, 'Fetishism', *The Standard Edition of the Complete Psychological Works of Sigmund Freud*, 23 vols., ed. James Strachey (London, 1966), vol. XXI.

centre, meaning that Stratford tourists began to demand that the memorialisation of Shakespeare match their expectations and correspond to their feelings.[11] Thus began a rivalry between Stratford and London concerning an 'appropriate' memorial location and monument design for Shakespeare. The ensuing dialogue proposed the disturbance of Shakespeare's bones, both figuratively and literally.

Central to determining the appropriateness for the new monument was the concept of 'greatness'. 'Greatness', as a character trait or as an attribute of family or dynastic reputation, pertains to status in both life and death. During the eighteenth century this concept was largely communicated through memorials to the aristocratic dead. Figural monuments described the high social rank in life of the individual buried at the location, but they also reflected the amount of esteem acquired by that person in death. As an aristocratic family grew in wealth and influence, its members included the dead in their demonstrations of self-celebration. Just as the building and expansion of manors and estates during the mid-eighteenth to early nineteenth centuries (such as Blenheim Palace in Oxfordshire,[12] Wentworth Woodhouse in Yorkshire, and Highclere Castle in Hampshire) celebrated the building and expansion of the status and memory of the families who lived there, so did the establishment and expansion of family sepulchral monuments and vaults celebrate the status and memory of the families who lay there. 'Greatness', in this sense, transcended status; it signified a measure of honour and rectitude that could only be found in the timeless moral superiority of the aristocracy as a group. For the patrons of sculptors and artists like Roubilliac, Scheemakers, Rysbrack, and others, figural monuments in churches and abbeys such as Westminster Abbey validated the social order within a sacred space of unimpeachable authority. In his poem 'A Night Piece, on Death' (1722), Thomas Parnell proclaims that English society in death remains divided into three levels: the poor, the 'half-ambitious' middle class, and the great.[13] Citing Parnell's poem, David Bindman and Malcolm Baker address the dissatisfaction with Shakespeare's Stratford grave that was felt by many of his eighteenth-century admirers. They state: 'In these terms, an anonymous burial was the mark of the poor and unregarded; a floor tablet indicated a member of the "middle race of mortals", while a large figural monument defined the dominant levels of society'.[14] By this logic, the most appropriate monument for Shakespeare would be one that proclaimed dominant social status and aristocratic 'greatness' for him. Although many aristocratic patrons of figural monuments were deeply sceptical

[11] Aaron Santesso, 'The Birth of the Birthplace: Bread Street and Literary Tourism Before Stratford', *English Literary History* 71, vol. 2, (Summer 2004): 386.

[12] Although Blenheim Palace was a gift from Queen Anne to the Duke of Marlborough, the home was completed, and later expanded, with the family's own money.

[13] Thomas Parnell, 'A Night Piece, on Death', *The Hermit. To which are Added, A Hymn to Contentment; Health, an Eclogue; and A Night Piece, on Death* (London, 1775), p. 22.

[14] David Bindman and Malcolm Baker, *Roubilliac and the Eighteenth-Century Monument* (New Haven, CT, 1995), p. 4.

about monuments erected by the bourgeoisie, an exception could be made in the case of Shakespeare. If Shakespeare could not be moved, he could be commemorated in a manner befitting his 'greatness': with an impressive figural monument. It would not be enough to provide a floor slab or a wall monument similar to the ones in Stratford; to do so would be to commemorate Shakespeare laterally in terms of status. The admirers of Shakespeare who commissioned the Westminster monument (led by Alexander Pope and including the Earl of Burlington, Dr Richard Mead, and Thomas Martin)[15] desired for Shakespeare to be elevated, both symbolically and literally, with a figural monument. Shakespeare's body could not be reinterred, but he could be translated socially in this way, his status elevated and ennobled.

The dedication engraved upon the Shakespeare monument by Scheemakers attests to the fact that the monument exists by public esteem. That esteem was linked to a steadily growing supposition of Shakespeare's greatness and its relation to the successes of the Empire. In viewing his talent as inborn, Shakespeare's devotees in Britain insisted upon his innate and distinctly *English* genius. It had been bestowed upon him by God for England's sake and benefit, and therefore Shakespeare's admirers in academia, the arts, and politics could argue in favour of a belated *pseudo*-aristocratic status for him. That being said, it was not easy to give Shakespeare what he did not have. Exceptions to accepted standards of nobility and to ideals of greatness were made for Shakespeare's sole benefit. Although he lived his early life as a member of the middle class and became a gentleman at the peak of his career, Shakespeare was a man about whom little was known. This fact proved to be useful. What little people knew about Shakespeare could be interpreted without reservation. Eighteenth- and nineteenth-century biographies of Shakespeare border on hagiographic in their portrayals of the playwright; and romantic novels of Shakespeare's life written in the nineteenth century are almost absurdly imaginative in their depiction of his creative process.[16] Books like *Shakespeare: The Poet, The Lover, The Actor, The Man: A Romance* by Henry Curling (1848), and *The Youth of Shakespeare, A Novel* (1846) and *Shakespeare and his Friends, or, The Golden Age of Merry England* (1838), both by Robert Folkenstone Williams, imagined that Shakespeare had not really been a glover's son of Stratford, a hardworking actor, a talented writer, and eventually a savvy theatre owner and director. Williams' novels argue that Shakespeare had been endowed with unique nobility by God as an accompaniment to his natural talent, and that he was destined to extend that nobility to England in order to enhance its greatness. The

---

[15] In addition to private funds, a public fund was raised by Charles Fleetwood of the Drury Lane Theatre, and John Rich of Covent Garden Theatre. It was common for figural monuments to be conceived and designed by committee, and for family members and well-wishers to donate funds.

[16] See especially Henry Curling, *Shakespeare: The Poet, The Lover, The Actor, The Man: A Romance* (London, 1848), and Robert Folkenstone Williams, *The Youth of Shakespeare, A Novel* (London, 1846), and *Shakespeare and his Friends, Or, The Golden Age of Merry England* (London, 1838).

issue of the translation of Shakespeare's *genius* to Westminster is therefore complex; as Bindman and Baker state, the Shakespeare monument does not merely reiterate his fame or assert social climbing on his part.[17] It is an ironic exercise in validation: of a valid reinterment without a body, and a valid celebration of nobility without an aristocrat. This is true of the time the monument was erected, and it was still true a century later when the novels by Curling and Williams were published.

The Shakespeare monument was in good company, for other figural monuments were erected to memorialise middle-class citizens around the same time. Indeed, during the eighteenth century, Westminster Abbey was transformed by the sheer number of figural monuments that filled the aisles and transepts of its great church. The vast majority of these monuments bore aristocratic names, but many of them represented wealthy commoners. Critics claimed that such monuments threatened to overwhelm the greatness of the aristocracy with spectacular materialism, and that there would soon be little distinction between those who were lauded in death for their nobility and those who congratulated themselves in death for their wealth. Those who conceived of the Shakespeare monument were concerned that the monument might make the Bard appear bourgeois; it was therefore not to be over-decorated or exaggerated, for that would negate the effort to emphasise greatness properly. It was necessary to make sure that Shakespeare was not counted among the 'wrong kind' of people.[18] The South Transept was the obvious place for the monument, as Chaucer, Spenser, and Dryden lay nearby, along with Beaumont, Drayton, and a growing host of others. Chaucer (who was buried at Westminster because of his status at court and his civil service in the reign of Richard II) had been reinterred during the sixteenth century by Nicholas Brigham, an effort that was supported by admirers and well-wishers who sought to commemorate the fame Chaucer had acquired in the century and a half since his death.[19] Spenser desired to be buried near Chaucer, and his interment subsequently established him as Chaucer's literary successor. Legend had it that John Dryden was placed in Chaucer's original grave as a laudatory gesture, making him a further successor to Chaucer. The increasing number of poets either buried or memorialised in the South Transept formed a cumulative effort to 'inherit' the greatness of the Father of English Poetry. It made sense that Shakespeare's monument should also establish him as a successor to Chaucer and a Patriarch of literature.[20]

---

[17] Bindman and Baker, p. 9.

[18] Bindman and Baker, p. 6.

[19] For a comprehensive discussion of the social and political issues contributing to the reinterment of Chaucer's remains, see Thomas Prendergast, *Chaucer's Dead Body: From Corpse to Corpus* (New York, 2004).

[20] Almost immediately after the construction of the Shakespeare monument in Westminster Abbey, a pedigree of sorts was indeed established for the playwright. David Garrick was buried nearby, and 'Poets' Corner' became established as an elite burial space for poets and playwrights, despite Shakespeare's corporeal absence rather than because of Chaucer or Spenser's corporeal presence.

The Shakespeare monument was meant, by its design and its placement, to argue in favour of a posthumous noble status for Shakespeare's reputation and also for his body. Shakespeare had been successful during his lifetime, but he had not been a 'new man' – ambitious or expedient – as many courtiers and hangers-on were. He was never knighted, and gave no indication of political interest outside that which was suggested by his plays. In his retirement he was comfortable, and lived out his twilight years as a prominent but not aspiring neighbor of Stratford. It is perhaps because of the understatement of Shakespeare's success that those who believe he deserved an ersatz aristocratic reburial in Westminster Abbey were so keen on the idea. What little was known about Shakespeare's life gave no indication of rakishness, as Marlowe's did, or political involvement, as Spenser's did. To his eighteenth-century admirers Shakespeare seemed to hold himself above such things; he appeared to embody virtues and hold values that a nobleman ideally was supposed to have. A 1775 poem entitled 'The Visitation' depicts the ghost of Shakespeare appearing to celebrated actor David Garrick. The ghost chides Garrick for producing extravagant stage adaptations filled with dances and music. In the poem, Garrick agrees that the performances are absurdly lavish, but protests that such performances attract the aristocracy to the theatre. He says, 'They in the Drama find no joys/But doat on Mimickry and Toys./Thus when a Dance is in my Bill/Nobility my Boxes fill'.[21] Unsatisfied with this explanation, the ghost of Shakespeare condemns the eighteenth-century aristocracy, claiming that in his day they had been far nobler. He laments, 'These Moths in Honor's sacred Flame/Noble in nothing, but in Name/Ah! How the Times are alter'd quite/Since last my eyes beheld the Light?/Then Nobles strove with noble Deeds/To cleanse the Land of all such Weeds'.[22] Poems like this one reflect the idea that Shakespeare was a champion of nobility for a bygone age; that he had a genuine understanding of the concept in life, and that he advocated for its ideals in death. Giving Shakespeare a knighthood posthumously was out of the question; his admirers could, however, give him a secondary burial fitting of someone in the elite group.

The importance of a figural monument, as opposed to a floor slab, wall plaque or monument with allegorical figures, is based largely on the relationship between the noble body in death and the monastic houses in which members of the aristocracy were interred.[23] Patronage of monastic houses was one of the ways the aristocracy built a substantial layer of social differentiation between themselves and the commons.[24] Aristocratic burials in monastic houses emphasised the idea of greatness in death by grouping ancestral interments together to demonstrate dynastic continuity; these

---

[21] Anonymous, 'The Visitation; Or, an Interview Between the Ghost of Shakespear and D-V-D G-RR-K, esq.' (London, 1775), ll. 91–4, in Maurice O'Sullivan, Jr, *Shakespeare's Other Lives: An Anthology of Fictional Depictions of the Bard* (Jefferson, NC, 1997).

[22] 'The Visitation', ll. 115–20.

[23] Danielle Westerhof, *Death and the Noble Body in Medieval England* (London, 2008), p. 34.

[24] Westerhof, p. 34.

groupings, supported by the family's ongoing patronage, established a continuous economic supremacy over other burials and maintained a close bond between the dynasty and the monastic order.[25] Danielle Westerhof says:

> Patronage could render visible the dynastic continuity of a social position, while maintaining the well-being of one's soul. Having close relationships with a monastic community offered the opportunity of exclusive burial while creating a focal point of familial commemoration, to which a monastery might oblige by creating a family genealogy, as for example at Llantony Secunda or Walden Abbey.[26]

Endowments for monastic houses created a culture of place for the aristocratic dead; for centuries the interment of noble bodies in monastic houses was used as a means to refine the concept of nobility and therefore disenfranchise non-aristocratic members of society who in life had accumulated enough wealth to compete with the aristocracy economically and politically.[27] By the eighteenth century, Westminster Abbey had become the premier monastic house for interment of the noble dead, although patronage and intercessions had long since stopped. The Abbey Church of St Peter stood as an assertion of royal and aristocratic authority in death as well as in life. Within this monastic space Shakespeare's monument was to be figural, large but not lavish, and it would stand amid noble graves and tombs, with endowments both public and private. Such a monument would reestablish and redefine the aristocratic ideal, with extraordinary irony: via a man who was not noble, whose body was not there.

Memorialising Shakespeare in Westminster Abbey while leaving his Stratford grave intact also indicates an imitation of aristocratic multiple burial, in which the heart or entrails of a nobleman might be buried in his homeland, while his bones are interred at the seat of the kingdom. Such burials gave aristocrats the opportunity to maintain a corporeal presence in their ancestral lands, and often included the establishment of a monastic house or parish church with the heart or viscera of the nobleman as a foundation upon which the family's dynastic continuity was based.[28] Burying the heart or other organs of a nobleman on his ancestral lands gave due respect to the land itself, and to his tenants who lived there. It also gave due reverence to the local clergy with whom he had dealt, and it gave benefaction to the church in which the part or parts were buried. In the case of a king for example, there might be multiple locations, with his heart and entrails buried in separate places, and his bones interred at his seat of power. Additional burial locations might be used if a nobleman died while he was away, or if he possessed lands outside his homeland; Richard Lionheart arranged for his heart to be buried in Rouen, his entrails to be buried in Châlus, and the rest of his body

---

[25] Westerhof, p. 69.
[26] Westerhof, p. 65.
[27] Westerhof, pp. 43 and 69.
[28] Westerhof, p. 82.

to be buried at Fontevrault Abbey.[29] In one unusual case, but one which connects the practice to one of the kings of Shakespeare's plays, the tomb of Richard II was treated as a proxy burial by the monks of Westminster Abbey while his whole body was still buried at King's Langley. Richard had commissioned a tomb for himself and Queen Anne for use at Westminster, but after his first burial at King's Langley only she lay in it. Still, the monks commemorated anniversaries and observances over his empty tomb for thirteen years as though the king, or part of him, were in it.[30]

The interment of the bones in a large church, cathedral, or monastic house kept the body of the nobleman near the centre of political power and influence. Furthermore, multiple burial provided a means by which the number of intercessory prayers on behalf of the dead could be increased, as devotions could be made in two or more locations. Aristocratic families could therefore maintain authority in death by way of a diverse corporeal presence, which was further regularised by clerical devotion. In this sense, the location of the heart or viscera of the nobleman is not considered a minor or secondary burial place; he is located completely, in both places. As Westerhof states, 'What is evident from the discussion of multiple burial is the clear separation of the body and the heart to represent different aspects of the aristocratic identity. The body was clearly viewed as a manifestation of the individual within the dynastic continuum and as a representative of the communal concept of nobility...'[31] The construction of Shakespeare's Westminster monument mimics this effort to provide a diverse locus for the body of the deceased. By translating his *genius* as a mystical medium for the *corpus* of his work the patrons of the monument achieved an imitation of an aristocratic multiple burial. Shakespeare's actual body would remain attached to his ancestral land in Stratford. His monument in Westminster Abbey would celebrate his greatness in London, the place where his career had flourished and the place that was presently the seat of British Imperial power. Both sites would provide opportunities for visitation and tribute, both secular and sacred.

The Bicentenary Jubilee (held three years late in 1769) shows how successful the imitation of aristocratic multiple burials was in Shakespeare's case. David Garrick's plans for celebrations at Stratford and Drury Lane recalled the long-held tradition of rivalry between an aristocrat's (or indeed, a saint's) burial site in his homeland and the site of his or her tomb or shrine.[32] Those who made the trip to Stratford in 1769, less than thirty years after the Westminster monument was erected, were aware of the fact that they were paying tribute to Shakespeare's body and homeland. They

---

[29] Westerhof, p. 82.

[30] Westerhof, p. 82. See also Paul Strohm, 'The Trouble With Richard: The Reburial of Richard II and Lancastrian Symbolic Strategy', *Speculum* 71, no. 1 (January 1996): 92.

[31] Westerhof, p. 87.

[32] See Johanne Stockholm, *Garrick's Folly; the Shakespeare Jubilee of 1769 at Stratford and Drury Lane* (New York, 1964); and Levi Fox, *A Splendid Occasion: The Stratford Jubilee of 1769* (Oxford, 1973); see also Anonymous, *Garrick's Vagary: Or, England Run Mad. With Particulars of the Stratford Jubilee* (London, 1769), for a contemporary account.

were aware that both his *genius* and the *corpus* of his work were commemorated in Westminster; but they were also aware that he had been memorialised in accordance with older traditions that located greatness within the context of aristocratic tradition and Imperial power. The word *bardolatry* emerged from the Jubilee phenomenon[33] because Garrick did his best to establish Stratford as a site of rural *pseudo*-pilgrimage, and London as a location for grand urban commemoration for the Empire's literary 'saint'. After the Bicentenary Jubilee, tourists poured into Stratford in far greater numbers than ever before, and many of them continued their honorific visitation to Shakespeare at Westminster Abbey. The suggestion of pilgrimage generated by their visit allowed tourists to experience the ceremonialism and ritualism that had been absent for over two centuries after the Reformers of the sixteenth century divested English religion of its pilgrimages and esteem for monastic houses.[34] The Westminster monument and the Bicentenary Jubilee aroused enthusiasm for traditional behaviours that had long been suppressed, but which were comforting nonetheless. When Garrick died in 1779 he was buried with great ceremony in Westminster Abbey in very close proximity to the Shakespeare monument. His large public funeral was a theatrical performance in and of itself, but it also served as a veritable second funeral for Shakespeare. William Shakespeare was eulogised and mourned almost as much as David Garrick was; Garrick had revived Shakespeare's work, and now Garrick's funeral revived death commemoration for Shakespeare. The funeral was a symbolic reenactment of Shakespeare's funeral for those who had not been alive to attend the first one. It replaced what had likely been a simple country funeral in 1616 with an urbanised public spectacle in 1779, and imagined for Shakespeare the type of funeral that a multiply-buried nobleman of the early seventeenth century might have had. Such imagination was certainly off the mark and was absurdly syllogistic; but as Aaron Santesso observes, tourists, pilgrims, and site managers conform sites of visitation to their imaginations until the site represents a 'false authenticity' manufactured for the purpose of meeting their expectations.[35] This is precisely what happened in the aftermath of David Garrick's funeral. Shakespeare was figuratively taken from his grave, translated, reburied, and memorialised in a grand style, creating a text of the corpse constructed of a false syllogism, but one that donned a mantle of authenticity in spite of itself.

To a great many who made assumptions about Shakespeare based on their interpretations of his plays, it was what the Bard would have wanted. Shakespeare's attitude toward the nobility in his plays appears to be deferential, even taking into

---

[33] For a comprehensive discussion of bardolatry, see Jack Lynch, *Becoming Shakespeare* (New York, 2006), and Stephen Greenblatt, *Will in the World* (New York, 2005).

[34] Without the practices of pilgrimage and intercession, aristocratic multiple burials diminished significantly after the Reformation.

[35] Santesso, 'The Birth of the Birthplace', p. 386; see also *A Careful Longing: The Poetics and Problems of Nostalgia* (Cranbury, NJ, 2006), for Santesso's discussion of literary nostalgia in the eighteenth century.

account his inclination toward favouring the ancestors of the current monarch, and his tendency to rely upon the tenuous claims of the Chronicles. As Catherine Canino states, Shakespeare was sympathetic to the aristocracy's sense of importance, relevance, and endurance, which is evidenced by his handling of the Oldcastle controversy, for example. The Oldcastle family took offence at the similarities they observed between the character Falstaff and their ancestor Sir John Oldcastle. Shakespeare adapted the character to distance the family's reputation from Falstaff's vulgar behaviour.[36] Shakespeare appeared to understand the intricacies of aristocratic lineage and their obligations to demonstrate allegiance and gratitude to their allies and their monarch.[37] Canino points to the history plays in particular, saying:

> They do not depict personas from the mythical past or the legendary past or the foreign past – they depict the progenitors and the consanguinity of the nobility of England. When the history plays appropriate identity, therefore, they are not only appropriating on the level of rank or status; they are also appropriating on the most deeply personal, evocative, and intrusive level of the family.[38]

Shakespeare's sensitivity was based on the realities of a playwright and theatre owner who relied upon the aristocracy for patronage. He might encounter them in London's great houses, in the environs of court, or in the theatre itself when they came to sit as privileged members of the audience.[39] As Shakespeare was transformed into an idealised figure and vaulted to an unprecedented position among poets, his relationship to the aristocracy was embellished by those who saw nationalist unity rather than problematic Tudor history proceeding from the plays.[40] Two centuries later, many aristocratic families took great pleasure in being associated with the characters in Shakespeare's plays. Shakespeare may have cast aspersion onto the Percys, or defamed the Oldcastles in the sixteenth century, but by the eighteenth and nineteenth centuries what was once defamation was now exotic appeal. The land disputes and wars between the houses of York and Lancaster were long over, and Britain was ruled by the houses of Hanover and Saxe-Coburg Gotha respectively. The Earls of Northumberland were created Dukes of Northumberland in 1766, and their relationship with the Hanoverians in the eighteenth century was certainly not the same as it had been with the Plantagenets in the fifteenth century or the Tudors in the sixteenth. By the eighteenth century the Percys were patronising the arts, serving in Parliament, and building lavish sepulchral monuments for themselves in Westminster Abbey.

---

[36] Catherine Grace Canino, *Shakespeare and the Nobility: The Negotiation of Lineage* (Cambridge, 2007), p. 2.
[37] Canino, p. 2.
[38] Canino, pp. 2–3.
[39] Canino, p. 2.
[40] Canino, pp. 2–3.

As an extension of the fantasist understanding of his life and work, Shakespeare was imagined to support the ideas of disinterment, reburial, and multiple burial that were used to maintain dynastic continuity, promote justice, and emphasise aristocratic 'greatness'. Interestingly, two of the kings closely associated with the idea appear as carvings on the Shakespeare monument itself: Henry V and Richard III. Shakespeare seems to have approved of the translation and reburial of Richard II in *Henry V*. He depicts the incident as a necessary step in the maturation of Prince Hal as he atones for the sins of his father and aids in the healing of the nation, saying, 'I Richard's body have interred anew;/And on it have bestow'd more contrite tears/Than from it issued forced drops of blood'.[41] Such healing allows the resentments created by the deposition and murder of Richard II to be suppressed long enough for the nation to enjoy Henry V's triumphant victory at Agincourt in Act IV. Henry V did in fact move the body of Richard II to Westminster Abbey in 1413, to give Richard a nobler place of rest than he had at King's Langley.[42] Although King's Langley was a respectable monastic house that was founded by Edward II, Henry V's choice to reinter Richard at Westminster was meant to remedy the dishonour Richard had suffered in being deposed.[43] The translation absolved Henry IV of interfering with Divine Right, and it the located the body of Richard II in an urbanised space appropriately close to the seat of power. Such an act was therefore auspicious for Henry V. The reinterment was a source of publicity for Henry V, what Strohm calls, 'a positive political stratagem',[44] for it kept Richard's corpse near the king's governing body, where agents of Henry V

---

[41] *Henry V*, IV.i.348–50. *The Norton Shakespeare*, ed. Greenblatt, et al. (New York, 2008).

[42] Raphael Holinshed, *Chronicles of England, Scotland, and Ireland*, 3 vols. (London, 1807–8). In the case of *Henry V*, Shakespeare prefers Raphael Holinshed's account of the translation of the body of Richard II to a popular story claiming that Richard had escaped from prison and lived out the remainder of his life among supporters in Scotland. Holinshed says that the Scots, '…untrulie write, that [Richard] escaped out of prison, and led a vertuous and a solitarie life in Scotland and here died & is buried (as they hold) in the blacke friers at Sterling' (3.13–14). Interestingly, Holinshed points to Richard's tomb at Westminster and its epitaph as proof that the story is false (3.15). Here, the existence of the tomb and epitaph serve as proof that Richard II is indeed interred there. It is an odd form of self-fulfilling verification, especially when Holinshed provides epitaphs for persons he considers deserving who do not have them, such as King John, Henry IV, and even Henry V himself (3.1040). See also Strohm, 'The Trouble With Richard', pp. 87–111.

[43] It was also meant to show that Richard was actually dead, for the reburial was accompanied by an extended public viewing of Richard's body in which thousands of Londoners viewed the corpse. Strohm, 'The Trouble With Richard', pp. 91 and 102. Shakespeare's use of the incident no doubt drew attention to the fact that Henry IV disinterred the body of Henry Hotspur after his death, and had him suspended between two millstones to prove that he was actually dead, an incident that goes unmentioned in I or II *Henry IV*. See Nicholas Harris, *A Chronicle of London from 1089 to 1483* (London, 1827), p. 88. The contrast between the two incidents suggested to enthusiasts that Shakespeare approved of disinterment when justice or atonement was concerned, but not where desecration or hubris was at the heart of the act.

[44] Strohm, p. 90.

could observe any visitation or devotion by Richard's loyalists at the tomb. At King's Langley such things might go unobserved or unreported.

Richard II was subsequently fictionalised by Shakespeare's play, and also in Westminster, via the famous portrait that hangs near his tomb. The haughty, overconfident fifteen-year-old king who was a legend of his own making is presented in contrast to the sombre tomb effigy that lies near it. Tourists visiting Shakespeare's monument could imagine the drama of *Richard II* as they gazed upon what appeared to be Richard before his deposition, and after – a dramatic demonstration of the power of fate. During the first half of the eighteenth century, a series of metal plaques was removed from the substructure of Richard's tomb, exposing the inner coffin. The inner coffin was easily opened by vandals who literally wanted a piece of one of Shakespeare's kings. Over the course of several years thieves and souvenir hunters removed bones and other items – someone even stole the dead king's mandible in 1766.[45] The remaining bones were inspected by two respected and well-published antiquaries: Sir Joseph Ayloffe, who at the time was Vice-President of the Society of Antiquaries of London, and Edward King, a prolific but controversial antiquary who eventually became President of that Society.[46] They examined the bones for signs of violence but found none. Richard was disinterred again by Arthur Penrhyn Stanley, Dean of Westminster, in 1871 and again examined for signs of violence.[47] This further examination meant to put to rest (literally and finally) apocryphal stories of violent murder that proceeded from centuries of rumour and that were immortalised in Shakespeare's play.[48] Dean Stanley oversaw the rearrangement of the bones in anatomical order, in a new subdivided coffin for their secure reinterment. George

---

[45] Aidan Dodson, *The Royal Tombs of Great Britain: An Illustrated History* (London, 2004), p. 72; also Arthur Penrhyn Stanley, *Historical Memorials of Westminster Abbey* (London, 1887), pp. 144–5. These and other sources suggest that much of the vandalism of various tombs in Westminster was carried out by schoolboys of the parish.

[46] King was accused of corruption in seeking his re-election to the Presidency of the Society. See J. A. Evans, *History of the Society of Antiquaries* (London, 1956).

[47] The coffins in the tomb were rotted through and partly collapsed. Among the materials found in the tomb were two copper crowns, a pair of iron plumbers' shears (probably used for the 1413 interment), the king's staff, two pairs of gloves, and fragments of a silk pall once used to cover the king's body. George Scharf, who sketched the remains, kept a few bone fragments, which he placed in a cigarette box and marked with the date (31 August 1871), and his initials, 'G.S.'. This item was lost for over a century until it was found in the National Portrait Gallery Archives in 2010; see www.theguardian.com/artanddesign/2010/nov/16/richard-second-national-portrait-gallery.

[48] The 1871 examination of Richard II found no signs of violence or poison. Another rumour about Richard's death claims that he had been starved to death, and such a murder would leave no marks. In his record, Dean Stanley references a switched-body theory stemming from the age of Henry V; that the body in the Westminster tomb was not Richard II but that of his chaplain, a man named Maudlin. There is no evidence for this theory and Stanley does not entertain it seriously. See Stanley, *Historical Memorials of Westminster Abbey*, pp. 144–5.

Fig. 17 Drawing by Sir George Scharf of the skull of Richard II upon its examination in 1871. Scharf also sketched what remained of Richard's brain, at the top left of the drawing. Photo reproduction courtesy of the National Portrait Gallery, London.

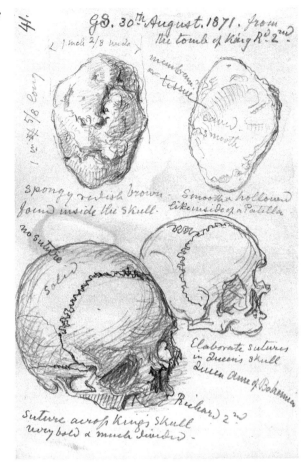

Scharf sketched the skull, inside of which was what remained of Richard's brain (Fig. 17).[49] Such was the power of the legacy of Shakespeare's work that it had a profound effect on antiquarian and scientific enquiry; both excavations sought in part to vindicate Henry IV and V, thereby validating Shakespeare's construction of heroism for those characters. Ironically, both excavations also established the posthumous, corporeal Richard as the sympathetic and tragic antihero of Shakespeare's play: a unification of corpse and text. Even in death Richard was in disarray, usurped, defeated, scattered. Richard's *body* was the Richard of the play, and putting things right was prudent because the corpse and the text of the play were inextricable.

To those attracted to such an idea, the face of Richard III on the Shakespeare monument suggested that Shakespeare also approved of the belated justice inspired by the issues of the play *Richard III*: the translation of the putative bones of the

---

[49] Eventually, Richard's mandible was returned in 1905, by the Rev. G.T. Andrews, whose great-uncle had been a schoolboy at Westminster in 1766 and had allegedly stolen it. Dodson, p. 72.

Two Princes from the Tower of London to Westminster Abbey. In 1674, workmen demolishing a staircase in the Tower of London made the discovery of the bones of two children in an elm chest, at around a depth of ten feet. At first the bones were thrown aside with rubble from the demolition; but the size and appearance of the bones[50] and their location (near the Chapel of the White Tower) led to speculation that they were the bones of Edward V and Richard, Duke of York.[51] King Charles II subsequently asked Christopher Wren to design a white marble container in which to house the bones in Westminster. They were interred in the Henry VII Chapel, near their presumed sister, Elizabeth of York.[52] The conspicuous marble ossuary stands as a symbol of Lancastrian triumph; it also stands as a form of poetic justice for those who knew the Two Princes best via their characterisations in Shakespeare's play. Tourists at the Henry VII Chapel could, by way of the ossuary, imagine the resolution of the issues of the play: the murders of the children appear to be avenged, and Richard's villainy appears to be foiled. Many were aware of the legend (now famously disproved)[53] of the fate of Richard's corpse, said to have been disinterred by

---

[50] The bones were mingled with traces of velvet cloth, which suggested their nobility.

[51] A number of accounts survive relating to the discovery of these bones. The following account, written on evidence presented by John Knight, Chief Surgeon to Charles II, was published in 1677: 'Upon Friday the ... day of July, An. 1674 ... in order to the rebuilding of the several Offices in the Tower, and to clear the White Tower of all contiguous buildings, digging down the stairs which led from the King's Lodgings, to the chapel in the said Tower, about ten foot in the ground were found the bones of two striplings in (as it seemed) a wooden chest, which upon the survey were found proportionable to ages of those two brothers viz. about thirteen and eleven years. The skull of one being entire, the other broken, as were indeed many of the other bones, also the chest, by the violence of the labourers, who ... cast the rubbish and them away together, wherefore they were caused to sift the rubbish and by that means preserved all the bones. The circumstances of the story being considered and the same often discoursed with Sir Thomas Chichley, Master of the Ordinance, by whose industry the new buildings were then in carrying on, and by whom the matter was reported to the King.' Repr. in A.J. Pollard, *Richard III and the Princes in the Tower* (London, 1991).

[52] The bones were disinterred and re-examined in 1933 by Lawrence Tanner, Westminster Abbey archivist, Professor William Wright, an anatomist, and George Northcroft, then president of the Dental Association. The bones were positively identified due to the fact that their size reflected the approximate ages of the princes, and that deformities of their teeth and of certain cranial bones suggested consanguinity (a common genealogical feature of royal families of the period). No present-day forensic examination has been made.

[53] In August 2012 archaeologists unearthed the corpse of Richard III on the grounds where Greyfriars Abbey once stood. The corpse lay buried in a hastily dug grave and bore no evidence of a shroud or coffin. It is still unclear as to whether there was ever a sepulchre above ground. The cause of death appears to be head trauma. Today, Richard III is interred in Leicester Cathedral, and the car park where his body lay for centuries is a visitors' centre where tourists can view a hologram of his bones. A host of books, articles, and television programmes tell the story. See The Grey Friars Research Team and Maeve Kennedy, eds., *The Bones of a King* (London, 2015), Matthew Morris, *The King under the Car Park* (Leicester, 2013), and *Secrets of the Dead: Resurrecting Richard III* (PBS Home video, 2014).

zealous Reformers as they demolished Greyfriars Church in Leicester in 1539. After tearing the evil Richard from his tomb, the Reformers were said to have thrown his hunchbacked body into the nearby Soar River. In the seventeenth century the antiquary John Evelyn reported a local story in Leicester that the sepulchre of Richard III was being used as a watering trough for horses, but this claim is unsubstantiated and unlikely.[54] These stories show the extent to which Richard's purported fate is connected to the popular image of Shakespeare as a hero of Protestantism by way of a dramatic, imaginative event illustrating the iconoclasm of the Reformation.[55] The story was embellished over time until it appeared that the play validated the story, rather than the story validating the play. For those who were most affected by these narratives, the location of 'The Two Princes' in Westminster Abbey performed an act of atonement for the interruption of dynastic continuity and the crime of murder; and that performance took place under the auspices of Shakespeare's *genius*, in the shadow of his monument.[56]

Ironically, creating such fictions did not involve much of a stretch of the imagination. The Tudors and Stuarts thoroughly fictionalised themselves in the Henry VII Chapel, using dynastic burials and conspicuous monuments to smooth over the controversies of their lives and reigns. Henry VII built the chapel, which changed the entire shape and layout of the Collegiate Church of St Peter. The large chapel proclaimed the supposed indomitable and enduring presence of the Tudors, and stood as a symbol of Henry VII's permanent victory over the Yorkists. Henry VIII paid for a lavish tomb for his parents to celebrate the establishment of a new dynasty and emphasise his parents' victory in the Wars of the Roses.[57] Elizabeth I and Mary I represented the tremendous oppositions of the Reformation, yet were commemorated alongside one another, beneath a large monument commissioned by James I. The Catholic Mary Queen of Scots had been displaced, imprisoned, and finally executed by Elizabeth, but was later endowed with an ornate tomb of unique beauty, also by James I, her son.[58] The two tombs reminded visitors that all three queens descended from Henry VII, and that despite the Reformation, Henry VIII's

---

[54] John Leland, *The Itinerary of John Leland*, vol. I, ed. Lucy Toulmin Smith (London, 1907), p. 15; and John Evelyn, '9th August 1654', *The Diary of John Evelyn*, ed. William Bray. 2 vols. (London, 1901), vol. I, p. 295.

[55] For further examples of how the legend of Richard III endured via the work and legacy of Shakespeare, see Philip Schwyzer, *Shakespeare and the Remains of Richard III* (Oxford, 2013).

[56] Other disinterments, such as the one in *Titus Andronicus*, also pointed toward Shakespeare's apparent 'support' for disinterment and reburial as a way to expose murder and dynastic interruption and ensure justice for the injured.

[57] Henry VIII himself chose to be buried at Windsor. He was buried next to his third wife, Jane Seymour, in a possible attempt to reestablish the Tudor dynasty with himself as progenitor. (See Chapter 5 and Fig. 9).

[58] Mary Queen of Scots was buried originally at Peterborough Castle, in a multiple burial. Her entrails are interred at Fotheringay Castle. In 1867 her tomb vault was opened to determine whether James I was buried within it. Although other members of the Stuart family were

six marriages, and a crisis of succession, little had been done to destroy the Tudors' dynastic continuity and Right. The tombs also validated James I as Elizabeth's rightful heir. Over the course of the seventeenth century other members of the Stuart dynasty were also interred in the Henry VII Chapel, in order to maintain dynastic continuity through the Tudors. Oliver Cromwell was buried in the Henry VII Chapel in 1658, reflecting his desire to become part of the fiction of the Tudors and Stuarts, and to validate his Protectorate as an extension of their legendary pedigree. In 1660 his effort was thwarted by Charles II, who had Cromwell disinterred so that the dynastic continuity of the Tudors and Stuarts would not be adulterated.[59] As Paul Strohm points out, dynastic burial is sometimes an exercise in the fiction of forgetting rather than the fiction of remembering. He says, 'Once a king's spirit is set down, its *dignitas* re-secured, the business, not of memory, but of forgetfulness can begin. Forgotten is the deposed king as the source of strident and unaccommodated demands. The memory that is tolerated is memory in its most narrowed and functional sense, with the king treated as a figure in a line of willing transmission and restored succession.'[60] Shakespeare's kings, their lives, stories, successes, and failures, became remembered largely through a reconstructed memory of Shakespeare. That reconstructed memory was represented materially by the Shakespeare monument in the same church where those kings were buried. This situation allowed the Shakespeare monument at Westminster to accomplish a performance of forgetting similar to that of the Henry VII Chapel: it encouraged the tourist or enthusiast to 'forget' that Shakespeare had not been a man of noble status.

The wide acceptance of the Shakespeare monument in Westminster after its completion in the eighteenth century did not ensure that Shakespeare was indeed resting in peace. In fact, in the century that followed, there continued a rivalry between Stratford and London in terms of which city was best for the celebration of Shakespeare's life, work, and death. As the Victorian era approached, so did that period's fascination with the very *greatness* of death and indeed, with what they supposed to be Shakespeare's *very great* death. Nineteenth-century discussions of Shakespeare's Stratford grave and London monument are characterised by an odd pairing of academic hubris and macabre romance. Many of those who belonged to Shakespearean appreciation societies and academic clubs wondered whether there were enough Shakespeare statues, monuments, and memorials in England. Interestingly enough, this sentiment flew in the face of Shakespeare's own ideas on the issue in Sonnet 55 ('Not marble, nor the gilded monuments/Of princes, shall outlive this powerful rhyme').[61] In looking for justification for the erection of a grand monument, many of Shakespeare's admirers ignored his emphasis on the undying nature of verse

buried in the vault, James I himself was found in the Henry VII vault. Alison Weir, *Mary, Queen of Scots and the Murder of Lord Darnley* (London, 2008), p. 509.

[59] For a discussion of the disinterment of Oliver Cromwell, see Chapter 8.

[60] Strohm, p. 103.

[61] ll.1–2.

as preferable to the transitory nature of stone and marble. In its self-published history of the Stratford memorial, The Council of the Shakespeare Memorial Association, for example, observed:

> Nothing is easier than to run down monuments, and to say that Shakespeare's works are his own monument; but the same argument will apply to any that was ever erected to any great man; and no one ever maintained that a Shakespeare memorial would be anything more than an expression of the sentiment which Shakespeare himself acknowledged when he described the Ruddock (or robin) as 'shaming those rich-left heirs that let their fathers lie without a monument'.[62]

Here, the members of the Council entertain the idea of the greatness of the noble body in death as it relates directly to the gratitude of the heirs the nobleman leaves behind. Their argument likens a lack of memorials to a neglect of the noble body. Frugality is an unsatisfactory virtue: the idea that a man's work is his memorial is refuted by a condemnation of the selfish attitudes of ungrateful heirs who refuse to spend money on a respectable memorial for their father by saying that memory of him is enough. The Council members, and others like them, felt that without sufficient statuary throughout the nation, and without sufficient money spent, England could not express its gratitude to Shakespeare in an appropriate way. The text of Sonnet 55 was negated by the Shakespeare Memorial Association and their supporters in favour of the text of monumental commemoration. Ideological interpretation of the body of Shakespeare's work, in reference to the memory of the actual corpse of the poet, contests and then overwrites the text produced by Shakespeare himself.

Arthur Penrhyn Stanley, Dean of Westminster and an esteemed Shakespearean scholar, was troubled by the fact that by the 1860s there was an absolute profusion of literary memorials and graves in Poets' Corner. Other names, faces, and in some cases bodies, threatened to overwhelm the Shakespeare memorial. Stanley favoured the exclusivity of Stratford and feared that if Stratford's country simplicity were neglected in favour of Westminster's urban appeal, Shakespeare might very well dissolve into a mere one among many. At the same time, Stanley was disappointed that so few tourists made the trip to Stratford in comparison to Westminster, favouring a visit to Shakespeare's memorial rather than to the playwright's actual grave. As Stanley catalogues the tombs and memorials in Westminster Abbey, he laments that Shakespeare's pen is 'mouldering away' in solitude in Stratford.[63] Using the word 'pen' as synecdoche for 'corpus' (and therefore corpse, in a double use of the device), Stanley envisions the pen of Shakespeare rotting away in a faraway gravesite, and imagines that Shakespeare must have attended the funerals of many of his contemporaries

---

[62] Council of the Shakespeare Memorial Association, *A History of the Shakespeare Memorial*, Stratford-upon-Avon, 2nd edn (London, 1882), p. 8.
[63] Stanley, *Historical Memorials of Westminster Abbey*, p. 330.

who, in his estimation, were of lesser talent.[64] His remark refers primarily to Spenser, who is buried near the Shakespeare monument in Poets' Corner. Citing the story that Spenser was buried with elegiac poems, and that his friends and fellow poets placed the pens with which they had written their tributes into the tomb, Stanley imagines that Shakespeare was (or perhaps should have been) also buried with poems and pens. Stanley pictures a more literary, and certainly more romantic funeral than Shakespeare likely had. In reimagining Shakespeare's funeral, he places himself at the heart of the fantasy as an attendee.

An essay entitled, 'The Enthusiast at Shakespeare's Tomb' by novelist Henry Curling (1841) creates a similar fantasy. In the essay, Curling sets out to view Shakespeare's tomb with two friends: one, a sea captain, the other 'a happy combination between the lunatic, the lover, and the poet'.[65] Upon seeing the Stratford gravesite, the poet imagines himself to be a phantasmic attendee at Shakespeare's funeral, saying, 'Methinks … I see at this moment his funeral procession advancing towards the church; the town hath cast her people out to follow him, "like Niobi, all tears"; the church, the "holy edifice", has not space sufficient to contain the mourning throng; they crowd amongst the very tombstones, and standing on Avon's banks, "Weep their tears into the stream"'.[66] Here, Curling's poet uses quotes from Shakespeare's own plays to narrate his dreamlike experience of viewing Shakespeare's interment as the final act in a grand drama, with the corpse of the playwright the drama's most tragic character.

Some discussions of the period reflect nineteenth-century forays into scientific enquiry. In these discussions the body of the dead man must be both celebrated and investigated in order to be commemorated appropriately. Doing so assures proper academic acknowledgment of Shakespeare's 'greatness'. Just as many of Shakespeare's eighteenth-century admirers sought to ennoble his body through the greatness of monument, many of Shakespeare's nineteenth-century admirers sought to do so via the greatness of scholarly investigation. Indeed, much of the nineteenth-century fantasist view of Shakespeare's death focuses on the physical body itself as the 'specimen' around which commemorative energy revolves. This attitude contrasts the eighteenth-century view, which uses the body as the 'subject' around which such energy revolves, with the tomb or monument used as an accompanying sign. In the nineteenth-century fantasist view the corpse as fetishised object becomes a 'specimen' for examination and analysis. Here, the 'specimen' is a representation of scientific fact, which, although it derives from an idea, ultimately transcends that idea. This issue is illustrated in a portrait said to be 'discovered' in 1885, and heralded in *Walford's Antiquarian* as a previously unknown portrait of Shakespeare, allegedly painted in 1616 (Fig. 18). This anonymous (and laughably dubious) portrait was purported by its

---

[64] Stanley, p. 330.
[65] Henry Curling, 'The Enthusiast at Shakespeare's Tomb' (1841), repr. in John Britton, *Essays on the Merits and Characteristics of William Shakspere* (London, 1849), p. 143.
[66] Curling, p. 143.

Fig. 18 Anonymous putative painting of William Shakespeare, oil on panel, possibly early seventeenth century. The scholar who claimed to have 'discovered' the painting imagined it to have been painted on the day Shakespeare died, 23 April 1616. Reproduced courtesy of the Huntington Library, San Marino, California.

vendor to have been painted on the day of Shakespeare's death, 23 April 1616.[67] Says the anonymous article, 'A single glance at the portrait will detect the lineaments of a man borne down by sickness: the face pale and wan, and the eyes deep sunk, but retaining their wonted lustre'.[68] The author of the article imagines that the painting has been done in great haste, the painter having been summoned on the news that Shakespeare was dying.

He cites as 'proof' an inscription, written on paper and fastened to the back of the portrait, that claims the portrait was painted as Shakespeare lay on his deathbed, on the very day he died.[69] Although he dismisses the artist as an amateur, the article's author allows for the possibility that the painting is genuine:

---

[67] Anonymous, 'A Previously Unknown Portrait of Shakespeare', *Walford's Antiquarian: A Magazine and Bibliographical Review*, VIII, no. 46 (July–December 1885): 156.

[68] 'Unknown Portrait', p. 157.

[69] Another, longer inscription, beneath the portrait, and painted on another board, reads: 'Howe speake thatte Browe soe pensive yet serene–/The lucidde Teare juste startynge to thine Eyne/ Dost thou nowe dwelle onne Romeo's ill-starr'd love?/Or doth the tortured Moore thy massion move?/None so. Alasse, no more shall phantsie's creatures/Adumbrate or enshrowde the Poet's features./To realle Illes hys frame nowe falls a Preye–/He feels approache the Ev'ninge of Lyfe's Daye–/And e'er another Dawne arise to cheere/Lyfe's busie Sonnes may droppe poore Wil: Shakspere./ Sic cecinit Cygnus Avoniae et obit 23 Aprilis, 1616 aet. 52'. Neither the painting nor its forced, mock-seventeenth-century verses are genuine. 'Unknown Portrait', p. 157.

On the whole it may be said that, although its proof does not reach to the point of absolute certainty, there is every probability that, in looking at this portrait, we are gazing on the features of the Immortal Bard as they must have appeared when he was approaching death; and on this account they are invested with a peculiar interest. But there is every evidence, short of positive proof, that it is a veritable portrait of Shakspere, taken from 'the life;' for the contention of its believers is that it would be impossible for the portrait, bearing as it does upon the features and visible signs of illness, to have been painted from memory.[70]

The author invites the viewer to meditate on the painting and gaze upon Shakespeare at the moment of death, at the moment when his *genius* became spirit. In so doing, the viewer effectively becomes both a voyeur and a student, the body of Shakespeare in death an object of fetish and an academic specimen at the same time. Moreover, the author suggests that the painting is genuine because its depiction of the last moments of life are too poignant to be produced by memory. He argues that this reading of the face in the last moments of life can only be a first-hand account. J.O. Halliwell-Phillipps produced a similar meditation in 1863, which was pseudo-historical rather than artistic. In *The Last Days of William Shakespeare* he places himself among the family members as they await Shakespeare's last moments on earth. He speculates upon the attitudes toward death and religious devotion of Shakespeare's family and relations, saying,

> So religious were they, that they could not but have consoled the dramatist in his last days; and so little prejudiced, that, even at a time when the serious world was one that involved an excess of puritanical thought, especially in regard to the drama, they never dreamed of deprecating the profession to which Shakespeare had belonged, and from which he had retired with a noble competency.[71]

In Halliwell-Phillipps' imagination, the Shakespeare family awaits the death of its patriarch with an emotional detachment meant to express their deep respect, and also their intellectual appreciation for his profession. They are mourning the loss of the nineteenth century's Shakespeare, not their own. *The Last Days of William Shakespeare* is a pocket-sized book of no more than twenty-three pages, designed to be carried by the tourist in Stratford through New Place, and at the Church of the Holy Trinity. The tourist is invited to meditate upon the death and funeral of Shakespeare in order to experience it imaginatively in the context of English grief in the contemporary age: the aftermath of the death of Prince Albert in 1861. The fantasy of Shakespeare's family gathering at his deathbed mirrors accounts of the royal family doing the same at the bed of Prince Albert, as he approached death. As Clare Gittings states in her study of deathbed depictions in the literature of the *ars moriendi*, there was a tendency to

---

[70] 'Unknown Portrait', p. 157.
[71] J. O. Halliwell-Phillipps, *The Last Days of William Shakespeare* (London, 1863), p. 9.

depict the deathbed as a trial of virtue for both the dying and the living.[72] In Halliwell-Phillipps' reconstruction, Shakespeare's family refuse to make a dramatic 'show' of grief; theirs is a virtuous expression of Victorian mourning that imitates the stoic nobility of the Royal Family in their grief.

Other academic sentiments reflected nineteenth-century pseudo-scientific trends. They stem from the dissatisfaction with the extent to which Shakespeare could be 'known' through literary or commemorative means. Shakespeare could not be moved, nor his gravesite be improved because of the curse; but he might be perceived and understood materially nonetheless. Via scientific enquiry, his body could become accessible to his admirers and understood in relation to their own bodies. 'Knowing' him in a corporeal way promised to reflect upon his admirers and their own humanity. Through him they could hope to discover secrets of humanity previously unknown. Anatomic caracteriology/phrenology was one 'science' that bore this promise. In an article entitled, 'Shakespeare's Physiognomy' by T. Fairman Ordish, the scholar and antiquary makes a case for the so-called 'Shakespeare death mask', a putative death mask of Shakespeare that made the rounds of the scientific and academic worlds after its alleged discovery in a rag picker's shop in 1842. Ordish, like others who were fascinated by the mask, cites its high forehead, prominent nose, and similarity to well-known Shakespeare portraits as proof that it is in fact the face of Shakespeare. In examining the death mask, the enthusiast is able to stand, Hamlet-like, holding the Bard's head, in full communion with the *genius* of the playwright.[73]

In another, no less fantastic example, renowned antiquary and topographer John Britton was intrigued by Shakespeare's life and work to the extent that he sought literally to have the Bard's head examined. Having contemplated the bust of the Stratford Shakespeare memorial in the Church of the Holy Trinity for many years, Britton desired to have a cast made for the purposes of scientific enquiry. He enlisted a man named George Bullock to produce a cast of the original. When the cast of the bust was studied, (an undertaking which Britton claims took place under the best of auspices), one of his companions was none other than Sir Walter Scott, and the other was the famed German phrenologist Dr Johann Spurzheim, who examined the cast. Britton writes:

… the peculiar formation of the Poet's skull, with all its superficial inequalities and curvatures … was descanted on [by Dr Spurzheim] with much ingenuity; with inferences from its peculiar developments, as indicating the possession of those talents which are evinced in his writings; also some personal traits of character which the ingenious and accomplished man of psychological science only could descry, or venture to comment on.[74]

---

[72] Gittings, 'Sacred and Secular', in *Death in England*, ed. Peter C. Jupp and Clare Gittings (New Brunswick, NJ, 1999), p. 183.

[73] See Ordish, T. Fairman. 'Shakespeare's Physiognomy', *The Bookworm: An Illustrated History of Old-Time Literature*, 2 vols. (London, 1888), vol. I, pp. 157–9.

[74] John Britton, 'Essays on the Merits and Characteristics of William Shakspere: Also Remarks on his Birth and Burial-Place, his Monument, Portraits, and Associations', repr. in *The*

During the phrenological examination it was observed that Sir Walter Scott bore a similarly wide distance between his nose and upper lip to the bust. Britton and Dr Spurzheim requested that a scientific measurement of Scott's face be made. Scott demurred, but soon relented to the measurement, which was made by a compass. Scott's upper lip proved to be of a shorter distance to his nose than that of the Stratford bust (most people's are), but Britton and Dr Spurzheim were convinced that the somewhat wide distance was indicative of Scott's literary genius. It was a psycho-physical trait that he shared with Shakespeare, and it correlated perfectly with the popular acclaim of Scott's work. As David Newsome states, Walter Scott's novels were seen to have 'a heroism tinged with pathos', which caused his work to evoke a great deal of nostalgia in his readers.[75] The assumption of physical similarity in the two poets led to a presumption of poetic genius shared by both men. The 'analysis' provided evidence to Britton that literary greatness was physically manifested in the body, not merely in the *corpus* of the poet's or novelist's work. The examination literally inscribed a reading of Shakespeare's dead body onto the living body of Sir Walter Scott.

By far the most fascinating meditation on the imaginatively disinterred corpse of Shakespeare is the experiment of composite photography by Walter Rogers Furness (Fig. 19).[76] Composite photography is a process by which a final photograph is obtained from the exposure to the same sensitised plate containing a series of individual photographs of human faces. Taking a cue from his mentor, Francis Galton, who produced composite photographs for medical research, Furness employed a meticulous and painstaking method.[77] He first made photographic transparencies of nine portraits of Shakespeare 'supposed to have the best authenticated pedigrees', including the Chandos portrait, the Stratford Bust, and the Death Mask.[78] He made sure the individual photographs were all of the same size, and were produced with the same lighting. He then laid the transparencies one over the other until they formed a composite human face, then exposed that composite to the plate. The effect is eerie and surreal, and the composite photograph is meant to generate an image of

---

    Complete Works of Shakespeare, ed. Charles Knight (London, 1849), p. 7.

[75] David Newsome, *The Victorian World Picture: Perceptions and Introspections in an Age of Change* (Princeton, NJ, 1997), p. 160.

[76] Walter Rogers Furness, *Composite Photography Applied to the Portraits of Shakespeare* (Philadelphia, 1885).

[77] Francis Galton, *Inquiries into Human Faculty and its Development* (London, 1883). Galton produced composite photographs that described ideal states of health; or, conversely, archetypes for illnesses and diseases. His composites also provided model templates for supposed criminal tendencies. See Fig. 20. For fun, Galton would make composites of an entire family to form a 'phantom' sibling or relative. Unfortunately, he also produced composite photographs illustrating racial archetypes. One of his most famous is that of the 'ideal' English solider, in which he used plates of Englishmen only, avoiding photographs of Scottish, Irish, or Welsh soldiers.

[78] Furness, p. 4.

Fig. 19 Composite photograph of nine portraits of Shakespeare by Walter Rogers Furness. Furness attempted to use composite photography to discover the 'true' face of Shakespeare, but only produced a portrait of more complex imaginative energy. Photo reproduction courtesy of the Huntington Library, San Marino, CA.

Shakespeare that looks at his admirers from beyond the grave. The effort, however, is a failure. Furness intended to produce a scientifically generated work based on reason, yet the composite photograph is no more indicative of Shakespeare's true face than is any one portrait, bust or mask. Although it is a sincere effort, the composite photo merely puts the nine mythic portraits into a different context, but still fails to demythologise them. What results is more fantasy and an unfortunate irony: the process by which Furness seeks to find truth only moves him closer to myth. Shakespeare's true face could no more be known than could his true motives in writing his plays. Again, what little was known about Shakespeare produced fantasist and fetishist speculation and observation that seemed to verify itself *because* it stood on such a tenuous basis.

Some felt it was time to get at the facts. And that meant it was time to get at Shakespeare, once and for all. It is not surprising that some members of the academic community wanted to defy the curse even as others held it in reverence; nor is it surprising that those who wished to disturb the bones directed their efforts toward pragmatic academic and even scientific enquiry rather than romantic commemoration. There are after all, as Kathryn Prince points out, 'multiple histories of Victorian Shakespeares'.[79] Those histories vary, depending on the decade and the

[79] Kathryn Prince, *Shakespeare in the Victorian Periodicals* (New York, 2008), pp. 2–3.

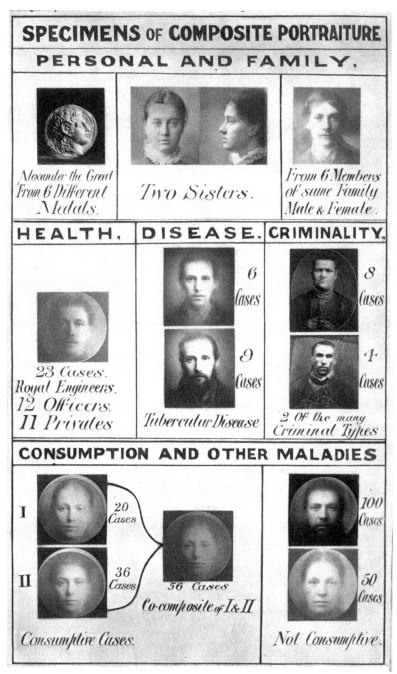

Fig. 20   Sample of composite photography by Francis Galton, innovator of the technique
and mentor of Furness. The sample suggests archetypes for various types of sickness,
criminality, and ethnic identity. Photo reproduction courtesy of the Huntington Library,
San Marino, California.

persons involved. Trends in the popular reception of Shakespeare could be affected by politics, commemorative events (such as the Tercentenary or the inauguration of the Crystal Palace), or movements within the theatrical milieu. Adrian Poole also addresses the subject, saying that attitudes toward Shakespeare during the nineteenth century varied greatly, especially concerning education, patriotism, and academic enquiry.[80] These subjects were definitely at the heart of discussions about whether Shakespeare might actually be disinterred, and why; and periodical literature was the forum for much of this discussion. The sheer volume and variety of literary periodicals from the mid- to late nineteenth century, on both sides of the Atlantic, allowed for varied discussions on all things Shakespeare. *The American Bibliopolist*, for example, was a periodical with a specific section entitled 'Shakespearean Gossip'. The section contained dozens of mini-discussions about Shakespeare among his enthusiasts both inside and outside academia that lasted over the course of decades.[81]

When it comes to the literal disinterment of Shakespeare, the articles and letters involved are remarkably devoid of superstition concerning the curse on Shakespeare's grave, although they do address peoples' sensitivity toward the legendary quatrain. More evident is a pragmatic concern for tourism and the need for continuous memorialism. As C.M. Ingleby argued,

> The sentiment which affects survivors in the disposition of their dead, and which is, in one regard, a superstition, is, in another, a creditable outcome of our common humanity; namely, the desire to honour the memory of our departed worth, and to guard the 'hallowed reliques' by the erection of a shrine, both as a visible make of respect for the dead, and as a place of resort for those pilgrims who may come to pay him tribute.[82]

If one were to disinter the bones, he says, it ought to be done with respect, as though one were viewing the body of a king upon translation of his corpse from one location to another. Identification and observation can be made, and the corpse can be returned to its resting place, or translated to a more fitting one, with no harm done, either to the deceased or to those who venerate his memory.[83] Hermann Schaafhausen agreed in a German periodical, saying:

> But there is no desecration in entrusting the noble remains of the poet to the enquiring eye of science; which will but learn something new from them, and place beyond doubt the value of another precious relic of him, and then restore them to the quiet of the grave.[84]

---

[80] Adrian Poole, *Shakespeare and the Victorians* (London, 2004), pp. 2–3.
[81] Prince, p. 11.
[82] C.M. Ingleby, *Shakespeare's Bones, The Proposal to Disinter Them, Considered in Relation to their Possible Bearing on His Portraiture* (London, 1883), p. 1.
[83] Ingleby, pp. 1–3.
[84] Hermann Schaafhausen, *Jahrbuch*, or *Annual, of the German Shakespeare Society* 10 (1875).

These scholars are emphatic in their view that the curse ought to be taken as a mere curiosity, and that it is an issue about which the scholar need not be sensitive. C.M. Ingleby dismisses the curse as doggerel, unworthy of Shakespeare's talent and no doubt written by an inferior poet. He also rejects the curse as a relic of a bygone age, and argues that England has modernised beyond the point to which such a curse would be truly meaningful.[85] One anonymous contributor agreed with this principle in an item in *The Atlantic Monthly*:

> Since the time seems to have come when a man's expression of his wishes with regard to what is to be done after his death is violently and persistently opposed by all who survive him, is it not a good opportunity to suggest that perhaps respect has been paid for a long enough time to the doggerel over Shakespeare's grave?[86]

Some scholars argued that the curse was redundant in any case: the grave had already been disturbed and the curse, if there ever was one, had been invoked on another man. In 1796 the grave was disturbed during the digging of a grave in its immediate proximity. The slab over Shakespeare's grave, having sunk below the level of the pavement, was removed, and a new one installed in its place. A contributor to *The Monthly Magazine* reported that the gravedigger was able to peer into the grave when he removed the old slab, and that he saw bones lying in it.[87] The story was well known, and some argued that the incident proved that concerns about disturbing the grave were unfounded. J.O. Halliwell-Phillipps, one of the most esteemed scholars of the time, notes in one of his books that the slab over Shakespeare's grave did not in fact lie in its original place, but had been replaced and moved. He says, 'The original memorial has wandered from its allotted station no one can tell whither – a sacrifice to the insane worship of prosaic neatness, that mischievous demon whose votaries have practically destroyed so many of the priceless relics of ancient England and her gifted sons'.[88] His point was that excavating under the slab might only result in finding the wrong bones – or no bones at all, and that other improvements to the Chancel may have already exposed Shakespeare's bones. Samuel Timmins states in his letter to *The Atlantic Monthly* that the curse, whether real or not, might easily be circumvented by having a woman disinter the bones, since the pronoun 'he' and the word 'man' are used in the curse itself. A lawyer friend had made the suggestion '… humorously – not professionally, of course'.[89] A few years later Ronald Gower agreed

---

85 Ingleby, p. 30.
86 Anonymous, Letter to *The Atlantic Monthly*, 'The Contributors' Club' (June 1878).
87 John Dowdall, *Traditionary Anecdotes of Shakespeare* (London, 1838), p. 11, and Anonymous, untitled item in *The Monthly Magazine*, 1 February, 1818, repr. in J.O. Halliwell-Phillipps, *Outlines of the Life of Shakespeare*, 4th edn (London, 1884), pp. 217–18.
88 Halliwell-Phillipps, *Outlines of the Life of Shakespeare*, pp. 217–18.
89 Samuel Timmins, Letter to J. Parker Norris in *The American Bibliopolist* 8 (April 1876): 39.

that Shakespeare's grave might be opened by 'a jury of matrons', and thus the curse would be nullified.[90]

By far the most outrageous story came from *Argosy* Magazine in 1879.[91] An essay written by 'A Warwickshire Man', claims to relate the story of a secret mission by Dr Frank Chambers to steal Shakespeare's skull and deliver it to none other than Horace Walpole.[92] The essay's source is unsurprisingly vague: the story, originating in 1794, comes purportedly from a fittingly mysterious 'Mr M', whose passing away at the age of seventy-five somehow has released the essay's author to repeat the story.[93] As the story goes, the uncle of 'Mr M', who was apparently a relative of Dr Chambers, reported to his nephew, who reported to the essay's anonymous author, that Dr Chambers and three cohorts stole the skull from the Church of the Holy Trinity 'some eighty years ago'.[94] The essay claims that Walpole had offered three hundred guineas to George Selwyn to deliver Shakespeare's skull to him.[95] Chambers had apparently brought the skull to Walpole, but Walpole had balked at it and refused to pay. An apocryphal legend stemming from the story holds that the skull was taken to St Leonard's Church in Worcester. Despite the tantalising material of the story, the old adage persists that if something sounds too good to be true, it probably is. *Argosy* magazine is known for fanciful and sometimes wildly embellished retellings of old stories, rumours, and legends, and its issues also contain a great deal of Gothic fiction. *Argosy* was not considered to be a serious source for literary history at the time; and as an academic resource in the present day *Argosy* fails utterly to live up to any scholarly standard. Moreover, if Horace Walpole ever made such an offer – to Selwyn or anyone else – it most likely reflected the bravado for which he was sometimes known rather than any specific act.[96]

---

[90] Ronald Gower, 'The Shakespearean Death-Mask', *The Antiquary* 2 (August 1880): 63.

[91] *The Argosy* 23, ed. Mrs Henry Wood (July to December 1879): 268–77. The story was repeated in a later issue in 1884.

[92] Wood, ed., *Argosy*, p. 268.

[93] Wood, ed., *Argosy*, p. 268.

[94] Wood, ed., *Argosy*, p. 268.

[95] Wood, ed., *Argosy*, p. 270.

[96] Regrettably, this story has made its way into twenty-first-century mainstream media. News sources from *The New York Times* to the *Guardian* to the *Daily Mail* repeated the story in March 2016. Archaeologist Kevin Colls, who apparently believed the *Argosy* story and the apocryphal accounts that accompany it, scanned Shakespeare's grave with ground-penetrating radar to see if any bones lay in it. The results were indeterminate, unsurprisingly. Tests on the skull in St Leonard's Church have revealed that the skull is that of an unidentified woman. Rumours, magazine articles, and Gothic melodrama aside, there is no evidence that Chambers stole Shakespeare's skull and no real evidence of an agreement with Horace Walpole to buy it. Perhaps more regrettably, the absence of facts or evidence in this case was not enough to prevent the production of a Channel 4 television documentary on the subject (*Secret History: Shakespeare's Tomb*, broadcast in March 2016). Christopher Shea, 'Alas, Poor William Shakespeare. Where Does His Skull Rest?' *New York Times*, 24 March, 2016, www.nytimes.com; Mark Brown, 'Shakespeare's Skull Probably

Some scholars in favour of disinterment cited the need to confirm that the grave's occupant was the 'real' Shakespeare – or, alternatively, to expose the corpse as an impostor. Ingleby argued that the face of the man under the Chancel floor might be compared to known portraits of Shakespeare to produce a positive identification.[97] J. Parker Norris offers that under the right conditions, corpses can retain much of their physical characteristics, and the faces of celebrated men and women have, throughout history, provided for their positive identification centuries after death. He says, 'Very often the features and the clothing of the dead are preserved for hundreds of years after burial, and on opening their graves wonderful sights have been seen. In a few minutes all crumble away, and nothing but dust remain, but for a short time the illusion is wonderful'.[98] Norris cites the discovery of the corpse of Charles I as a perfect example of how well a body might be preserved if it were undisturbed – according to the official account, his skin had been supple and his one open eye was still blue.[99] He also cites the opening of the tomb of the Princess Mary, a daughter of Edward IV, who died in 1482. Her eyes were still blue and her hair blonde. Timmins agreed with Norris. In a letter to Norris he conceded that Shakespeare's face might appear healthy, and cites the probable use of a lead coffin as the reason. Other disinterments of seventeenth-century figures, he says, prove that those laid to rest during Shakespeare's time could be excellently preserved if they were properly embalmed, wrapped in cerecloth, and sealed in lead coffins.[100] Here, Timmins assumes that Shakespeare would have been given the type of burial reserved for the aristocracy and very wealthy of the seventeenth century: he does not account for the possibility of a far less comprehensive middle-class burial that would result in Shakespeare's corpse being reduced to bones relatively quickly. In his wish to look the dead Shakespeare in the face, Norris demonstrates the same attitude toward the noble body that was demonstrated during the eleventh through fifteenth centuries: the noble body in death was not subject to the same grotesque transformations as that of the commoner. Norris' desire to gaze upon the face of the 'living' Shakespeare fetishises the playwright. Norris imagines the emotional gratification he will experience at enjoying the illusion of life – including the exchange of eye contact with the deceased – for a brief moment before the corpse crumbles to dust, as it transforms from subject to object in a matter of seconds.

Stolen by Grave-Robbers, Study Finds', *Guardian*, 23 March, 2016. www.guardian.co.uk; Chris Kitching, 'Was Shakespeare's Skull Stolen for a £300 Bet'? *Daily Mail*, 27 March, 2016, www.dailymail.co.uk.

[97] Ingleby, p. 29.

[98] J. Parker Norris, untitled item in 'Shakespearean Gossip', *The American Bibliopolist* 8 (April 1876): 38; repr. in *The Philadelphia Press*, 4 August, 1876.

[99] Norris, 'Shakespearean Gossip', p. 38; and Sir Henry Halford, *An Account of What Appeared on Opening the Coffin of King Charles the First ... on the first of April, MDCCCXIII ...* (London, 1813), pp. 6–7. See also Chapter 8 and Fig. 9.

[100] Timmins, p. 39.

Although the attitudes of Norris and his fellow contributors are rooted in ancient ideas about the noble body in death, and even in the veneration of relics and the bodies of saints, they are also unexpectedly modern. They reflect contemporary ideas about scientific enquiry into the state of human development. Darwinism allowed scientists and those appreciative of scientific principles to focus on the body in a new way. The corpse was not merely a thing, it was *the* thing; it was precisely that which illustrated Darwin's principles so completely. The corpse of the reptile, the arboreal quadruped, the bipedal 'ape-man', and of Man himself, was the centrepiece of any museum's or university's natural history collection. Human skulls were sorted to determine class and racial groups and displayed according to what observation appeared to dictate; phrenology and anatomic characterology were employed on skulls and bones to determine the characteristics of the dead and apply those generalisations to the living; and composite photography was used on skulls to form ideals of race and class based on the shapes of the crania, the mandibles, the cheekbones, and the teeth. By the 1880s, The Royal College of Surgeons had by far the most impressive exhibition illustrating Darwin's principle of evolution. The 'climbing series of skeletons' displayed specimens from fish and reptilia, to the smallest mammals, and proceeding via *genus* and *species* to the larger mammals, to the monkeys, apes and Man. The exhibition showed that the body in death was not merely an artefact, nor was it merely the relic of a personal or dynastic history. It was part of a living narrative; it demonstrated Man's place on an ever-developing scale and it made continuous and relevant contributions to the discourse of science. It was to this exhibit that an anonymous contributor to the *Cincinnati Gazette* made reference in 1883. He states that Shakespeare should indeed be disinterred, so that his body could be examined anatomically and its superiority to other poets (or perhaps even to other men) determined. Particular attention should be paid to the skull. He states, 'His skull, if still not turned to dust, should be preserved in the Royal College of Surgeons, as the apex of the climbing series of skeletons, from the microscopic to the Divine'.[101] The recommendation of the Anonymous contributor goes far beyond the adaptation of the Medieval notion of the noble body, or of the uncorrupted saint. It looks forward to a new definition of nobility and divinity: superiority via natural selection. He views Shakespeare's skull not as a specimen of *homo sapiens*, but as a representation of what Man is capable of, what he could become. To the contributor, Shakespeare's skull represents the apex of human classification: Divinely Endowed Poet, or perhaps absurdly, *homo poetas*. The skull of Shakespeare would change the scientific discourse of the climbing series of skeletons and also effectively change the literary and cultural discourse on Shakespeare. The contributor desires that the discussion about Shakespeare evolve – literally – from who Shakespeare the man had been, to what humanity had become. This text of the corpse is a form of *prolepsis*: the dead poet living. Despite the extraordinary eccentricity of his suggestion, the

---

[101] Anonymous. 'Shakespeare at Home', in *The Cincinnati Commercial Gazette* 43, 26 May, 1883.

contributor's article nonetheless invites his fellow scholars to look deeply into their understanding of their world, and into their ideas about the place Shakespeare should have in that world. He was not alone in this understanding.

Such ideas are at the heart of the fascination with Shakespeare's death, his burial site, and his corpse. Shakespeare is considered in terms of who he is supposed to have been, and enthusiasts of the eighteenth and the nineteenth centuries relate to him on that ground. This consideration points to the desire for an original, or authentic, experience of the body in death, what Marjorie Garber calls the 'originary wholeness' of Shakespeare's body.[102] Ironically, this sense of 'wholeness' is specific to the experience of his death and burial. This phenomenon occurs precisely because of the discomforting absence of the details of his life. Since his life appears to enthusiasts to be less than whole, the corpse, and indeed the death, must be envisioned as whole in order to compensate for what is missing. To provide a 'whole death' for Shakespeare is to preserve a sense of wholeness for the body of his work as well.[103] This practice seeks to put 'more on the bones' where Shakespeare is concerned, to return the avid enthusiast to an originary wholeness that never was, to a place where neither the enthusiast nor Shakespeare has ever been.

[102] Garber, p. 245.
[103] Garber, p. 245.

8

THE CONVERSANT DEAD

Charles I and Oliver Cromwell

When the now-famous statue of Oliver Cromwell was erected outside Whitehall in November 1899, it stood unassumingly just across from the west wall of St Margaret's Church (Fig. 21). There, a bust of Charles I, erected a few decades earlier, appeared to gaze upon the Lord Protector (Fig. 22). The two monuments stood as reminders that since the seventeenth century Charles I and Oliver Cromwell had been made by poets, statesmen, and polemicists to coexist, and even converse, in death. They had been featured in pamphlets and poems, in sermons and treatises, and also in folklore; and when they 'spoke' to or about each other they did so as dead men whose relationship extended beyond the grave. This pattern was supplemented by a series of occurrences that over

Fig. 21 Statue of Oliver Cromwell by Hamo Thornycroft erected in 1899 outside Whitehall in London. Photo courtesy of iStock by Getty Images.

Fig. 22 Bust of Charles I, outside St Margaret's Church in London. The creative tourist imagines that the statue of Cromwell appears to be casting his gaze down in the face of the King's triumphant glare. Photo courtesy of iStock by Getty Images.

the next two centuries encouraged many people in literature and politics to imagine the two men in continuous juxtaposition: their bodies had suffered physical violence, and their supporters had depicted them as triumphant in the afterlife. Both men were memorialised in royal chapels, and both graves had at one point been lost. By 1899, neither man enjoyed a lavish tomb or figural monument. The tomb of Charles I was marked by a simple slab in the floor of St George's Chapel, Windsor. Cromwell's burial place, long emptied of its occupant, was marked by a plaque in the floor of the Henry VII Chapel in Westminster Abbey (Fig. 23). The quiet commemoration of the burial sites was deceptive.

Fig. 23 Floor plaque marking the burial place of Oliver Cromwell, Westminster Abbey, London. The plaque, which is near the tomb of Henry VII, lies under a carpet in the nave of the Henry VII Chapel. Photo courtesy of Westminster Abbey Library and Archives.

Since their respective deaths, the language of historical memory had been employed with great fervour to keep the king and the Lord Protector talking about – and to – each other. The cooperation of literature, history, and folklore produced a comprehensive fantasist view of the relationship between Charles I and Oliver Cromwell that resulted in a unique effect: the corpses of the two men became intercommunicative texts.

Many scholars and politicians of the nineteenth century viewed the English Civil War with fascination and nostalgia. As Blair Worden, Roger Howell, and H.F. McMains have demonstrated, there was an attraction to the discourse of the seventeenth century in the wake of the military triumphs of the early part of the nineteenth century. Amid the growing power of the Labour movement in Parliament in the latter half of that century, historians, churchmen, and politicians cited the contemporary work of Thomas Carlyle and earlier work by Edward Hyde, Earl of Clarendon (among others), as texts that contributed to their views of the seventeenth century as an archetypal time that reflected upon contemporary issues and concerns.[1] Such politicians and scholars expanded the rhetoric of the Civil War by creating new political and historical texts to replace the ghost pamphlets, commemorative epitaphs, and broadsheet ballads of the seventeenth century. Still, Charles I and Oliver Cromwell continued to be sensationalised in imaginative ways, just as they had been in those earlier texts. Charles I and Oliver Cromwell continued to 'speak' to each other through their respective supporters, who cooperated with persistent popular legends and folklore. Their efforts to re-envision both Oliver Cromwell and Charles I not as living men, but as dead men in mutual engagement produced innovative literary and political views of each man's dead body. These views were invigorated by folk legends that placed the corpse of each man at the centre of historic sites, landmarks, and monuments. The historical memory of Oliver Cromwell and of Charles I in the nineteenth century is profoundly affected by the enduring presence of each man's corpse as a readable document that simultaneously recalls the past and speaks to the present.

Charles I died a most dramatic death, as a deposed king suffering execution at the hands of revolutionaries – indeed, he had given the signal for the axeman with his own hand. There was a large crowd, many of whom cheered the death of a man they saw as a tyrant, and many others who cried out against the death of a man they saw as a martyr. No one, of course, disputed that the king was dead. That was perfectly evident – or at least it should have been. After the execution, the severed head of Charles I was sewn onto the body so that the king could be viewed as he lay in state. As Clarendon would later say, 'His body was immediately carried into a room at Whitehall; where he was exposed for many days to the public view, that all men might know that he was not alive. And he

---

[1]   See especially Roger Howell, 'Who Needs Another Cromwell? The Nineteenth-Century Image of Oliver Cromwell', *Images of Oliver Cromwell: Essays for and by Roger Howell, Jr* (Manchester, 1993), pp. 98–9; H.F. McMains, *The Death of Oliver Cromwell* (Lexington, KY, 2000); Blair Worden, *Roundhead Reputations: The English Civil Wars and the Passions of Posterity* (New York, 2002); Edward Hyde, Earl of Clarendon, *History of the Rebellion and Civil Wars in England Begun in the Year 1641* (1702–4) (Oxford, 1888), 4 vols., vol. III, Books IX–XI; and Thomas Carlyle, *Letters and Speeches of Oliver Cromwell* (London, 1904).

was embalmed, and put in a coffin, and so carried to St James's [sic] where he likewise remained several days.'² The situation, however, immediately lent itself to rumours. One story, which by the beginning of the nineteenth century had become legendary, holds that before this posthumous re-memberment took place, Cromwell himself had inspected the body of the king for assurance that the deed was done, and done correctly. The story reflects concerns held by the regicides and their supporters that the king's body could remain formidable in death as he lay in state. Because the king's subjects would be able to see his body intact, their memories would be permitted to preserve the image of the king's 'whole' body. Despite the fact that the admirers of Charles I accepted his death, there was a risk that they could adopt the belief that the king was being interred as a 'whole man'. Such a belief would be tantalisingly mythic, and dangerously accessible to royalists. It was therefore necessary to prevent the king's supporters (some of whom were suspected of having Catholic sentiments) from making any sort of pilgrimage to the tomb to pray for, or to, the dead king and establish communication with him in death as a martyr figure. It was also necessary to prevent access to the corpse for the collection of relics. Although the veneration of relics had long since been banned, a clandestine tradition continued and was often politicised: after the execution of King Charles many of his supporters dipped their handkerchiefs in his blood. It was still believed in many quarters that relics were objects of communication between the martyr and the devotee, under the auspices of Divine Will; that relics were texts constructed from the remnants of the martyr's corpse. In the light of these issues, the story of Cromwell's inspection acknowledged that even in a decapitated state the king could 'speak' volumes, and that the Republic needed to be protected from this 'voice'. The king's body was taken away from London, therefore, by a small group of lords to Windsor, and interred at the Chapel of St George with a great deal of secrecy and discretion.³ This action pleased Parliament, for it promoted security, as Windsor was a military fortification behind locked gates. Although the king's entire (albeit not *whole*) body was interred there, no one would be able to access it. In a further effort to combat any power wielded by the dead king, Parliament denied Charles I a

² Edward Hyde, Earl of Clarendon, *History of the Rebellion*, vol. IV, Books IX–XI, p. 492. See also a similar account by Anthony Wood, in *Athenae Oxonienses* (London, 1721), 3 vols., vol. II, p. 703. Thomas Herbert also relates that many people wished to view the king's body, some to be sure he was dead, and some to see him restored to a state of regal dignity after his execution. Sir Thomas Herbert, *Threnodia Carolina* (1678), repr. in Allan Fea, *Memoirs of the Martyr King; Being a Detailed Record of the Last Two Years of the Reign of His Most Sacred Majesty King Charles I* (London, 1905), pp. 146–50.

³ See Hyde, Earl of Clarendon, *History of the Rebellion*, vol. IV, pp. 492–3, for an informed, but somewhat speculative account of the king's interment at Windsor. Further observations on Clarendon's account are made by Sir Henry Halford in his own account of the disinterment of Charles I in 1813. Sir Henry Halford, *An Account of What Appeared on Opening the Coffin of King Charles the First … on the First of April, MDCCCXIII …* (London, 1813). Anthony Wood states that among the lords were some who claimed to have licence from Parliament, to make sure the king was buried discreetly and not taken out from the grounds of Windsor Castle. *Athenae Oxonienses* (London, 1813), vol. II, p. 703.

burial in the Chapel of Henry VII. This act interrupted the dynastic continuity of the Tudors and Stuarts. Neither the king's whole body nor the Stuarts' whole dynasty could remain intact.[4]

The occasion of Cromwell's death on a stormy night nearly 10 years later was fraught with rumours that the Lord Protector was not really dead. He was in Ireland, in hiding perhaps, or abroad. Much of this disbelief was a reaction to Cromwell's death by natural causes, and by the popular belief that his death was premature. But in large part the rumours can be attributed to the fact that Cromwell's body was buried quickly in Westminster Abbey, secured behind a wall and adjacent to the tomb of Henry VII (Fig. 24).[5] Interestingly, there was a desire for security similar to that of the interment of Charles I. There was a fear of relic hunting, or worse: of disinterment for the purposes of revenge. Placing Cromwell adjacent to the tomb of Henry VII 'secured' the burial from desecration because of its proximity to that of a national hero. The placement of Cromwell's body also 'secured' his legacy in a place among the very kings whose dynasty he had interrupted. The body of Cromwell took the place of that of Charles I, lying in its stead among the Tudors and Stuarts.[6] There was also a practical concern for security. Cromwell had planned his funeral years earlier, devising a grand pageant based on the funeral of James I in 1625.[7] Because the planning and implementation of the funeral took months, effigies were necessary for lying in state and for the procession and funerary rite.

---

[4] As Anthony Wood noted a generation later, '...they thought no place more fit to inter the corpse than in the Chapel of King Henry VII at the end of the church of Westminster Abbey, out of whose loins King Charles I was lineally extracted, &c. whereupon Mr Herbert made his application to such as were then in power for leave to bury the King's body in the said chapel, among his ancestors; but his request was denied, for this reason; that his burying there would attract infinite numbers of all sorts thither, to see where the king was buried; which, as the time then were, was judged unsafe and inconvenient. Mr Herbert, acquainting the Bishop with this, then resolved to bury the King's Body in the Royal Chapel of St George within the Castle of Windsor, both in regard that his Majesty was Sovereign of the Most noble Order of the Garter, and that several kings had been there interred; namely, King Henry VI, King Edward IV, and King Henry VIII, &c'. Wood, vol. II, p. 703.

[5] J.L. Chester reports, 'The vault was under the easternmost end of the chapel's middle aisle; it abutted Henry VII's vault, located centrally under the middle aisle and just to the west.' Within the Lord Protector's vault 'massive walls, abutting immediately on the royal vault of Henry VII, are the only addition to the structure of the Abbey dating from the Commonwealth'. J.L. Chester, *Registers of the Collegiate Church or Abbey of St Peter* (London, 1876), p. 521. This same report mentions that the Abbey's record of the burial and exhumation of Oliver Cromwell were destroyed by an overzealous loyalist.

[6] Clarendon glibly reports the suggestion of Cromwell's regality in death: 'The dead [Cromwell] is interred in the sepulchre of the kings, and with the obsequies due to such: and his son inherits all his greatness and all his glory, without that public hate that visibly attended the other'. Hyde, Earl of Clarendon, vol. IV, Book XVI, p. 98.

[7] Cromwell probably began planning his funeral as he made preparations for the funeral of Henry Ireton, his son-in-law, some years earlier. Ireton had also been given permission by Parliament to be buried in the Henry VII Chapel at Westminster, and royalists were outraged at the idea of one of the regicides being buried in the royal mausoleum.

Fig. 24 Grille tomb of Henry VII and Elizabeth of York, Henry VII Chapel, Westminster Abbey, London. Cromwell's burial place was adjacent to this tomb so that he could lie as near as possible to the founder of the Tudor dynasty. Photo courtesy of Westminster Abbey Library and Archives.

By the time of Cromwell's public funeral his body had rested in Westminster, unseen and essentially uncommemorated, for over two months. In that sense, the *whole* body of Cromwell was no more present at his funeral in 1658 than the king's had been at his own burial in 1649. Rumours spread that the Lord Protector was not dead at all.

These rumours disturbed Andrew Marvell, who held a deep admiration for Cromwell. Marvell did not wish for any suggestions of myth or ritualism to attend upon Cromwell's death. In 'A Poem upon the Death of his Late Highness the Lord Protector' (1658), Marvell sought to emphasise the fact that the Lord Protector was not only definitively dead, but was better off that way. In the poem, Marvell states boldly the fact of the matter: 'I saw him dead'.[8] This statement is in part an assertion of Marvell's

---

[8] Andrew Marvell, 'A Poem upon the Death of his Late Highness the Lord Protector', in *Andrew Marvell: The Complete Poems*, ed. Elizabeth Story Donno (New York, 1996), pp. 148ff, l. 247.

Parliamentarian authority. As a Member of Parliament, Marvell had the privilege of seeing Cromwell's corpse up close, unlike the majority of London's populace, who had to wait months for the funeral only to see him in effigy. He therefore had an exclusive claim, which was supported by his reputation as an MP and as a loyal servant of the Protectorate. Unaffected by superstition or rumour, Marvell held a detached, yet pious view of death. He saw himself as a most reliable witness to the fact that the man was dead. Marvell saw Cromwell in the simplicity of death, by viewing his body laid out plainly. For the poet this was an appropriate appearance for Cromwell. At the funeral, Cromwell's effigy had been dressed in royal robes, and adorned with a sceptre and a crown. Marvell was distressed by this depiction, and in his poem he resists the sentimentality that he knew accompanied such ritualism, and which he believed to be strongly linked to royalism. Indeed, Marvell felt that the funeral and its use of effigy threatened to 'crown' Cromwell posthumously. If such an effort were to succeed, it would only result in a resurrection of the monarchical body of Charles I. It would also argue in favour of one of the defining elements of monarchy – that the king had a mystical connection to God and therefore ruled by Divine Right.[9] In such a case, although his physical body was dead, Charles I would continue to live, mystically, in the bodies of Oliver, and then Richard Cromwell – indeed in the body politic of the Protectorate itself. The king would thereby intrude, continuously, upon the Protectorate, and speak through it. As Ashley Marshall points out in his analysis of 'A Poem Upon the Death of his Late Highness the Lord Protector', Marvell abhors this idea and uses his poem to emphasise that Cromwell's body is a *dead* body, without a voice.[10]

Marvell describes the decayed state of the corpse in particular, saying that death has reduced the great man to a state less than human: 'That port which so majestic was and strong,/Loose and deprived of vigour, stretched along:/All withered, all discoloured, pale and wan–/How much another thing, nor more that man'?[11] This is not a regrettable state, however. It means that both Cromwell and kingship are dead. By placing himself in the same room with the corpse, and by de-emphasising any sense of pomp or adornment of the body, Marvell is, according to Marshall, attempting to 'reabsorb Cromwell into the known patterns of human experience'; in effect disenfranchising the concept of 'the King's two bodies' completely.[12] Marvell asserts in his poem that although Cromwell does not have a mystical, monarchical connection to God, he will live again, albeit spiritually rather than physically. Marvell writes, 'Yet dwelt that greatness in his shape decayed,/That still though dead, greater than death he laid:/And

---

[9] See Ernest Kantorowicz, *The King's Two Bodies* (1957) (Princeton, NJ, 1997). Kantorowicz argues that a monarch possesses both a physical body and a mystical one. Upon the death of the king's physical body, his mystical body is immediately transferred to the new king, so that the mystical connection between the Monarch and God is uninterrupted.

[10] Ashley Marshall, 'I Saw Him Dead: Marvell's Elegy for Cromwell', *Studies in Philology* 103, no. 4 (Autumn 2006): 501–3.

[11] Marvell, ll. 251–4.

[12] Marshall, 'I Saw Him Dead', p. 502, and Kantorowicz.

in his altered face you something feign/That threatens death he yet will live again'.[13] In de-mystifying monarchy, Marvell both humanises Cromwell and associates him with the Elect, thereby making his poem an act of devout iconoclasm. As Marshall says, 'In short, Marvell's poem emphasises the absence of a king. There is no king because there had been no king.'[14] Cromwell's body must be inspected just as the king's has, and he must be as dead as the king is.

Almost immediately after Cromwell's death, pamphlets appeared that sought to establish a posthumous conversant relationship between the Lord Protector and the king. In these pamphlets, the ghosts of Cromwell and Charles I engage in rhetorical combat as they struggle for primacy from beyond the grave. There was a well-established tradition of these 'ghost pamphlets', which used the parlay of the dead to continue the unfinished business of earthly polemic. Highly imaginative, they used what Joad Raymond calls 'a patchwork of widely accessible forms, including prose, verse dialogue, and dramatic dialogue, to combine humour, criticism, and revenge fantasy, and to reveal diabolical machinations occluded from the sight or understanding of the living'.[15] The ghost pamphlets sought to fill the gaps of information left by incompletely or poorly reported news during times of crisis, and presented themselves as testaments to historical and cultural memory. Beginning during the later years of the Reformation, ghost pamphlets and broadside ballads featuring ghosts appealed to readers (and hearers) who were looking for ways to justify confusing, threatening, or otherwise unstable events in their changing world. During the Elizabethan period ghost pamphlets could be used for continued attacks on a dead enemy: Robert Greene appears posthumously in pamphlets such as *Greenes Newes Both from Heaven and Hell* (1593) and *Greene in Conceit, New Raised from his Grave* (1598); in the latter piece Greene condemns the art of pamphleteering and the war of words it has caused.[16] Such attacks continued in ghost pamphlets of the seventeenth century: the Earl of Leicester is the subject of Thomas Roger's attack in *Leicester's Ghost* (1605, pub. 1641), while Thomas Nash is the subject of *Crop-Eare Curried* (1644); in the pamphlet, Nash confesses to the deficiencies of intellect and personality that his enemies had claimed all along.[17] Ghost pamphlets acted as enhancements and accompaniments to polemical tracts, often making reference to political pamphlets and their authors. As

---

[13] Marvell, ll. 257–60.

[14] Marshall, 'I Saw Him Dead', p. 511.

[15] Joad Raymond, *Pamphlets and Pampheteering in Early Modern Britain* (Cambridge, 2003), pp. 353–4.

[16] Anonymous, *Greenes Newes Both from Heaven and Hell Prohibited the First for Writing of Bookes, and Banished Out of the Last for Displaying of Conny-Catchers* (London, 1593); and *Greene in Conceit, New Raised from his Grave to Write the Tragique Historie of Faire Valeria of London. Wherein is Truly Discouered the Rare and Lamentable Issue of a Husbands Dotage, a Wiues Leudnesse, & Children of Disobedience*. Received and Reported by I.D. (London, 1598).

[17] Thomas Rogers, *Leicester's Ghost* (1605, pub. 1641), ed. Franklin B. Williams, Jr (Chicago, 1972); and John Taylor, *Crop-Eare Curried, Or, Tom Nash His Ghost: Declaring the Pruining of Prinnes Two Last Parricidicall Pamphlets...* (London, 1644).

political pamphlets argued in general for certainty and justice amid controversy, ghost pamphlets added to those arguments by compensating for the inconveniently absent voices of the dead. The ghost pamphleteer uses the figure of the ghost to provide a sense of rightness that, for circumstantial reasons, cannot be reproduced by the voices of the living. As Joad Raymond points out in his discussion of pamphleteering during the Stuart period, living people have sensibilities and opinions, and they can be swayed by arguments in matters of consequence. The dead, however, have no pretences in this respect. They speak the truth in ways living witnesses cannot, because living witnesses cannot provide evidence of God's judgment. Since the dead have experienced God's judgment, they do not merely speak the truth; they are incarnations of the truth. Even as they demand justice, they represent God's justice.[18]

The ghost of Charles I appears in pamphlets soon after his death, and most of the pamphlets place the king in heaven, asserting his martyrdom and condemning the Protectorate. One pamphlet, however, takes an interesting approach – it nods at traditionalism while it describes a contemporary issue. *A Coffin for King Charles* (1649)[19] was published anonymously as a polemical ballad and was meant to be sung to the tune of a popular song.[20] In the ballad, a living Cromwell sings triumphantly from a throne, as a usurper whose republican rhetoric has been set aside in favour of a desire to be king. In response, Charles I sings from his coffin in the crypt of St George's Chapel. Compellingly, Charles I sings not as a ghost *per se* but as a revenant figure, a living dead man lying in his coffin, protesting the injustice of his death. He cries out to Cromwell: 'Think thou base slave, though in my grave/Like other men I lie:/My sparkling fame and Royal name/Can (as thou wishest) die[?]'[21] Cromwell dismisses the voice from the grave, proclaiming the king to be dead 'without all remedie',[22] but the dead king asserts his right, by way of his physical and mystical body, even in death, stating that soon his son will inhabit the monarchical body and restore the Crown.[23]

Although the king states that he is in heaven, and singing among angels,[24] he also sings from his coffin, as an animated corpse. His body and soul are separated, yet both are reunified via his consciousness. Similar to the revenant of Medieval *exempla*, who returns from the grave to warn others of impending danger or to identify his murderer, Charles I defends himself from his tomb in the name of justice.[25] He does

---

[18] Raymond, p. 253.
[19] Anonymous. *A Coffin for King Charles. A Crown For Cromwell. A Pit for the People* (London, 1649).
[20] The song is 'Fain I Would'.
[21] *A Coffin for King Charles*, 2.1–4.
[22] *A Coffin for King Charles*, 4.8.
[23] *A Coffin for King Charles*, 2.6.
[24] *A Coffin for King Charles*, 14. 1–4.
[25] For a representative assortment of Medieval *exempla* containing ghosts and revenants, see Caesarius of Heisterbach, *Dialogos Miraculorum* (Cologne, 1481); William of Newburgh, *Historia Rerum Anglicarum* (Antwerp, 1567); Peter the Venerable, *The Book of Miracles*, in

not, however, appeal for prayers for his soul, as revenants in the *exempla* tradition often do – although the anonymous author imagines the king to be a hagiographic figure, he does not openly promote Catholicism. Still, the headless king recalls an early tradition of martyr saints who are termed *cephalophoric*; namely, saints who speak or sing after they have been beheaded.[26] As he sings in his grave, Charles I empowers and modernises the *cephalophoric* tradition, which is characterised by St Edmund the martyr and St Denis, among others.[27] These figures defy, via Divine Will, the most dramatic act of silencing: the severing of the head from the body. Here, the hagiographic tradition is acknowledged, but is redefined by the Church of England via the body, and specifically via the singing head of the king. The king is both ghost and saint, an embodiment of both traditionalism and Protestantism, and his body is at once severed but whole.

Upon his death Cromwell appeared in ghost pamphlets as well. In many of them Cromwell speaks from Hell, often as a rival to the devil. Even when he is not speaking from Hell he is an aggressive, haughty figure, who is eager to perturb the Stuarts, and in particular the dead king. In *A New Conference Between the Ghosts of King Charles and Oliver Cromwell* (1659), the two men again speak to each other in death.[28] Still eager for power, the upstart ghost of Cromwell returns to England and disturbs the peaceful rest of the dead King Charles as he lies in his tomb:

King: How now! Who's this that disturbeth my dust, at rest now some years?
Oliver: I am he that gave thee no rest when we lived together upon the Earth.
King: What? Is it Oliver Cromwell that great enemy of mine?
Oliver: The same.
King: What? Hast thou left thy station on earth and durst thou here also to own thy
    self my enemy?
Oliver: What is it that I ever wanted impudence to do?[29]

Patrologiae Cursus Completus, Series Latina, ed. J.P. Migne, 220 vols. (Paris, 1844–1906), vol. CLXXXIX; Gregory the Great, *The Dialogues of St Gregory*, ed. and trans. Odo John Zimmerman (New York, 1959); and Bede, *Ecclesiastical History of the English People*, ed. and trans. J. McLure and R. Collins (Oxford, 1994). See also Jean Claude Schmitt, *Ghosts in the Middle Ages: The Living and the Dead in Medieval Society*, trans. Teresa Lavender Fagan (Chicago, 1994), for a comprehensive discussion of the ghost tradition before the Reformation.

[26] For a discussion of cephalophoric saints in hagiography, see Jacobus De Voragine, *The Golden Legend; Readings on the Saints* (13th century) (Princeton, NJ, 1993); for a literary discussion, see *Heads Will Roll: Decapitation in Medieval Literature and Culture*, ed. Larissa Tracy and Jeff Massey (Leiden, 2012).

[27] Cephalophoric saints range from Roman martyrs such as St Denis, and Felix and Regula, to later saints like Valerie of Limoges and Minias of Florence.

[28] Adam Wood, *A New Conference Between the Ghosts of King Charles and Oliver Cromwell* (London, 1659).

[29] Wood, *A New Conference*, p. 2.

A New Conference backs away from conventional ideas of liminal space that had accompanied the Medieval ghost tradition for centuries. Typically, ghosts either haunt places – most commonly, the places of their deaths or burials – or they haunt the living, visiting humans in moments of solitude or emotional vulnerability. In *A New Conference,* the two men haunt each other instead of haunting a physical location or a living person or party. Interestingly, neither figure inhabits the Christian afterlife. Although in some pamphlets Cromwell is depicted in Hell as a rival to the devil,[30] and in others Charles I is depicted in Heaven amongst angels,[31] in *A New Conference* the earthly (or un-earthly) location of their conversation is less important than the conversation itself.

On 26–30 January 1661, the nightmare of Cromwell's supporters came true. Cromwell was disinterred, and his body desecrated and hanged at Tyburn. Cromwell's corpse, along with those of Bradshaw and Ireton, lay among other members of the Cromwell family, whose graves had to be disturbed in order to get to the bodies of the regicides. Jonathan Fitzgibbons theorises that Parliament was aware that the juxtaposition of the Cromwell family vault to that of the Tudors and Stuarts represented a dynastic rivalry.[32] This indeed appears to be the case. As Sgt James Norfolke and his attendants disturbed the Cromwells in order to get to their patriarch, the men engaged in a similar type of dynastic interruption that the regicides had engaged in when they buried Cromwell among the ancestors and predecessors of Charles I. Once the men located the coffin, which was hidden in the wall and protected with several layers of wood and lead, they laid the coffin out in the open. Upon the coffin was affixed a gilt copper plate naming Cromwell as Protector of England, Ireland, and Scotland, along with the arms of England, and Cromwell's own family arms.[33] Crowds of Cromwell's supporters, enemies, and those who were just plain curious filed into the church, paying sixpence apiece to see the corpse.[34] It was far from the dignified 'inspection' Marvell had encouraged, although it put to rest the rumours that Cromwell had escaped the hand of death – or justice. The body, along with those of the other two regicides, was dragged to Tyburn and hung at the gallows for more gawking crowds. After a time, Cromwell's body was cut down, decapitated, and his body was buried under the gallows in a pit dug

---

[30] Such as, Anonymous, *The Case is Alter'd, or, Dreadful News from Hell* (London, 1660).

[31] Such as, Anonymous, *Bradshaw's Ghost, A Poem. Or, A Dialogue Between John Bradshaw, Ferry-Man Charon, Oliver Cromwell, Francis Ravilliack, and Ignatius Loyola* (London, 1660).

[32] Jonathan Fitzgibbons, *Cromwell's Head* (Richmond, VA, 2008), p. 36.

[33] The arms were engraved on the obverse. On the reverse it read, 'Oliverus Protector Reipublicae Angliae, Scotiae, & Hiberniae, Natus 25. April 1599, Ignaturatus 16. Dec.ris 1653, Mortuus 3. Sept.ris 1658. Hic situs est'. Recorded in Robert Harley, *Harleian Miscellany* (London, 1808–11). Norfolke, thinking the plate to be made of gold, claimed it for himself. Although he was disappointed to learn later that the plate was made of gilt copper, he nonetheless took possession of the body's official identifying marker, which had been meant to lie on the corpse for posterity.

[34] Thomas Rugge, *The Diurnal of Thomas Rugge*, ed. W.L. Sachse (London, 1961), p. 143.

for that purpose. His head was placed upon a pike above Westminster Hall in a final act that was meant to parallel the death of the king.

Epitaphs by ghost pamphleteers and polemicists described the posthumous relationship between the king and the Lord Protector in the shadow of the disinterment of the regicides. As Scott Newstok points out in his book on epitaphs in Early Modern England, epitaphs are at once the literature *in* the graveyard and the literature *of* the graveyard.[35] The audience of this literature extends beyond the readership of those looking upon the tomb. It includes the dead as witnesses to the verses that describe them. Moreover, since epitaphs are sometimes written in the first person, from the point of view of the deceased, epitaphs also function as voices of the dead. Although epitaphs had been in use for millennia, Newstok points out that during the Early Modern period epitaph writing was elevated to an art form in an unprecedented way. Early Modern epitaph writers (whether they wrote them for public view or for private circulation) sought to engage in a conversation with the dead in order to reconstruct, and, in a sense, recuperate English history.[36] Epitaph writers of the Early Modern period were profoundly affected by events such as the Royal Supremacy, the Reformation, the creative explosion and prosperity of the Elizabethan era, the plague, the Great Fire, and the Civil War. As Newstok argues, they did more than continue the tradition of a classical genre; they reinvented it.[37] Indeed, as epitaph writers sought to reconstruct fragments of their history they also sought to reconstruct communication with the dead. This effort is a reaction to the ecclesiastical policies of the sixteenth century that forbade Purgatory, pilgrimage, intercessory prayer, and ritual observations. Without such means of communication, the dead are effectively cut off from human experience. In cultivating the art of epitaph writing, Protestant polemicists of the Early Modern era sought to reestablish this communication in the years following these changes. In doing so, they created a liminal space defined by the epitaph, in which the living and the dead could speak to each other without ritual aids.

Ghost pamphleteers of the seventeenth century are particularly aware of this fact, using their skills to communicate with (and via) the dead, and to reconstruct history. The royalist author of a pamphlet called *A New Meeting of the Ghosts at Tyburn* (1660/1661) provides each of the regicides with his own epitaph.[38] Any epitaphs Bradshaw and Ireton once had on their graves at Westminster were broken up when they were disinterred; Cromwell's grave had been unmarked for security, and his only epitaph was the descriptive plaque, which was stolen; in any case, it was written in very plain language. Since the graves under the Tyburn gallows afforded the regicides

[35] Scott Newstok, *Quoting Death in Early Modern England* (New York, 2009), p. 2.
[36] Newstok, pp. 2–4.
[37] Newstok, pp. 2–4.
[38] Anonymous, *A New Meeting of the Ghosts at Tyburn: Being a Discourse of Oliver Cromwell, John Bradshaw, Henry Ireton, Thomas Pride, Thomas Scot, Secretary to the Rump. Major Gen. Harrison, & Hugh Peters the Divells Chaplain* (London, 1660/1661), p. 5.

no tombstones, the author of *A New Meeting* provides epitaphs that he feels are fitting to identify each burial and 'mark' each dead man the way a gravestone would. Cromwell's reads:

> Here lies that Beast made up of blood
> That murdered Charles the First so good:
> And for his deeds, as they were evill,
> Let him not want fire, good Devill.[39]

The 'marking' of the figure of Cromwell is an act of revenge upon the deceased that parallels the 'marking' of the desecration of his body and functions as a text inscribed upon his corpse.

George Bate (d.1669) is one of the few controversialists who dared sign his name to his work. His book, *The Lives, Actions, and Execution of the Prime Actors, and Principall Contrivers of that Horrid Murder of our Late Pious and Sacred Soveraigne, King Charles the First* (1661), places itself in the context of burial space, both the king's and Cromwell's.[40] Here, Bate imagines an epitaph for Cromwell that vandalises the tomb, even after its tenant has been pulled from it. Knowing that the vault containing Cromwell's body had been concealed from view for security, Bate intends for his epitaph to mark the spot, rather than the man, in case the disinterment should succeed in suggesting that Cromwell had never desecrated the Chapel of Henry VII by resting there. He says:

> Here lies ignominious dust
> Which was the only seat of lust;
> A man and yet a Monster too,
> That did both King and State undo.
> Most people say, this is his doom:
> That here he don't deserve a tomb.[41]

Part of Scott Newstok's important discussion of epitaphs includes the idea that the epitaph 'places' the body, particularly by way of the words 'Here lies X'. The words of an epitaph do more than locate the body; they announce and describe the body. Furthermore, epitaphs demand aural participation from the visitor to the tomb,

---

[39] *A New Meeting*, p. 4.

[40] Other tracts provide similar epitaphs with royalist sentiments. See Joseph Glanvill, *A Loyal Tear Dropt on the Vault of our Late Martyred Sovereign in an Anniversary Sermon on the Day of his Murther* (London, 1667); also Thomas Swadlin, *King Charles His Funeral: Who Was Beheaded by Base and Barbarous Hands January 30, 1648, and Interred at Windsor, February 9, 1648, with his Anniversaries Continued until 1659* (London, 1661).

[41] George Bate, *The Lives, Actions, and Execution of the Prime Actors, and Principall Contrivers of that Horrid Murder of our Late Pious and Sacred Soveraigne, King Charles the First...* (London, 1661), p. 10.

literally, that he or she 'hear' the epitaph.[42] As Newstok points out, Early Modern epitaph writers mean to describe, locate, and, occasionally accuse, as Bate does here. Hearing and pronouncing the epitaph at the location where the body is (or was), allows the visitor to participate in the events of the life, death, and burial of the deceased.[43] Bate wants his reader to know that Cromwell once *lay* here, but no longer *lies* here; he does not deserve a tomb, but he deserves an epitaph which leaves the location marked, yet vandalised.

Because he is a royalist, Bate does not end his treatise without providing an epitaph for Charles I. He relates a poignant (but unconfirmed) report about the burial of Charles I, saying, 'A Gentleman standing at his sad interment, threw this Distick into the Vault: Non Carolus magnus, nec Carolus quintus,/Sed Carolus Agnus his Iacet intus'.[44] Bate invites his readers to locate themselves at the sites of burial and disinterment, to engage in an imaginative reenactment of events they had not attended. Because he supports the king, Bate uses the second epitaph to attest to the injustice of the king's execution by placing the text in immediate proximity to the body. Bate's posthumous epitaph for Cromwell marks the external location of the body with text; the king's epitaph is placed in the coffin, internalising the relationship between Charles I and the anonymous 'Gentleman', who represents those members of the public who could not be there. Bate's anecdote also attempts to compensate for the tradition of hagiographic adoration that could not take place at the time of the king's actual interment. Hagiographic adoration and incorruptibility were issues that attended the deaths of both men, precisely because the Chapel of Henry VII had been involved. A follower of the cult of Henry VI, Henry VII at first wanted to be buried at Windsor next to his predecessor, whom he expected to be canonised. His tomb at Westminster was meant to establish a hagiographic dynasty for his family when a canonisation for Henry VI was not granted. It did not go unnoticed that Cromwell had been buried next to Henry VII, while Charles was buried near Henry VI. After Cromwell's disinterment, the body of the king's nemesis was displayed publicly, with people paying sixpence to see a desiccated corpse instead of making a donation at the tomb of an uncorrupted one.

John Quarles (1624–1665) includes an epitaph for the king in *Reglae Lectum Miserae: Or, a Kingly Bed of Misery* (1649).[45] In a dream about the dead king, Quarles goes to kiss the king's hand, but the phantom disappears before Quarles can venerate it. Upon

---

[42] Newstok, pp. 1–3, and 39–40.

[43] Newstok, pp. 1–3, and 39–40.

[44] Bate, p. 144. The phrase reads, 'Not Charles the Great, nor Charles the Fifth, but Charles the Lamb lies within'. Bate likely invented the story, or heard it as a rumour. There is no mention of papers inside the coffin in the record of the disinterment of Charles I in 1813, although the record does state that only the top part of the coffin was opened, so that the face of Charles I might be identified. In any case, such a paper, if it existed, had probably disintegrated by then.

[45] John Quarles, *Reglae Lectum Miserae: Or, A Kingly Bed of Misery: In Which is Contained, a Dream: With an Elegy Upon the Martyrdom of Charles, Late King of England, of Blessed Memory: And Another Upon the Right Honourable the Lord Capel. With a Curse Against the Enemies of Peace, and the Authors Farewell to England* (London, 1649).

waking, he admits: 'And then I found my active fancy play'd/The Politician'.[46] He then proceeds with an elegy, wishing that every heart could spend a few drops of blood on the tomb of the king, so that the tomb would soon be covered with blood from loyal and well-meaning hearts '... And send/Millions of sighes to Heav'n, that may expresse/His death was Englands great unhappinesse'.[47] Here, the blood of aggrieved and penitent royalists produces sighs, which are heard by Heaven. Quarles also recounts that his dream featured a second funeral for Charles I; one in which the Thames, filled with the tears of loyal subjects, provided a more fitting conveyance for the king's funeral barge than the earthly river had.[48] Again, an author envisions that the king is reinterred, his funeral reproduced as an imaginative, literary reenactment so that his body can rest in peace. A reimagined public funeral replaces the secretive first one, and produces, in the mind of the author, a secondary reality. The epitaph at the end of Quarles' piece likens this imaginative reinterment to a state of gestation, which will give birth to dynastic continuity and allow Divine Right to pass to the king's son, Charles II. It reads: 'I may presume to say, a Tombe/Never had a richer wombe'.[49] The tomb itself is a womb that will nurture kingship during the years of the Interregnum, until kingship is reborn upon the restoration of the Monarchy. John Quarles did live to see the Restoration, and he was very likely proud of his prophetic epitaph.

There were many rumours that ran wild in the aftermath of the disinterment of the regicides, but the most sensational was the one that claimed that the body which had been dragged out of the Chapel of Henry VII, hung, and decapitated, was not that of Oliver Cromwell. This rumour (which persists in some quarters today)[50] owes much of its persistence to the fact that it revisited an issue that troubled both Royalists and Roundheads in 1649 and again in 1659: that the great man (either Charles I or Cromwell) was not dead; that he had escaped, and that the body interred (or disinterred), was not his. Even if one had witnessed the posthumous hanging of Cromwell, one might still not be able to say, as Marvell once had, 'I saw him dead'. The fantasy that Cromwell's body had been switched fed the imaginations of both camps, and it was used by each to weaken the position of the other for centuries afterwards. One facet of the rumour looked to Samuel Pepys' diary for legitimacy: Pepys cites

---

[46] Quarles, p. 3.
[47] Quarles, p. 61.
[48] Quarles, pp. 86–7.
[49] Quarles, p. 91.
[50] See H.F. McMains, *The Death of Oliver Cromwell* (Lexington, KY, 2000), and Jonathan Fitzgibbons, *Cromwell's Head* (Richmond, 2008) for recent discussions of this idea. There is, expectedly, a switched-head theory that stipulates that the head owned and displayed by the Wilkinson family for generations was not the head of Oliver Cromwell. In 1875, George Rolleston, Professor of Anatomy and Physiology at Oxford, used the Cromwellian death mask at the Ashmolean Museum for his guide and decided that Horace Wilkinson indeed owned the original. It is possible (but not probable), that the authentication was made simply to get the head out of the public eye and off the market. In any case, the head was buried in 1960 at Sidney Sussex College, Cambridge, in an undisclosed place.

that he read 'in a French book' a rumour that while Cromwell was alive, he translated the bodies of many English kings from one place to another; and that it could not be known whether the body hanged at Tyburn 'be that of Cromwell or one of the kings'.[51] With this rumour there arose the horrible possibility that the royalists, in their zealous desire to exact revenge on Cromwell's corpse, accidentally desecrated the body of one of their own kings. The rumour likely started after the deaths of some of the members of the Cromwell family, who were interred at Westminster in the Henry VII Chapel. It may have seemed to persons of a cynical attitude that royal bodies were being moved or rearranged so that anyone seeking to desecrate Cromwell's body in death might mistakenly disinter the wrong corpse. Citing participation of aptly named 'resurrection men', proponents of the switched-body theory could comfort themselves with the idea that Cromwell's body was still safe, enshrined in the Abbey. Interestingly, whether one was a royalist or a republican one could find comfort in such an idea, since it places the bodies of both men, once again, on common ground after death. Those who believed the switched-body rumour could rest assured that the body of their hero lay unmolested, protected within a sacred space and among kings, hidden from the eyes of all but God. In any case, by 1684 both Cromwell and Charles I lay buried in unknown, unmarked graves.[52]

During the nineteenth century there was renewed interest in the Civil War. Just as the Henrician era and the Reformation were being reimagined, and even relived, so was the Interregnum. Nonconformists had taken a generally positive view of Cromwell throughout the eighteenth century, largely because of his support for religious toleration;[53] but as Roger Howell states, in the nineteenth century came the cry, 'We need another Oliver'.[54] How one got another Oliver was a complicated matter. In his study of the subject, Roger Howell breaks down what he calls 'the extensive recall' of Cromwell into three defining factors. First, reference to Cromwell as a political symbol had already been established in the eighteenth century, not infrequently with radical overtones. He says, 'During the Wilkes crisis of 1769, for

---

[51] Samuel Pepys, 'Diary entry for 13 October 1664', *The Diary of Samuel Pepys*, ed. Henry B. Wheatley (London, 1899), www.gutenberg.org.

[52] See McMains, who argues against Cromwell's burial at Tyburn, maintaining that Cromwell's final resting place is completely unknown. Also see Sir Henry Halford for a persuasive assertion that until the vault containing Charles I was stumbled upon, no one could remember where it was.

[53] Roger Howell, 'The Eighteenth-Century View of Oliver Cromwell', *Cromwelliana* (1979), pp. 19–25, www.olivercromwell.org/cromwelliana.htm. PDF format.

[54] Howell, 'Eighteenth-century View', pp. 98–9; Olive Anderson, 'The Political Uses of History in Mid-Nineteenth Century England', *Past and Present* 36 (1967): 85; T.W. Mason, 'Nineteenth-Century Cromwell', *Past and Present* 40 (1968): 187–91; and J.P.D. Dunabin, 'Oliver Cromwell's Popular Image in Nineteenth-Century England', in *Britain and the Netherlands: Papers Delivered to the Third Anglo-Dutch Historical Conference* 5, ed. J.S. Bromley and E.H. Kossman (London, 1968): 141–63.

example, Cromwell's image was used as a threat of deposition or regicide'.[55] Second, the folk memory and oral tradition with respect to Cromwell were strong in the nineteenth century, with a focus on working-class evocations of his image. While not all that tradition was positive, there was a significant association in the popular mind of Cromwell with prosperous, or at least better, times.[56] Third, various issues that agitated nineteenth-century politics had what Howell calls 'distinct echoes of the great seventeenth-century struggle' and could easily be fitted to a Cromwellian frame.[57] His forceful foreign policy and the perception that he had made England respected abroad especially cooperated with British Imperialism of the nineteenth century.

Cromwell was reestablished as a national hero, in great part by the work of Thomas Carlyle, especially *Letters and Speeches of Oliver Cromwell*,[58] which defined the English view of Cromwell for nearly a century. In Carlyle's book, Cromwell was lionised as a virtuous, morally upright and patriotic figure, a man who Jonathan Fitzgibbons claims, 'was something that most Victorian families could admire'.[59] Ironically, Cromwell's image was subject to a switching of sorts – from that of a Puritan Lord Protector who committed regicide and brutally repressed the Irish, to a champion of religious sectarianism and the working class, a man who reflected nineteenth-century republican ideals. Just as the monarchical body stood resurrected intact in the body of Victoria, the republican body politic was resurrected in a refreshed Cromwellian figure. As Blair Worden states, 'If many Victorians were against what Charles had been against, by the middle of the century few people were in favour of what, in political and constitutional matters, he had been for'.[60] This complex but convenient notion allowed Cromwell to approach political unison with the monarchical body. People could respect the authority and tradition of the monarchy while admiring the progressive aspects of republicanism. These issues, says Worden, when combined with a rising admiration for military heroism in the aftermath of the Napoleonic Wars, produced a Cromwell who could stand alongside Wellington and Nelson.[61]

Around the same time as some of England's greatest victories in those wars,[62] the body of Charles I was literally stumbled upon by workers in St George's Chapel who were cutting a passage leading from under the choir to a new mausoleum. A hole was broken in a brick wall along the passage, and upon inspection, the workers were able

---

[55] Howell, 'Eighteenth-century View', pp. 98–9.
[56] Howell, 'Eighteenth-century View', pp. 98–9.
[57] Howell, 'Eighteenth-century View', pp. 98–9.
[58] Thomas Carlyle, *Letters and Speeches of Oliver Cromwell*; see also J.R. Green, *History of the English People*, 3 vols. (London, 1878–80).
[59] Fitzgibbons, p. 178.
[60] Worden, p. 229.
[61] Worden, p. 233.
[62] Although Nelson had died in 1805, he was still lauded feverishly in 1813; Wellington, in 1813, defeated the French at Vitoria and would defeat Napoleon at Waterloo two years later.

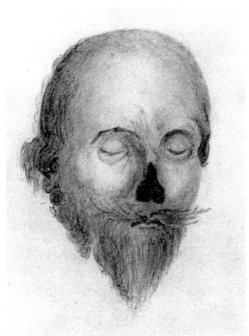

Fig. 25 Drawing by Sir Henry Halford of the head of Charles I as it appeared on 1 April 1813. The King's head was attached to his body with sutures. After examining the head, Halford passed it to the Prince Regent and George III for identification before returning it to the coffin.

to see three coffins (Fig. 9). Since one of the coffins was very large, they supposed it to be that of Henry VIII, which, although its whereabouts was not known, was said to be located in that area of the chapel. The coffin next to it was presumed to be that of Jane Seymour, and the third was determined to be that of Charles I.[63] The Prince Regent (later George IV) ordered the opening of the vault shortly after. It was done on 1 April 1813, under the auspices of the Prince Regent, the Duke of Cumberland, Count Munster, the Dean of Windsor, Benjamin Charles Stevenson, Esq., and Sir Henry Halford, physician to the king and the Prince Regent. Despite his illness, George III himself was also present. Dr Halford recorded the event as the coffin was opened, and noted that the only words inscribed upon the coffin were 'King Charles 1648' – an identifying marker strikingly similar to Cromwell's in its simplicity. The head of Charles I was loose, the sutures at the neck long since having disintegrated, and it was easily removed from the coffin. Upon inspection by all present it was agreed that the head was definitely that of Charles I (Fig. 25). Halford records:

> At length, the whole face was disengaged from its covering. The complexion of the skin of it was dark and discoloured. The forehead and temples had lost little or nothing of their muscular substance; the cartilage of the nose was gone; but the left eye, in the first moment of exposure, was open and full, though it vanished almost immediately;

[63] Sir Henry Halford, pp. 6–7.

and the pointed beard, so characteristic of the period of the reign of King Charles, was perfect. The shape of the face was a long oval; many of the teeth remained; and the left ear, in consequence of the interposition of the unctuous latter between it and the cere-cloth, was found entire.[64]

With no further disturbance, the coffin was soldered shut. This time no one would forget where the king lay. The Prince Regent commissioned a simple monument of black stone, upon which was inscribed the names and dates of those buried in the vault.[65] Locating the body of Charles I was a victory for monarchists, because it presented them with an opportunity to reiterate the tragedy of regicide and the failure of the short-lived Protectorate. The identification of Charles I also promoted the idea of monarchical continuity in the face of uncertainty: the Prince Regent reigned in the place of his father George III, who was ill with porphyria; in the following years as George IV he left no heir, and was succeeded by his brother, William IV, who, similarly leaving no heir, was succeeded by his niece, Victoria. 'Locating' the body – saying, 'Here lies Charles I' – demonstrated dynastic endurance in the face of adversity.

Giving 'voices' to Cromwell and Charles I allowed both men to speak to the Victorians in the political rhetoric people already understood. This renewed interest also allowed both men to 'speak' to Victorians folklorically, through that culture's fascination with ghosts. Ghosts of the nineteenth century differ markedly from the polemical spirits that moralise in seventeenth-century pamphlets and broadsheet ballads. The spirits of Cromwell and Charles I were imagined to participate in afterlife communication, albeit with a subtler, more arcane rhetorical sense. Victorians actively pursued proof of life after death, with séances, spirit mediums, and various types of pseudo-scientific ghost investigation. Amid this fervour for ghosts, Charles I and Cromwell were given the opportunity to defend themselves, albeit in language that the Victorians, rather than the people of the Stuart era, were comfortable with. Here, the conversant dead make their pleas directly to the living via hauntings, rather than to each other in pamphlets and ballads. When it comes to such hauntings, there are few, if any, words. Moreover, there is almost no literary context – no metre or formality of address.[66] The ghost of Charles I was reported in various places associated with battles and political intrigues of the Civil Wars.[67] He appeared, for example, at Marple Hall,

---

[64] Halford, p. 8.

[65] In addition to Charles I, Henry VIII, and Jane Seymour, the vault also contained the coffin of an infant child of Queen Anne.

[66] For a comprehensive discussion of the changes in ghost legend between the Early Modern period and the Georgian through Victorian periods, see Owen Davies, *The Haunted: A Social History of Ghosts* (New York, 2007).

[67] For an overview of the competitive field of nineteenth-century spiritualism and ghost hunting in Britain and America, see Tatiana Kontou and Sarah Wilburn, eds., *The Ashgate Research Companion to Nineteenth-Century Spiritualism and the Occult* (Farnham, 2012), and Deborah Blum, *Ghost Hunters: William James and the Search for Scientific Proof of Life After Death* (New

Cheshire, where he was associated with the apparition of a free-floating decapitated head;[68] at Christ Church, Oxford, where he walked the grounds while holding his head under his arm;[69] and at Pencait Castle, Lothian, where his death mask was displayed.[70] He was also seen at Court House in Painswick, where his headless ghost was said to drive around the grounds in a phantom coach.[71] In each case the ghost is headless; this state serves as a continual reminder of the severance of the monarchy from the people, and of the dynastic interruption of the Stuarts. Although the head and body are reunited in the tomb, the king is nevertheless not a *whole* man. The headlessness of the ghost is a form of political rhetoric in its own right, even without words. It represents conflict, unresolved issues, and dynastic uncertainty. It represents a futility of sorts, as well, since no amount of political reconciliation or cooperation can restore the whole man. The ghost of Charles I remains connected to the circumstances of his death, and seeks out living witnesses with whom to interact. The Charles I of the Victorian ghost

York, 2006). For a specific example of the influence of spiritualism on one writer's career, see Matt Winget, *Sir Arthur Conan Doyle and the World of Light 1887–1920* (Portsmouth, 2016).

[68] These stories are based in local folklore, much of which today is related via ghost tours of residences, public houses, castles, and battlefields. None of these ghost legends predates the eighteenth century, and many go back no farther than the mid-nineteenth. Much of the cataloguing of stories of this type was done by nineteenth- and early twentieth-century folklorists and folklore societies. They compiled tales and conducted interviews with people who demonstrated qualities of acceptable credibility for their time, such as a good name, a stoic demeanour, deep religious faith, and aristocratic or military honour. See Anthony D. Hippisley-Coxe, *Haunted Britain* (London, 1973); also see Christina Hole, *English Folklore* (London, 1940), and *Haunted England* (London, 1941); also T.M. Jarvis, *Accredited Ghost Stories* (London, 1823). Jarvis attaches ghost legends to people by name in order to emphasise their credibility; but Catherine Crowe, in her study of such legends, mentions a family's or individual's greatness but discreetly avoids giving names. Catherine Crowe, *The Night Side of Nature, Or, Ghosts and Ghost-Seers*, 2 vols. (London, 1848).

[69] Hole, *Haunted England*, p. 65.

[70] Coxe, pp. 11 and 189. Coxe attended tours, interviewed curators and keepers of castles, and inspected sites. He also utilised sources such as The British Tourist Authority Information Library, which has, over the years, printed guides of haunted castles, inns, and other sites for tourists. Such catalogues and guides offer institutional legitimacy for long-told stories that can be traced to no real source and which are told in many variations. They provide the basis for much of the relationship between a local tourist site and the government when it comes to declaring a site to be of historical value. Camille Flammarion discusses the role of catalogued experiences in the exhaustive (and rather absurd) process by which haunted houses in England and France were deemed 'legal', for the purpose of negotiating tenancy contracts during the nineteenth century. Camille Flammarion, *Haunted Houses* (New York, 1924), pp. 70–111.

[71] Tales of phantom coaches are common in England and Ireland (especially in Dunkerron and Cumberland). They feature the headless spectre of a famous or historical person travelling in a fast-moving coach, sometimes with a headless driver, and sometimes pulled by headless horses. For a discussion of the tale and its sources see Maurice O'Leary, 'The Phantom Coach', *Journal of American Folklore* 11 (1898): 235; and also Christina Hole, *English Folk-Lore*, p. 151, and *Haunted England*, pp. 139ff.

legend is the same Charles of the seventeenth-century ghost pamphlets: restless and eternally seeking justice. It is a frustrating but permanent state, and one with which the Victorians were familiar, since after the 1689 Bill of Rights and the 1707 Acts of Union the monarchical body was forever changed, forever severed from the Royal Prerogative it once enjoyed. Stories of the headless ghost of Charles I are rooted deeply in the vast differences between those who stood firmly upon the tradition of monarchy and the authority of Victoria, and those who looked toward republicanism and social reform, for whom Cromwell had become a modern hero.

The legend of the ghost of Cromwell is related to the 'switched-body' theory that had captivated the English imagination since the seventeenth century. One story stated that the headless bodies of Cromwell, Ireton, and Bradshaw were not thrown into a pit below the gallows at Tyburn, but were buried secretly in a field in Holborn, near a pub called the Red Lion, where their bodies had been held for a few days before their posthumous hanging. By the eighteenth century this field was known as Red Lion Square, and it sported a lone obelisk bearing a mysterious epigraph: *Obtusioris Ingenii Monumentum. Quid me respicis, viator? Vade.*[72] Those who wished to could find great meaning in such an epigraph, and the verse provides much fuel for the imagination. The most inspired of Cromwell's admirers imagined him to be buried under the spot, commemorated cryptically, and therefore safe from the hands of royalists.

The ghost legend that grew up around Red Lion Square involves the phantom figures of Cromwell, Ireton, and Bradshaw walking about the Square on foggy nights. The three men are conversant, with their heads attached. Their conversation is unheard by human ears but understood by the keen nineteenth-century politico/ghost enthusiast: they speak of the Commonwealth and its best interests. They are hale and hearty, a far cry from the dessicated corpses which were pulled from Westminster. Cromwell's head is where it is supposed to be, his body whole and functional. The imagination which fuels this ghost legend memorialises Cromwell in a different way than does the ghost legend of Charles I: here, the language of cultural memory literally re-members him. It also rewrites the ghost legend of the earlier pamphlets and enfranchises the ghost of Cromwell into the world of the living. The ghosts of the regicides interact with each other as active men of Parliamentary politics, with no acknowledgment of their ghostly state.[73] They act as whole men of the modern world. However, although these ghosts are conversant, their language assumed to be fittingly political, they are nonetheless wordless phantoms, whose exchanges are not meant for the living. Although they rewrite the pamphlets, they do so metaphorically, in a way not meant to be understood by the everyday reader, as the pamphlets were. Here, the text of the corpse is as phantom-like as the spectre of the dead man himself; it is a sort of palimpsest, a text that communicates invisibly, but alongside another set of words

---

[72] Hole, *Haunted England,* pp. 65–6. The cryptic inscription reads: 'Bear witness to this clever monument. How do you regard me, traveller? Go.'

[73] Hole, *Haunted England,* pp. 65–6.

and ideas. As it was, the obelisk in Red Lion Square was probably not the spot where Cromwell's body lay; it is not known what or whom it was meant to commemorate. The monument fell into decay, and was removed by 1790. Cromwell's body, or the idea of its location, went uncommemorated until the mid-nineteenth century, when a plaque was laid in the floor of the Henry VII Chapel in Westminster Abbey (probably in 1866) on the spot where Cromwell's vault had been (see Fig. 23). It is a simple plaque, inscribed with the name and dates, much like the nineteenth-century stone laid for Charles I at Windsor. By the end of the nineteenth century, both Cromwell and Charles I were 'located' and commemorated, but simply, without monuments or epitaphs.

Ghost legends of the nineteenth century cooperate with the monument culture of the period. Just as burials locate the body of the dead person, stating, 'here lies X', tales of hauntings locate the dead *persona* within a specific, memorialised space, which may be different from the locus of interment. Ghost legends announce, 'here haunts X'. Monuments perform a similar function in that they locate the *personage* of a celebrated figure, who is most often dead. They announce the celebrated figure to his or her admirers in an ideal state of nobility, victory, or youth, pronouncing, 'here *is* X'.[74] Locating and announcing the personage of Cromwell were precisely the motives of Lord Rosebery when he proposed in 1894 that a majestic statue of Cromwell be erected at Westminster Hall.[75] The Prime Minister had long been an admirer of Cromwell, who he proclaimed to be '…the raiser and maintainer of the power of the Empire in England'.[76] Rosebery called for a Cromwell of the Victorian age, one whose persona would be different from that of the seventeenth-century Cromwell but who would nonetheless retain his well-known qualities as a military leader and statesman.[77] Many of Rosebery's fellow politicians, especially the Irish MPs and Tory monarchists, did not hold this view. Despite the generally favourable reassessment of Cromwell's legacy in nineteenth-century England, and the continuous reiteration of that reassessment in the historiography of the period, the Lord Protector remained controversial.[78] Requests for public funds were temporarily dropped, but Rosebery did get his statue in time for the tercentenary of Cromwell's birth, in 1899.

The statue was not, however, as majestic as Rosebery and other admirers of Cromwell wanted it to be. Instead of striking a victorious pose on horseback (which Rosebery had wanted in order to recall the 1633 statue of Charles I in Trafalgar Square),[79] the statue

---

[74] A haunted cemetery filled with monuments would provide all three scenarios, but neither Charles I nor Cromwell could enjoy these circumstances.

[75] Rosebery's request for the statue had been made years earlier, but the plans were not put into place until he became Prime Minister in 1894. The statue was designed by Hamo Thornycroft.

[76] Lord Archibald Rosebery, *Oliver Cromwell: A Eulogy and an Appreciation* (London, 1900), p. 5.

[77] Rosebery, pp. 10, 11, 19, and 33–4.

[78] Much of the controversy revolved around Cromwell's putative toleration for non-conformity in religion, his foreign policy, and in particular his treatment of the Irish. See Anderson, p. 85.

[79] The statue of Charles I stands on the spot where Charing Cross once stood. During the Interregnum the statue was hidden in a garden, and was later reinstalled by Charles II. Timothy Lang also cites the equestrian statue of Richard I outside Westminster Hall as inspiration for an early design for the Cromwell statue. Timothy Lang, *The Victorians and the*

of Cromwell stands humbly, the text of his body communicating humility and piety rather than triumph. In one hand he holds a Bible, in the other, a sword, with its blade pointed down (Fig. 21). The location of the statue was also less than majestic. In 1882, the new Royal Courts of Justice were opened in the Strand, and the old buildings, which were adjacent to Westminster Hall, were demolished. The demolition site was known as 'The Pit', and although a new stone façade covered the unsightly brick on the exposed wall of Westminster Hall, 'The Pit' remained a London joke for some time. By 1899 the overall pit-like qualities of the area had been mostly remedied, but it still made for a tongue-in-cheek location for the Cromwell statue. The statue was erected near the site of Cromwell's disinterment as a form of reconciliation for the act of desecration that had occurred nearby at Westminster Abbey. It located the personage of the great man near the place where his body once enjoyed a king's burial – and it also located (metaphorically and ironically) the disposal of his body in a pit. When it debuted, the statue was not granted a dramatic presentation before cheering crowds, but was unveiled before a small group of enthusiasts at seven-thirty in the morning on 14 November 1899.[80] This was due partly to the political controversy caused by the statue, and also to the fact that the disturbing narrative of Cromwell's desecrated corpse and the pit it lay in were inscribed metaphorically upon the statue.

It is perhaps most fitting that a lead bust of Charles I had been installed in the west-facing exterior wall of St Margaret's Church, Westminster, some years earlier. (Fig. 22). Set near a plaque commemorating the burial of several of the regicides in St Margaret's churchyard, the bust looks out upon Whitehall and directly (so it seems) across the street at the statue of Cromwell. The expression on the bust is convivial, and yet its gaze (as tour guides are wont to point out) appears to be aiming a triumphant look at Cromwell, who, in deference to the restored Monarchy, averts his glance. The disembodied head of Charles I is recalled by the bust, and it communicates contentment and a sense of justice in death. Via these figural monuments, the two men are 'located' on the common ground of both Whitehall and Westminster, where Charles I had reigned and died, and where Cromwell had ruled, been buried, and been disinterred. The 'conversation' between Charles I and Oliver Cromwell continues uninterrupted, protected by the liminal space between the world of the living and that of the dead. Both men intended to complete successful careers at Whitehall and intended to rest undisturbed at Westminster; both experienced the interruption of power and the failure of dynasty; and both were removed from the spaces in which they intended to

---

Stuart Heritage: Interpretations of a Discordant Past (Cambridge, 1995), pp. 309–13. See also Patrick Maume, 'Cromwell's Statue in Westminster', *History Ireland* 16, no. 6 (Nov.–Dec. 2008): 12–13.

[80] Despite the controversy surrounding the statue, the Tercentenary was celebrated fervently all over the country. In London, at City Temple in Holborn, a series of commemorative meetings and presentations lasted from morning until night. The City Temple was filled to its 3,000-person capacity, and hundreds stood outside. The Tercentenary also produced a slew of new biographies of Cromwell, and reprintings of Carlyle's work. Worden, p. 215.

be defined in life and in death. The statues 'locate' this absence and communicate it to
onlookers. Tourists bear witness to both figural monuments as documents of the past
and the present: they 'read' them in life and in death, and they 'locate' the bodies of the
two men, albeit in their absence. Because neither man is buried in that space, a visitor
cannot claim 'I saw him dead', as he or she can within the Abbey church, where a
monument locates the dead personage in his or her tomb, uniting commemoration and
the physical body. The visitor must therefore say, 'I see Cromwell', or 'I see Charles I', as
they read the continuing discourse of the political and monarchical bodies of Church
and State. Although they are immobile and silent, with neither heads nor crowns, the
two men are enduringly and exclusively conversant in death – but still, as it were, not
seeing eye to eye.

CONCLUSION

Antiquaries of the Georgian through the Victorian periods were aware that nostalgia could be used to interrupt and rewrite memory as well as construct it, and that disinterment was an important tool for such a task. They believed that their efforts would energise their ideals of the past and make those ideals newly relevant for the present. In this sense the idea of 'The English Renaissance' as a Golden Age is located in stereotypes of the sixteenth and seventeenth centuries that revolve around the dead.[1] By disinterring important figures from this era (if 'the English Renaissance' can be called an era in and of itself) the antiquaries discussed in this book, and many of their colleagues, constructed texts of a Golden Age that could, in part, be read via the bodies of its celebrated dead. By 'reading' the corpse in this way one could argue, for example, that Shakespeare had always enjoyed god-like status; that Henry VIII had always been a grotesque tyrant; that Oliver Cromwell had always been a champion of religious tolerance; that Catherine Parr had always been a bold Protestant heroine, and that Anne Boleyn was a *femme fatale* from the start. One could argue that long-held scepticisms about the legends of King John and Thomas Becket could be upheld. When antiquaries looked into the tombs and graves of kings, queens, poets, and churchmen, they expected to read these truths in the bodies of the dead.

The idealism for the Middle Ages during the period 1700–1900 (including the Tudor and Stuart eras in the popular imagination) reflects more than an attachment to the aesthetic of art, literature, or legend. It relates to innovations of urban governance, to ideas of patriotism and the expansion of the Empire, and to what Billie Melman calls 'the civilising process'.[2] For many there was a real desire to project the ideals of 'Medieval' England onto Imperial urbanised London, while at the same time making continual distinctions between the present and the past. The result was what Melman calls a 'mixed modernity',[3] as the desire to draw the past closer to the present was

---

[1] Peter Mandler, 'Revisiting the Olden Time', in Tatiana String and Marcus Bull, eds., *Tudorism: Historical Imagination and the Appropriation of the Sixteenth Century* (Oxford, 2011), p. 29. In his chapter Mandler argues that eighteenth- and nineteenth-century medievalism is a subject distinct from its 'Tudorism'.

[2] Melman, p. 55.

[3] Melman, 'The Pleasure of Tudor Horror', in Tatiana String and Marcus Bull, eds., *Tudorism: Historical Imagination and the Appropriation of the Sixteenth Century* (Oxford, 2011), p. 55.

met with a desire to appropriate and redefine it via scientific investigation, academic enquiry, and political rhetoric. The result is a series of well-constructed fictions of which society is conscious and which people accept willingly. Britain's victories over France during the early nineteenth century, for example, were juxtaposed with idealised views of Henry VIII's military campaigns against the French. George IV modelled himself on the Tudor monarchs (sans Mary I); he drew heavily upon the power of the Crown, he obtained the first public royal divorce since Henry VIII, and he styled much of his ceremonial dress after the Tudor manner (a style enhanced perhaps by his fifty-inch waist).[4] The emergence of women's literary groups was juxtaposed with idealised views of Katherine Parr's intellectualism. Shakespeare's career was idealised to the extent that it lent credibility to any facet of society that cared to attach his name to it.

Jonathan Gil Harris states that the study of 'things' is connected to a culture's national sovereignty and its notions of temporality.[5] In establishing such a complex sense of temporality, it is important for a culture to assure itself that the 'things' it studies do not conflict with the current time, but complement it. This is particularly important for a state like Imperial Britain, which was focused on building and maintaining an Empire that simultaneously idealised and appropriated the Tudor and Stuart pasts. In doing so, Britain was able to affirm its assumptions about its cultural and political superiority. The corpse of a literary or historical figure that becomes the object/subject of fascination fits into this model. The corpse goes from being 'one of them' to 'one of us'. In this sense, the disinterred Tudor/Stuart corpse has its own moment in the temporality of Imperial Britain, a moment different from that of the excavated Roman soldier, Medieval saint, or Egyptian mummy. For the scholars of the eighteenth and of the nineteenth centuries, the Roman soldier, like the Medieval saint, is a figure of the past, a symbol of a struggle overcome. The Egyptian mummy (for the nineteenth-century Egyptologists who incorporated the study of the Egyptian dead into their scholarship about death and memory) is also a symbol of an ancient past whose history, its glories lost, has been absorbed into that of the British Empire; but the mummy is an exotic object fit for a display case in a museum (or, for the wealthy collector, a parlour or library). The Tudor/Stuart corpse is polytemporal, what Jonathan Gill Harris calls 'untimely'. He says, 'In its polychronicity, an object can prompt many different understandings and experiences of temporality – that is, of the relations between now and then, old and new, before and after'.[6] The temporal meaning of disinterment describes the present time and validates notions of cultural and political superiority that were conceived long after the death of the figure in question. The moment of unity comes when the corpse is not merely seen, but *read*; and the experience goes beyond simple observation. As antiquaries gazed at the corpses of the historical dead they unified the moment of their cultural present

---

[4]   See Steven Parissien, 'The Tudors Reinvented: The Regency and the Sixteenth Century', in *Tudorism: Historical Imagination and the Appropriation of the Sixteenth Century*, ed. Tatiana String and Marcus Bull (Oxford, 2011), p. 119.

[5]   Harris, *Untimely Matter in the Time of Shakespeare* (Philadelphia, 2009), p. 2.

[6]   Harris, p. 4.

with that of the past. They were aware that the same process had once been employed for hagiographic inspection; but they were determined that the corpse should validate social, cultural, and political truths, rather than supernatural ones.

Their enquiries nevertheless represent an incomplete demystification. Although they intended to de-centre the corpse from Medieval ideas of sanctification, antiquaries were nevertheless driven by intellectual energy that was charged with emotion. The sentimental values they held concerning the belief that Britain was a superior cultural force and political power approached sanctification. The effort to validate the present via the past creates a hagiography of concepts and ideas, at the centre of which is the corpse. No miraculous healings are expected; but the notion that the scholars, churchmen, and politicians discussed in this book were right about who they believed they were, and what they believed Britain to be, is phenomenal nonetheless. Monarchic dignity was written on the face of Charles I; Republican resolve was written on the corpse of Cromwell; tyranny was written on the corpse of Henry VIII; injustice was written on the body of King John; Catholic determinism was certainly written upon the bones of Thomas Becket (if only they would identify themselves); and Protestant determination was written in the expressive, excellently preserved face of Katherine Parr. The disarray of Anne Boleyn's bones reflected the inconvenient untidiness of her legend; the shameful state of the corpse of Katherine de Valois told a complex story of tragic romance and negligence; and the genius of Shakespeare was surely written upon his bones (if they could ever be reached). As they could not, monuments representing his body proved the existence of his natural genius.[7]

In his seminal book, *Metahistory: The Historical Imagination in Nineteenth-Century Europe*, Hayden White argues that the philosophy of history shares the same rhetorical structure and archetypal models as the literary tradition. This method of 'reading' histories (and artefacts) began in the eighteenth century, and contributed to the development of antiquarianism over the course of the next century. The fact that the writing of the philosophy of history was expressed in the same rhetorical structures as literature means that histories and artefacts – including corpses – can indeed be 'read' as part of a larger epistemological context that includes the literary imagination.[8] The association in this book of each corpse with one or more forms of rhetoric (auxesis, enthymeme, epideictic, euphemism, hyperbole, parenthesis, phallogocentrism, syllogism, and syncope) encourages White's view of the relationship between history, literature, art, language, and death. It is a surprising combination of elements, but it nevertheless produces an epistemological context that encourages new understandings of the vocation of antiquarianism, the professions of academic study and of politics, and the cultural phenomenon of death fascination between 1700 and 1900.

---

[7]   Absent from this volume is a chapter on the translation of and posthumous speculation upon the bones of Geoffrey Chaucer. This subject is discussed thoroughly in Thomas Prendergast, *Chaucer's Dead Body: From Corpse to Corpus* (New York, 2004).

[8]   Hayden White, *Metahistory: The Historical Imagination in Nineteenth-Century Europe* (Baltimore, 1973).

There are far more disinterments over the course of the period 1700–1900 than are discussed in this book. There are so many, in fact, that in order to discuss a great many of them (although hardly most of them) one would need to publish a catalogue of disinterments. Arthur Penrhyn Stanley created several such catalogues in *Historical Memorials of Westminster Abbey* (London, 1887), in *Historical Memorials of Canterbury* (London, 1888), and in other similar publications. In London he was assisted by Sir George Scharf, who provided the sketches of the bones for the majority of the excavations. In the present time, Aidan Dodson has done so, painstakingly, in his book *The Royal Tombs of Great Britain: An Illustrated History* (London, 2004). Records of other disinterments of figures both celebrated and notorious of the Medieval through the Stuart periods appear in various journals, books, and letters by a wide variety of academics, clergy, and amateur scholars with antiquarian interests. Disinterment was an important – even necessary – accompaniment to the study of one's own time. It was not merely a byproduct of architectural renovation, nor was it merely a macabre side-interest. It was essential to understanding the role of the dead in the progressive course of the events of the contemporary age. That role was historical, theological, and rhetorical – and it was also literary. The corpses discussed in this book form a group that demonstrates this theory as comprehensively as possible – this is true because in each case a wide-ranging narrative proceeds clearly from the record of the disinterment. This is the story of the corpse, one that supersedes the history of the corpse or the lifetime of the deceased; the story of the corpse, where the seven examples of this book are concerned, includes the entire cultural and political milieu into which the disinterred subject/object is admitted. The story is different in the case of each corpse, and – most interestingly – it does not always lead to the truth. In fact, more often than not, the story of the corpse leads to rumours, legends, misperceptions, and prejudices. What is important concerning this study is not simply that the disinterment produces a story, but that the story leads us in new and interesting directions by which we might understand why the practice of disinterment developed, how it was affected and informed by culture, politics, art, drama, and literature, and why it persisted. Ultimately, antiquarian study aided the development of the modern sciences of archaeology, and of physical and cultural anthropology. Its persistence, therefore, is important, and its view of the past is essential to an understanding of how a culture constructs narratives both on and off the page.

BIBLIOGRAPHY

Primary Sources

Addison, Joseph. *Dialogue upon the Usefulness of Ancient Medals* (London, 1726).

Anonymous. *Account of the Funeral of Katherine Parr*. College of Arms MS R20.

——. *Account of the Funeral of Katherine Parr*. College of Arms MS RR21C.

——. 'Box Containing the Bones of Thomas Becket'. Engraving. BL MS Cotton Tiberius E. viii, repr.

——. *Bradshaw's Ghost, A Poem. Or, A Dialogue Between John Bradshaw, Ferry-Man Charon, Oliver Cromwell, Francis Ravilliack, and Ignatius Loyola* (London, 1660).

——. *The Case is Alter'd Or, Dreadful News from Hell* (London, 1660).

——. *A Coffin for King Charles. A Crown for Cromwell. A Pit for the People* (London, 1649).

——. *An Excellent Ballad of King John and the Abbot of Canterbury. To the Tune of, The King and Lord Abbot* (Newcastle, c. 1711–69).

——, *Garrick's Vagary: Or, England Run Mad. With Particulars of the Stratford Jubilee* (London, 1769).

——. *Greene in Conceit, New Raised from his Grave To Write the Tragique Historie of Faire Valeria of London. Wherein is Truly Discouered the Rare and Lamentable Issue of a Husbands Dotage, a Wiues Leudnesse, & Children of Disobedience*. Received and Reported by I.D. (London, 1598).

——. *Greenes Newes Both from Heaven and Hell Prohibited the First for Writing of Bookes, and Banished Out of the Last for Displaying of Conny-Catchers* (London, 1593).

——. *Ivanhoe; Or, The Knight Templar: Adapted from the Novel of that Name*. (London, 1820).

——. Letter to *The Atlantic Monthly*, 'The Contributors' Club' (June 1878).

——. *A Mery Geste of Robyn Hoode: And of Hys Life, With a Newe Playe for to Be Played in Maye Games Very Pleasaunt and Full of Pastime* (London, 1560, repr. 1590).

——. 'The Murder of Thomas Becket'. *Manchester Times*, Saturday 30 September, 1865.

——. *A New Meeting of the Ghosts at Tyburn: Being a Discourse of Oliver Cromwell, John Bradshaw, Henry Ireton, Thomas Pride, Thomas Scot, Secretary to the Rump. Major Gen. Harrison, & Hugh Peters the Divells Chaplain* (London, 1660/1661).

——. *A Pleasant Comedie, Called Look About You* (London, 1600).

——. 'Shakespeare at Home'. *The Cincinnati Commercial Gazette* 43 (26 May, 1883).

——, 'Thomas à Becket'. *The Bristol Mercury and Daily Post,* Wednesday 1 February, 1888, issue 12393.

——. 'Thomas Becket's Remains'. *The York Herald,* Saturday 11 August, 1888, issue 11606.

——, *The Troublesome Raigne of King John* (London, 1591).

——, Untitled item in *The Monthly Magazine,* 1 February, 1818, repr. in J.O. Halliwell-Phillipps, *Outlines of the Life of Shakespeare,* 4th edn (London, 1884).

——. 'The Visitation; Or, An Interview Between the Ghost of Shakespear and D-V-D G-RR-K, esq'. (London, 1775), in O'Sullivan, Maurice, *Shakespeare's Other Lives: An Anthology of Fictional Depictions of the Bard* (Jefferson NC, 1997).

Arkasden. 'Letter to the Editor'. *The Standard* (London), Saturday 17 October, 1896.

——. 'Letter to the Editor'. *The Standard* (London), Tuesday 27 October, 1896.

Bale, John. *Acts of the English Votaries* (London, 1546).

——. 'Epitaph on the Discovery at Worcester of the Most Illustrious John, King of the English', in Trevet, Nicholas. *Annales Regum Angliae.* Parker Library, Corpus Christi College, Cambridge MS 152 fol. 48.

——. *Index Brittaniae Scriptorum,* ed. Reginald Poole and Mary Bateson (Oxford, 1902).

——. 'Kynge Johan' (1539), ed. Peter Happe. *The Complete Plays of John Bale.* 2 vols. (Cambridge, 1985).

Bate, George. *The Lives, Actions, and Execution of the Prime Actors, and Principall Contrivers of that Horrid Murder of our Late Pious and Sacred Soveraigne, King Charles the First...* (London, 1661).

Beazeley M. 'Letter to the Editor'. *The Morning Post,* 28 January, 1888, repr. in M. Beazeley , *The Canterbury Bones* (London, 1913).

Bede, *Ecclesiastical History of the English People,* ed. and trans. J. McLure and R. Collins (Oxford, 1994).

Bell, D.C. *Notices of the Historic Persons Buried in the Chapel of St Peter ad Vincula* (London, 1877).

Boker, George H. *Anne Boleyn, A Tragedy* (Philadelphia, 1850).

Bunn, A. *Ivanhoe; Or, The Jew of York: A New Grand Chivalric Play* (Birmingham, 1820).

Burke, Edmund. *Reflections on the Revolution in France and the First Letter on a Regicide Peace* (1790) (Cambridge, 2014).

Caesarius of Heisterbach. *Dialogos Miraculorum* (Cologne, 1481).

Chester, J.L. *Registers of the Collegiate Church or Abbey of St Peter* (London, 1876).

Cibber, Colley. *The Dramatic Works of Colley Cibber, Esq.* 5 vols., vol. I (London, 1767).

Curling, Henry. 'The Enthusiast at Shakespeare's Tomb' (1841), repr. in John Britton, *Essays on the Merits and Characteristics of William Shakspere* (London, 1849).

——. *Shakespeare: The Poet, The Lover, The Actor, The Man: A Romance* (London, 1848).

Darley, George. Thomas à Becket: A Dramatic Chronicle in Five Acts (London, 1840).

Davenport, Robert. King John and Matilda, a Tragedy (1623?) (London, 1662).

Drayton, Michael. *Mathilda, the Faire and Chaste Daughter of Lord R. Fitzwater* (London, 1594).

Erasmus, Desiderius. 'De Copia', ed. Craig R. Thompson, trans. Betty Knott and Brian McGregor, in *Collected Works*, vol. XXIV (Toronto, 1978).

Evelyn, John. *The Diary of John Evelyn*, ed. William Bray. 2 vols. (London, 1901).

Fiddes, Richard. *The Life of Cardinal Wolsey* (London, 1724).

Foxe, John. *Acts and Monuments*. 12 books (London, 1570), book IV.

——. *The Unabridged Acts and Monuments Online* or *TAMO* (1570 edition) (HRI Online Publications, Sheffield, 2011), https://www.johnfoxe.org [Accessed: 17.01.15].

Freud, Sigmund. 'Fetishism', *The Standard Edition of the Complete Psychological Works of Sigmund Freud*, 23 vols., ed. James Strachey (London, 1966), vol. XXI.

G.I.H. 'Letter to the Editor'. *The Standard* (London), Monday 19 October, 1896, issue 22559.

Geoffrey of Monmouth. *Historia Regum Brittaniae: A Variant Version Edited from Manuscripts* (Cambridge, MA, 1951).

Glanvill, Joseph. *A Loyal Tear Dropt on the Vault of our Late Martyred Sovereign in an Anniversary Sermon on the Day of his Murther* (London, 1667).

Great Britain, Public Record Office. *Calendar of Letters and Papers, Foreign and Domestic, of the Reign of Henry VIII*. 21 vols. (London, 1888, impr. 1965), vols. IX and X.

——. *Will of Henry VII*. E 23/3.

Gregory the Great, *The Dialogues of St Gregory*, ed. and trans. Odo John Zimmerman (New York, 1959).

H.W.B. 'The Shrine and Bones of St Thomas à Becket'. *The Graphic* (London), Saturday 24 March, 1888, issue 956.

Halford, Henry. *An Account of What Appeared on Opening the Coffin of King Charles the First ... on the First of April, MDCCCXIII ...* (London, 1813).

Hall, Edward. *Hall's Chronicle, Containing the Story of England During the Reign of Henry the Fourth and the Succeeding Monarchs, to the End of the Reign of Henry the Eighth* (1548) (London, 1809).

Hearne, Thomas. *A Collection of Curious Discourses*. 2 vols. (London, 1773), vol. I.

Herbert, Thomas. *Threnodia Carolina* (1678), repr. in Fea, Allan, *Memoirs of the Martyr King; Being a Detailed Record of the Last Two Years of the Reign of His Most Sacred Majesty King Charles I* (London, 1905).

Heywood, Thomas. *The Life of Merlin Surnamed Ambrosius, his Prophecies and Predictions Interpreted* (London, 1641) (Carmarthen, 1812).

Holinshed, Raphael. *Holinshed's Chronicle of England, Scotland, and Ireland* (1577). 6 vols. (London, 1807–8).

Holland, Hugh. *Pancharis* (1603), repr. in *Illustrations of Old English Literature*, ed. J. Payne Collier. 2 vols. (London, 1866).

——. 'Upon the Lines and Life of the Famous Scenic Poet, Master William Shakespeare', *Mr. William Shakespeare's Comedies, Histories & Tragedies, Published According to the True Originall Copies* (London, 1623), facsimile, Huntington Library, San Marino, CA).

An Improved History and Description of the Tower of London (London, 1817).

Jacobus de Voragine. *The Golden Legend; Readings on the Saints.* (Princeton, NJ, 1993).

Kingston, William. 'Letter to Thomas Cromwell', 19 May, 1536. MS Cotton Otho C x 223.

Knight, Thomas. 'Letter to Thomas Cromwell', 5 October, 1538'. Public Record Office. *Calendar of Letters and Papers, Foreign and Domestic, of the Reign of Henry VIII*, vol. XIII (London, 1893).

Knox, John. *The First Blast of the Trumpet Against the Monstrous Regiment of Women* (London, 1558).

Leland, John. *The Itinerary of John Leland*, vol. I, ed. Lucy Toulmin Smith (London, 1907).

Maitland, S.R. *Essays on Subjects Connected with the Reformation in England* (London, 1849, repr. 1899).

——. *Six Letters on Foxe's Acts and Monuments* (London, 1837).

Manning, Henry, Cardinal-Archbishop of Westminster. 'Archbishop Manning on St Thomas à Becket'. *London Daily News*, Thursday 3 September, 1868, issue 6970.

Marvell, Andrew. 'A Poem upon the Death of His Late Highness the Lord Protector', in *Andrew Marvell: The Complete Poems*, ed. Elizabeth Story Donno (New York, 1996).

Middleton, Thomas. *A Chaste Maid in Cheapside* (1613), in *English Renaissance Drama: A Norton Anthology*, ed. David Bevington et al. (New York, 2002).

Milman, H.H. *Anne Boleyn, A Dramatic Poem* (London, 1872).

Moncrieff, W.T. *Ivanhoe! Or, The Jewess; A Chivalric Play* (London, 1820).

Morris, Father. 'Letter to the Editor'. *The London Times*, Friday 10 February, 1888.

Morris, J. 'Letter to *The Morning Post*' (London). 3 February, 1888.

Mühlbach, L. *Henry VIII and his Court; Or, Catharine Parr: A Historical Novel in Two Volumes.* 2 vols., trans. Rev. H.N. Pierce (Mobile, AL, 1865).

Munday, Anthony. *The Death of Robert, Earle of Huntington: Otherwise Called Robin Hood of Merrie Sherwodde: With the Lamentable Tragedie of Chaste Matilda, His Faire Maid Marian, Poysoned at Dunmowe by King Iohn* (London, 1601).

——. *The Downfall of Robert, Earle of Huntington, Afterward called Robin Hood of Merrie Sherwodde* (1597–8) (London, 1601).

Nicolson, William. *The English Historical Library.* 3 vols. (London, 1697).

Norris, J. Parker. 'Letter to the Editor'. *The American Bibliopolist* 8 (April 1876): 38; repr. in *The Philadelphia Press*, 4 August, 1876.

Paris, Matthew. *Chronica Majora.* 3 vols. (London, 1852–4), vol. II.

Parnell, Thomas. 'A Night Piece, on Death'. *The Hermit. To Which are Added, A Hymn to Contentment; Health, an Eclogue; and A Night Piece, on Death* (London, 1775).

Pepys, Samuel. *The Diary of Samuel Pepys*, ed. Henry B. Wheatley (London, 1893), www.gutenberg.org (full text).

Pepys Library, *Catalogue of the Pepys Library at Magdalene College Cambridge* (Woodbridge, 2004).

Percy, Thomas. *Reliques of Ancient English Poetry, Consisting of Old Heroic Ballads, Songs, and Other Pieces of our Earlier Poets (Chiefly of the Lyric Kind).* 2 vols. (London, 1765).

Peter the Venerable, *The Book of Miracles*, in *Patrologiae Cursus Completus, Series Latina*, ed. J.P. Migne. 220 vols. (Paris, 1844–1906).

Pix, Mary. *Queen Catharine, or the Ruines of Love* (London, 1698).

Pope Paul III. Bull of Excommunication, 16 January 1538/9, in R.W. Heinze, *The Proclamations of the Tudor Kings* (Cambridge, 1976).

Prynne, William. *An Exact Chronological Vindication and Historical Demonstration of our British, Roman, Saxon, Danish, Norman, English Kings' Supreme Ecclesiastical Jurisdiction Over All Prelates, Persons, Causes, within their Kingdoms and Dominions* (London, 1666).

——. 'Letter to Sir Harbottle Grimston', 9 September, 1661, in *Report on the Manuscripts of the Earl of Verulam, Preserved at Gorhambury* (London, 1906).

Pynson, Richard. *A Little Gest of Robin Hode* (London, 1500).

Quarles, John. *Reglae Lectum Miserae: Or, A Kingly Bed of Misery: In Which is Contained, a Dream: With an Elegy upon the Martyrdom of Charles, Late King of England, of Blessed Memory: And Another upon the Right Honourable the Lord Capel. With a Curse Against the Enemies of Peace, and the Authors Farewell to England* (London, 1649).

Ralph of Coggeshall. *Chronicon Anglicanum*, ed. J. Stevenson (London, 1875).

Robert of Gloucester, *fl.* 1260–1300. *The Life and Martyrdom of Thomas Becket, Archbishop of Canterbury, from the Series of Lives and Legends Now Proved to Have Been Composed by Robert of Gloucester*, ed. and trans. William Henry Black (London, 1845).

Rogers, Thomas. *Leicester's Ghost* (1605, pub. 1641), ed. Franklin B. Williams, Jr (Chicago, 1972).

Rowley, Samuel. *When You See Me You Know Me, or the Famous Chronicle Historie of Henry the Eight* (London, 1605).

Rugge, Thomas. *The Diurnal of Thomas Rugge*, ed. W.L. Sachse (London, 1961).

Sander, Nicholas *The Rise and Growth of the Anglican Schism* (1589) (London, 1877).

Sandford, Francis. *A Genealogical Historie of the Kings of England, and Monarchs of Great Britain* (London, 1677).

Scott, Walter. *Ivanhoe* (1820), ed. Graham Tulloch (Edinburgh, 1998).

Shakespeare, William. *Henry V*, in *The Norton Shakespeare, Second Edition*, ed. Stephen Greenblatt et al. (New York, 2008).

——. *The Life and Death of King John*, in *The Norton Shakespeare, Second Edition*, ed. Stephen Greenblatt et al. (New York, 2008).

Stow, John. 'The Citie of Westminster', in *A Survey of London, by John Stow: Reprinted from the Text of 1603* (London, 1908).

Swadlin, Thomas. *King Charles His Funeral: Who Was Beheaded by Base and Barbarous Hands January 30, 1648, and Interred at Windsor, February 9, 1648, with his Anniversaries Continued until 1659* (London, 1661).

Swift, Jonathan. 'Marginal Note in Herbert of Cherbury's *Life and Raigne of Henry VIII* (1649)'. *Miscellaneous and Autobiographical Pieces, Fragments, and Marginalia*, ed. Herbert Davis Oxford (London, 1959).

Taylor, John. *Crop-Eare Curried, Or, Tom Nash his Ghost: Declaring the Pruining of Prinnes Two Last Parricidicall Pamphlets...* (London, 1644).

Tennyson, Alfred, Lord. *Becket* (London, 1884).

Thornton, W. Pugin. 'Surgical Report on a Skeleton Found in the Crypt of Canterbury Cathedral'. *Archaeologia Cantiana* 18 (1889).

Timmins, Samuel. 'Letter to J. Parker Norris', *The American Bibliopolist* 8 (April 1876), 39.

Trevet, Nicholas. *Annales Regum Angliae.* Parker Library, Corpus Christi College, Cambridge MS 152.

Vatican Library Codex Ottobonianus Latinus 1474, fols. 1r–4r. Transcribed by Carl Greith, *Spicilegium Vaticanum* (Frauenfeld, 1838).

de Vere, Aubrey. *St Thomas of Canterbury, a Dramatic Poem* (London, 1876).

Waith, Eugene. 'King John and the Drama of History', in *King John and Henry VIII: Critical Essays*, ed. Francis Shirley (New York, 1988).

Warner, William. *Albion's England* (London, 1586).

Weever, John. *Ancient Funerall Monuments Within the United Monarchie of Great Britaine, Ireland and the Islands Adjacent, with the Dissolved Monasteries Therein Contained* (London, 1631).

Wendover, Roger. *Chronica*, ed. H.O. Coxe. 5 vols. (London, 1831–44).

William of Newburg, *Historia Rerum Anglorum: Chronicles of the Reigns of Stephen, Henry II, and Richard II* (1567), ed. Richard Howlett. 4 vols. (London, 1884–9).

Williams, Robert Folkenstone. *Shakespeare and his Friends, Or, The Golden Age of Merry England* (London, 1838).

——. *The Youth of Shakespeare, A Novel* (London, 1846).

Wood, Adam. *A New Conference Between the Ghosts of King Charles and Oliver Cromwell* (London, 1659).

Wood, Mrs Henry, ed. *The Argosy* 23 (July–December 1879).

Wriothesley, Charles. *A Chronicle of England during the Reigns of the Tudors.* 2 vols. (London, 1875–7).

Wyatt, George. *Extracts from the Life of the Virtuous, Christian and Renowned Queen Anne Boleyn* (1605) (London, 1817).

Secondary Sources

Abbott, Edwin. *St Thomas of Canterbury: His Death and Miracles* (London, 1898).

Ainsworth, W. Harrison. *Windsor Castle* (London, 1843).

Anderson, Olive. 'The Political Uses of History in Mid-Nineteenth Century England', *Past and Present* 36 (1967): 85.

Aungier, George. *History and Antiquities of Syon Monastery* (London, 1840).

Ballard, George. *Memoirs of Several Ladies of Great Britain, Who Have Been Celebrated for their Writings or Skill in the Learned Languages, Arts, and Sciences* (Oxford, 1752).

Bann, Stephen. *The Clothing of Clio: A Study of the Representation of History in Nineteenth-Century Britain and France* (Cambridge, 1984).

Barczewski, Stephanie. *Myth and National Identity in Nineteenth-Century Britain: The Legends of King Arthur and Robin Hood* (Oxford, 2000).

Bartlett, Robert. *Why Can the Dead Do Such Great Things?* (Princeton, NJ, 2015).

Beazeley, M. *The Canterbury Bones* (London, 1913).

Behrendt, Stephen. *Royal Mourning and Regency Culture* (New York, 1997).

Bentley, Samuel. *Excerpta Historica* (London, 1833).

Biddick, Kathleen. *The Shock of Medievalism* (Durham, NC, 1998).

Bindman, David and Baker, Malcolm. *Roubilliac and the Eighteenth-Century Monument.* (New Haven, CT, 1995).

Birch, W.G. *Catalogue of Seals in the Department of Manuscripts in the British Museum*, 2 vols. (London, 1887).

Blum, Deborah. *Ghost Hunters: William James and the Search for Scientific Proof of Life After Death* (New York, 2006).

Braunmuller, A.R. 'King John and Historiography', *English Literary History* 55, no. 2 (Summer 1988): 309–32.

Britton, John. 'Essays on the Merits and Characteristics of William Shakspere: Also Remarks on his Birth and Burial-Place, his Monument, Portraits, and Associations', in *The Complete Works of Shakespeare*, ed. Charles Knight (London, 1849).

——. *The History and Antiquities of the Cathedral Church of Worcester* (London, 1835).

Broadway, Jan. *'No Historie So Meete': Gentry Culture and the Development of Local History in Elizabethan and Stuart England* (Manchester, 2006).

Bronfen, Elisabeth. 'Dialogue with the Dead: The Deceased Beloved as Muse', in *Sex and Death in Victorian Literature*, ed. Regina Barreca (Bloomington, IN, 1990).

Brown, Mark. 'Richard II Relics found in National Portrait Gallery Archive'. *The Guardian*, Tuesday 16 November, 2010, www.theguardian.com/artanddesign/2010/nov/16/richard-second-national-portrait-gallery.

——. 'Shakespeare's Skull Probably Stolen by Grave-Robbers, Study Finds'. *The Guardian*, 23 March 2016. www.guardian.co.uk.

Bryden, Inga. *Reinventing King Arthur: The Arthurian Legends in Victorian Culture* (Aldershot, 2005).

Bulfinch, Thomas. *Bulfinch's Mythology: The Age of Fable, The Age of Chivalry, and Legends of Charlemagne* (1855) (New York, 1991).

Burke, S.H. *The Men and Women of the English Reformation, from the Days of Wolsey to the Death of Cranmer.* 2 vols. (New York, 1872), vol. I.

Burnet, Gilbert. *The History of the Reformation of the Church of England* (1679) (Oxford, 1865).

Butler, John. *The Quest for Becket's Bones: The Mystery of the Relics of St Thomas Becket of Canterbury* (New Haven, CT, 1995).

Caciola, Nancy Mandeville. *Afterlives: The Return of the Dead in the Middle Ages.* (Ithaca, NY, 2016).

Canino, Catherine Grace. *Shakespeare and the Nobility: The Negotiation of Lineage.* (Cambridge, 2007).

Carlyle, Thomas. *Letters and Speeches of Oliver Cromwell* (London, 1904).

——. *On Heroes, Hero-Worship, and the Heroic in History*, ed. Michael K. Goldberg, Joel J. Brattin, and Mark Engel (Berkeley, 1993).

Carpenter, D. A. 'Abbot Ralph of Coggeshall's Account of the Last Years of King Richard and the First Years of King John', *The English Historical Review* 113, no. 454 (November 1998): 1210–30.

——. *The Reign of Henry III* (1996) (London, 2006).

Carruthers, Mary. *The Book of Memory* (Cambridge, 1990).

Carver, Martin. 'Burial as Poetry: The Context of Treasure in Anglo-Saxon Graves', in *Treasure in the Medieval West*, ed. Elizabeth M. Tyler (York, 2000).

Centerwall, Brandon. 'Who Wrote Basse's Elegy on Shakespeare?' *Shakespeare Survey* 59 (2006): 267–84.

Cervone [Tomaini], Thea. 'The King's Phantom: Staging Majesty in Bale's *Kynge Johan*', *Studies in Medievalism* 17 (2009): 185–202.

——. *Sworn Bond in Tudor England* (Jefferson, NC, 2011).

——. 'Tucked Beneath Her Arm: Culture, Ideology, and Fantasy in the Curious Legend of Anne Boleyn', in *Heads Will Roll: Decapitation in Medieval Literature and Culture*, ed. Larissa Tracy and Jeff Massey (Leiden, 2012).

Chapman, Hester. *Anne Boleyn* (London, 1974).

Chapter Archives of St George's Chapel, Windsor (Corporate Author). 'Henry VIII's Final Resting Place: Background notes'. Pdf Format. http://www. stgeorges-windsor.org/assets/files/LearningResources/BackgroundNotesHenry VIII.pdf.

Chester, J.L. *Registers of the Collegiate Church or Abbey of St Peter* (London, 1876).

Chrimes, S.B. *Henry VII* (New Haven, CT, 1999).

Collinson, Patrick. 'Through Several Glasses Darkly: Historical and Sectarian Perceptions of the Tudor Church', in *Tudorism: Historical Imagination and the Appropriation of the Sixteenth Century*, ed. Tatiana String and Marcus Bull (Oxford, 2011).

Costain, Thomas B. *The Conquering Family* (New York, 1962).

Council of the Shakespeare Memorial Association. *A History of the Shakespeare Memorial*, Stratford-upon-Avon, 2nd edn (London, 1882).

Coxe, Anthony D. Hippisley. *Haunted Britain* (London, 1973).

Craigie, James. 'Materials for the History of Archbishop Thomas Becket', in *Chronicles and Memorials of Great Britain and Ireland During the Middle Ages*. 99 vols. Vol. LXVII, no. iv (London, 1879).

Crook, John. *English Medieval Shrines* (Woodbridge, 2011).

Crowe, Catherine. *The Night Side of Nature, Or, Ghosts and Ghost-Seers*. 2 vols. (London, 1848).

Crull, Jodocus. *The Antiquities of St Peters, Containing the Inscriptions and Epitaphs Upon the Tombs and Gravestones* (London, 1711).

Curl, James Stevens. *The Victorian Celebration of Death* (Stroud, 2000).

Curley, Michael J. 'A New Edition of John of Cornwall's *Prophetia Merlini*', *Speculum* 57, issue 2 (April 1982): 217–49.

Curll, Edmund. *The Rarities of Richmond: Being the Exact Descriptions of the Royal Hermitage and Merlin's Cave, With His Life and Prophecies* (London, 1736).

Darby, Elizabeth and Smith, Nicola. *The Cult of the Prince Consort* (New Haven, CT, 1983).

Dart, John. *Westmonasterium, Or, the History and Antiquities of the Abbey Church of St Peter, Westminster* (London, 1723).

Davies, Owen. *The Haunted: A Social History of Ghosts* (New York, 2007).

Davies, W.T. 'A Bibliography of John Bale'. *Oxford Bibliographic Society Proceedings and Papers*, vol. V, part IV (Oxford, 1940).

Davis, J.F. 'Lollards, Reformers, and St Thomas of Canterbury', *University of Birmingham Historical Journal* 9 (1963): 13.

Derrida, Jacques. *Specters of Marx, the State of the Debt, the Work of Mourning, & the New International*, trans. Peggy Kamuf (New York, 1994), https://www.marxists.org/reference/subject/philosophy/works/fr/derrida2.htm.

——. *The Truth in Painting*, trans. Geoff Bennington and Ian McLeod (Chicago, 1987).

Dodson, Aidan. *The Royal Tombs of Great Britain: An Illustrated History* (London, 2004).

Dowdall, John. *Traditionary Anecdotes of Shakespeare*, (London, 1838).

Duffy, Eamon. *The Stripping of the Altars* (New Haven, CT, 1992).

Duffy, Mark. *Royal Tombs of Medieval England* (Stroud, 2003).

Dugdale, William. *Monasticon Anglicorum* (1655), 3 vols. (London, 1846).

Duggan, Anne. *Thomas Becket* (London, 2004).

Dunabin, J.P.D. 'Oliver Cromwell's Popular Image in Nineteenth-Century England', *Britain and the Netherlands: Papers Delivered to the Third Anglo-Dutch Historical Conference*, ed. J.S. Bromley and E.H. Kossman (London, 1968).

Dutton, Richard. '"Methinks the Truth Should Live from Age to Age": The Dating and Contexts of *Henry V*, *Huntington Library Quarterly* 68, no. 1–2 (March 2005): 173.

Ellis, Roger. *Catalogue of Seals in the Public Record Office*, 2 vols., vol. I (London, 1986).

Elton, G.R. *Policy and Police: The Enforcement of the Reformation in the Age of Thomas Cromwell* (Cambridge, 1972).

Engel, Ute. *Worcester Cathedral: An Architectural History* (Chichester, 2007).

Evans, J. A. *History of the Society of Antiquaries* (London, 1956).

Evison, V.I. 'Dover: Buckland Anglo-Saxon Cemetery', *English Heritage Archaeological Report* 3 (London, 1987).

Fairfield, Leslie. *John Bale: Mythmaker for the English Reformation* (Indianapolis, IN, 1976).

Faull, M.L. 'British Survival in Anglo-Saxon Northumbria', *Studies in Celtic Survival*, ed. L. Laing, *British Archaeological Reports* 37 (1977): 1–55.

Fay, Elizabeth. *Romantic Medievalism: History and the Romantic Literary Ideal* (New York, 2002).

Fiddes, Richard. *The Life of Cardinal Wolsey* (London, 1724).

Field, John. *Kingdom, Power, and Glory: A Historical Guide to Westminster Abbey* (London, 1996).

Fitzgibbons, Jonathan. *Cromwell's Head* (Richmond, VA, 2008).

Flammarion, Camille. *Haunted Houses* (New York, 1924).

Fosbroke, T. D. *British Monachism*, 2nd edn, vol. I (London, 1817).

Fox, Adam. *Oral and Literate Culture in England* (Oxford, 2000).

Fox, Levi. *A Splendid Occasion: The Stratford Jubilee of 1769* (Oxford, 1973).

Furness, Walter Rogers. *Composite Photography Applied to the Portraits of Shakespeare* (Philadelphia, 1885).

Galton, Francis. *Inquiries into Human Faculty and its Development* (London, 1883).

Garber, Marjorie. 'Shakespeare as Fetish', *Shakespeare Quarterly* 41, no. 2 (Summer 1990): 243.

Garton, Stephen. 'The Scales of Suffering: Love, Death, and Victorian Masculinity', *Social History* 27, no. 1 (January 2002): 40–58.

Geary, Patrick J. *Living With the Dead in the Middle Ages* (Cornell, 1994).

Giles, John. *The Life and Letters of Archbishop Thomas à Becket*. 2 vols. (London, 1846).

Gittings, Clare. 'Sacred and Secular', in *Death in England: An Illustrated History*, ed. Peter C. Jupp and Clare Gittings (New Brunswick, NJ, 1999).

Goldberg, Michael. 'Introduction', in Carlyle, Thomas. *On Heroes, Hero-worship, and the Heroic in History*, ed. Michael K. Goldberg, Joel J. Brattin, and Mark Engel. (Berkeley, 1993).

Gough, Richard. *British Topography Or, An Historical Account of What Has Been Done for Illustrating the Topographical Antiquities of Great Britain and Ireland.* 2 vols. (London, 1753).

———. *Sepulchral Monuments in Great Britain.* 2 vols. (London, 1796), vol. II.

Gower, Ronald. 'The Shakespearean Death-Mask', *The Antiquary* 2, (August 1880): 63.

Gransden, Antonia. *Historical Writing in England 500–1307* (New York, 1974).

de Grazia, M., Quilligan, M. and Stallybrass, P. *Subject and Object in Renaissance Culture* (Cambridge, 1996).

Green, J.R. *History of the English People*, 3 vols. (London, 1878–80).

Green, Valentine. *An Account of the Discovery of the Body of King John, in the Cathedral Church of Worcester, July 17th, 1797, from Authentic Communications; with Illustrations and Remarks* (London, 1797).

——. *History and Antiquities of the City and Suburbs of Worcester* (London, 1796).

——. *Survey of the City of Worcester* (Worcester, 1764).

Greenblatt, Stephen. *Will in the World* (New York, 2005).

Greg, W.W. *English Literary Autographs* (Nendeln, Liechtenstein, 1968).

The Grey Friars Research Team and Kennedy, Maeve, eds. *The Bones of a King* (London, 2015).

Halliwell-Phillipps, J. O. *The Last Days of William Shakespeare* (London, 1863).

Halsall, Guy. 'Burial Writes: Graves, "Texts", and Time in Early Merovingian Northern Gaul', in *Erinnerungskultur im Bestauttungsritual*, ed. J. Jarnut and M. Wemhoff (Munich, 2003).

Happe, Peter. *John Bale* (New York, 1996).

Harley, Robert, *Harleian Miscellany* (London, 1808–11).

Harris, Jonathan Gil, *Untimely Matter in the Time of Shakespeare* (Philadelphia, 2009).

Harris, Nicholas. *A Chronicle of London from 1089 to 1483* (London, 1827).

Harvey, P.D. and McGuiness, Andrew, eds. *A Guide to British Medieval Seals* (London, 1996).

Henry, David. *An Historical Account of the Curiosities of London, in Three Parts*. 3 vols. (London, 1753).

Herbert, Henry William. *Memoirs of Henry VIII* (New York, 1855).

Hill, Geoffrey. *A Treatise of Civil Power* (New Haven, CT, 2008).

Hilton, Lisa. *Queens Consort: England's Medieval Queens* (London, 2008).

Hines, John. *Voices in the Past: English Literature and Archaeology* (Cambridge, 2004).

Hoffman, C. Fenno. 'Catherine Parr as a Woman of Letters', *Huntington Library Quarterly* 23, no. 4 (August 1960): 350–1.

Hole, Christina. *English Folklore* (London, 1940).

——. *Haunted England* (London, 1941).

Holland, Agnes. *Letters to Miss Lisa Rawlinson*, in Mason, James Arthur, *What Became of the Bones of St Thomas?* (Cambridge, 1920).

Hollister, C. Warren. 'King John and the Historians', *Journal of British Studies* 1, no. 1 (November 1961): 1–19.

Howell, Roger. 'The Eighteenth Century View of Oliver Cromwell', *Cromwelliana* (1979), www.olivercromwell.org/cromwelliana.htm. PDF format.

——. 'Who Needs Another Cromwell? The Nineteenth-Century Image of Oliver Cromwell', in *Images of Oliver Cromwell: Essays for and by Roger Howell, Jr* (Manchester, 1993).

Hughes, Paul L. and Larkin, James Francis, eds. *Tudor Royal Proclamations* (New Haven, CT, 1964).

Hume, David. *History of England under the House of Tudor* (London, 1759).

Hutchinson. Robert. *The Last Days of Henry VIII: Conspiracies, Treason, and Heresy at the Court of the Dying Tyrant* (New York, 2005).

Hutton, Ronald. *The Rise and Fall of Merry England: The Ritual Year 1400–1700.* (Oxford, 1996).

Hutton, William Holden. *S. Thomas of Canterbury, An Account of his Life and Fame from the Contemporary Biographers and Other Chroniclers* (London, 1889).

Hyde, Edward, Earl of Clarendon. *History of the Rebellion and Civil Wars in England Begun in the Year 1641* (1702–4). 4 vols. (Oxford, 1888), vol. III.

Ingelby, C.M. *Shakespeare's Bones, The Proposal to Disinter them, Considered in Relation to their Possible Bearing on his Portraiture* (London, 1883).

Janes, Regina. 'Beheadings', in *Death and Representation*, ed. Sarah Webster Goodwin and Elisabeth Bronfen (Baltimore, 1993).

——. *Losing Our Heads: Beheadings in Literature and Culture* (New York, 2005).

Jarvis, T.M. *Accredited Ghost Stories* (London, 1823).

Jenkyns, Henry. *The Remains of Thomas Cranmer.* 4 vols. (Oxford, 1833).

Jenkyns, Richard. *Westminster Abbey* (Cambridge, MA, 2005).

Jerrold, Douglas William. *Thomas à Becket: A Historical Play in Five Acts.* As Played at the Surrey Theatre (London, 1829).

Jones, Fred L. '*Look About You* and *The Disguises*', *PMLA* 44, no. 3 (September 1929): 836–7.

Jones, Richard. *Haunted Britain and Ireland* (London, 2003).

Jupp, Peter C. and Gittings, Clare, eds. *Death in England: An Illustrated History* (New Brunswick, NJ, 1999).

Kantorowicz, Ernest. *The King's Two Bodies* (1957) (Princeton, NJ, 1997).

Keepe, Henry. *Monumenta Westmonasteriensa, Or, An Historical Account of the Original, Increase, and Present State of St. Peter's, Or, The Abbey Church of Westminster* (London, 1683).

Kelly, Jason M. *The Society of Dilettanti: Archaeology and Identity in the British Enlightenment* (New Haven, CT, 2009).

Kitching, Chris. 'Was Shakespeare's Skull Stolen for a £300 Bet?' *Daily Mail*, 27 March 2016, www.dailymail.co.uk.

Knight, Stephen. *Robin Hood: A Mythic Biography* (Ithaca, 2003).

Kontou, Tatiana and Wilburn, Sarah, eds. *The Ashgate Research Companion to Nineteenth-Century Spiritualism and the Occult* (Farnham, Surrey, 2012).

Koopmans, Rachel. *Wonderful to Relate: Miracle Stories and Miracle Collecting in High Medieval England* (Philadelphia, 2011).

Kucich, John. 'Death Worship Among the Victorians: The Old Curiosity Shop'. *PMLA* 95, no. 1 (January 1980): 58–9.

Lacan, Jacques. *Feminine Sexuality*, ed. Juliet Mitchell and Jacqueline Rose (New York, 1985).

Lang, Timothy. *The Victorians and the Stuart Heritage: Interpretations of a Discordant Past* (Cambridge, 1995).

Le Fanu, Sheridan. *Carmilla*, ed. Cathleen Costello Sullivan (Syracuse, NY, 2013).

Levin, Carole. *Propaganda in the English Reformation: Heroic and Villainous Images of King John* (New York, 1988).

Levine, Joseph M. *The Autonomy of History: Truth and Method from Erasmus to Gibbon*. (Chicago, 1999).

——. *Humanism and History: Origins of Modern English Historiography* (Ithaca, NY, 1987).

Levine, Philippa. *The Amateur and the Professional: Antiquarians, Historians, and Archaeologists in Victorian England 1838–1886* (Cambridge, 1986).

Lindley, Philip. 'The Funeral and Tomb Effigies of Queen Katharine of Valois and King Henry V', *Journal of the British Archaeological Association* 160 (2007): 165–77.

——. Tomb Destruction and Scholarship: Medieval Monuments in Early Modern England (Donington, 2007).

Llewellyn Nigel. *The Art of Death: Visual Culture in the English Death Ritual* (London, 1991).

Lynch, Jack. *Becoming Shakespeare* (New York, 2006).

Lyons, Sherrie Lynne. *Species, Serpents, Spirits, and Skulls: Science at the Margins in the Victorian Age* (New York, 2009).

Macaulay, Thomas Babington. *History of England*. 3 vols. (London, 1849–61).

MacDonald, Robert. *The Language of Empire: Myths and Metaphors and Popular Imperialism, 1880–1918* (Manchester, 1994).

Maitland, S.R. *Essays on Subjects Connected with the Reformation in England* (1849) (London, 1899).

——. *Six Letters on Foxe's Acts and Monuments* (London, 1837).

Mancoff, Debra. 'Albert the Good: Public Image and Private Iconography', *Biography* 15, no. 2 (Spring 1992): 140–64.

Mandler, Peter. 'Revisiting the Olden Time: Popular Tudorism in the Time of Victoria', in *Tudorism: Historical Imagination and the Appropriation of the Sixteenth Century*, ed. Tatiana String and Marcus Bull (Oxford, 2011).

Manning, Henry Edward. Lord Archbishop of Westminster. 'Archbishop Manning on St Thomas à Becket', in Henry Edward, *Sermons on Ecclesiastical Subjects*. 2 vols. (New York, 1872).

Markovitz, Stephanie. 'Form Things: Looking at Genre through Victorian Diamonds', *Victorian Studies* 52, no. 4 (Summer 2010): 591–619.

Marshall, Ashley. 'I Saw Him Dead: Marvell's Elegy for Cromwell', *Studies in Philology* 103, no. 4 (Autumn 2006): 501–3.

Marshall, Peter. *Beliefs and the Dead in Reformation England* (Oxford, 2002).

Mason, Arthur James. *What Became of the Bones of St Thomas?* (Cambridge, 1920).

Mason, T. W. 'Nineteenth Century Cromwell', *Past and Present* 40 (1968): 187–91.

Matheson, W. 'Notes on Mary Macleod', *Transactions of the Gaelic Society of Inverness* 41 (1951): 11–25.

Matus, Jill. *Unstable Bodies: Victorian Representations of Sexuality and Maternity* (Manchester, 1995).

Maume, Patrick. 'Cromwell's Statue in Westminster', *History Ireland* 16, no. 6 (November–December 2008): 12–13.

Maxwell-Stuart, P.G. *Ghosts: A History of Phantoms, Ghouls, and Other Spirits of the Dead* (Stroud, 2006).

McMains, H.F. *The Death of Oliver Cromwell* (Lexington, KY, 2000).

Melman, Billie. 'The Pleasure of Tudor Horror: Popular Histories, Modernity, and Sensationalism in the Long Nineteenth Century', in *Tudorism: Historical Imagination and the Appropriation of the Sixteenth Century*, ed. Tatiana String and Marcus Bull (Oxford, 2011).

Meyer-Hochstetler, Barbara. 'The First Tomb of Henry VII of England', *The Art Bulletin* 58, no. 3 (1976): 364–5.

Millican, Charles B. 'Spenser and the Arthurian Tradition', *The Review of English Studies* 6, no. 22 (1930): 167.

——. *Spenser and the Table Round: A Study in the Contemporaneous Background for Spenser's Use of the Arthurian Legend* (Cambridge, MA, 1932).

Milner, John. *The History, Civil and Ecclesiastical, and Survey of the Antiquities of Winchester*. 2 vols. (London, 1809).

Morris, Matthew. *The King under the Car Park* (Leicester, 2013).

Nash, Treadway. 'Observations on the Time of Death and Place of Burial of Queen Katherine Parr', *Archaeologia: Or, Miscellaneous Tracts Relating to Antiquity*, vol. IX (London, 1789): 1–7.

Newsome, David. *The Victorian World Picture: Perceptions and Introspections in an Age of Change* (Princeton, 1997).

Newstok, Scott. *Quoting Death in Early Modern England* (New York, 2009).

Norgate, Kate. *John Lackland* (London, 1902).

Norton, Elizabeth. *Catherine Parr* (Stroud, 2010).

O'Leary, Maurice. 'The Phantom Coach', *Journal of American Folklore* 11 (1898): 235.

Okell, J. *A Brief Historical Account of the Castle and Manor of Sudeley, Gloucestershire, Including Curious and Interesting Particulars Relative to Queen Katherine Parr* (Tewkesbury, 1844).

Ordish, T. Fairman. 'Shakespeare's Physiognomy', *The Bookworm: An Illustrated History of Old-Time Literature*. 2 vols. (London, 1888).

Orgel, Stephen. *Imagining Shakespeare* (New York, 2003).

Orr, Clarissa Campbell, ed. *Queenship in Britain 1660–1837* (Manchester, 2002).

Pafford, J.H.P. 'King John's Tomb in Worcester Cathedral', *Transactions of the Worcestershire Archaeological Society for 1958* 35, new series (1959): 58–60.

Parish, Helen. *Monks, Miracles, and Magic: Reformation Representations of the Medieval Church* (New York, 2005).

Parry, Graham. *The Trophies of Time: English Antiquarians of the Seventeenth Century* (Oxford, 1995).

Parsloe, J. 'The First Issue of Samuel Rudder's *The History and Antiquities of Gloucester*', *Transactions of the Bristol and Gloucestershire Archaeological Society* 117 (1999).

Perkins, Jocelyn. *Westminster Abbey, its Worship and Ornaments*. 2 vols. (Oxford, 1940).

Poe, Edgar Allan. *The Fall of the House of Usher and Other Writings*, ed. David Galloway (London, 2011).

Pollard, A.J. *Richard III and the Princes in the Tower* (London, 1991).

Pollen, J.H. 'Henry VIII and St Thomas Becket, Part I', *The Month* 137 (February 1921): 119–28.

———. 'Henry VIII and St Thomas Becket, Part II', *The Month* 137 (April 1921): 324–33.

Poole, Adrian. *Shakespeare and the Victorians* (London, 2004).

Prendergast, Thomas. *Chaucer's Dead Body: From Corpse to Corpus* (New York, 2004).

Price, Jonathan. '*King John* and Problematic Art', *Shakespeare Quarterly* 21, no. 1 (Winter, 1970): 26.

Prince, Kathryn. *Shakespeare in the Victorian Periodicals* (New York, 2008).

Raine, James. *Saint Cuthbert: With an Account of the State in which His Remains Were Found upon the Opening of His Tomb in Durham Cathedral in the Year MDCCCXXVII* (Durham, 1828).

Ralph, James. *A Critical Review of the Publicke Buildings, Statues, and Ornaments in and about London and Westminster* (London, 1734).

Rankin, Mark. *Henry VIII and His Afterlives: Literature, Politics, Art*, ed. Mark Rankin, Christopher Highley, and John N. King (Cambridge, 2009).

Raymond, Joad. *Pamphlets and Pamphleteering in Early Modern Britain* (Cambridge, 2003).

Reed, John. *Victorian Conventions* (Columbus, OH, 1975).

Reynolds, Andrew. *Anglo-Saxon Deviant Burial Customs* (Oxford, 2009).

Richards, Judith. 'Unblushing Falsehood: The Strickland Sisters and the Domestic History of Henry VIII', in *Henry VIII and History*, ed. Thomas Betteridge and Thomas Freeman (Farnham, 2012).

Ritson, Joseph. *Robin Hood: A Collection of all the Ancient Poems, Songs and Ballads, Now Extant, Relative to that Celebrated English Outlaw: To Which are Prefixed Historical Anecdotes of his Life*. 2 vols. (London, 1795).

Roberts, Peter. 'Politics, Drama, and the Cult of Thomas Becket', in *Pilgrimage: The English Experience from Becket to Bunyan*, ed. Colin Morris and Peter Roberts Cambridge, 2002).

Rosebery, Archibald. *Oliver Cromwell: A Eulogy and an Appreciation* (London, 1900).

Routledge, C.F. and Field, Thomas. *Canterbury Official Guide to the Cathedral Church* (Canterbury, 1897).

Routledge, C. F., Sheppard, J., and Scott Robertson, W.A. 'The Crypt of Canterbury Cathedral', *Archaeologia Cantiana* 18 (1889): 253–6.

Rudder, Samuel. *A New History of Gloucestershire, Comprising the Topography, Antiquities, Curiosities, Produce, Trade, and Manufactures of that County* (Cirencester, 1779).

Santesso, Aaron. 'The Birth of the Birthplace: Bread Street and Literary Tourism Before Stratford', *English Literary History* 71, no. 2 (Summer 2004): 385.

——. *A Careful Longing: The Poetics and Problems of Nostalgia* (Cranbury, NJ, 2006).

Schaafhausen, Hermann. *Jahrbuch*, or *Annual, of the German Shakespeare Society* 10 (1875).

Schmitt, Jean Claude. *Ghosts in the Middle Ages: The Living and the Dead in Medieval Society* (Chicago, 1994).

Schor, Esther. *Bearing the Dead: The British Culture of Mourning from the Enlightenment to Victoria* (Princeton, NJ, 1994).

Schwyzer, Philip. *Archaeologies of English Renaissance Literature* (Oxford, 2007).

——. *Shakespeare and the Remains of Richard III* (Oxford, 2013).

Scott, George Gilbert. 'Letter to the Dean and Chapter of Westminster', 4 March, 1878, in Stanley, Arthur Penrhyn. *Historical Memorials of Westminster Abbey*. 2 vols. (Philadelphia, 1899).

Secrets of the Dead: Resurrecting Richard III, dir. Gary Johnstone (PBS Home video, 2014).

Seel, Graham. *King John: An Underrated King* (London, 2012).

Sharpe, Kevin. *Sir Robert Cotton, 1586–1631: History and Politics in Early Modern England* (Oxford, 1979).

Shea, Christopher. 'Alas, Poor William Shakespeare. Where Does His Skull Rest?' *New York Times*, 24 March 2016, www.nytimes.com.

Sheppard J.B. and J.C. Robertson, eds. *Materials for the History of Thomas Becket, Archbishop of Canterbury*. 7 vols. (London, 1875–85).

Sherlock, S.J. and Welch, M.G. 'An Anglo-Saxon Cemetery at Norton, Cleveland', *Council for British Archaeology Research Report* 82 (London, 1992).

Simmons, Clare. *Popular Medievalism in Romantic-Era Britain* (New York, 2011).

Sims, Michael, ed. *The Phantom Coach: A Connoisseur's Collection of Victorian Ghost Stories* (New York, 2014).

Sinnema, Peter. *The Wake of Wellington: Englishness in 1852* (Athens, OH, 2006).

Smith, Anthony. *National Identity* (London, 1991).

Smith, Bruce R. *The Key of Green* (Chicago, 2008).

Smith, George. *The Religion of Ancient Britain: A Succinct Account of the Several Religious Systems Which Have Obtained in this Island from the Earliest Ties to the Norman Conquest* (London, 1844).

Smith, R.J. *The Gothic Bequest: Medieval Institutions in British Thought 1688–1863.* (Cambridge, 2002).

Stallybrass, Peter. 'Drunk with the Cup of Liberty', in *The Violence of Representation: Literature and the History of Violence* (London, 1989).

Stanley, Arthur Penrhyn. *Historical Memorials of Canterbury: The Landing of Augustine, The Murder of Becket, Edward the Black Prince, Becket's Shrine* (London, 1888).

———. *Historical Memorials of Canterbury Cathedral, Second American Edition* (New York, 1888).

———. *Historical Memorials of Westminster Abbey.* 2 vols. (Philadelphia, PA, 1899), vol. I.

———. 'On the Depositions of the Remains of Katherine de Valois, Queen of Henry V, in Westminster Abbey', *Archaeologia* 46 (January 1881): 287.

Starkey, David. *The English Court* (London, 1987).

———. 'The Tudors: Famous for Five Centuries'. Lecture delivered at the Colston Research Symposium on 'Tudorism', University of Bristol, 6 December 2008, in *Tudorism: Historical Imagination and the Appropriation of the Sixteenth Century*, ed. Tatiana String and Marcus Bull (Oxford, 2011).

Starkie, Andrew. 'Henry VIII in History: Gilbert Burnet's *History of the Reformation* (v.1), 1679', in *Henry VIII and History*, ed. Thomas Betteridge and Thomas Freeman (Farnham, 2012).

Stockholm, Johanne. *Garrick's Folly; the Shakespeare Jubilee of 1769 at Stratford and Drury Lane* (New York, 1964).

Stott, Rebecca. *The Fabrication of the Late Victorian Femme Fatale* (London, 1992).

Stow, John. *Annales, or a General Chronicle of England* (1580) (London, 1631).

Strickland, Agnes and Elizabeth. *Lives of the Queens of England from the Norman Conquest.* 12 vols (London, 1840–4).

String, Tatiana. 'Myth and Memory in Representations of Henry VIII, 1509–2009', in *Tudorism: Historical Imagination and the Appropriation of the Sixteenth Century*, ed. Tatiana C. String and Marcus Bull (Oxford, 2011).

String, Tatiana and Bull, Marcus, eds. *Tudorism: Historical Imagination and the Appropriation of the Sixteenth Century* (Oxford, 2011).

Strohm, Paul. 'The Trouble With Richard: The Reburial of Richard II and Lancastrian Symbolic Strategy', *Speculum* 71, no. 1 (January 1996): 92.

Strong, Roy. *And When Did You Last See Your Father? The Victorian Painter and British History* (London, 1978).

———. *Recreating the Past: British History and the Victorian Painter* (London, 1978).

Strype, John. *Ecclesiastical Memorials.* 3 vols. (London, 1751).

Stubbs, William. *Historical Introductions to the Rolls Series*, ed. A. Hassall (New York, 1902).

Stubbs, William, ed. 'The Historical Works of Gervase of Canterbury', *Chronicles and Memorials of Great Britain and Ireland during the Middle Ages*, Vol. LXXIII, no. i (London, 1879–80).

Sweet, Rosemary. *Antiquaries: The Discovery of the Past in Eighteenth Century Britain* (London, 2004).

Tarlow, Sarah. 'Wormie Clay and Blessed Sleep: Death and Disgust in Later Historic Britain', in *The Familiar Past?* ed. Sarah Tarlow and Susie West (London, 2002).

Tatton-Brown, Tim and Mortimer, Richard, eds.. *Westminster Abbey: The Lady Chapel of Henry VII* (Woodbridge, 2003).

Taylor, Rupert. *The Political Prophecy in England* (New York, 1911).

Thaden, Barbara. *The Maternal Voice in Victorian Fiction: Rewriting the Patriarchal Family* (New York, 1997).

Thomas, Keith. *The Perception of the Past in Early Modern England* (London, 1983).

——. *Religion and the Decline of Magic* (New York, 1971).

Thomas, William. *A Survey of the Cathedral Church of Worcester* (London, 1736).

Townsend, R.D. 'Hagiography in England in the Nineteenth Century: A Study in Literary, Historiographical, and Theological Developments'. Unpublished D. Phil. Thesis. Oxford, 1981.

Tomaini, Thea. See Cervone, Thea.

Tracy, Larissa. 'For Our Dere Ladyes Sake: Bringing the Outlaw in from the Forest—Robin Hood, Marian, and Normative National Identity', *Explorations in Renaissance Culture* 38 (Summer and Winter 2012): 35–66.

Tracy, Larissa and Massey, Jeff, eds. *Heads Will Roll: Decapitation in Medieval Literature and Culture* (Leiden, 2012).

Tracy, Robert. 'Loving You All Ways: Vamps, Vampires, Necrophiles, and Necrofilles in Nineteenth Century Fiction', in *Sex and Death in Victorian Literature,* ed. Regina Barreca (Indianapolis, IN, 1990).

Valdez del Alamo, Elizabeth and Pendergast, Carol, eds. *Memory and the Medieval Tomb* (Aldershot, 2000).

Walford's Antiquarian: A Magazine and Bibliographical Review 8, no. 46 (July–December 1885): 143–57.

Walker, Greg. *Persuasive Fictions: Faction, Faith, and Political Culture in the Reign of Henry VIII* (London, 1996).

Wallace, Jennifer. *Digging in the Dirt: The Archaeological Imagination* (London, 2004).

Walvin, James. 'Dust to Dust: Celebrations of Death in Victorian England'. *Historical Reflections* 9, no. 3 (Fall 1982): 353–71.

Warren, W.L. *King John* (London, 1961).

Warton, Thomas. 'Remarks on Worcester Cathedral and the Churches of Eversham and Pershore', in Green, Valentine. *History and Antiquities of the City and Suburbs of Worcester* (London 1796).

Watson, Nicola. *The Literary Tourist* (New York, 2006).

Webb, Charles Le Bas. *The Life of Thomas Cranmer*. 2 vols. (New York, 1833).

Weir, Alison. *Mary, Queen of Scots and the Murder of Lord Darnley* (London, 2008).

Westerhof, Danielle. *Death and the Noble Body in Medieval England* (London, 2008).

Wheeler, Michael. *Heaven, Hell, and the Victorians* (Cambridge, 1994).

White, Hayden. *Metahistory: The Historical Imagination in Nineteenth-Century Europe* (Baltimore, 1973).

Wilkins, David. *Concilia Magnae Brittaniae et Hiberniae*. 3 vols. (London, 1737).

Williams, Ann. *The English and the Norman Conquest* (Woodbridge, 1995).

Williams, Howard. *Death and Memory in Early Medieval Britain* (Cambridge, 2006).

Willis and Sotheran (Corporate Author). *A Catalogue of Superior Second-Hand Books, Ancient and Modern, Comprising Works in Most Branches of Literature and Offered at Very Low Prices for Ready Money*, no. xxxv. new series, vol. XXV (London, 1867).

Winget, Matt. *Sir Arthur Conan Doyle and the World of Light 1887–1920* (Portsmouth, 2016).

Wood, Anthony. *Athenae Oxoniensis, An Exact History of all the Writers and Bishops Who Have Had their Education in the University of Oxford*. 2 vols. (London, 1721).

Woolf, D.R. 'The Power of the Past: History, Ritual, and Political Authority in Tudor England', in *Political Thought and the Tudor Commonwealth: Deep Structure, Discourse, and Disguise*, ed. Paul Fideler and T.F. Meyer (London, 1992).

——. *The Social Circulation of the Past: English Historical Culture 1500–1730* (Oxford, 2003).

Worden, Blair. *Roundhead Reputations: The English Civil Wars and the Passions of Posterity* (New York, 2002).

Yalom, Marilyn. *The Birth of the Chess Queen: A History* (New York, 2005).

Yates, Frances. *The Art of Memory* (Chicago, 1966).

Zimmerman, Susan. *The Early Modern Corpse and Shakespeare's Theatre* (Edinburgh, 2005).

INDEX